DISRUPTING AFRICA

In the digital era, many African countries sit at the crossroads of a potential future that will be shaped by digital-era technologies with existing laws and institutions constructed under conditions of colonial and postcolonial authoritarian rule. In *Disrupting Africa*, Olufunmilayo B. Arewa examines this intersection and shows how it encompasses existing and new zones of contestation that are based on ethnicity, religion, region, age, and other sources of division. Arewa highlights specific collisions between the old and the new, including in the 2020 #EndSARS protests in Nigeria, which involved young people who engaged with varied digital-era technologies, provoking a violent response from rulers threatened by the prospect of political change. In this groundbreaking work, Arewa demonstrates how colonial and postcolonial lawmaking and legal processes continue to frame contexts in which digital technologies are created, implemented, regulated, and used in Africa today.

Olufunmilayo B. Arewa is the Murray H. Shusterman Professor of Transactional and Business Law at the Temple University Beasley School of Law. She writes about music, technology, and Africa, and has worked as a practicing lawyer in emerging growth company space in Silicon Valley, New York, and Boston. This book, which involved extensive archival research, brings together her training as an anthropologist and lawyer.

Disrupting Africa

TECHNOLOGY, LAW, AND DEVELOPMENT

OLUFUNMILAYO B. AREWA
Temple University, Philadelphia

CAMBRIDGE
UNIVERSITY PRESS

CAMBRIDGE
UNIVERSITY PRESS

University Printing House, Cambridge CB2 8BS, United Kingdom

One Liberty Plaza, 20th Floor, New York, NY 10006, USA

477 Williamstown Road, Port Melbourne, VIC 3207, Australia

314–321, 3rd Floor, Plot 3, Splendor Forum, Jasola District Centre, New Delhi – 110025, India

103 Penang Road, #05–06/07, Visioncrest Commercial, Singapore 238467

Cambridge University Press is part of the University of Cambridge.

It furthers the University's mission by disseminating knowledge in the pursuit of education, learning, and research at the highest international levels of excellence.

www.cambridge.org
Information on this title: www.cambridge.org/9781107156692
DOI: 10.1017/9781316661482

First published 2021

A catalogue record for this publication is available from the British Library.

Library of Congress Cataloging-in-Publication Data
NAMES: Arewa, Olufunmilayo B., author.
TITLE: Disrupting Africa : technology, law, and development / Olufunmilayo B. Arewa, Temple University, Philadelphia.
DESCRIPTION: Cambridge, United Kingdom ; New York, NY : Cambridge University Press, 2021. | Includes bibliographical references and index.
IDENTIFIERS: LCCN 2021009263 (print) | LCCN 2021009264 (ebook) | ISBN 9781107156692 (hardback) | ISBN 9781316610039 (paperback) | ISBN 9781316661482 (ebook)
SUBJECTS: LCSH: Technological innovations – Law and legislation – Africa, Sub-Saharan. | Law and economic development – Law and legislation – Africa, Sub-Saharan. | Law – Social aspects – Africa, Sub-Saharan. | Disruptive technologies – Social aspects – Africa, Sub-Saharan. | Postcolonialism – Africa, Sub-Saharan.
CLASSIFICATION: LCC KQC90 .A74 2021 (print) | LCC KQC90 (ebook) | DDC 344.67/095–dc23
LC record available at https://lccn.loc.gov/2021009263
LC ebook record available at https://lccn.loc.gov/2021009264

ISBN 978-1-107-15669-2 Hardback
ISBN 978-1-316-61003-9 Paperback

For my father (in memoriam), my mother, and my husband, who helped make this project possible

Contents

Preface

I am a daughter of two diasporas from Africa. The first, an involuntary one of enslaved people, brought my mother's ancestors to the New World. The transatlantic slave trade caused disruptions in Africa and in the New World that continue to reverberate today. In Africa during the slave trade, disruption was present in areas in West Africa, the Congo region, and other places that were primary sources of slaves. My father was born in Nigeria in present-day Ondo state in what was at the time the western region of Nigeria, then a British colonial possession. He came to the United States around the time of Nigeria's independence in 1960. His coming to the United States reflected new patterns of migration at the end of the colonial period when large numbers of people from Nigeria and other African countries went abroad to study with the idea that these people would return to their home countries. Migration for my father and others has been driven in some instances by a search for available education, work, or other opportunities. Nigeria is now the largest source of immigrants from Africa to the United States. My father, like many others, did not return permanently to Nigeria.

As a person of Nigerian American heritage, I grew up with a vision of Nigeria as a source of potential future greatness. My late father was proud of his Nigerian heritage. Like many Nigerians in the most recent postcolonial diaspora, he worked hard and was highly educated, eventually becoming a professor. He is not an anomaly. Nigerians are one of the most well-educated immigrant groups in the United States.

My father instilled in us a conception of Nigeria and other African countries as having great, but as yet unrealized, potential. As someone once reflected to me in a conversation about Nigeria: Nigeria is a continuing paradox, a country of enormous capacity and potential that never seems realized. Despite this significant capacity, which is not always the case in sub-Saharan Africa (SSA),[1] the potential that my father hoped to be Nigeria's future path has never been realized and more importantly, is not likely to be realized without significant legal and other reforms that involve disruption of past approaches, policies, and laws.

This book emerged from something that puzzled me about the origins of a single law in Nigeria. Untangling one piece of this puzzle led me on a quest of close to a decade during which I continued to untangle multiple intertwined pieces of an ever larger puzzle. This puzzle came to be closely intertwined with my personal and professional background and experience. My quest has taken me to multiple archives, including Archives and Special Collections, SOAS Library, British Library, the National Archives of the UK, Bodleian Library, and Parliamentary Archives in the United Kingdom, the Library of Congress and National Archives in the United States, and the *Archives nationales d'outre mer* in France. The focus of my work in these archives has been to examine laws, regulations, and law and policymaking processes during colonialism in order to understand the continuing impact of precolonial and colonial policies and processes today. I have reviewed thousands of pages of documents related to law, lawmaking processes, and legal administration, with a primary focus on colonial Nigeria.

This book is also an exploration of potential future paths for African countries, particularly Nigeria, with a focus on implications of digital economy technologies that have now disseminated throughout the world, including in Africa. Many within and outside of Africa see the potential future of such technologies as offering an opportunity to disrupt past disadvantageous patterns that have diminished opportunities for far too many people in Africa. New technologies, however, spread in contexts defined by a collision of the past, the present, and visions of the future that may be preconditioned by what has come before.

This book seeks to illuminate some reasons that legal, business, and other institutions in sub-Saharan African countries have repeatedly failed or proven ineffective for the vast majority of people living within these countries. Consideration of the impact of the external in Africa can illuminate much about the past, the present, and likely future paths. Although media sensationalism may overemphasize negative aspects of the state of affairs in many African countries,[2] today, more than half a century after the end of colonialism for most countries in Africa, far too many remain poor. High rates of economic growth in the early years of the new millennium have decreased, while African countries could account for more than half of global population growth between 2018 and 2050, with the population of some countries likely to at least double during that time.[3] Unemployment and underemployment are pervasive in many African countries today, driven by a lack of demand for labor rather than by worker characteristics.[4] The current state of affairs many countries in Africa today attests to the gulf between past visions and present, and likely future, realities.

This book focuses on sub-Saharan Africa, which includes countries in Africa south of the Sahara Desert, a dominant geographical feature of the continent. Although North Africa is clearly part of the African continent geographically with longstanding cultural, historical, and other connections to the rest of the continent, it is not a focus of my discussion. The exclusion of North Africa from dominant scholarly and popular approaches to the rest of the continent is rooted in past assumptions largely based on race that are themselves ripe for disruption.[5] These past approaches are being increasingly questioned today. In a study of nineteenth-century trans-Sahara trade, historian Ghislaine Lydon notes "[d]espite perceptions to the contrary, the countries bordering the Sahara are united by a common history ... I treat West and North Africa as one region with the Sahara sealing the continent rather than dividing it."[6]

This book does not involve extensive consideration of whether colonialism on balance was good or bad. As discussed in the coming chapters, it seems pretty apparent that colonialism was generally a bad thing for the vast majority of people in Africa. That said, however, colonialism had winners and losers, often identified and defined in terms of external needs and decisions, as discussed in this book. Further, many policies and laws that were implemented before, during, and even after colonialism have been poorly conceived, ineffectively implemented, and deleterious to the fabric of laws and institutions, even when undertaken with the best of intentions. Because law is comparable to a blob that accumulates over time, the impact of these laws, even if old, may be significant and continuing. More importantly, governments in many African countries today reflect the institutional structure of colonial governance, which often included unchecked executive power and weak legislatures and judicial institutions. These institutional structures have contributed to declining fortunes after colonialism in many countries. As Leander Heldring and James Robinson note: "we will argue that, in most cases, postindependence economic decline in Africa can be explicitly attributed to colonialism, because the types of mechanisms that led to this decline were creations of colonial society and institutions that persisted."[7]

The current state of political, economic, and human conditions in countries in SSA has long been a topic of discussion, particularly in the postindependence era when such countries seemingly had the ability to chart their own future paths. This book discusses why future hopes at the time of independence have not been fully realized and also considers why past patterns of external domination and determination have not been sufficiently disrupted.

Notes

1. Capacity was particularly limited in the legal profession. Although Ghana and Nigeria had a small number of African lawyers at independence, many other African countries had few lawyers, which was a significant problem given the legal nature of the colonial state. At independence, Tanganyika had only twenty-five lawyers in the country, only two of whom were African. Belgian and Portuguese colonies had "virtually no trained legal professionals to handle disputes in the national court system." Joireman, 2001: 580–581.
2. Hunter-Gault, 2007: 107.

3. United Nations Department of Economic and Social Affairs, 2019: 1, 10; Mo Ibrahim Foundation. 2013. *Africa Ahead: The Next 50 Years*, p. 5, accessed October 23, 2020, https://mo.ibrahim.foundation/sites/default/files/2019-03/2013-facts-%26-figures-an-african-conversation-africa-ahead-the-next-50-years.pdf.
4. Golub and Hayat, 2015: 137.
5. Countries in North Africa are typically considered together with countries in the Middle East as part of the Middle East and North Africa (MENA) region. Iman Amrani. "Why Don't We Think of North Africa as Part of Africa? *Guardian*, September 25, 2015, accessed October 23, 2020, www.theguardian.com/commentisfree/2015/sep/09/north-africa-algeria-black-africa-shared-history.
6. Lydon, 2012: 5.
7. Heldring and Robinson, 2017: 299.

Acknowledgments

This book is a collaborative project in varied ways. It reflects engagement with past and contemporary scholarship about issues related to Africa, technology, law, anthropology, and other fields. I thank my family for their continuing support and assistance. I also thank friends and current and former colleagues who contributed to this project over a number of years. I have received academic support from deans at the universities where I have worked as I have completed this book. I also thank past mentors and academic advisors, who have directly and indirectly contributed to this book. I am also indebted to the staff of libraries and archives in the United Kingdom and in the United States.

This book was made possible by research funding from the University of California, Irvine School of Law, and Temple University Beasley School of Law. This book was significantly influenced by my time spent as a Fellow at the Käte Hamburger Center for Advanced Study in the Humanities at Universität Bonn in Germany. My time at the center and interactions with center faculty, staff, and other fellows was particularly helpful and assisted me in conceptualizing my thinking about commercial law in African countries today, as well as relationships between law and the humanities in colonial and postcolonial contexts in Africa.

Abbreviations and Acronyms

AfDB	African Development Bank
AI	Artificial Intelligence
ANOM	Archives nationales d'outre mer
AU	African Union
Bodleian	Bodleian Libraries, University of Oxford, Bodleian Archives & Manuscripts
CBK	Central Bank of Kenya
CBN	Central Bank of Nigeria
DRC	Democratic Republic of the Congo
DSS	Nigerian Department of State Service
ECOWAS	Economic Community of West African States
EDB	World Bank Ease of Doing Business Index
EFCC	Nigerian Economic and Financial Crimes Commission
FAO	Food and Agriculture Organization of the United Nations
fintech	financial technology
GDP	Gross Domestic Product
ICJ	International Court of Justice
IFC	International Finance Corporation
IFFs	illicit financial flows
IMF	International Monetary Fund
IoT	Internet of Things
IPO	Initial Public Offering
NGO	Nongovernmental organization
NJC	Nigerian Judicial Council
R&D	Research and Development
RNC	Royal Niger Company
SAPs	Structural Adjustment Programs
SDGs	Sustainable Development Goals
SOAS Archive	Archives and Special Collections, SOAS Library

SSA	sub-Saharan Africa
TNA	The National Archives of the UK
TPA	The Parliamentary Archives – UK Parliament
UN	United Nations
UNCTAD	United Nations Conference on Trade and Development
UNDP	United Nations Development Program
UNECA	United Nations Economic Commission for Africa
UNICEF	United Nations Children's Education Fund
USNA	The United States National Archives

Map

AFRICA

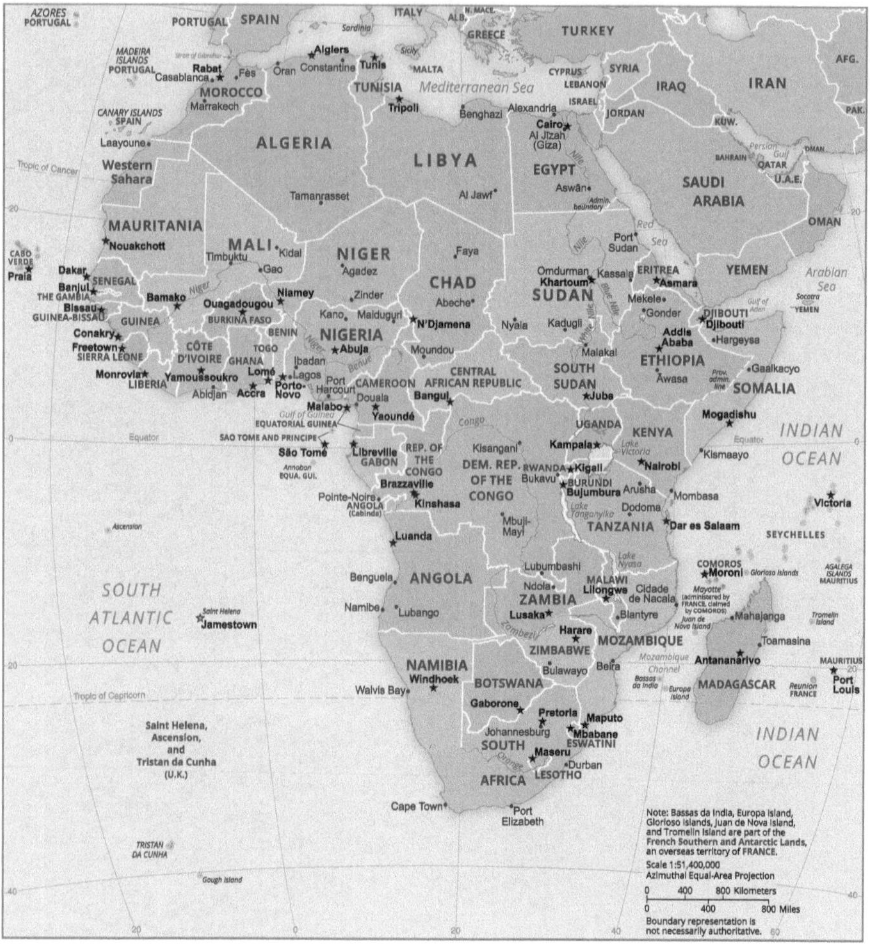

Political Map of Africa[1]

Note

1. www.cia.gov/library/publications/the-world-factbook/attachments/docs/original/africa_pol .pdf?1558019469

1

Introduction

Colonialism and Africa's Future Paths

The European ways were considered modern, the African old-fashioned. Lagos culture was such an unfortunate conglomeration of both that you ended up not knowing to which you belonged.

Buchi Emecheta, *The Bride Price* (1976)

This book examines past, present, and likely future paths for Nigeria and other countries in Africa through a lens of disruption. The *Oxford English Dictionary* defines *disrupt* as meaning "to break apart, burst, shatter, separate forcibly, interrupt the normal continuity of (an activity, etc.) or to throw into disorder." This book combines this commonplace understanding of disruption with conceptions of disruption that have become prominent in digital economy discussions, significantly influenced by the work of Clayton Christensen. In his seminal 1997 book, *The Innovator's Dilemma* and in later work, Christensen characterized disruptive innovation as a process "by which a product or service initially takes root in simple applications at the bottom of a market – typically by being less expensive and more accessible – and then relentlessly moves upmarket, eventually displacing established competitors."[1]

Disruptive innovation has become an influential concept in technology, finance, and other arenas, with much discussion about what constitutes a disruptive innovation. Disruption is celebrated in Silicon Valley, a global epicenter of technology disruption. This book is not an intervention into the extensive discourse about digital economy disruption. Rather, this book discusses how varied forms of disruption have had an impact in countries in sub-Saharan Africa (SSA) in the past, the impact of such past disruptions today, and potential future paths, given disruptive digital economy technologies and innovations.

This book uses contemporary and historical events, particularly as they relate to law, to both highlight the impact of disruptive technologies in SSA today and the pressing need to disrupt past patterns of external relationships, external networks, and uses of external models within African countries that reflect significant colonial era overhang. This book focuses on Nigeria, but also discusses commonalities in experiences related to law in British and other colonial contexts. Pervasive patterns of legal borrowing link Britain with its former colonies inside and outside of Africa, which are typically categorized as having common law legal systems. Examining laws and lawmaking processes can also reveal much about the shifting interface between the internal and external in SSA. Nigeria, which is thought to contain some 20 percent of the population of SSA,[2] reflects important aspects of colonial lawmaking and other policies.

As a background to understanding these patterns, a brief summary of the interface with the external, including during colonialism, is advisable, particularly for readers who may not be as familiar with African history. The experiences of African countries are diverse in important aspects, particularly as they relate to experiences of the colonized.[3] At the same time, however, significant commonalities exist among British colonies in relation to law and the design of legal institutions, and as a result of persistently unequal and exploitative relations between external powers and African countries. The external relationships that are the focus of this book have unfolded at times in contexts of significant internal change within Africa. This book focuses on the internal implications of external contacts and relationships, which is just one perspective from which to view disruption in Africa.

Relationships between African countries and European powers that have shaped current conditions throughout the continent have involved a series of disruptions that have continuing impact today. As a result, understanding outcomes in Africa today requires examination of the internal, the external, including assumptions and theories guiding external actors, and hybrid systems and other institutions developed under conditions of external domination. As Achille Mbembe notes:

> From a narrow methodological standpoint, this means that, from the fifteenth century, there is no longer a 'distinctive historicity' of these [African] societies, one not embedded in times and rhythms heavily conditioned by European domination. Therefore, dealing with African societies' 'historicity' requires more than simply giving an account of what occurs on the continent itself at the interface between the working of internal forces and the working of international actors. It also presupposes a critical delving into Western history and the theories that claim to interpret it.[4]

We tend to speak of African countries in terms of historical time periods defined by reference to actions of external powers. Consequently, like many others, I refer to eras such as precolonial and colonial, which refer to time periods before and during formal colonialism in Africa. I also refer to a postcolonial era of independence, which began in SSA in 1957 with the independence of Ghana. However, these demarcations contain significant illusory aspects because essential patterns of relationships, particularly external ones, did not necessarily change as countries in Africa became independent, for example. Furthermore, from a legal perspective, we have seen significant continuity of law and legal and policymaking processes, even after countries in Africa became formally independent.

People in Africa have had contacts with varied external actors for a long time. Long before widespread contacts with European powers, Africans developed varied trading networks, including across the Sahara Desert via the trans-Sahara trade and across the Indian Ocean. From the ninth through the fifteenth centuries, a series of kingdoms, many with names that remain familiar today, such as Ghana, Mali, and Songhai, arose in West Africa between the Niger River and the Atlantic Ocean.[5] East Africa has had a long association with South Asia and China with trade links developing between the seventh and tenth centuries.[6] Coastal merchant towns in East Africa that traded across the Indian Ocean developed in the context of these trading relationships.[7] These examples of early external contacts illustrate ways in which trading networks and various forms of interchange have played an important role in various times and places in Africa. By the thirteenth and fourteenth centuries, West African gold constituted two-thirds of the gold in the world. Caravans of up to 10,000 camels passed through the legendary Timbuktu, which became part of the Mali Empire in the fourteenth century.[8] Interchanges and networks across the Sahara Desert became prominent in the middle of the fourteenth century when Mansa Musa, the emperor of the Mali, made a famous pilgrimage to Mecca in 1324–1325, accompanied by thousands of slaves, state officials, and guards, as well as immense amounts of pure gold. Mansa Musa spent so much gold on his journey that the price of gold dropped, leading to price inflation.[9]

In addition to ongoing contacts with external actors, significant internal population movements have occurred in Africa, including the migration of Bantu-speaking peoples. Early Portuguese explorers had noted close similarities between languages in the southern half of Africa as early as 1498.[10] Bantu language speakers are the largest language group in Africa, with 300 million people (of some 1.2 billion in Africa) speaking some 500 Bantu languages. Bantu language speakers began their migration from somewhere in the area of Cameroon around 4,000 to 5,000 years ago, reaching the southernmost area of Africa approximately 1,200 to 1,500 years ago.[11] Internal and external population movements, contacts, and other activities are a key background for external engagement in Africa by Europeans and others.

European activities on the ground in Africa began long before formal colonialism in the late nineteenth century. The Portuguese were early in expanding outside of Europe in Africa and elsewhere. Early Portuguese activities in Africa began during the early fifteenth century with the capture of the Moroccan coastal town of Ceuta. From the sixteenth to nineteenth centuries, prior to the advent of formal colonialism, commercial relationships initially centered in coastal areas often around the slave trade, particularly in West Africa and parts of Central Africa. Britain, then a global naval power, began to enforce its 1807 abolition of the slave trade,[12] which did not mean that Britain did not continue to benefit from forms of involvement in the slave trade.[13] During the nineteenth century, however, other avenues of trading developed, including so-called legitimate trade in products such as palm oil, although the slave trade did not peak until 1820; the slave trade and palm oil trade were both present at the same time in areas such as the Bight of Biafra in present-day Nigeria.[14]

Formal colonialism, through which European countries established ownership-like relationships over territories in Africa, came in the late nineteenth century and lasted for just two or three generations. The countries that emerged at the end of the colonial period reflected arbitrary divisions by external powers based on incomplete maps. The United States did not formally take a piece of Africa when it was arbitrarily divided by European and other powers. However, the United States and other powers who did not take colonies in Africa, including Austria-Hungary, Sweden-Norway, Russia, and the Ottoman Empire, participated in the Berlin Conference of 1884–1885, which formalized the division of Africa into colonies. The papers and maps for the Berlin Conference, available at the United States National Archives, reflect a strong sense of ownership by external powers, coupled with a lack of knowledge about what they were dividing. The Berlin Conference did not include participation by African peoples or governments or representatives that adequately considered local interests or concerns. The outcome of processes with such a starting point have been largely negative for people in the territories so divided.

As Heldring and Robinson have noted, despite its short duration, colonialism impeded economic outcomes throughout Africa:

> Colonialism blocked further political development, and indirect rule made local elites less accountable to their citizens. After independence, even if these [centralized] states had a coherence that others lacked, they had far more predatory rulers. It is true that the colonial powers brought technology and institutions that Africans did not have, but Africans in these types of polities were busy adopting these developments in the nineteenth century, as they were the most capable of doing so.[15]

As Heldring and Robinson note, some colonies, including South Africa, Zimbabwe (called Southern Rhodesia during colonialism), and Kenya, were settler colonies where European settlers came in significant numbers. Other colonies incorporated centralized states that existed at the time of the Scramble for Africa, including Botswana, Benin, Ethiopia, and Rwanda. A third category of colonies had little or no centralized state formation or a mixture of societies with centralized forms of governance and those without such centralized forms. Examples of this third category would include Nigeria and Sierra Leone. Heldring and Robinson's empirical study also suggests that unlike the rest of the world, where the impact of colonialism was more heterogenous, the impact of colonialism in Africa, though diverse, was negative:

> There is no success story in Africa similar to Australia or the United States, from which economically dynamic settler economies emerged . . . . All in all, we find it

difficult to bring the available evidence together with plausible counterfactuals to argue that there is any country today in sub-Saharan Africa that is more developed because it was colonized by Europeans. Quite the contrary.[16]

Colonialism was also part of broader networks of relationships between Africa and external forces, which, by the nineteenth century, had become dominated by European governments and other European actors. Many have noted the three C's of European colonialism: Christianity, Commerce, and Civilization. Although the assumption that Europeans could impart civilization in Africa was often at odds with their actual practices in Africa and elsewhere, the civilizing mission was a major part of how Europeans conceptualized and justified their actions in their African colonial possessions.

A wide range of commercial actors were present in Africa before, during, and after the colonial era. Commercial actors in British colonies included companies that had received British royal charters, such as the Royal African Company, which played a significant role in the slave trade and whose investors and beneficiaries included the British royal family and composer Georg Friedrich Handel,[17] and the Royal Niger Company. In addition to companies with royal charters, smaller enterprises that included merchants from Liverpool, participated in the slave trade and palm oil trade. Participants in commerce in Africa also included involuntary and voluntary African laborers, migrants to West Africa from Lebanon,[18] and Indian laborers and businesspeople, primarily present in East Africa and southern Africa. Indian laborers came voluntarily at times, long before colonialism, but were brought as involuntary indentured servants during colonialism to replace freed slaves.[19] Migrants in West Africa also included thousands of ex-slaves from Brazil (referred to in Nigeria as Amaro) and ex-slaves from Sierra Leone (referred to in Nigeria as Saro).[20] Patterns of migration have shaped the local and the global before, during, and after colonialism.[21]

The Christianity part of the three C's underscores the impact of world religions in Africa. World religions have spread throughout Africa, with Christianity being adopted in Ethiopia as early as the fourth century. Islam spread in West Africa in the eighth century and is present in many parts of the continent. Catholic Jesuit missionaries were present in the Kingdom of Kongo in central Africa as early as the late fifteenth century.[22] Christianity became more widespread with the Christian mission movement, which had become prominent by the early nineteenth century. Christian missionaries, who included Europeans, Americans, including African Americans, and former African slaves, were a key factor in the spread of Christianity in Africa. Missionary education became an important force within many African countries because missionary schools provided education, which became a gateway for access to opportunities, including for those who might have lacked such access prior to the coming of Europeans. Through these and other activities, missionaries have had a continuing impact in many African countries.

I have organized this book around key themes that highlight interactions of the past, the present, and potential future paths. These themes include consideration of intertwined strands of connectivity between the external and the internal as they relate to governance in Africa. Consideration of governance includes examination of the governed and those who govern. Related themes explored in this book include relationships between the global and the local in ever-shifting local and global contexts, types of competition, migration and diaspora, as well as power, authority, and accountability.

Wherever possible, this book also notes how cultural activities interact with these key themes. In African contexts, varied forms of artistic activity have been present and relevant to activities in other spheres. These artistic forms include music, metal work, sculpture, architecture, painting, oral and written literature, fiber art, and dance, to name a few. As was the case elsewhere in the broader African diaspora, forms of cultural expression such as music have become zones of contestation in varied contexts. Given this, artistic expression can shed light on questions of governance and control in both colonial and postcolonial contexts. For example, contestation in music illustrates that governance and control were about more than formal institutions. Colonial governance extended to the cultural realm and attempted to regulate and control ways of being and ways of doing.

This introductory chapter serves as an introduction to key themes discussed in the book, and contextualizes current circumstances in Nigeria and elsewhere in Africa in light of past experiences of interactions with external actors.

Chapter 2 examines questions of governance in colonial contexts, with consideration given to how conceptions about governance of corporations bear similarities to approaches to colonial governance by colonial powers. The thin European staffing that was typical during colonialism, emphasis on reducing costs and covering colonial costs with local taxes, and focus on extraction draw attention to ways in which colonial corporate governance reflected decision-making and investment choices that were more appropriate for short-term corporate decision-making than for long-term decisions about entire societies that might impact millions of people. Chapter 2 also looks at the internal construction of colonial governance and the often problematic bifurcation between English law and customary law in British colonial contexts.

Chapter 3 focuses on relationships and accountability and looks at the role of colonial rule in contributing to continuing state fragility in Africa today. This chapter also considers colonialism from the perspective of internal and external relationships. Chapter 3 ends with discussion of the implications of colonial governance and legal structures for accountability and recourse in instances of harm.

Chapter 4 analyzes the operation of colonial legal structures and examines implications of parallel customary and English law frameworks in the context of legal imperialism in British colonies. This chapter also considers structures of government, separation of powers, and the construction of legislative, judicial, and executive branches during colonialism. The colonial executive power was largely unconstrained, which has contributed to structural problems in the organization and operation of postcolonial governmental structures that carried over to a significant degree from colonialism.

Chapter 5 considers issues related to colonialism, language, and law. Colonial policies have had a sustained impact in the language arena. Language policies also play a critical role in law. Language choices initially made during colonialism continue to shape questions of access, justice, and fairness in legal and other contexts in African countries.

Chapter 6 begins discussion of how past paths play a role in present-day questions related to the digital economy. This chapter examines how past legal and other institutions have influenced the diffusion of digital economy technologies and the tension between such technologies and existing institutions. This is an issue of global concern, not just in Africa. African countries, however, have significant issues related to colonial legal and institutional overhang that casts a shadow over digital economy laws and policies.

Chapter 7 examines digital technology issues in Nigerian contexts where today we see competing narratives about Nigerian start-ups that exist side by side with older narratives about scams involving Nigerian Princes, which are probably perceived by many to be the most well-known Nigerian digital economy export. This chapter also discusses how conceptions about technology uplift exist side by side with profound sources of insecurity from a range of sources for many people in countries in Africa.

Chapter 8 considers implications of digital economy trends for issues related to insecurity and precarity. It discusses rural and urban spaces in the context of digital economy trends. It ends with a consideration of implications of protest movements such as #EndSARS in Nigeria that illustrate ways in which digital technologies are creating digital communities and having an impact in contested spaces that exist around societal fissures, including intergenerational and other forms of conflict.

Chapter 9 takes note of the important role of elite formation during colonialism in defining elite spaces, particularly in Nigeria. These elite spaces are important for understanding patterns of governance and the persistence of poverty. Although this is of critical importance because so many are poor in Africa, discussions about poverty may not take sufficient note of elite attitudes that shape policies that may contribute to or alleviate poverty. Elite formation during colonialism has been important in shaping attitudes about governance and conceptions of internal responsibility of those who govern to those over whom they rule.

Chapter 10 returns to issues related to colonialism and commerce by examining how activities of colonizers have shaped opportunities, business institutions, and competitiveness throughout Africa. This chapter also discusses the implications of colonial portfolio approaches for law and commerce and the ways in which attitudes about governance have shaped the construction of the public and private in former colonies in Africa.

Chapter 11, the Conclusion, begins with consideration of a viral video of a young boy dancing ballet in the mud in Lagos that was viewed by tens of millions of people in the summer of 2020. This video highlights potential dreams and hopes of future paths, the potential of which may not be realized because of the paucity of available opportunities. Chapter 11 then discusses potential future paths in the digital economy era given past and present paths.

Notes

1. Disruptive Innovations, Christensen Institute, www.christenseninstitute.org/disruptive-innovations/
2. According to World Bank figures, the total estimated SSA population in SSA in 2019 was 1,106,957,900, with an estimated population in Nigeria 200,963,599, which would make Nigeria's population 18.15 percent of the total population of SSA. The World Bank, Population, Total – Sub-Saharan Africa, https://data.worldbank.org/indicator/SP.POP.TOTL?locations=ZG.
3. Vansina, 2010.
4. Mbembe, 2001: 6.
5. Mcintosh, 2012.
6. Pollard and Kinder, 2017.
7. Kusimba, 2018.
8. Levtzion, 1980: 132; Eaton, 2011: 3.
9. Levtzion, 1980: 211, 213; Eaton, 2011: 3.
10. Maret, 2018.
11. Barbieri et al., 2014.
12. Slave Trade Act 1807, An Act for the Abolition of the Slave Trade, 47 Geo III Sess. 1 c. 36.
13. Sherwood, 2007.
14. Northrup, 1976: 354.
15. Heldring and Robinson, 2017: 299–300.
16. Ibid. at 297, 300.
17. Hunter, 2019: 27.
18. Arsan, 2014.
19. Modi and Taylor, 2017.
20. Animashaun, 2018; Castillo, 2016; Dixon-Fyle, 1989; Ralston, 1969.
21. Modi and Taylor, 2017: 917.
22. Thornton, 1984: 148.

2

Colonialism, Governance, and Law

The white man's court has decided that it should belong to Nnama's family '. . . ' He has put a knife on the things that held us together and we have fallen apart.

Chinua Achebe, *Things Fall Apart* (1958)

COLONIALISM AND THE ART OF GOVERNMENT

Chinua Achebe's groundbreaking novel *Things Fall Apart*, a literary masterpiece by an author whom many consider to be the father of modern African literature, attests to the disruption that came with colonialism. Hierarchies of authority that elevated the external over the internal were pervasive in colonialism. However, varieties of models of colonialism,[1] involving overlapping, interactive, hierarchical, and at times, competing spheres of governance, are essential for understanding the impact of colonialism. Varied actors oversaw these spheres of governance, including colonial administrators, missionaries, settlers (in settler colonies such as Kenya and South Africa), varied commercial interests, and *traditional* local rulers.

The legal and regulatory fabric of British colonial possessions, including Nigeria, illustrate key features of colonial governance. British colonial rule involved large-scale experiments that have proven to a significant degree to be problematic and prone to dysfunction and failure long after the formal end of colonialism. Although Africans have often been blamed for governance failures in Africa, systems and institutions put in place in Africa during colonialism were in many instances neither suitable nor robust. Failures within Africa have undoubtedly played a role in continuing postcolonial governance failures. Recent events outside of Africa draw attention to potential points of failure in external models of governance that have been primary sources for borrowing in many African contexts.[2]

Discussions of reform in Africa typically incorporate recommendations about desired forms of governance. As the World Bank noted in a 1989 report: "[u]nderlying the litany of Africa's development problems is a crisis of governance. By governance is meant the exercise of political power to manage a nation's affairs."[3] Promoters of good governance often do not directly connect current perceived governance failures to colonial policy design and legal structures. However, structures and processes that became commonplace during the colonial era have played a significant and continuing role in shaping institutions all over Africa. Further, those charged internally within African countries with rectifying governance failures have been, in at least some instances, questionable stewards for implementation of good governance practices.

Questions about governance and the power of states are not limited to African contexts. Michel Foucault notes that government "as a general problem seems to me to explode in the sixteenth century."[4] Governmentality or the "art of government" as conceptualized by Foucault centers on the nation-state and involves questions about "[h]ow to govern oneself, how to be governed, how to govern others, by whom the people will accept being governed, how to become the best possible governor."[5] Discourse about governance has exploded in discussions about and within Africa, particularly in the last twenty years. Interrogating contexts of good governance discourse about Africa is critical for understanding the impact of conceptions about governance on potential future paths for African countries.

Good governance proposals in Africa arose in the post-Cold War and post-debt crisis era.[6] These proposals were initially the product of external actors, who sought to connect conceptions of economic development and political freedom: "amidst the backdrop of a general climate in favor of free markets and liberal democracy."[7] By the beginning of the 1990s, varied external actors, including Western governments that provide development assistance to African countries and international financial institutions, such as the World Bank and International Monetary Fund (IMF), were focusing on governance and indicia of democracy as a condition for receiving development aid and other assistance.[8]

Prevailing opinions that may change according to the notions of external actors have long shaped external prescriptions for future paths for African countries. Prior to the 1990s, academics, donors, and international financial institutions were not as concerned about democracy. In fact, they "expressed few misgivings about funneling billions of dollars in development aid through repressive regimes as long as the latter accepted the appropriate policy advice . . . . Western governments, with one eye on Cold War geopolitics and the other on safeguarding their own economic and political interests in Africa, openly supported a succession of friendly 'strongmen'."[9]

Internal prodemocracy social movements had also become active by the late 1980s and early 1990s, influenced by the release of Nelson Mandela, the liberation movement in South Africa, and upheavals in Eastern Europe.[10] These internal social movements agitated for improved conditions and highlight the complexity of internal terrains and presence of zones of internal contestation that exist within African countries. The presence of internal and external pressures to embrace democracy also raise questions about what democracy means in African contexts: "[t]he existence of electoral systems, a multiplicity of political parties, and independent legislatures and courts may not, by themselves indicate very much about the extent of real democratic change."[11]

By the 1990s, a new external prescription had emerged that promoted conceptions of democracy largely based on historical experiences of developed countries in the West.[12] However, the countries and experts suggesting particular prescriptions often did not sufficiently engage with local contexts, goals, capacity, and likely outcomes. This meant that proposed cures for governance and other perceived failures could actually lead to worse outcomes. As part of the promotion of greater democracy in Africa, external support and funding became based on African countries' meeting new benchmarks, with political conditionality and "democratic sanctions."[13] As varied external powers have identified policy prescriptions to cure governance and other failures in Africa, many more people in Africa have become poor. World Bank estimates suggest that the percentage of people in extreme poverty in Africa declined from 57 percent in 1990 to 43 percent in 2012. However, during that same time period, the number of people living in extreme poverty increased by more than 100 million because of population growth.[14] The World Bank defines extreme poverty as living on less than $1.90 per person per day.[15]

Good governance discourse represents a current iteration of a familiar pattern in Africa – use of policy and governance models derived from outside of Africa to create and shape institutions within Africa. This is problematic due to processes of adoption of such models in many African contexts. The essential problem is not that African countries relate to external powers and policies or use external models, but how African countries have internalized the external, all too often in indiscriminate ways. These cut-and-paste borrowing processes have also often failed to take sufficient account of local considerations and local needs.

In colonial Nigeria, lawmaking reflected an unquestioned assumption that laws in Nigeria should follow in line with English law. A report in colonial records discussing the Nigerian Wireless Telegraphy (Amendment) Ordinance 1927 reflects typical attitudes that saw law principally through the lens of the external and exercised power in lawmaking and other contexts accordingly: "[i]f, at sometime in the future, the Imperial Acts are amended to cover television more specifically, the Nigerian legislation can then fall into line."[16] Cut-and-paste patterns of borrowing during colonialism did not end with formal independence. However, borrowing comes with past histories, disputes, understandings, conflicts, and resolutions that may not be readily apparent, but which may nonetheless be part of the thing being borrowed. As a result, it may be difficult to sort out what is really relevant to local contexts of borrowings.

These patterns of adoption of the external have been evident in the legal sphere before, during, and after colonialism. During colonialism, people within most colonial possessions in Africa had little ability to modify external legal models or externally influenced adaptation of local customary law. Even during a time of seeming independence, this pattern of external policy, governance, and legal models being readily adopted in Africa with insufficient scrutiny and inadequate attention to local considerations has not been sufficiently disrupted. Since independence, for example, African countries have signed many treaties, adopted model law and other recommended laws, and followed laws and legal processes recommended by varied external actors, including international institutions and external governmental and nongovernmental actors, and their recommended experts. Many of these legal interventions have not been sufficiently flexible or customized to fit the contexts of their implementation.

In addition to continuing local colonial legacies, global colonial legacies remain. As a result of these global legacies, African countries are underrepresented in global institutions such as the World Bank and the IMF that serve as central nodes for the development of policies of external determination. These global institutions, created after World War II, continue to reflect power arrangements established during colonialism. As António Guterres, the United Nations Secretary-General, noted in July 2020:

> The legacy of colonialism still reverberates .... We see this in the global trade system. Economies that were colonized are at greater risk of getting locked into the production of raw materials and low-tech goods – a new form of colonialism. And we see this in global power relations. Africa has been a double victim. First, as a target of the colonial project. Second, African countries are under-represented in the international institutions that were created after the Second World War, before most of them had won independence. The nations that came out on top more than seven decades ago have refused to contemplate the reforms needed to change power relations in international institutions.[17]

In the economic policy realm, African countries have followed external recommendations concerning a wide range of policies, including import substitution policies,[18] Structural Adjustment Programs,[19] investment climate reform, and various macroeconomic and other policy proposals. Although bad luck and poor policy implementation within Africa undoubtedly played a role,[20] countries outside of Africa that did not adhere so closely to external policy recommendations have performed better than most countries in Africa.[21] Some "countries have closely followed the dictates of the model, but have not seen especially strong economic performance. Other countries have ignored many of the dictates – at least with respect to the crucial details of sequencing – and have experienced some of the highest rates of sustained growth the world has ever seen."[22] In contrast, African countries, which produced over 3 percent of global manufacturing output in the 1970s, were producing 1.5 percent by 2016.[23]

Continued adherence to external models with insufficient local input based on actual local needs has contributed to institutional and policy incoherence and inflexibility in Africa. These approaches have also failed to ameliorate the poverty and marginalization of so many in Africa. Past contexts of imposed, coerced, and voluntary uses of external models remain relevant today. By the middle of 2020, several African countries were thought to be on the cusp of another debt crisis, in part as a result of the COVID-19 pandemic. The global economic slowdown in 2020 from COVID-19 increased concerns about an impending debt crisis in Africa. Many African countries had incurred significant external debt prior to the pandemic. The pandemic will likely make it difficult for countries to service their existing debt.[24] In October 2020, Zambia failed to make a $42.5 million interest payment on $1 billion in Eurobonds maturing in 2024,[25] becoming the first African country to default on its debt obligations in the aftermath of COVID-19. Zambia's default reflects the increasing need of African countries to navigate among different external actors, including increasingly China, which has given loans throughout Africa for varied projects, including infrastructure lending as part of its Belt and Road Initiative.[26] Holders of Eurobonds had asked Zambia for more information about its debts held by China; Zambia required these debtholders to sign confidentiality agreements before disclosing information about these loans, which the bondholders apparently did not sign.[27] The circumstances of Zambia's default reflect continuing issues about transparency in relations between African countries and external powers.

In the aftermath of the 1980s debt crisis, Structural Adjustment Programs (SAPs) were a dominant external policy response to deal with highly indebted countries in Africa and Latin America. Countries that needed financial assistance from the IMF and the World Bank were required to meet certain conditions as a requirement of having their loans approved.[28] SAPs were implemented by the IMF and World Bank in ways that led them to be called "the overlords of Africa" in the 1990s.[29]

The effectiveness of SAPs has been debated. SAPs expanded external trade in Africa, enmeshing African countries to a greater extent within global trade networks. SAPs may also have led to increased poverty and lower incomes and adversely affected vulnerable populations in Africa.[30] SAPs included deficit reduction measures that typically required significant budget cuts and privatizations. SAPs have been associated with increased food insecurity and undernutrition, and decreased access to health care.[31] SAPs have also devastated education, becoming a major factor contributing to an ongoing education crisis in Nigeria.[32] Education is beneficial to society in various ways, including enhancing human capital, promoting economic growth, creating building blocks for inclusive institutions, encouraging civic engagement, and promoting longer and healthier lives.[33]

In 1989, United Nations Children and Education Fund (UNICEF) reported that SAPs "have often been devastating to achievements of the past and to confidence of the future ... Africa ... has undoubtedly been hardest hit. 'Adjustment programs,' said representatives of 30 African countries . . .early in 1988, 'are rending the fabric of African society.' In the process, what safety nets existed for many of Africa's poor have been torn away."[34] The impact of SAPs and other experiences in Africa with uses of external models and recommendations highlight the need for greater robust internal intermediation of policy, laws, and proposals for action, particularly those that might reflect past patterns of indiscriminate borrowing of the external. This would also mean giving closer attention to contexts of origin of proposed external policies and thoroughly assessing and modifying such policies in light of past impact in previous implementations of such policies and likely potential local effects in Africa. This type of scrutiny may play an important role in preventing African countries from again becoming an experimental lab for failed, untested, or poorly considered policies that reflect significant external determination. Preventing such experiments could potentially disrupt externally dominated approaches to policy and law within Africa that were established during colonialism.

Discussions about good governance in African have become widespread. The Mo Ibrahim Foundation, established in 2006 by Mo Ibrahim, the Sudanese-born billionaire,[35] focuses on the importance of governance and leadership for Africa. The Mo Ibrahim Foundation defines governance as "the provision of the political, social and economic public goods and services that every citizen has the right to expect from their state, and that a state has the responsibility to deliver to its citizens."[36] The African Development Bank (AfDB) is a regional development finance bank that was established to contribute to the economic development and social progress of African member countries. The AfDB Group Policy on Good Governance states that good governance "should build on (i) effective states; (ii) mobilized civil societies; and (iii) efficient private sectors, three factors necessary for sustained development . . . . There is also wide consensus that the key elements of good governance include accountability, transparency, combatting corruption, participator governance, and an enabling legal/judicial framework."[37] Although they are not identical, these conceptions of governance from the Mo Ibrahim Foundation and the AfDB sketch out key features of good governance recommendations.

The models from which recommended governance templates are drawn are typically not specifically identified. However, they clearly reflect recommendations drawn on from settings outside of Africa. They may also reflect top-down abstractions about what governance should be that may, to a significant degree, be decontextualized. Abstractions of sources of ideas about what constitute good governance goals and practices for African countries represent a missed opportunity to instill greater understanding about the interaction of policy and context. Failing to discuss origins of these models also deters consideration of the actual operation of good governance in contexts of origin, the historical development of good governance processes in such contexts, and how abstract governance concepts have related to concrete local conditions in varied contexts. Instances of governance failure in such contexts would also be helpful for understanding governance in more practical, rather than abstract ways.

Contexts and histories of sources of models for recommended governance goals are essential for the development of strategies for good governance in Africa at local levels. Context and history are also important for understanding potential limitations of such models in Africa. This is even more important because the state of affairs in many African countries that has led to the widespread emphasis on the need for good governance is itself in part a consequence of the indiscriminate adoption of varied types of laws, policies, and initiatives based on external models with insufficient attention to local needs, considerations, and outcomes.

Foucault contextualizes his discussion of governmentality within European contexts in which discourse about government became prominent. Foucault's assumptions about the nation-state do not fit well with past or present governance in many contexts in Africa. However, governmentality is important for understanding both the formation of states and legal systems and conceptualizations of government and governance structures by those in positions of authority.

Foucault also notes that the "introduction of economy into political practice" is an essential issue in the establishment of the art of government.[38] Discussions about governance in Africa are closely tied to the economic status and performance of countries in Africa and the continued poverty of so many in Africa. This is evident in Nigeria, which has become the poverty capital of the world. In 2018, World Poverty Clock noted that Nigeria had surpassed India as the country with the greatest number of people in extreme poverty, which is particularly notable because India's population is more than six times that of Nigeria. Nearly 50 percent of Nigerians or some 86.9 million people live in extreme poverty, according to June 2018 figures. Nigeria, like many other countries in Africa, faces a significant population boom. This population boom may lead to Nigeria's replacing the United States as the third most populous country in the world after China and India by 2050.[39] Nigeria is not alone in Africa in having high levels of both poverty and population growth. In June 2018, seven of the ten countries with the highest absolute number of people in extreme poverty were in Africa. Without fundamental policy reform, poverty levels in Nigeria and other countries in Africa will likely increase, potentially significantly. In 2018, World Bank statistics suggested that people in SSA comprised more than half of extremely poor people in the world in 2015. By 2030, forecasts suggest that 9 in 10 extremely poor people will live in SSA.[40] Population growth and poverty forecasts make the necessity of significant reform even more urgent.

The history of lawmaking and legal processes in Africa offers a window into understanding the continuing impact of history and context on governance. The art of government in colonial Africa has had continuing negative effects long after the end of colonialism. Although formal colonialism has ended in most of Africa, Western Sahara, a former Spanish colony, has remained under occupation, first by its neighbors Mauritania and Morocco, and by Morocco alone since 1979.[41] In December 2020, the United States and Morocco engaged in a trade involving Western Sahara that is reminiscent of the monopoly games of colonial powers. The United States recognized Moroccan control over the Western Sahara, ending its prior policy of neutrality, in exchange for Morocco's opening diplomatic relations with Israel.[42]

COLONIAL CORPORATE GOVERNANCE AND LEGAL CULTURES

Colonial policies, institutions, and laws in Africa were largely motivated by goals of external powers who sought to extract benefits from their African territories. These powers talked about civilization and used rhetoric about civilization to justify colonialism. However, their conception of law, as implemented in colonies such as Nigeria, reflected governance and strategies based on goals of extraction for external benefit rather than development for internal improvement. Continuing structures of colonial governance and postcolonial policies implemented with an external orientation are part of why so many in Africa remain so poor. The externalized governance solidified during colonialism and continued after independence represents a significant impediment to fundamental transformation within Africa to approaches to governance that benefit most people within African countries.

Problems of governance in postcolonial Africa have long been recognized. Over the past twenty years, multiple initiatives have focused on governance or incorporated recommendations about governance into broader reform efforts. The New Partnership for Africa's Development (NEPAD), an economic development program of the African Union (AU) launched in 2001, has played an important role in putting good governance at the forefront of the development agenda. NEPAD seeks to address "challenges of poverty, development and Africa's marginalization internationally".[43]

The UN 2030 Agenda for Sustainable Development, adopted in 2015, establishes a fifteen-year timeline for countries to achieve seventeen Sustainable Development Goals (SDGs). The SDGs are intended to "free the human race from the tyranny of poverty" and "shift the world onto a sustainable and resilient path."[44] Effective governance is critical for achievement of the SDGs.[45] Notably, although progress has been made toward meeting some SDGs within Africa, most African countries are not on track to meet the SDGs.[46]

The AU has also launched Agenda 2063, which it describes as "Africa's blueprint and master plan for transforming Africa into the global powerhouse of the future … [and a] strategic framework that aims to deliver on its goal for inclusive and sustainable development … [breaking from the past] to prioritize inclusive social and economic development, continental and regional integration, democratic governance and peace and security amongst other issues aimed at repositioning Africa to becoming a dominant player in the global arena."[47] The Agenda 2063 goal of breaking from the past will require disruption of past approaches that have led to the current state of affairs.

These initiatives may be incomplete in not sufficiently considering the continuing impact of institutions, practices, legal arrangements, and bureaucratic structures, introduced during colonialism that must be transformed to truly address the challenges of poverty, development, and marginalization. African countries must disrupt legacies of colonial institutional, bureaucratic, and legal structures to a far greater extent than has been the case.

Colonial governance was external in origin, ultimate authority, and orientation. The administration of colonialism could be complex with activity at varied locations, including local colonial administrations and colonial metropolitan centers. Wider colonial power networks linked colonial and other global powers, as well as colonial possessions of the same power. This book does not delve deeply into the complexity of many of these aspects of the administration of colonialism. The British style of colonial governance eventually came to be based upon indirect rule in which the British ruled through local rulers. In contrast, the French style of colonial governance was based on direct rule, and colonial officers had direct authority over local rulers, which tended to reduce the power of local rulers and traditional institutions.[48] Although direct rule was more centralized in conceptualization and structure, differences between these two approaches may not always have been as evident in practice on the ground, in part due to the extensive reliance on local intermediaries that led all colonial powers to develop some form of indirect rule in a manner that left significant power in the hands of colonial administrators.[49] As a British colonial official described indirect rule in Dagomba in Ghana in the 1920s:

> Yendi has an elaborate system of nomination of chiefs . . . but in spite of this well-defined system, the administration in the past has interfered many a time with its working, and almost succeeded in breaking it down . . . . In reality, the administration is a direct one; the chiefs are practically powerless; they have neither revenue nor authority; they have tended to become mere sergeant-majors, through whom the administration can address the rank and file.[50]

British indirect rule in Nigeria involved extensive British supervision and guidance of local rulers. The administration of the Emirate of Katsina, a city in northwestern Nigeria, is described as follows in a dossier prepared in 1939 in anticipation of the Emir of Katsina's audience in London with King George VI: "[t]he administration of the Emirate is in the hands of the Emir, assisted by a Council of 9 hereditary officeholders and 22 District Heads. British Administrative Officers reside in the Emirate to supervise and guide the Administration."[51]

Both direct and indirect rule were based on patterns of borrowing from external models and sources. This borrowing entailed transfer of more than just laws and legal systems. Laws and legal orders do not exist in isolation, but rather, in specific sociocultural contexts. These contexts shape law in ways that may not always be adequately recognized, particularly in instances of coercive borrowings. Greater interrogation of context, legal cultures, and legal meaning is an essential element for disruption of existing deleterious patterns of external borrowing in African countries. Legal culture reflects the "cultural background of law which creates the law and which is necessary to give meaning to law . . . [and] is . . . important in explaining and predicting the effect of law on society, such as in the extent to which promulgated laws will be adhered to and judgments will be implemented."[52]

Any discussion of law, culture, and meaning should take account of both institutional and interpretive aspects of legal frameworks. One potential source of frameworks for understanding the role of culture in the legal arena comes from symbolic anthropology as espoused by Clifford Geertz, who conceptualizes culture as involving "webs of significance" that humans spin and within which humans are also suspended.[53] Geertz's conceptualization of culture focuses on the interpretive aspects of culture and draws attention to the implicit cultural meanings within which law and other sociocultural elements may be shaped. Consideration of sociocultural context must also encompass the ways in which human agency may also act to shape the webs within which we are suspended.[54] Attention to the reality of human agency has implications for legal discourse where conceptions of sociocultural processes and human actors are often incomplete and unsatisfactory.[55] Questions of agency can also reveal something central to colonialism itself: "[u]nderstandings of agency were at the core of the colonial encounter. The ways in which Africans and Europeans thought about power and the ability to act underwrote foreign rule and Gabonese reactions to it, shaping innumerable decisions in everyday life."[56]

Human agency and social institutions may help to illuminate the "concrete processes of social life."[57] Consideration of law and sociocultural context thus necessitates closer scrutiny of law as a "constructed social world that could be constructed differently."[58] Understanding the cultural vision at least implicit in laws and legal doctrine is an important step in elucidating the actual operation of law in practice.

Legal cultures that came with colonialism to Nigeria were to a significant degree inconsistent with widespread cultural and community values that existed prior to colonialism, including values evident in customary law. These values were varied and by no means static and reflected ongoing internal processes of interchange, as well as changes that came with varied internal and external interactions, including with Europeans. The large-scale translation of external bodies of law in colonial contexts occurred as European colonizers established colonial administrative structures in Africa in the late nineteenth and twentieth centuries. In British colonies, colonial administrations in conjunction with colonial officials in London undertook the wholesale imposition of legal frameworks that involved significant borrowings from English law in circumstances that were radically different from contexts of origin.

These laws were imposed along with new colonial economic, political, and social structures.[59] Although colonial administrators spoke about continuity of traditional legal structures that they believed had existed from time immemorial, colonialism itself entailed significant disruption, which is evident in the emergence during colonialism of a form of power "not merely coincident with colonialism ... concerned above all with disabling old forms of life by systematically breaking down their conditions, and with constructing in their place new conditions so as to enable – indeed, so as to oblige – new forms of life to come into being."[60] Further, as Sally Falk Moore notes in her ethnographic study of the historical development of customary law among the Chagga in Tanzania, customary law is "itself a cultural construct with political implications. The term sounds as if it designates a straightforward set of traditional rules. But the entity to which it refers is a set of ideas embedded in relationships that are historically shifting. The label 'customary law' has its own history in colonial and postcolonial worlds."[61]

Because law was central to colonialism, it "provides an excellent window through which to view the colonial period,"[62] as well as what has come after the formal end of colonialism. New legal structures were imposed by external powers with little internal input: "forms, institutions and processes of a 'contractual' legal system were imposed upon local societies rather than 'evolved' by them."[63] The transplantation of English law in British colonial contexts was a core aspect of colonialism. Rule of law was presented as a key benefit of colonialism that was used to justify colonial rule.[64] Although British and other colonizers talked about rule of law, their practices on the ground in Africa often did not reflect adherence to robust conceptions of rule of law. Failure to respect rule of law with respect to African colonial possessions did not end with colonialism. This has been evident, for example, in the International Court of Justice case brought by Mauritius against the United Kingdom. This case arose from events at the time of independence:

> In 1964, a UK/US survey of the Indian Ocean revealed that Diego Garcia, in the remote Chagos Archipelago, would make an ideal site for a US military base. The Archipelago was a distant dependency of the Non-Self-Governing Territory of Mauritius and home to the Chagossians ... the United Kingdom ... detach[ed] the Chagos Islands from Mauritius. It applied considerable pressure to obtain consent and the transaction was tied up with the decision to grant Mauritius its independence. The British Indian Ocean Territory (BIOT) was created in 1965 and the Chagos Islands were separated from Mauritius accordingly. In 1966, the United Kingdom and United States concluded a treaty regarding the use of Diego Garcia. Pursuant to the planned construction of a U.S. base on this island, the Chagossians were forcibly removed from the entire Archipelago. Most were transported to Mauritius where they have experienced chronic impoverishment.[65]

The United Kingdom has consistently refused to permit the displaced Chagossians to return to the Chagos Islands. The Chagos Archipelago case is important for understanding decolonization processes and ways in which patterns of domination established during colonialism continue to play an important role globally as well as within former colonies. Events at the time of independence led to a long-standing dispute about the sovereignty of the Chagos Archipelago that led the

International Court of Justice (ICJ) to issue an advisory opinion on the request of the United Nations General Assembly.[66] The 2019 ICJ advisory opinion concluded that the occupation of the Chagos Archipelago by the United Kingdom was unlawful: "as a result of the Chagos Archipelago's unlawful detachment and its incorporation into a new colony, known as the BIOT, the process of decolonization of Mauritius was not lawfully completed when Mauritius acceded to independence in 1968."[67] The ICJ also considers power relationships of the colonizer and the colonized in reaching its opinion that the detachment of the Chagos Archipelago was unlawful:

> In the Court's view, it is not possible to talk of an international agreement, when one of the parties to it, Mauritius, which is said to have ceded the territory to the United Kingdom, was under the authority of the latter. The Court is of the view that heightened scrutiny should be given to the issue of consent in a situation where a part of a non-self- governing territory is separated to create a new colony. Having reviewed the circumstances in which the Council of Ministers of the colony of Mauritius agreed in principle to the detachment of the Chagos Archipelago on the basis of the Lancaster House agreement, the Court considers that this detachment was not based on the free and genuine expression of the will of the people concerned.[68]

The ICJ concluded that "the United Kingdom is under an obligation to bring an end to its administration of the Chagos Archipelago as rapidly as possible, thereby enabling Mauritius to complete the decolonization of its territory in a manner consistent with the right of peoples to self- determination."[69] The United Nations General Assembly overwhelmingly adopted a resolution on May 22, 2019 by a vote of 116 to 6. This resolution affirmed the 2019 ICJ Advisory Opinion and demanded that the United Kingdom "withdraw its colonial administration from the Chagos Archipelago unconditionally within a period of no more than six months from the adoption of the present resolution, thereby enabling Mauritius to complete the decolonization of its territory as rapidly as possible."[70] As of late 2020, more than one year after the deadline established in the General Assembly resolution, the United Kingdom had refused to withdraw from the Chagos Archipelago.[71] Mauritius has indicated that it would lease the Diego Garcia military base to the United States once the United Kingdom withdraws.[72] The Chagos Archipelago case reveals something important about both external and internal implications of colonial governance. It also underscores the potential malleability of rule of law in colonial contexts and ways in which colonizing powers and their allies (in this case the United Kingdom and the United States) may operate in partnership with one another to the detriment of countries once colonized. Examining the art of government touches upon what decolonization means and whether and when colonialism actually ended.[73] From a legal perspective, as the Chagos case illustrates, decolonization processes may be at best works in progress.

Within colonial possessions, British colonial governance came to be based on particular forms of governance. Colonial governance in Northern Nigeria became the model for indirect rule in Africa.[74] In theory, at least, British indirect rule shared functions of government between the colonial administration and *native* administrations. In practice, colonial power was predominant. European powers often rationalized colonial rule in Africa using two types of arguments. These arguments reflect the dual mandate advanced by Frederick Lugard, one of the best-known officers to serve in British colonial Africa. The first type of arguments justify colonialism because of the barbarous or savage state of Africans, who would benefit from a civilizing European influence, including notably, European law. The second type of arguments justify exploitation of Africa's resources and raw materials based on perceived inadequacies of African people and African cultural practices, including land use practices. Lugard uses both arguments in justifying colonialism:

> These products [raw materials] lay wasted and ungarnered in Africa because the natives did not know their use and value. Millions of tons of oil-nuts, for instance, grew wild without the labour of man, and lay rotting in the forests. Who can deny the right of the hungry people in Europe to utilize the wasted bounties of nature, or that task of developing these resources was, as Mr Chamberlain expressed it, a 'trust for civilization' and for the benefit of mankind? Europe benefitted by the wonderful increase in the amenities of life for the mass of her people which followed the opening up of Africa at the end of the nineteenth century. Africa benefited by the influx of manufactured goods, and the substitution of law and order for the methods of barbarism.[75]

W. E. B. Du Bois saw colonial practices regarding land and natural resources as constituting theft: "To-day Africa is being enslaved by the theft of her land and natural resources . . . shameless monopolizing of land and natural resources to force poverty on the masses and reduce them to the 'dumb-driven-cattle' stage of labor activity."[76] The positioning of colonialism as a necessity because of local *failures* to use adequately land and other natural resources reflects a discourse based in ideologies of European superiority that treated any European uses of such resources as justified. These justifications were used to sanction a wide range of European actions and practices, including some that entailed considerable brutality for local people. Furthermore, the structure of argument used by Lugard and other colonizers in relation to raw materials had a direct connection to allocations of legal rights regarding such resources. Local *failures* to use such resources in accordance with European use expectations became the basis for European ownership of and extraction of such resources, seemingly in perpetuity.

Lugard's assertions about law reflected pervasive use of legal rationales within discourses of empire by British and other colonizers where discourse about possession and occupation actually reflected competition among competing colonial empires rather than an attempt to defend property claims or the moral legitimacy of such claims:

> [t]he European discourse on possession and occupation developed both in metropolitan centers and in empire ... imperial agents engaged in and encouraged an inclusive, not to say scattershot, approach to legal rationales ... .Their main objective was to show *better* title to territories vis-à-vis competing empires rather than to defend claims to absolute title or moral legitimacy....[77]

Within this indiscriminate approach, asserting and defending claims involved "multiple, overlapping, and even conflicting arguments being addressed to various, sometimes imagined, audiences."[78] Underlying rationales justifying colonialism, at least from a legal perspective, were not always fully thought out or consistent. As with rationales for colonialism, legal frameworks implemented in British colonial Africa were inconsistent and at times incoherent.

British colonialism reflected the extractive goals of the dual mandate to a significant degree. The first mandate of extraction subsumed second part of the dual mandate of African development: "[c]olonialism was first and foremost a search for super-profits rather than a 'civilizing mission'."[79] This extractive focus was apparent in British investment decisions within Africa. Infrastructure investments, for example, reflected an external focus that facilitated extraction rather than implementation for internal benefit. This does not mean that no internal benefit occurred, but rather, that internal benefit was often an incidental outcome of externally driven and oriented processes. The development of colonies as a locus for extraction has played an important role in creating vulnerable and unstable political systems and economies in a number of African countries:

> It was far more efficient for the raw materials to be produced where the labour was actually sited and Africa became transformed into a mineral and agricultural exporter for the burgeoning European manufacturing centres. Colonisation was in no small measure concerned with establishing this system ... not only were the raw materials provided for the metropolitan countries but the money paid to the African peasants and the mine and plantation workers provided them with the cash to meet their tax obligations, and this covered the costs of colonial rule .... Ghana became dependent on the export of cocoa, Zambia on copper. Fragile, unstable and vulnerable economies were the legacy.[80]

The British colonial emphasis on extraction also reflected an underlying approach to governance in British colonies that was much like that of a corporation in orientation. This corporate orientation was apparent in activities of chartered private companies, such as the Royal Niger Company (RNC) and other private companies, as well as in activities of British colonial authorities. In contexts of indirect and other rule overseen by the British government, local authorities were agents for the colonial power, but were not necessarily respected by them or thought to be worthy political leaders.[81] As with other colonial political and legal institutions, indirect rule originated "largely in a doctrine of expediency."[82]

Colonial Nigeria was to a significant degree run like a business enterprise, focusing continually on cost containment and ensuring that colonialism would pay for itself: "imperial rulers of British Africa and India strove to balance budgets and minimize costs by hiring local recruits for petty administrative jobs."[83] This reflects an ethos of what Sara Berry has referred to as "hegemony on a shoestring."[84] Extractive colonial economies were also built on cheap labor, which facilitated the creation of profitable enterprises built upon extraction of raw materials.

Private companies played a significant role in colonialism. In India, for example, colonial conquest was undertaken initially by the British East India Company, "a dangerously unregulated private company headquartered in one small office, five windows wide, in London, and managed in India by a violent, utterly ruthless and intermittently unstable corporate predator .... India's transition to colonialism took place under a for-profit corporation, which existed entirely for the purpose of enriching its investors."[85] Chartered companies such as the RNC were essential layers in the overlapping and competing zones that characterized colonialism.[86] Approaches of the RNC included soft approaches reflected in treaties and agreements and hard approaches that used military power, which led to many atrocities.[87]

Mass violence was an essential part of colonialism in varied contexts. Colonial wars tended to "degenerate into genocidal slaughter."[88] Colonial wars descended into slaughter at least partly as a result of competition among European powers: "colonial powers are ready to act against their economic interests and to use genocidal violence in order to avoid or avenge humiliating defeats against 'semi-civilized' adversaries. Europeans perceived indigenous resistance not only as a threat to their ambitions in the colonies but to their imperial project as such because a possible failure diminished their prestige in the eyes of imperial rivals."[89]

In the early 2000s, representatives of the Hereros, an ethnic group in southern Africa, filed a series of lawsuits in federal courts in the United States, seeking reparations relating to colonial-era atrocities committed by representatives of the German government and German companies during colonialism in German South West Africa (today the Republic of Namibia).[90] The slaughter of Herero and Nama:

> is generally recognized as the first genocide of the twentieth century. Following an uprising of Herero against German settlers, the German *Schutztruppe* chased the Herero into the Omaheke Desert, forcing thousands of women and children to die of thirst while others were shot on sight. Many of those who escaped death were sent to concentration camps, or coerced into working commercial farms, where many died from inhumane conditions.[91]

The Herero lawsuits, which were ultimately not successful, brought attention to the German genocide in its South West Africa colony. In German, prisoner camps during the 1904–1908 war, for example, German documentation suggests that death rates were close to 50 percent.[92] During the 1904–1908 war, German General Lothar von Trotha issued an extermination order that "stated that within German territory

Herero men with or without guns were to be shot and that no more Herero prisoners would be taken."[93] Some 80 percent of Herero people were killed and their land "transferred to German settlers with long-term loans subsidized by the German government. These farms remain the heart of Namibian agriculture to this day."[94] In 2020, Germany and Namibia were said to be negotiating an official apology. In August 2020, Namibia reportedly rejected a compensation offer from Germany of €10 million.[95]

The Congo Free State (today the Democratic Republic of the Congo (DRC)) was owned by King Leopold II of Belgium. In his quest for personal enrichment, Leopold implemented a bloody and barbaric governance regime in his personal domain:

> To harvest ivory and, more importantly, rubber, required conscription of the 'natives.' In the process all manner of hideous acts were committed. Rubber quotas were assigned, and if the output was too low, villages would be burned and Africans shot. Others were flogged or mutilated – the chopping off of hands was by no means uncommon. Women were kidnapped and held as hostages .... Massacres were not rare. As was the case with the Nazi-sponsored Holocaust, slave labor led to many deaths, as did deliberate starvation and disease. In addition, the Congolese birth rate dropped precipitously. Precise mortality statistics are difficult to come by, but historians estimate the death toll to have been six to eight million, perhaps even ten million. In the opinion of ... Belgian scholar Jan Vansina, the Congolese population was reduced by 50% over a 40-year period beginning in 1880.[96]

The atrocities in the Congo Free State were disclosed to the world by two African American missionaries, one of whom, George W. Williams,[97] wrote an open letter to King Leopold that has been characterized as the "first comprehensive, systematic indictment of Leopold's colonial regime written by anyone."[98]

Colonial violence was related to the profit-seeking goals of colonialism as a form of essentially corporation-like governance. The Herero and Congo Free State cases particularly reveal various profit motivations at the core of many colonial endeavors. Although European justifications for colonialism often focused on bringing *civilization* to Africa, structures of governance revealed other more important priorities. In the case of Congo Free State, King Leopold sought to wring profit from his personal domain. As Adam Hochschild notes, "[r]eading the king's correspondence is like reading the letters of a CEO of a corporation that has just developed a profitable new product and is racing to take advantage of it before competitors can get their assembly lines going."[99] Governance in German South West Africa reflected recognition by the German government of the "necessity of having German companies assume responsibility for the economic exploitation of South West Africa."[100]

Colonialism in Congo Free State and German South West Africa reflected the violence that came with colonial undertakings, as well as the corporate orientation that was characteristic of colonialism, even in instances that did not involve actual corporations. In Nigeria, the takeover of RNC territories by the British government did not displace its corporate orientation or governance approach. Reflecting an ethos that echoed forms of governance established by chartered companies, Nigeria, which was an entity constructed by the British, was a "administered . . . as a corporatized entity . . . imagined and governed not as a nation but as an industrial corporate entity."[101] The colonial administration in Nigeria and elsewhere in Africa was thinly staffed, reflecting a "thin white line" of official European staff in African colonies:[102] in the late 1930s, 3,000 European administrators ruled over an African population of some 90 million.[103] The thinness of this line varied among colonies and is an enduring legacy of colonialism. The thinly staffed nature of European colonialism also meant that activities on the ground in Africa were implemented through various types of intermediaries. How colonial powers conceptualized, selected, and empowered these agents of colonial powers have had continuing consequences in former colonies in Africa.

The structures put in place to facilitate extraction for the most part did not contribute to development in the long term, but led to structures that created incentives for agents of colonial powers that have been detrimental for many in Africa. Decision-making by British colonizers often reflected a short-term orientation that largely considered British interests and needs. These decisions also showed a portfolio mindset that led British decision makers to make investment and other decisions across their portfolio of colonial possessions in ways that accrued to their benefit, often in ways that were not to the benefit of local people or institutions in contexts within which such decisions unfolded.

GOVERNANCE, AGENCY, AND COLONIAL LEGAL SYSTEMS

British colonial authorities conceptualized governance as a duality of British created and native administrations. Despite the appointment or designation of local rulers as local authorities under indirect rule, any authority granted to such rulers was subject to advice and supervision by colonial political officers and was part of a system with questionable legal underpinnings. These legal underpinnings involved various hybrid forms of governance that were often messy, ad hoc, and a poor basis for independent nations with functional and effective legal systems that incorporate rule of law.

Both indirect and direct rule involved laws derived from the laws of the colonial power and laws that were categorized as *traditional* or *customary*. In British colonies, this typically led to a distinction between customary law and English law, at times with Islamic law as an additional body of law that was applicable in some local areas. British officials viewed customary law as an *immutable tradition*, and British colonial rule entailed identification of chiefs, who were put in place even where none had existed before, including in the Warrant Chief system in southeastern Nigeria:

In seeking to apply this policy [of Indirect Rule] to the Ibo and their neighbors, the British selected certain natives who they thought were traditional chiefs and gave them certificates of recognition and authority called warrants. The warrant entitled each of these men to sit in the Native Court from time to time to judge cases. It also empowered him to assume within the community he represented executive and judicial powers which were novel both in degree and territorial scope . . . . One striking characteristic of the Ibo, Ibibio, Ijo and Ogoja peoples at the time of British advent was their decentralization ... each of these people was split into a large number of tiny, politically equivalent and autonomous units.[104]

The Warrant Chief system "was set up to serve as an instrument of political 'pacification' and consolidation ... busying the supposed chiefs with the work of local administration, especially where this brought some material reward to act as a bribe, was an effective way of limiting the time and inclination they might have to plan mischief."[105] The selection and maintenance of native authorities led to circumstances where selected intermediaries were agents with problematic incentives. These agents were not necessarily rewarded for representing the interests of those whom they ostensibly ruled. Rather, the establishment of native authorities reflected a process by which agents were chosen to represent British interests. This has had continuing implications for governance throughout Africa.

British indirect rule began in northern Nigeria with the use of Emirs to carry out administrative functions. In parts of southern Nigeria, paramount chiefs of the emir type did not exist. In such instances, "the creation of a paramount chief, while fitting perfectly into the working of the Lugard system, was bound to create difficulties in practice, as it was tantamount to granting whosoever was appointed to the office arbitrary paramountcy over a large area."[106] In some cases, this led to the appointment of a single chief in areas with multiple ethnic groups. In Warri Province in the Niger Delta, a translator and intermediary who was loyal to the British was given the status of *Recognized Chief* for the Warri division, which included the Itsekiri, Urhobo, and Ijaw peoples due to the fact that "the British were pre-occupied with the working of a system, and failed to realize that in the Warri Province with no less than five different ethnic groups, there could be no traditional or paramount chief acceptable to all the groups."[107] In other places, *native alien* subcolonialism was put in place, including in the diverse Middle Belt region of Nigeria between north and south, where

an actually existing cultural and religious divide sustained a narrative of difference and deviation and enabled British colonizers to insinuate Muslim Hausa-Fulani officials as 'natural' overlords over non-Muslim Middle Belt communities . . . .The British sat atop their pyramid of sociopolitical sophistication and authority. The Hausa-Fulani inheritors of the caliphate's heritage sat below them . . . . The non-Muslim peoples of the Middle Belt, described in both [Sokoto] caliphate and British discourse as benighted tribesman, sat on the lowest rung.[108]

Because of inattention or indifference to the realities on the ground of dual governance, intermediaries were given opportunities to undertake an extractive approach to the people whom they governed through practices such as jurisdictional arbitrage and other forms of corruption. Not all rulers did this. Although some were penalized, the British response to these extractive behaviors did not typically lead to broad institutional constraint of such practices. This reflects prioritization given to expediency over institutional coherence, integrity, and constraint of those in power.

Native chiefs were incorporated as local rulers within a system in which customary law governed most contexts involving local people. Customary law was treated as if it had existed in a static state. The view of customary law as immutable was incorporated into local understandings of customary law and was evident in petitions submitted to colonial administrators in Nigeria. These petitions typically included a standard recital about customary law that indicated its immutable and implicitly unchanging existence "from time immemorial."[109] This phrase is still used today in discussions about customary law in Nigeria. How to determine whether something has existed from time immemorial raises evidentiary questions. In a 1931 case involving a land dispute in Onitsha, the Supreme Court of Nigeria notes:

> one of the essentials of a custom which will be given effect to by a Court of Law is that it must be immemorial though proof that it has existed during living memory will establish a presumption of immemorially. This at once puts plaintiffs in a difficulty since it is obvious that they cannot date the custom further back than the advent of European civilization before which such a conception as to payment of yearly rent for land was unknown .... Native custom may change with the advent of European ideas, and I should not be inclined to exclude a custom from recognition if it could be shown that it has existed substantially back to the time of European settlement ... the custom contended for by plaintiffs lacks three of the essential elements of a custom which the Courts will enforce, namely, antiquity, certainty, and free consent."[110]

The view of customary law as ancient and unchanging did not take sufficient account of ways in which customary law was a response to colonialism itself, but instead reflected a view that customary law was not really law. The implementation of customary law frameworks in Nigeria and other British colonies in Africa led to invention of tradition and zones of contestation.[111]

British approaches in colonial Africa conceptualized and applied law in racialized ways, with English law applying to Europeans and customary law applying to most *natives* in British colonies. Although other European powers also had colonies in Africa, Britain's colonizing activities touched many more people in Africa than activities of other European colonizers. British colonies had a larger population than French, Belgian, and Portuguese colonies combined.[112] French colonies distinguished between persons of "state civil français" and "status personnel," the former of which applied to French people and the latter to Africans who had not been granted French citizenship.[113] Mozambique, a Portuguese colony, distinguished between white colonists and elite natives, "who made up the central state, had access to citizenship rights and were ruled by civil law"; in contrast, the rural majority "located in ethnic enclaves, were ruled by 'traditional authority' through customary law."[114] In postcolonial contexts, this continuing bifurcation has contributed to the continuing wide divide between law as written and law in practice that is evident in Nigeria and elsewhere in Africa.

COLONIAL LEGAL SYSTEMS, COURTS, AND CONFLICT OF LAWS

In addition to offering opportunities for jurisdictional arbitrage and blocking activities by intermediaries, the dual colonial legal system that combined elements of English law and customary law raised continuing issues about conflict of laws. Conflict of law principles are important in contexts where multiple bodies of law may interact. The importance of conflict of law principles was evident in the United Kingdom following the eighteenth century Anglo–Scottish union and later union between Great Britain and Ireland. This situation led to potential questions to arise concerning jurisdiction, choice of law, and recognition and enforcement.[115] Jurisdiction deals with the ability of a court to either assert power over a defendant in a lawsuit (personal jurisdiction) or the entitlement of a court to hear the subject matter of a lawsuit (subject matter jurisdiction).[116] Choice of law principles determine which law should be applied in a case when more than one law governs disposition of the case.[117]

In colonial Nigeria, conflict of laws might have existed, for example, between various customary laws and Islamic law, English law and customary law, or English law and Islamic law. Conflict of laws might also exist between different customary law frameworks. Conflict of law issues were evident in colonial Nigeria in courts with oversight authority over customary law, which were typically given a fairly nebulous jurisdiction. Native Courts Law 1956 deals with native courts in northern Nigeria. Under this law, the court's jurisdiction extends to what the law refers to as "natives," meaning Africans. The provisions of the law dealing with jurisdiction, however, do not directly say this, which gives those administering or interpreting the law tremendous discretion. This law gives native courts in northern Nigeria jurisdiction over "person and classes of persons who have ordinarily been subject to the jurisdiction of native tribunals (Section 15)." Under this law, native courts also have jurisdiction over people who consent to jurisdiction of the court, people who institute proceedings in native court, and people (African or non-African) whom colonial administrators direct to be subject to the jurisdiction of a native court.[118]

Most provisions in the statute that define the jurisdiction of native courts are qualified by the requirement that native courts have jurisdiction over persons "whose general model of life is that of the general native community."[119] The language concerning general models of life and inclusion of non-Africans in the category of people who could be subject to the jurisdiction of a native court are instructive. These legal provisions demonstrate that the law was intended to give native courts jurisdiction over Africans but not Europeans, and, at the same, time give significant discretion to colonial administrators.

The jurisdiction of native courts under the Native Courts Law 1956 raises conflict of law issues,[120] some of which the law anticipates and attempts to address. The law includes Islamic law within the definition of *native law and custom*. It also defines *mixed cause* to mean a cause in which two or more of the parties are normally subject to different systems of native law and custom. Native courts were structured to eliminate native court jurisdiction over Europeans unless colonial administrators desired otherwise. Conceptions and definitions of natives also reflect the racialized nature of colonial societal and legal contexts. This was evident when these laws were applied to people who were neither European nor African and people with *mixed-race* backgrounds. The vagueness of definitions of the native was present in other colonial African contexts. In British colonial administrations in eastern, central, and southern Africa in the late 1920s and 1930s, a lack of consensus existed as to how to define the term *native*, despite the fact that the term was widely used and applied.[121]

The 1929 *Carr* v. *Karim* case reflects how legal definitions of who is a native can play an important role in case outcomes.[122] Christopher J. Lee described the events in this case, which took place in the British protectorate of Nyasaland, which is part of Malawi today. Ernest Carr sold a truck to Suleman Abdul Karim, who lived in a neighboring town. Carr and Karim entered into a written contract that set forth payment for the car in monthly installments. After making two payments, Karim defaulted on the remaining payments and failed to pay an insurance premium that the two had agreed upon. Karim did not return ownership of the truck to Carr. Carr then brought a claim against Karim before the High Court of Nyasaland in 1929. During the trial, Karim sought *non-native* status. The case involved application of the Credit Trade with Natives Ordinance 1926, which prohibited giving credit to "natives." Karim would thus have been protected from prosecution if he had claimed native status because Carr would have been in violation of the Ordinance for having given credit to a native. It is not clear from the case documents why Karim took the position that he was not a "native."[123] The court determines that Karim held non-native status but a "half-caste Indian ... of Indian origin."[124] In reaching the determination of Karim's racial status, the court notes:

> Defendant states that he does not wish to take the defense that he is a native. The Court however must consider this, and I therefore ask him who were his parents. He says his father was an Indian and his mother a native.... By the Credit Trade with Natives Ordinance 1926 (15) a native is defined as a native of Africa not being of European or Asiatic race or origin; accordingly for this Ordinance a native means

a native of Africa who is not of European or Asiatic race or origin, and all others are non-natives .... A person's race or origin does not depend on where he or she is born, just as being born in a manger does not make a person a cow, or a child of European parents being born in India or China is not therefore an Indian or a Chinaman.[125]

This case led to unintended consequences, including the "formation of a politically active 'Anglo-African' community that sought state recognition and various social benefits such as civil service jobs and separate educational facilities."[126] The case also circulated among colonial officials in east, central, and southern Africa regarding the categories of *native* and *non-native*, and eventually reached British colonial administrations throughout Africa, the Colonial Office in London and "served as an unanticipated catalyst for addressing questions of race, legal status, and legal uniformity in British colonial Africa."[127] This case provides important "insight into colonial state formation and state power, specifically the ambiguities, contradictions and organic, improvisational nature of their existence."[128] This case is also notable in illustrating forms of economic exclusion of local people in colonial African contexts. The ordinance at issue in *Carr* v. *Karim* limited access to credit and prohibited loans to "natives." The ordinance was intended to protect Africans from predatory loans and exploitation, particularly by Whites.[129]

In colonial contexts, expediency and lack of foresight led to colonial legal and other institutions not being fully developed. As a result, adequate conflict of law principles were often not established. Customary law was by its nature fragmented, which fit well with a key underlying colonial policy of divide and rule. Furthermore, a "system of ethnic identification underlies customary law," with a "jurisdiction limited to particular cultural boundaries," and constituting "the possession and right of a restricted ethnic group."[130] For example, in Cameroon, part of which was a British colony and part of which was a French colony, each of over 250 ethnic groups has its own customary rules.[131]

Although customary law has offered an avenue for application of internal local norms and legal practices, the colonial law assumption of a separate body of customary law for each discrete group as defined by the colonizing country is potentially problematic. It is rigid and may ossify law in a structure based in some instances on invented traditions. It is not a structure of law that promotes unification across internal boundaries, which is something an internal country builder would attempt to address. Assumptions that underlie how customary law that became norms during colonialism should be applied, and the rigidity of the structure of its implementation, have become more difficult to justify and administer. Customary law tended to be consigned to private law matters related to family and inheritance and land rights. Cut-and-paste versions of English law were applied in most other areas, including to the overall structure and operation of legal institutions, criminal law and procedure, and economic and business matters. Customary law was secondary to English law and could be void to the extent that it was "repugnant" to the laws of England.[132]

The colonial legal system in Nigeria involved a mix of English law and customary law that could be confusing. This confusion involved legal structures and was also a consequence of lack of care taken in a broad range of legal undertakings, from the drafting statutes and ordinances to documentation of treaties and other agreements. This has had a significant negative impact long after colonialism in varied areas, including in relation to land claims.

Colonial administrators in Nigeria in the 1920s describe early RNC treaties as "nebulous treaties, which only referred to sovereign rights over undefined areas."[133] As a result, the Nigerian colonial government itself was confused about the origins and scope of its own rights in varied contexts. In a discussion of land rights in relation to a petition involving a dispute related to Itsekiri land rights, a report marked *Confidential* notes that the RNC entered into treaties and separate agreements regarding land rights.

According Sir William Geary, an English solicitor who represented Nigerian clients in claims relating to land and other matters, the RNC acquired titles as follows: "according to repute . . . the agent of the Niger Co went in a launch with armed police and with an offer of gin, dane guns, and trade gunpowder . . . an African made little difficulty in affixing his mark to any paper."[134] When the British government took over RNC territories after revocation of its charter, the colonial government's title to lands governed by the Royal Nigeria Company was "confused" by incorrect information about the source of such rights: "the Government was under the impression that its rights were derived from the Treaties instead of the later Agreements. (This confusion seems to find an echo in the last sentence of the extract from Lord Lugard's memorandum quoted above). It was not until 1926 that the original Agreements were re-discovered."[135]

In an opinion contained in the same colonial administration file discussing Atani lands said to be acquired by the RNC, the writers of the opinion note that

> it does not appear anywhere, that the chiefs and people of Osibite possessed any sovereign rights over the Atani lands . . . . It would appear from the general character of the treaties and agreements, that the [Royal Niger] Company were anxious to obtain an option on all land which could be used with advantage for development purposes, with a view to furthering their own ends, and excluding competitors from the best sites for trading . . . . In the papers before us, there does not appear to be any document the equivalent of conveyance . . . the documents could hardly be called Agreements for sale.[136]

The Nigerian colonial government was aware that at least some land claims based on the RNC treaties and agreements were of doubtful validity. After a report concerning land claims was completed in 1933, the Nigerian colonial government determined that

> in cases where it appeared that the Government had no claim or only a claim of doubtful validity it should merely cease quietly to make any claim to rights over the land: it was pointed out that for the most part the areas affected were occupied by people who had no idea that the Government had any claim in regard to them. On the other hand lands occupied by Government or leased to nonnatives were to be retained as Crown lands, it being left to future administrations to hand them back to people if the land ceased to be required by Government or when the lease fell in. This line of action was approved by the Secretary of State . . . . Mr. Williams' report indicates that of the eighty-nine Agreements covering lands in Southern Nigeria, sixty-five are in a stereotyped form and are of particularly dubious validity. Indeed there is a strong suspicion that the majority of them are forgeries. He admits, however, that this is almost wholly conjecture and that it is based almost entirely on the statements of those most interested to disprove the validity of the agreements . . . Sir Williams' conclusion was that the Government would be justified in retaining its title in a number of cases. *The policy which was approved by the Secretary of State in 1935, and which it is still desired to pursue, is that the Government should withdraw from the large majority of the titles, only retaining as Crown land those actually occupied by Government or leased to non-natives . . . . The Government's position with regard to those lands which it desires to retain would be that anyone who wished to contest the Crown's title would be able to do so in the Courts. This policy is admittedly one of expediency. The title to the lands which it is desired to retain may be no better than that of lands which are to be abandoned and the decision whether to abandon or to retain is taken not in light of the probable validity of the title, but of the use to which the land has or has not been put by government.*[137]

The colonial government approach was rooted in expediency in the pursuit of British interests and convenience, even in cases based on dubious claims. This approached prioritized expediency over other desirable principles upon which functional legal systems tend to be based, including rule of law, justice, and fairness. Allowing people to challenge government claims was also unlikely to have been a satisfactory remedy in an environment in which the legal system was predominantly an alien one, imported by a government that was retaining rights in property that it knew to be questionable, and in which many were poor, few spoke English, and even fewer were likely to have had access to legal representation by a lawyer with knowledge of this alien legal system.

The Nigerian government approach also meant that sources of disputes were not addressed but pushed into some future time to be addressed. Colonial government actions and legal approaches in this and other cases reflect why the executive power in colonial Nigeria needed to be constrained and how rights about land and many other things emanating from colonial government legal practices and policies continue to be contentious in Nigeria and elsewhere in Africa.

Land was a particular point of contestation during colonialism between British colonizers and local people, as well as among local people themselves. Limiting

African access to land during colonialism made people more likely to be forced to provide labor for plantation, mines, and infrastructure projects.[138] In colonial Tanganyika, a former German colony that after independence was combined in 1964 with the island of Zanzibar to create Tanzania, British colonizers adopted the German hut and poll tax, which was aimed at extracting labor: "[i]n many cases the district administration actually planned their tax drives so as to flush out labour during periods when the employer needed it most . . . throughout the early period of colonialism, tax continued to be an important weapon in stimulating labour supplies."[139] British colonizers imposed hut and poll taxes multiple colonies, including in Kenya, where payment of such taxes was a prime burden for African agricultural producers.[140] Labor conditions under German colonial rule had been severe, with an average of 5,000 workers sentenced to corporal punishment each year from 1901 to 1913.[141] Labor law in Tanganyika, reinforced processes of labor extraction. Colonial administrative officers could require tax defaulters to work; defaulters who were required to work, but refused or failed to work, committed a criminal offense that made them subject to imprisonment for up to three months.[142]

The dual colonial legal system was not truly dual because the same people were ultimately in charge of making decisions about both legal systems in ways that typically prioritized their interests. Colonial officers had significant oversight over both customary and English law legislation and adjudication. Criminal law matters in Nigeria were principally governed by laws adopted in the early twentieth century, including the Criminal Procedure Ordinance of 1914, which was discussed in the case of *Shorunke* v. *The King*,[143] decided on appeal to the Privy Council. The Privy Council is an advisory body to the British sovereign that played an important legal role in colonial contexts, particularly in relation to its judicial functions, which are carried out by the Judicial Committee of the Privy Council. At the time of the *Shorunke* case, the Privy Council was the highest court of appeal in colonial Nigeria.[144] The appeal to the Privy Council occurred after the West African Court of Appeal upheld Shorunke's conviction. Thomas Shorunke was a police constable who was charged with three other constables and three other persons with breaking and entering a store in Ogbomosho and stealing £300 from the store.

At trial, the person whom Shorunke indicated was his legal counsel did not appear in court to any significant degree. Shorunke was mostly silent during the trial court proceedings. The trial judge did not subpoena the witnesses whom Shorunke had sought to call to testify. The judge proceeded with the trial and found Shorunke guilty and sentenced him to imprisonment of seven years with hard labor. In his appeal to the West African Court of Appeal, Shorunke complained about the refusal of the trial court to issue subpoenas and gave an alibi for his defense by filing affidavits and applying to be called to give evidence along with his witnesses. The Court of Appeal refused the application and affirmed his conviction in April 1940. Notably, during the Shorunke litigation, representatives for the Crown tried to draw a distinction between legal treatment of subpoenas in Nigeria from that in England by stating that common law was the basis for legal treatment under English law while appropriate local ordinances and procedures applicable under such ordinances were the basis for legal treatment in Nigeria. This view of representatives for the Crown is important from a legal perspective because it reflects an underlying treatment of law in Nigeria as something other than common law, at least as common law is typically understood. This draws attention to ways imposed, and coercive implementations of common law in colonial contexts represent a distinctive, and at times very different, type of common law that may be radically at odds with understandings of common law in its contexts of origin in England.

Following Shorunke's conviction at trial and his failure to persuade the appeals court to overturn his conviction or hear his application concerning the failure of the trial court to issue subpoenas in his case, William Geary, who was his lawyer at the time, wrote a letter to the Lord Chancellor of Great Britain,[145] who was then the head of the judiciary. In his letter, Geary notes that Shorunke's conviction "seems a miscarriage of justice ... [m]y client Thomas Shorunke ... was convicted of a robbery, whereto his defense was alibi, but the Appeal Court would not hear, and the Crown object to a hearing of his witnesses (including the lady superior of a convent) ... Can I solicit you to use your influence that my client's evidence of alibi may somehow be heard."[146] Geary also requested that his client be pardoned. After the Governor refused to pardon Shorunke, Geary indicated that Shorunke would appeal to Privy Council in forma pauperis represented by a solicitor appointed by the Privy Council clerk.[147] Colonial officers were opposed to the Privy Council appeal, suggesting that the matter did not fall within the scope of the Lord Chancellor's jurisdiction.[148]

The only question that the Privy Council examined in Shorunke's appeal was whether the trial judge should have issued the requested subpoenas without attaching conditions, or whether the trial judge was justified in requiring that Shorunke demonstrate a likelihood that the witnesses could give material evidence on Shorunke's behalf. The Privy Council noted that it "was conceded by the Crown's representatives that if this question had arisen in England, an accused man could have applied for and must have been furnished subpoenas without the imposition of any conditions."[149] Those arguing on behalf of the prosecution at the Privy Council noted that Shorunke was told in a meeting with the trial judge that he would get no further assistance and could make his own arrangements about subpoenas. The Privy Council decision noted that the Lordships did not understand this argument and that "it is difficult to see how a man under arrest in the midst of a trial could take steps to ensure that subpoenas would be issued without the assistance of the Court."[150]

The Lordships rejected the assertion that the Nigerian Ordinances and Rules provide the only method by which subpoenas can be obtained and stated that "[i]n their view there exists, side by side with them in appropriate cases, the English Common Law right of subpoena."[151] They also state that "they are unable to say that a grave miscarriage of justice has not occurred."[152] The Shorunke case highlights the confusion that may exist in determining how to navigate the multiple bodies of law that may apply in colonial and postcolonial legal contexts. The *Shorunke* case offers an important lesson in how due process and rule of law should have operated in colonial Nigeria at the level of trial courts.[153] This case underscores tensions and contradictions in ideas about what common law actually was in colonial contexts.

The *Shorunke* decision also highlights the overlaps between the executive and judiciary in colonial contexts such as Nigeria and the importance of institutions such as the judiciary that can effectively constrain decisions of the executive that are contrary to law. The Privy Council issued its decision in April 1946. By November 1946, colonial administrators were discussing whether Shorunke should be entitled to compensation for his loss of liberty.[154] Thomas Shorunke also asked for reinstatement in a letter where he speaks about the suffering and irreparable losses he experienced due to his imprisonment.[155]

Notes

1. Comaroff, 1997: 178–181.
2. McConnell and Tormey, 2020; George Packer. "We Are Living in a Failed State." *Atlantic*, June 2020.
3. World Bank, 1989: 60.
4. Foucault,1991: 87.
5. Ibid. at 87.
6. Ezenwe, 1993.
7. Gathii, 1998: 65.
8. Harsch, 1993: 7–9.
9. Ibid. at 7.
10. Ibid. at 16.
11. Ibid. at 24.
12. Gorm Rye Olsen notes that "In Europe and other OECD countries as well, these statements gave impetus to the formulation of demands for political reforms in developing countries towards Western-type democracy, and thereby Europe and the EC/EU came to support the international trend to replace 'development' with 'democracy' as one of the slogans of its development assistance in the 1990s." Olsen, 1998: 344.
13. Soest and Bohnenberger, 2016.
14. Beegle, Christiaensen, Dabalen, and Gaddis, 2016: 4.
15. "Ending Extreme Poverty." Interview with Ana Revenga, Senior Director of the Poverty and Equity Global Practice at the World Bank, June 8, 2016, accessed October 24, 2020, www.worldbank.org/en/news/feature/2016/06/08/ending-extreme-poverty.
16. TNA CO 583/155/4.
17. United Nations Secretary-General, António Guterres, Nelson Mandela Annual Lecture, July 18, 2020, accessed October 24, 2020, www.un.org/sustainabledevelopment/a-new-social-contract-for-a-new-era/.

18. Import substitution approaches typically assume that low-income countries must reduce the dominance of agricultural and mineral activities and industrialize by protecting their economies from imports from more developed countries in the North and put in place new activities to produce manufactured products that would over time change the structure of the economy. Import substitution may be contrasted with export-oriented approaches to development. Bruton, 1998: 904.
19. In the 1980s, African countries had a serious debt crisis that led to the role of the International Monetary Fund (IMF), a leading multilateral creditor to Africa, to shift "from that of primary provider of loans to one of policy advisor and certifier of the quality of the countries' policy regimes and economic conditions," which led to strained relations between the IMF and many African countries "because of resentment over the Fund's emphasis on 'structural' adjustment as the basis for its lending arrangements with low-income countries and with the increased use of detailed structural policy conditions in Fund-supported programs." "Looking to the Future: The IMF in Africa." (2000): 677–738, www.imf.org/external/pubs/ft/history/2012/pdf/c14.pdf.
20. John Page. Africa's Failure to Industrialize: Bad Luck or Bad Policy?" Brookings Africa In Focus Blog, November 20, 2014, accessed October 24, 2020, www.brookings.edu/blog/africa-in-focus/2014/11/20/africas-failure-to-industrialize-bad-luck-or-bad-policy/.
21. Notably, models undertaken in Northeast Asia and Southeast Asia incorporated export promotion strategies. Jung and Lee, 1986; Rodrik, 1996.
22. Joseph E. Stiglitz. "Knowledge for Development: Economic Science, Economic Policy, and Economic Ideas." Annual World Bank Conference on Development Economics, April 1998, http://documents.worldbank.org/curated/en/769861468765277458/pdf/multi-page.pdf.
23. Economist Intelligence Unit. "Manufacturing in Africa: Still Struggling with the Basics. March 16, 2016, accessed October 24, 2020, http://country.eiu.com/article.aspx?articleid=754034459&Country=South%20Africa&topic=Economy&subt_2.
24. Organization for Economic Cooperation and Development. *COVID-19 and Africa: Socio-Economic Implications and Policy Responses*, May 7, 2020, www.oecd.org/coronavirus/policy-responses/covid-19-and-africa-socio-economic-implications-and-policy-responses-96e1b282/.
25. Matthew Hill and Taonga Clifford Mitimingi. "Zambia Trades Blame With Bondholders Following Default." Bloomberg.com, November 16, 2020, accessed December 2, 2020, www.bloomberg.com/news/articles/2020-11-16/zambian-finance-minister-says-bondholders-to-blame-for-default. A Eurobond is debt issued in a currency other than that of the country issuing the bond. African countries issued some $115 billion in Eurobonds in the decade prior to the COVID-19 pandemic.
26. The Belt and Road Initiative has involved significant infrastructure investment in Africa by China that has led to concern about China's lending leading to a debt trap for governments that borrow. Andrew Chatzky and James McBride. Backgrounder: China's Massive Belt and Road Initiative. Council on Foreign Relations, January 28, 2020, accessed December 2, 2020, www.cfr.org/backgrounder/chinas-massive-belt-and-road-initiative.
27. Ollie Williams. "Zambia's default fuels fears of African 'debt tsunami' as Covid impact bites." *Guardian*, November 25, 2020, accessed December 2, 2020, www.theguardian.com/global-development/2020/nov/25/zambias-default-fuels-fears-of-african-debt-tsunami-as-covid-impact-bites.

28. Mosa and Noosa, 2019.
29. John Darnton. "In Poor, Decolonized Africa, Bankers Are New Overlords." *New York Times*, June 20, 1994, at A1, accessed October 24, 2020, www.nytimes.com/1994/06/20/world/in-poor-decolonized-africa-bankers-are-new-overlords.html.
30. Easterly, 2003; Thomson et al., 2017; Ismi, 2004.
31. Loewenson, 1993.
32. Babalola, Lunwangwa and Adeyinka, 1999: 88.
33. World Bank, 2018: 38–43.
34. UNICEF, 1989.
35. Ken Auletta. "The Dictator Index." *New Yorker*, February 28, 2011, www.newyorker.com/magazine/2011/03/07/the-dictator-index.
36. Mo Ibrahim Foundation. 2019. *Agendas 2063 and 2030: Is Africa on Track? African Governance Rep*ort, p. 17, https://mo.ibrahim.foundation/sites/default/files/2019-10/African_Governance_Report_2019.pdf.
37. African Development Bank. 1999. Bank Group Policy on Good Governance, www.afdb.org/en/documents/document/bank-group-policy-on-good-governance-27134.
38. Foucault, 1991: 92.
39. John Campbell. "Nigeria Faces a Crippling Population Boom. Council on Foreign Relations Blog." April 20, 2018, accessed October 24, 2020, www.cfr.org/blog/nigeria-faces-crippling-population-boom.
40. Divyanshi Wadhwa, "The Number of Extremely Poor People Continues to Rise in Sub-Saharan Africa." World Bank Blogs, September 19, 2018, accessed October 24, 2020, https://blogs.worldbank.org/opendata/number-extremely-poor-people-continues-rise-sub-saharan-africa.
41. Shelley, 2004.
42. Jared Malsin and Dion Nissenbaum. "Trump Wades into Western Sahara Conflict with Morocco-Israel Deal." *Wall Street Journal*, December 11, 2020, accessed December 11, 2020, www.wsj.com/articles/israel-morocco-deal-thrusts-u-s-into-western-sahara-conflict-11607705049.
43. www.un.org/en/africa/osaa/peace/nepad.shtml.
44. https://sustainabledevelopment.un.org/post2015/transformingourworld.
45. Glass and Newig, 2019.
46. Begashaw, 2020.
47. https://au.int/en/agenda2063/overview.
48. Munslow, 1983: 226.
49. Lawrance, Osborn, and Roberts, 2006: 9-10; Sharkey, 2003: 1.
50. Ferguson and Wilks, 1970: 332.
51. Visits of Native Chiefs. TNA CO 583/243/21.
52. Michaels, 2012: 2–3.
53. Geert, 1972: 4–5.
54. Ortner, 2006: 3.
55. Lessig, 1995: 947.
56. Bernault, 2019: 9.
57. Giddens, 1984: xvii, 30.
58. Kahn, 1999: 30.

59. Elias, 1963: 3–4.
60. Scott, D., 1999: 26.
61. Moore, 1986: xv.
62. Roberts and Mann, 1991: 4.
63. Chanock, 1998: 224–229.
64. Roberts and Mann, 1991: 4.
65. Stephen Allen. "The Chagos Advisory Opinion and the Decolonization of Mauritius." ASIL Insights, April 15, 2019, accessed December 2, 2020, www.asil.org/insights/volume/23/issue/2/chagos-advisory-opinion-and-decolonization-mauritius.
66. Legal Consequences of the Separation of the Chagos Archipelago from Mauritius in 1965, Advisory Opinion (February 25, 2019), at ¶ ¶1, 132.
67. Ibid. at ¶ 174.
68. Ibid. at ¶ 172.
69. Ibid. at ¶ 178.
70. General Assembly resolution 73/295, *Advisory opinion of the International Court of Justice on the legal consequences of the separation of the Chagos Archipelago from Mauritius in* 1965, A/RES/73/295 (May 22, 2019), https://undocs.org/pdf?symbol=en/A/RES/73/295.
71. Stephen Allen. "The U.K.'s Intransigence on the Chagos Islands Dispute Is a Self-Inflicted Wound." World Politics Review, July 29, 2020, accessed December 2, 2020, www.worldpoliticsreview.com/articles/28948/the-u-k-s-refusal-to-abide-by-the-icj-chagos-verdict-is-a-self-inflicted-wound.
72. Jagdish Koonjul. "Diego Garcia: The US Has a Clear Choice." The Interpreter, August 14, 2020, accessed December 2, 2020, www.lowyinstitute.org/the-interpreter/clear-choice-us-diego-garcia.
73. Thomas and Thompson, 2018.
74. Crowder, 1964.
75. Lugard, 1922: 615.
76. Du Bois, 1915: 713.
77. Benton and Straumann, 2010: 3–4.
78. Ibid. at 29.
79. Sumner, 1982: 23.
80. Munslow, 1983: 222.
81. Falola, 2009: 34–35.
82. Hailey, 1947: 338.
83. Sharkey, 2003: 2.
84. Berry, 1993: 24–25.
85. Dalrymple, 2019: 23.
86. Stern, 2013: 22.
87. Falola, 2009: 174–175.
88. Schaller, 2010: 350.
89. Ibid.
90. *Herero People's Reparations Corp.* v. *Deutsche Bank*, AG, 370 F.3d 1192, 361 U.S. App. D.C. 468 (D.C. Cir. 2004), Court Opinion (06/11/2004); *The Herero People's Reparations Corp.* v. *Deutsche Bank* AG, No. 03 Civ. 0991 (RLC)., 2006 BL 49655, 2006 WL 903197 (S.D.N.Y. Apr. 05, 2006), Court Opinion (04/05/2006); *Hereros* v. *Deutsche Afrika-Linien GMBLT & Co.*, Civil Action

No. 05-1872 (KSH)., 2006 BL 10959, 2006 US Dist. Lexis 2761 (D.N.J. January 17, 2006), Court Opinion (01/17/2006).

91. Cooper, 2006: 113.
92. Schaller, 2010: 359.
93. Gewald, 1994: 67.
94. Cooper, 2006: 114.
95. Jason Burke and Philip Olterman. "Namibia rejects German Compensation Offer over Colonial Violence." *The Guardian*, August 12, 2020, accessed October 23, 2020, www.theguardian.com/world/2020/aug/12/namibia-rejects-german-compensation-offer-over-colonial-violence.
96. Weisbord, 2003: 36.
97. Williams, 1890.
98. Hochschild, 1998: 109.
99. Ibid. at 159.
100. Voeltz, 1988: x.
101. Maiangwa, Dan Suleiman and Anyaduba, 2018: 3.
102. Kirk-Greene, 1980.
103. Richens, 2009: 36.
104. Afigbo, 1972: 6–7.
105. Ibid. at 50.
106. Ikime, 1965: 314.
107. Ibid. at 318.
108. Ochonu, 2014: 8.
109. TNA CO 583/254/8.
110. *Mgbelekeke* v. *Ijayi*. The Supreme Court of Nigeria, William Butler Lloyd Judge, Suit No. 4 of 1931, at Onitsha, August 23, 1931, TNA CO 583/199/9.
111. Roberts and Mann, 1991: 4.
112. Stauder, 1974: 39.
113. Opoku, 1974: 139–153.
114. Obarrio, 2014: 77.
115. Hood, 2007: xlvi.
116. Michaels, 2017.
117. Kramer, 1990: 280–281.
118. Northern Nigeria Native Courts Law 1956, Section 15(d).
119. Ibid. at Section 15(1)(a)(ii), Section 15(1)(b), and Section 15(1)(c)(ii).
120. Nwabueze, 2001.
121. Lee, 2005.
122. CO 822, Case No. 46 of 1929, *Ernest Carr* v. *Suleman Abdul Karim*. The events in this case are described by historian Christopher J. Lee. Lee, 2005: 455–457.
123. Christopher J. Lee notes that although "there is no clear evidence, Karim probably decided to risk punishment as a means of maintaining good relations in a small business community, even if it meant a financial penalty in the short term." Lee, 2011: 498.
124. Lee, 2005: 456.
125. Ibid. at 456.

126. Lee, 2005: 457.
127. Lee, 2011: 499.
128. Lee, 2005: 457.
129. Lee, 2011: 498.
130. Kiye, 2015: 86.
131. Ibid.
132. T. O. Elias notes that the main principles of repugnancy of Nigerian legislation may be stated as follows: "Under the Colonial Laws Validity Act 1865, any Nigerian legislative enactment contrary to the provisions of any Act of Parliament extending to the Colony is void for repugnancy." Elias, 1954: 23, 26. The Colonial Laws Validity Act 1865, 28 & 29 Vic. c. 63, Section 2 states: "Colonial laws, when void for repugnancy.-Any colonial law which is or shall be in any respect repugnant to the provision of any Act of Parliament extending to the colony to which such law may relate, or repugnant to any order or regulation made under authority of such Act of Parliament, or having in the colony the force and effect of such Act, shall be read subject to such Act, order, or regulation, and shall to the extent to such repugnancy, but not otherwise, be and remain absolutely void and inoperative."
133. Letter from Sir Graeme Thompson, Colonial Governor of Nigeria to Leo Amery, Colonial Secretary dated January 13, 1927. TNA CO 583/148/3.
134. Letter from Sir William Geary to O. G. R. Williams, Colonial Office dated August 8, 1942. TNA CO 583/255/6.
135. Report on Niger Lands marked *Confidential*. Petitions. Sir William Gary – Acquisition of the Itsekeri and Claim to Ataniland. TNA CO 583/264/4.
136. Instructions to Counsel for Opinion. Elliot Gorst and Valentine Holmes. TNA CO 583/264/4.
137. Niger Lands. TNA CO 583/255/6 (emphasis added).
138. Shivji, 1982: 42.
139. Ibid. at 43.
140. Anderson and Throup, 1985: 328.
141. Paton, 1995: 182.
142. Ibid. at 44.
143. *Thomas Shorunke* v. *The King*, [1946] A.C. 316 (P.C.) (Nigeria).
144. The Privy Council's role in disallowing colonial statutes was an important mechanism of imperial control. Beth, 1977.
145. Smith, 2005.
146. Letter from William Geary to The Lord Simon, Lord Chancellor November 18, 1940. TNA CO 583/254/9. The Lord Chancellor is a member of the Cabinet and has traditionally served as the head of the judiciary. The role of the Lord Chancellor was significantly modified in constitutional reforms that took effect in 2005. *See* The Office of the Lord Chancellor, accessed on October 23, 2020, https://publications.parliament.uk/pa/ld201415/ldselect/ldconst/75/7504.htm
147. Letter from William Geary to Mr. Cohen dated September 9, 1943. TNA CO 583/254/9.
148. TNA CO 583/254/9.
149. Thomas Shorunke (Appeal No. 85 of 1944) v The King (West Africa) [1946] UKPC 11 (April 11, 1946), p. 3, www.bailii.org/uk/cases/UKPC/1946/1946_11.pdf.

150. Ibid.
151. Ibid. at 5.
152. Ibid.
153. Rotimi and Ogunyemi, 2016.
154. N. 1326 Saving From the Secretary of State for the Colonies To the Officer Administering the Government of Nigeria, November 5, 1946. TNA CO 583/264/1.
155. Extracts from letters from Thomas K. M. Shorunke dated May 17, 1946 and May 21, 1946. TNA CO 583/264/1.

3

Relationships and Accountability

[C]ustomary law... provided a ... form of international law [that regulated relations between different states and peoples of West Africa].

Robert Sydney Smith (1989)[1]

COLONIALISM, STATE KNOWLEDGE, AND FRAGILITY

State Knowledge and Legibility

In *Seeing Like a State*, James Scott discusses state knowledge in terms of legibility. His discussion of how state functionaries apprehend reality has implications for the construction of states in Africa during colonialism and after formal independence. Scott examines how acts by officials regarding things like mapmaking, measurement, and codification involve a lens that defines what the state sees and acknowledges. The knowledge and information generated by state instruments of control renders reality legible to those in or with power.

The tools of observation used by the tax officials in Vietnam discussed by Scott "have the power to transform the facts they take note of."[2] This transformative power of the state through its officials and other intermediaries has been largely to the detriment of many, but not all, local people in colonial and postcolonial African contexts. Local people were disadvantaged because the new systems, laws, policies, and processes imposed have been external and often alien. They were also often legible to only a small portion of local people within such countries. Being able to decipher new structures and systems because they are legible gives advantages to people who can translate such new interventions, often with far-reaching, and, for many for whom these new structures are not legible, negative consequences.

Acts by states in colonial contexts were also far-reaching due to the authoritarian nature of the colonial state and the administrative discretion granted to colonial administrators. Determinations of who qualified as a *native*, what legal regime would apply to a dispute, and what court might hear a dispute highlight the broad discretion given to colonial officials in many contexts. This discretion meant that decision-making could be ad hoc, even improvisatory, which has contributed to postcolonial instability and chronic problems.[3]

Colonial governance thus draws attention to legal process. Laws in colonial settings such as Nigeria reflected extensive borrowing from external models and sources of law that typically were not appropriately customized for local conditions. This mismatch between source and target of borrowing has contributed to a gap between law on the books and law in practice. Global tax policies in the Caribbean, for example, may constitute a form of *new tax colonialism* in contexts in which differences already exist between laws applicable in France and its overseas departments that are part of France; the tradition of *nèg mawon*, which symbolizes "runaway slaves' creation of their own societies in the French Caribbean," captures the gap between French law as written and its actual application on "islands in the Caribbean that are part of though far distant from France."[4] Gaps between law on the books and law as practiced in postcolonial contexts in Africa and elsewhere reflect Scott's recognition that state simplifications to transform the world may encounter various types of resistance because society has the capacity to "modify, subvert, block and even overturn the categories imposed upon it." This is apparent in Nigeria and other African countries in significant areas of continuing contestation about a broad range of things, but most particularly relating to the shifting and potentially nebulous interface between the internal and the external.

Assumptions made in the development of colonial legal systems, including in relation to customary law, have contributed to a problematic postcolonial legal legacy in Nigeria. In British colonies in Africa, laws in the business and commercial arena were primarily derived from English law. This has significant implications for development, which is often identified as an important goal for countries in Africa today. The legal foundations and legal processes developed during colonialism are not conducive to future paths that take sufficient account of the needs of the many, or to those that can really form a basis for future paths of sustained prosperity for the many.

Although local rulers may have had some authority under indirect rule, local rulers under colonialism were selected and evaluated to a significant degree based on their loyalty to Britain, not on satisfactory governance of local people under the local ruler's authority. Lord Lugard described the essential features of indirect rule as involving two sets of rulers in a single government of complementary duties in which the "chief himself must understand that he has no right to place and power unless he renders his proper services to the State."[5]

In colonial Sudan, people "quickly caught on to the British habit of rewarding loyal supporters and providing jobs and school places to those from prestigious families. Petitioners for jobs, wage increases, and pension supplements made the most of their connections and went out of their way to emphasize a history of family loyalty to the regime. The British considered these histories seriously."[6] In colonial Nigeria, when discussing the 1939 visit of Alhaji Muhammadu Dikko, the Emir of Katsina, to London for cataract surgery, colonial administrators noted:

> he was appointed Emir for courageous loyalty at a time when the local situation in Nigeria was difficult. He has amply justified his choice as he has proved to be the most progressive chief in the Northern Provinces . . . . He was the first Emir to open a school for girls . . . .He is a keen sportsman . . . and is an ardent supporter of polo . . . .The Emir is a very able administrator and is keenly interested in the welfare of his people.[7]

Under indirect rule, British administrators selected native rulers with the goal of holding such rulers primarily accountable to the British, rather than those over whom they ostensibly ruled.[8]

Although no single prescription exists for what constitutes good governance, selection of native rulers in British colonial Nigeria did not have a goal of promoting good governance. These rulers were typically not selected for the primary benefit of those over whom they had authority, and were not placed in a broader institutional context in which good governance was even a goal. A lack of concern for governance was also evident in the colonial administration, particularly in instances where local people or others dissented, petitioned, or otherwise wished to express opposition to laws, policies, or practices. Intolerance of criticism and opposing views by those who govern has persisted long beyond the end of colonialism in many former colonies in Africa.

Local rulers under indirect rule were not without power. However, in colonial Nigeria, their power was typically circumscribed, at least with respect to British authority. Colonial records contain many discussions and petitions related to removal of local rulers. Rulers with whom colonial officials were displeased were readily removed. This highlights the fact that choices about local rulers were not neutral and were highly contested. Choices by the British and other colonial powers regarding local rulers and their incorporation into colonial law and government "meant supporting one claimant over others and privileging one form of authority with its linked moral and political ideas over many alternative forms."[9] The manner of implementation of indirect rule may, however, have given such rulers greater power locally than they might have had traditionally. Indirect rule in northern Nigeria strengthened the power of traditional rulers,[10] while creating distinct governance structures that continue to be a basis for division and conflict in Nigeria today. In British West Africa, traditional checks and balances were often ineffective within colonial governance structures, although educated elites did temper authoritarian inclinations of local rulers under indirect rule. The power that was accorded to at least some local rulers during colonialism reflected a view of absolute power of local rulers expressed by Lord Lugard: "[t]he authority the Emir over his people is absolute."[11] Nigerian legal cases from the early twentieth century illustrate the legal importance and status of traditional rulers within colonial legal infrastructures: "Now what is the chieftaincy? I say without hesitation that it is a mere dignity, a position of honour, of primacy among a particular section of the native community".[12]

Processes for selecting local rulers by British colonial officials continue to have significant implications today for a broad range of institutions in countries that were once colonized by Britain. The legacy of indirect rule is apparent in the continuing power of incumbent elites in many African countries today.[13] The continuing power of incumbents in Nigeria and other countries in Africa has significant implications for disruption of ineffective institutional frameworks from which such elite incumbents may continue to derive benefit.

The externalized nature of colonial governance is apparent in the treaties, laws, regulations, and other legal structures and processes that have been adopted in Nigeria and elsewhere in Africa. This legal infrastructure is still largely present, thus operating as a visible and ongoing force in many former colonies. Although legal reform has been discussed, if not undertaken, in the postcolonial era in Africa, these legal reforms have typically not fundamentally disrupted the legal architecture and processes derived from British colonial rule.

The externalized governance of colonialism might be contrasted with a path that might reflect governance principles and practices that focus on internal needs in which those in charge make all efforts to be the best possible governors who rule for the benefit of the local population, even in contexts of significant external constraint, and who effectively govern themselves. This future path of internal governance with an intent to benefit local people is likely not possible within an inflexible architecture derived from governance structures and processes that continue to reflect an external gaze.

Development in Nigeria and other former colonies in Africa will require freedom from the legacy of colonial legal overhang and colonial institutional design that remains a vital force, even long after the end of colonialism. Colonialism in Nigeria and elsewhere in Africa involved the creation of pervasive unfreedoms, in the meaning of Amartya Sen. As Sen notes, development requires "the removal of major sources of unfreedoms: poverty as well as tyranny, poor economic opportunities as well as systematic social deprivation, neglect of public facilities as well as intolerance or overactivity of repressive states."[14]

Governance, Measurement, and the Nigerian Census

Colonialism and its institutional legacies have contributed to state fragility and failure.[15] A significant discourse exists today concerning state failure, weakness, and fragility. African countries often play a featured role in discussions about failed states, which often focus on issues related to governance. In a 2002 Brookings Institution report, former US National Security Adviser Susan E. Rice defined failed states as "countries in which the central government does not exert effective control over, nor is it able to deliver vital services to, significant parts of its own territory due to conflict, ineffective governance or state collapse."[16] Of the nearly twenty weak or failing states on Rice's list in the paragraph in which she defines failed states, ten are in Africa.

As with so many things today, we even have a quantitative index to rank fragile states. The Fund for Peace produces the Fragile States Index (FSI), which identifies and assesses cohesion, economic, political, and social indicators of state fragility.[17] In 2020, the Fund for Peace produced the downloadable FSI Heat Map. In the 2020 heat map, Africa is awash in hues of yellow, orange, and red, indicating high levels of state fragility. The heat map contains just one visible spot of green in Botswana in southern Africa, making it one of just five countries in Africa that is not in the top 100 of those on the FSI list. In 2020, Nigeria was the fourteenth most fragile state on the FSI list.

African countries are overrepresented on the fragile side for the 2020 Fragile State Index. All of the countries ranked as least fragile are in Europe, except Singapore, Australia, New Zealand, and Canada. Mauritius, an island nation in the Indian Ocean 1,200 miles off the southeast coast of the African continent, is alone among African countries in the *Very Stable* or higher category.[18] Given that African countries comprise approximately 30 percent of the countries on the list, the ranking of two-thirds of countries in Africa in the top fifty of those on the FSI list is striking.[19]

The FSI is one of many seemingly objective indicators in which African countries often rank poorly. Quantitative rankings may have "the patina of objectivity [and] . . . show what is 'really going on,'"[20] and the quantification employed in the FSI may illuminate important things. Quantification and the creation of rankings enable us to "reduce vast amounts of information to a figure that is easy to understand."[21] This process of reductive quantification to create an index echoes the type of simplification noted by James Scott. Simplification may accompany activities of states in standardization, creation of legal frameworks, and other types of activities. However, "despite their appearance of objectivity and impartiality, measures are often the product of political processes and contain biases."[22] Indicators also reflect assumptions about desired future paths, "often express ideologies about the ideal society and the process of achieving it," and "play roles in shaping highly decentralized or nonformal governance structures such as networks."[23]

Although the FSI and other rankings may provide information about outcomes today in many African countries, they are abstractions that may not actually be helpful in understanding the complex history and topography of governance in many African countries. As with other rankings, uses of the list may be more revealing than the ranking itself. In a critical review of the literature on state failure, weakness, and fragility in Africa, Mxolisi Notshulwana of the Development Bank of South Africa discusses theoretical and methodological problems with concepts of state fragility, weakness, and failure and calls for dynamic approaches that recognize states as "the terrain of contestation." Notshulwana also notes that "state fragility involves a complex combination of causes and effects that have proven impervious to quick, template-driven external solutions."[24]

Indexes draw attention to state knowledge about, and measurement of, local phenomena. State knowledge is an area of continuing tension between the external and internal in many African countries. States may attempt to define reality by imposing systems of measurement, law, and administrative processes. In many African countries, the externalized nature of key aspects of these activities remains prominent, even long after the end of formal colonialism.

Colonial powers determined standards within their African colonies that reflected standards of the colonial power. Railroads offer an example of colonial infrastructure built with an external orientation. Colonial railroads in Africa were typically built for various purposes, including military control and extraction. These railway lines promoted European mining interests or connected to agriculturally rich areas where export crops could be grown. Railroads were built with an external perspective in ways that minimized costs, and did not follow routes that made the most sense. This led to construction of railways "'going from nowhere to utterly nowhere" that, with the Kenya–Uganda railroad line, the *Lunatic Express*, "bypassed highly populated areas en route to Kisumu (Lake Victoria) and Uganda."[25]

Neighboring countries may also have different infrastructure standards, including rail gauges, which has contributed to development of train networks that are not interoperable, even between neighboring countries: "African railway networks are characterized by different gauges (metric and standard) as well as by a host of other technical standards and specifications. This has resulted in the inability of Africa to develop interconnected and interoperable railway systems for most of the continent."[26] This makes internal connectivity in Africa for trade and transport quite challenging. Although 60 percent of railway lines in the world are standard gauge, 85 percent of rail lines in Africa are narrow gauge railways, mostly built during colonialism.[27] Furthermore, nine different rail gauges are used in Africa.[28] The limited and non-interoperable rail infrastructure built during colonialism and widespread failure to maintain rail lines after independence, partially explain why China's construction of rail infrastructure in Africa has been in such demand.

Besides potential problems emerging from past uses of external models and standards, governments in Nigeria and other countries in Africa do not adequately collect data about key internal demographics.[29] The population of Nigeria is an ongoing mystery with varying estimates (some say 180 million; others say 200 million). Like so much else, census numbers in Nigeria are politicized with internal contestation between groups that might benefit or be harmed by census data. The census in Nigeria has been politicized since the first postcolonial attempt in 1962. The 2006 Nigerian census gave provisional results and a total population count of 140 million, with 75 million in northern states and 65 million in southern states.[30] Notably, the definitions of *north* and *south* in Nigeria continue to track geographic boundaries used during colonialism. Responses to the 2006 census reflect ongoing contestation about the distribution of population between the North and the South in Nigeria: "[l]ike earlier censuses that provoked an outcry, the reaction followed a set pattern. The south, which made up less than half the population, rejected figures, while the north endorsed them."[31]

Internal failure to collect basic demographic information highlights yet another aspect of how the external reaches deep in Nigeria. Various sources outside of Nigeria are likely the most reliable sources of information about Nigeria. Technology companies and applications that collect information about their users, including Facebook, Instagram, and Google, likely have greater knowledge and information about Nigerians than the Nigerian government. In the absence of reliable data from within Nigeria, institutions such as the World Bank and International Monetary Fund (IMF) are important suppliers of estimates and forecasts about Nigeria. In late 2019, Nigerian President Buhari tweeted about the importance of reliable data for planning and his dissatisfaction with the accuracy of external data about Nigeria:[32]

> Mohammadu Buhari@MBuhari – October 9, 2019 10:06 AM
>
> We can only plan realistically when we have reliable data. As a government we are taking very serious steps to improve the quality of data available for policy-making, and today I charged the Presidential Economic Advisory Council to prioritize the collection of Primary Data.
>
> Mohammadu Buhari @MBuhari – October 9, 2019
>
> Replying to @MBuhari
>
> This must extend to data collection as well. Today, most of the statistics quoted about Nigeria are developed abroad by the World Bank, IMF and other foreign bodies. Some of these statistics are wild estimates that bear little relation to the facts on the ground.

One Twitter comment in response to President Buhari's tweet asked: "Can we start first by having a national census? It's hard to plan when we don't know exactly how many people we are planning for. I don't believe we are anywhere near the about 200 m people we claim to be."

Implementation of policies that meet local needs requires the ability to measure those needs and evaluate outcomes. The lack of reliable data, however, is not likely an accident: "the lack of availability of data locally enables a culture which lacks transparency and allows political leaders [to] [*sic*] paint their preferred versions of reality."[33] This reflects James Scott's recognition of the power of state measurement to transform and shape reality. The intentional nonmeasurement of things by states may enable particular visions of reality that might well be inconsistent with the actual state of affairs.

Problems of measurement in Africa are not unique to Nigeria. In former British colonies, an urgent need exists for reliable statistics.[34] Simply updating national income accounting measurements can make a significant difference. National income accounting measurements are used to assess a country's economic activity during a specified time period, and are used to calculate gross domestic product (GDP), the most frequently used indicator in national accounts.[35] In 2014, Nigeria updated its national income accounting measurements for the first time in twenty-four years to include booming sectors such as film and telecommunications. As a result of this update, Nigeria surged to become the largest economy in Africa, displacing South Africa, and the size of its economy immediately rivaled that of Poland and Belgium.[36]

The Mo Ibrahim Foundation 2019 African Governance Report notes that "African countries face enormous challenges both in terms of working on the measurability of the targets of the development Agendas and developing the statistical capacity required to collect the data to measure those targets."[37] Collection of data to undertake needed measurements may, however, raise other issues of concern in the digital economy era, particularly in contexts of states that are authoritarian or that have authoritarian tendencies. Data and information raise questions about legibility. Digital-era technologies may make citizens more legible to states and others that might have access to their data. Whether states become more legible to their citizens in such contexts is not as clear.

COLONIALISM, DIVIDE AND RULE, AND INTERNAL RELATIONSHIPS

The Asante Empire and Divide and Rule

Colonialism changed networks of internal relationships in Africa in significant ways. Groups within Nigeria and elsewhere in Africa had a high level of interaction prior to the coming of Europeans.[38] In West Africa, customary law was the basis for a bond between states and peoples.[39] Customary law also provided a type of international law that regulated relationships between such states and people. Reports of early travelers to West Africa show that West African states had long sent representatives on diplomatic missions to each other, and the earliest reference to diplomatic relations within West Africa is from the tenth century.[40]

Precolonial diplomatic relationships included issues related to politics and commerce. Diplomats carried credentials or badges of office, including canes, batons, whistles, fans, and swords. In the Asante Empire, spokespersons or linguists carried staffs.[41] Spokespersons were essential as counselors, ambassadors, legal experts, and historians. The Asante Kingdom and Empire was a major West African state in present-day Ghana, founded in the late seventeenth century, that ceased to be independent during colonialism. The establishment and growth of the Asante Empire reflected both diplomatic and war making capacity.

A subgroup of the Akan people, the largest ethnic group in Ghana and the Ivory Coast today,[42] founded the Asante Kingdom. Material symbols of power and authority may be demonstrative of governance and law. Akan staffs reflect the rich cultural history of Akan peoples, serve as a medium of communication, and may contain iconography and symbolism, including representations of proverbs that communicate ideas about rule of law or about the king or chief. The staff may be painted black or covered with gold leaf "as gold is the social prestige and material wealth of the Akan."[43]

Other material symbols of power and authority are also important in Akan culture, including stools. Hierarchies of male and female stools have significant social significance in Akan culture.[44] Stools serve as a "bond between the living, the dead, and those yet to be born."[45] Governing power among the Asante has long been associated with the Golden Stool of the Asantehene, the ruler of the Asante Empire. The Golden Stool is sacred and is the royal and divine throne of Asante rulers. It is a symbol of Asante unity. It never touches the ground, and no one may sit on it.

The Golden Stool is the stool of the first Asante king, Nana Osei Tutu, and is traditionally said to have been brought down from the sky by Asantehene Osei Tutu's priestly counselor. This priestly counselor gave laws to the nation upon the descent of the Golden Stool; these laws ranged from broad moral injunctions to a type of civil and criminal code.[46] The cultural significance of the Golden Stool and manners of governance and law among the Asante were lost on Governor Hodgson, the governor of the Gold Coast Crown Colony at the beginning of the last British war with the Asante in 1900. Hodgson regarded the Asante as "lesser breeds without the law."[47] This view made Hodgson unable or unwilling to understand the cultural contexts into which he sought to become paramount. The view that Africans lacked law reflects evolutionary assumptions about the development of law that were greatly influenced by Sir Henry Sumner Maine. In the House of Commons debate about the Asante in 1901, Joseph Chamberlain describes what he sees as a lack of Asante understanding of law:

> The hon. Member speaks of these savage tribes of Africa as though he was speaking of a modern European Power. He talks of the Ashantis fighting for their "constitutional rights." The Ashantis, if they understood what constitutional rights meant, would explain that their constitutional rights were to exercise absolute power and authority over all neighbouring tribes, to make slaves of them, to procure from them all the labour they required; and, if they did not get it, and tribute also whenever they desired it, to torture them, sacrifice them to their fetish, and generally treat them with the utmost barbarity. Seeing the condition of civilisation in which they were, we may make allowance for the Ashantis that they knew no better; but it is absurd to treat these tribes as if they were members of a civilised community.[48]

The Asante Empire became subject to British authority following a series of wars between the British and Asante that began in 1807 and ended in 1901. As the most powerful state in West Africa, the Asante presented one of the longest and most effective resistance to European conquest and were "the only West African army to defeat a European army in more than one major engagement."[49] The breakup of the Asante Empire exemplifies the role of military force in creating the British Empire and the importance of divide and rule policies. In 1896, the British overthrew Asantehene Agyeman Prempe I and exiled him with many senior Asante officials, first to Sierra Leone and later to the Seychelles; Asantehene Prempe was not permitted to return to Ghana until 1924.[50]

Wars between the British and Asante continued even after the exile of Asantehene Prempe, breaking out in 1900 after Governor Hodgson demanded that the Asante hand over the Golden Stool in a speech to the Assembly of Ashanti Chiefs in Kumasi on March 28, 1900. In this speech, the governor laid out expectations of British primacy that was characteristic of British approaches throughout Africa:

> What must I do to the man, whoever he is, who has failed to give to the Queen, who is the paramount power in this country, the stool to which she is entitled? Where is the Golden Stool? Why am I not sitting on the Golden Stool at this moment? I am the representative of the paramount power; why have you relegated me to this chair? Why did you not take the opportunity of my coming to Kumasi to bring the Golden Stool and give it to me to sit upon?[51]

The Asante defended the Golden Stool in the Yaa Asantewaa War and never surrendered the stool to the British. The Golden Stool is housed today in the Asante Royal Palace in Kumasi, Ghana. After the defeat of the Asante Empire, a resident commissioner was appointed who reported to the Governor of the Gold Coast Crown Colony along the coast of Ghana. British policies of divide and rule led the Asante Empire to be broken up into its components parts, segments of which were "persuaded to sign separate treaties by which they placed themselves under the protection of the British government."[52] At the end of this last war, those opposing the British were exiled to the Seychelles where they joined King Prempe. After annexation by the British Crown, the Asante Empire was administered separately.[53]

Art, Looting, and External Relationships

Precolonial settings highlight patterns of internal relationships within Africa that existed long before the coming of Europeans. These relationships were, in many instances, diffuse and not organized around central nodes connected to external European powers. In these earlier time periods, connectivity existed among groups and interchanges occurred that involved, for example, religion, language, culture, war, and trade. The archeological record gives evidence of people who spread out across central Nigeria beginning around 1500 BCE and "were in contact through relationships, trade, and traditions."[54] We know little about the contexts of these people, but they left behind their terracotta sculptures. These Nok terracotta sculptures, named after the village in central Nigeria where they were uncovered, are among the oldest in SSA and "represent the origins of the West African tradition of portraying people and animals."[55] Nok terracottas were uncovered during colonialism – in 1928 and 1943 – in tin mines near Nok, a village in central Nigeria. Nok terracottas are highly sought in global art markets and have been looted and exported illegally out of Nigeria.[56]

The looting of African art has become an increasingly visible issue of contention. Colonial powers looted a significant amount of art during colonialism, much of which ended up in private collections and various museums. An ongoing dispute exists concerning Nigeria's Benin Bronzes, which participants in the punitive British Expedition of 1897 looted and took to Britain. In 2018, French President Emmanuel Macron commissioned a report by Felwine Sarr and Bénédicte Savoy that recommends permanent repatriation of African art looted during colonialism:

> Organizing the return of African objects is a task with a number of dimensions. The first dimension – and the one which will constitute the rupture with the prior situation – is to institute, through national law, a definitive path toward restitution, according to the requests, through the creation of an ad hoc procedure proposing the basis for a calm process toward restitution.[57]

The presence of African art in museums in Europe and elsewhere is increasingly a point of contestation because the taking of such art and refusals for much of the twentieth century to return this art encapsulates much about the nature and continuing impact of colonialism:

> The memory here which must be recalled to allow other pasts to re-emerge, to be no longer silenced, is a memory of loss through extraction, where the bronze plaques and other royal and sacred objects looted from Benin City were no more side effects of empire than palm oil or rubber were side effects of empire; in fact, they form an enduring part of the ecology of militarist colonialism.[58]

Continuing contestation has forced museums to address issues related to colonial era takings and lootings, including planning for a return of 309 of the Benin Bronzes to Nigeria for a museum in Benin City with a planned 2023 opening date.[59] In March 2019, German culture ministers from all sixteen states met and agreed to establish procedures for repatriation of colonial-era objects from public collections across Germany that were "acquired 'in ways that are legally or morally unjustifiable today'."[60]

Colonial looting has inspired activists. In September 2020, Congolese activist Emery Mwazulu Diyabanza and four others went on trial in France, accused of theft, and were acquitted in November 2020.[61] The *New York Times* describes Diyabanza's visit to the Quai Branly Museum in Paris, which houses art from former French colonies:

> Early one afternoon in June ... Mwazulu Diyabanza walked into the Quai Branly Museum, the riverfront institution that houses treasures from France's former colonies, and ... began denouncing colonial-era cultural theft while a member of his group filmed the speech and live-streamed it via Facebook ... he then forcefully

> removed a slender 19th-century wooden funerary post, from a region that is now in Chad or Sudan, and headed for the exit. Museum guards stopped him before he could leave. ... The next month, in the Southern French city of Marseille, Mr. Diyabanza seized an artifact from the Museum of African, Oceanic and Native American Arts in another live-streamed protest, before being halted by security... [in October 2020], in a third action that was also broadcast on Facebook, he and other activists took a Congolese funeral statue from the Afrika Museum in Berg en Dal, the Netherlands, before guards stopped him again.[62]

Diyabanza began his trial for trying to seize a funerary staff from the Quai Branly in Paris on September 30, 2020. He and four other people faced up to ten years in prison and fines of up to €150,000 for the charge of attempted theft of a registered work of art.[63] He and his associates have brought significant visibility to their movement that seeks reparations for colonialism, slavery, and cultural expropriation, drawing attention to France's colonial record and the estimated 90,000 objects taken from Africa in French museums. A video posted on YouTube shows his activities in the Afrika Museum in Berg en Dal, the Netherlands.[64]

The longstanding contention over looted art highlights the importance of culture and cultural objects, particularly for former colonies. Contestation about looting and repatriation are part of a continuing dialogue about the past, present, and future and draws attention to patterns of involvement of the external in Africa. Resolution of contestation about looted art may be an important path to reconciliation of past wrongs and future possibilities. As Sarr and Savoy note:

> The implicit act of the gesture of restitution is very clearly the recognition of the illegitimacy of the property that one had previously claimed ownership of, no matter what the duration of time was. As a consequence, the act of restitution attempts to put things back in order, into proper harmony. To openly speak of restitutions is to speak of justice, or a re-balancing, recognition, of restoration and reparation, but above all: it's a way to open a pathway toward establishing new cultural relations based on a newly reflected upon ethical relation.[65]

Exploration about and connection with the past may play an important role in connecting people in Africa today with past paths that were disrupted by imperialism and colonialism. As a result, research about the Nok, among others, is important. However, research about the Nok repeats key elements of past patterns of external engagement in Africa, in ways that suggest that approaches to the external have not fundamentally changed in at least some contexts. Much of the Nok terracotta archeological work has been undertaken through collaborations with external researchers. The National Commission for Museums and Monuments in Nigeria has partnered with Goethe University at Frankfurt am Main in Germany to undertake archeological research in Nigeria. This research collaboration has explored the cultural development of the last 4,000 years, including the Gajiganna Culture, the earliest farming culture in Northeast Nigeria (ca. 1800 BCE to 500 BCE). In

May 1987, near the village of Dufana in northeastern Nigeria, a Fulani cattle rearer digging a well to water his cattle discovered a dugout canoe estimated to be 8,000 to 8,500 years old, which made the boat at the time of its discovery the oldest in Africa.[66] The University of Maiduguri, in northeastern Nigeria, undertook excavations of the site, but neither the university nor the government of the Borno State nor the Nigerian federal government could support full excavation of the site.[67] This led to establishment of a research collaboration with researchers from Goethe University, who were brought in to undertake a second excavation of the site.[68]

This important research about Nigeria's past has been funded externally, to a significant degree by the Deutsche Forschungsgemeinschaft (German Research Foundation), with significant external technical assistance. This research collaboration has illuminated important aspects of Nigeria's early history that would likely not have been revealed without external assistance. This work has uncovered greater knowledge about Nok terracottas, the "oldest large-scale sculptures in sub-Saharan Africa."[69] Although research collaborations like this one are critical and important, academic research and many other things in Nigeria rely to a significant degree on external collaboration and external funding. This pattern pervades relationships between the internal and external in Nigeria and other African countries and echoes patterns of relationships established under colonialism.

Colonial Policy Design, Extraction, and Internal Relationships

Along with imposing external dominance in policy and decision-making, colonialism changed internal connectivity and relationship configurations in important ways. The British presence in Nigeria and elsewhere in Africa involved potential multiple points of interaction with missionaries, colonial administrators, commercial interests, including chartered companies, and, in some cases settlers. External interests, needs, and conceptions of governance became key aspects of the institutional architecture in Nigeria and other colonies. This led to changing configurations of internal relationships, particularly as colonial institutions became solidified around indirect rule in the early twentieth century in British colonies in Africa.

Traditions of cultural exchange have long been present among groups within what later became Nigeria, reflecting rich tapestries of history, culture, interchange, and contestation that illustrate networks of local relationships. Colonialism and the interactions with Europeans that preceded it changed this tapestry and led to new networks that refocused ties through various British-affiliated intermediaries. These new networks that came with colonialism fostered internal competition among local groups within colonies for access to this center and scarce opportunities and resources over which British had established forms of centralized control. The process by which British decision makers and institutional structures became embedded in colonial Nigeria led to new and often deeper cleavages, changed existing configurations of and activity across local networks, and generally formed a poor basis for interaction across preexisting and new internal boundaries after independence.

The colonial state was hierarchical and often authoritarian with means of political, economic, social, and military control. The priorities of British colonial officials played a significant role in defining what opportunities were made available to local people and which local people might benefit from such opportunities. As an externally oriented government, the British colonial administration did not have a goal of facilitating internal opportunities for all or the development of infrastructures beyond those needed for extraction, which often meant that the center of the colonial state did not always have deep geographic reach. Colonial states were "gatekeeper states" that "had weak instruments for entering into the social and cultural realm over which they presided, but they stood astride the intersection of the colonial territory and the outside world."[70] The colonial state in Nigeria was structured to provide opportunities to locals necessary to meet perceived needs of colonial projects in Nigeria, which again, were externally focused.

This degree of effective central control may have made sense during colonialism because extraction was a primary goal of colonial policy design, so a strategy of coordination by centralized control was likely easier to organize and coordinate across multiple colonies in the British colonial portfolio. However, if one were to undertake nation-building with a goal of internal improvement, this type of centralization would not be advisable in a country as young and as diverse as Nigeria.

Except for perhaps Ghana, colonial rule did not prepare former colonies very well for functioning as independent and democratic countries after independence:

> Colonial rule was by no means a preparation for postindependence democratic government. It was extremely hierarchical, at best paternalist, and at worst, authoritarian. Britain's army of colonial administrators have been described as 'inbred and insular' . . . .There was no possibility of creating the necessary environment within which these [Westminster model] institutions could survive. In the educational sphere, to take but one example, rates of illiteracy were very high and the numbers of well-educated small indeed. Belgium gave precisely twelve months notice of its intention to decolonize the Congo, leaving the princely sum of thirteen trained African graduates within the country.[71]

At independence, countries in Africa typically replicated the government structure of the power that colonized them. In cases where former colonies adopted the British Westminster model, including in Ghana, Tanzania, and Kenya, a stronger executive power was put in place, along with a curtailment of multiparty competition.[72] This contributed to even greater centralization of political and economic power. Many African countries, including Nigeria, have since adopted presidential style systems of government. Nigeria's current constitution, adopted in 1999 and modeled after the US Constitution, "provides for separation of powers among a strong executive, an elected legislature, and an independent judiciary."[73]

The centralization of economic control in Nigeria and elsewhere in Africa is a legacy of colonialism that has continuing and significant distributional consequences. This centralization also has implications for economic development, the economic autonomy of local areas, and the relationship between the private and public sectors. Colonial administration in British colonies also had a significant military aspect and the "thin white line of colonial administrators was also tipped with steel."[74] This militaristic aspect of colonialism has contributed to active military engagement in political processes after independence, including, through coups: the "militaristic influence in colonial administration laid a foundation for post-independence army rule by officers frequently trained in Britain's Sandhurst Military Academy."[75]

From a legal and institutional perspective, the postcolonial state in Nigeria reflects the architecture of colonial policy design applied with some modifications in postcolonial contexts. This legal and institutional architecture based on pervasive use of external models has not been fundamentally changed since independence. In the postcolonial era, this background has made the state a zone of intense contestation in Nigeria and elsewhere as elites compete to control the state, which due to colonial policy design, confers considerable benefits on winners in battles for state control. Winners of such contests in Nigeria and elsewhere in Africa may direct proceeds from such control to themselves, their foreign bank accounts, or their favored interests or regions, but often not the country as a whole, at least in sufficient amounts to meet the basic needs of people internally. The benefits to winners in this state contestation further deepen contestation and battles for control and access to state resources.

This legal and institutional architecture has also led to contested relationships among groups that might seek to control or believe that they might deserve control or who would like to break away from the center or have greater autonomy. This ongoing internal contestation can lead to violence and led to a brutal civil war with Biafra, which included states in the Eastern Region of Nigeria that sought to declare independence. Multiple military coups, religious and ethnic violence, and other acts reflect deep cleavages along divides and fissures that were created or deepened and then weaponized during colonialism. This contestation is not unique to Nigeria. In the first two decades of independence, forty successful coups occurred in Africa with countless attempted coups.[76] Frequent military intervention, authoritarian rule, and corruption in postcolonial African countries reflect a continuing competition for resources.[77]

Colonial powers facilitated external control by fragmenting and disrupting existing institutions and relations. British colonial policies contributed to disruption by fostering division within colonial possessions by drawing ever finer distinctions based on classifications into groups based on language, religion, ethnicity, and skin color, for example.[78] This strategy fragmented potential opposition to colonialism, at least for a time. This division of communities and societies was part of a divide and conquer strategy that continues to resonate to the present day:

> When the problems of multi-ethnic states and political fragmentation are examined at the present time, a significant input from the British imperial heritage may be discerned . . . all derive in no small measure many of their problems from the British colonial attempt to divide the population into distinct groups . . . . Boundary lines drawn on the ground in colonial times have been remarkably difficult to erase in the post-colonial era.[79]

The consequences of this focus by colonial powers on division did not end with colonialism in Africa. Policies of division effectively weaponized difference by reinforcing and even creating bases for separating populations into more manageable groups, at least from the perspective of British colonial authorities. Divide and rule, co-option of local elites, and European settlement in some colonies both facilitated colonial control and became important elements in postcolonial internal competition and strife.[80]

Practices that emerged before and during colonialism have become a template for power allocation and adoption of the external in African contexts. The persistent failure to adapt such models for local contexts with a more bottom-up approach is a key failing in the adoption of laws, regulations, and policies in far too many contexts in Africa, and is one reason that varied African legal systems and institutions may not operate coherently. As Chinua Achebe notes: "Africa's postcolonial disposition is the result of people who have lost the habit of ruling themselves. We have also had difficulty running the new systems foisted upon us at the dawn of independence by our 'colonial masters'."[81]

One key fissure in Nigeria is between the North and the South, which sheds light on the continuing contestation about the Nigerian census. Within an institutional structure where control of the central government confers significant benefit, given the regional cleavages present in Nigeria and focus on control of the state, census data that show a larger population in the northern part of Nigeria are likely to determine which region would control Nigeria in democratic elections. The legacy of colonial and postcolonial lawmaking and legal institutions has not provided adequate tools to deal with this contestation.

Contestation in Nigeria has been apparent in frequent military coups that began shortly after independence. Although Nigeria has had no military coups since the most recent return to civilian rule in 1999, Nigeria has in the past swung between military and civilian rule, with attempted and successful military coups in 1966, 1975, 1983, 1985, 1990, and 1993. Nigeria was under military rule from 1966 to 1979 and from 1983 to 1999. From 1993 to 1998, Nigeria was ruled by General Sani Abacha, who, like other Nigerian military rulers, had been a player in past Nigerian coups. The title of Sani Abacha's 1998 obituary in the *New York Times* referred to him as "a Beacon of Brutality In an Era When Brutality Was Standard."[82]

By the time of Abacha, the Nigerian military had become highly politicized. The military in its first extended period of military rule from 1966 to 1979 "was perceived to be an agent of order and stability, in contrast to the institutional chaos that accompanied civilian politicians."[83] Nigeria's military rulers eventually became "infected by the ills it came to cure . . . . Soldiers were corrupted by politics as quickly and absolutely as civilians had been. Although the military claimed to bring law and order, communal, criminal, and religious violence increased under its watch. It continually promised to eradicate corruption; yet, military officers were indicted for corruption."[84] Past support for military rule in Nigeria, at least with early military regimes, reflects a common pattern where "[s]upport for illiberal politics in the name of stability and prosperity remains common in Africa."[85]

Authoritarian Rule, Legal Process, and Institutions

The extended period of military rule after independence has had significant implications for Nigerian legal frameworks and legal institutions. British colonial authorities adopted laws during colonialism with little real internal input. This meant that internal discussion and debate about proposed laws and regulations did not include much, if any, input from Africans. Military rulers tend to adopt laws by decree, which also typically leaves little room for internal debate and discussion. Military regimes in Nigeria have also fused legislative and executive functions and "institutionalized a system and culture of government that was extremely executive-centered."[86] Sani Abacha, for example, began his rule with a series of decrees that defined his power as an authoritarian ruler, including by suppressing internal dissent, placing his government over the judiciary, constraining trade unions, and eliminating the free press.[87] Abacha's decrees illustrate how authoritarian rule may unfold and take shape. Decrees issued by Abacha and other military rulers in Nigeria typically exclude courts from entertaining matters or proceedings relating to such decrees.[88]

The Abacha decrees targeting trade unions were critical in constraining an important internal counterbalancing force in Nigeria. Trade unions, another import from Europe, were an important force in anticolonial movements throughout Africa.[89] Trade unions in Africa have interacted with labor movements outside of Africa. In colonial Nigeria, the Labour Department also received significant training and investment from Britain,[90] which has contributed to the development of trade unions as an important institutional force in Nigeria. Trade unions remain a critical force throughout Africa, including in South Africa, where trade unions played a critical role in the anti-Apartheid movement. Trade unions in Nigeria have been an important part of anti-authoritarian, prodemocracy social movements: "labor movements in Nigeria have evolved into a robust, intellectual, vibrant, militant, national liberator movement in the country, taking on successive military and civilian regimes."[91]

One of Abacha's early decrees dissolved the Nigeria Labour Congress, an umbrella labor organization formed in 1978 from the amalgamation of trade unions into a single labor federation by military decree.[92] Decree No. 9 of 1994 issued by

General Sani Abacha is explicit in targeting the Nigeria Labour Congress on account of its opposition to military rule:

> WHEREAS the Nigeria Labour Congress (hereinafter referred to as the 'Congress') ... has of recent and intermittently embarked on, and has persistently keeps threatening to call for, nation-wide strikes over political matters ... the Congress embarked on the said strike action without the endorsement of its constituent affiliates contrary to its constitution and its declaration did not follow the prescribed Industrial Dispute Resolution Processes ... the Congress strikes have been calculated to sabotage a vital and essential sector of the economy and indeed resulted in untold hardship to law-abiding citizens and wrecked incalculable damage to the economy ....
>
> NOW THEREFORE THE FEDERAL MILITARY GOVERNMENT hereby decrees as follows: 1. The national bodies of the Congress specified in the schedule to this Decree are hereby dissolved ... 3. (1) Any person, who on the direction of the appropriate authority had on commencement of this Decree, acted in compliance with this Decree shall stand indemnified in respect thereof and no suit or any other proceedings whatsoever shall lie at the instance of any person aggrieved in respect of any act, matter or thing done or purported to be done in respect of such direction or compliance, and whether any such suit or other proceedings has been or is instituted in any court, it shall abate and be of no effect whatsoever.[93]

Dissolution of the Nigeria Labour Congress highlights its importance as an internal opponent to military rule. The decree also reflects how authoritarian rulers can significantly neuter institutions, at least from a formal legal perspective, with the stroke of a pen. The language of the decree authorizes the government and its agents to undertake any action and insures people who act in compliance with the decree from any act they undertake. These types of legal accommodations, combined with the reality of authoritarian military rule, results in military decrees' having real effects on the people whom they target.

Other targets of Abacha decrees include internal institutions within the government structure that might work in opposition to military rule. Prominent among these is the judiciary, which Abacha targeted less than one week after attempting to eliminate labor opposition. Abacha Decree No. 12 of 1994 states that:

> WHEREAS by section 5 of the said Constitution (Suspension and Modification) Decree, no question as to the validity of any Decree or any Edict ... shall be entertained by any Court of law in Nigeria.[94]

In one paragraph, this decree essentially eliminates the power of the judiciary. The explanatory note to this Decree states: "This Decree re-emphasises the supremacy of the Federal Military Government by giving protection to the act, matter or thing done or purported to be done under any Decree or Edict in consequence, excluding the application of Chapter 4 of the Constitution of the Federal Republic of Nigeria 1979."[95] Chapter 4 of the 1979 Nigerian Constitution contains fundamental rights.[96]

Although authoritarian rulers may be constrained by mechanisms such as protests, lawmaking processes in Nigeria reflect a problematic legacy. Authoritarian rule during colonialism and after independence is woven into Nigeria's legal fabric. Many laws on the books in Nigeria were adopted with little visible process and a paucity of public consideration, discussion, or debate. The institutional structure of colonial rule and military rule in past Nigerian governments raises serious issues about what democracy means in Nigeria from the perspective of law, lawmaking process, and the role of the judiciary. Postcolonial lawmaking processes in Africa, even in democratically elected governments, may reflect significant authoritarian elements. Authoritarian tendencies are of critical concern as Nigeria and other countries in Africa become further enmeshed in the digital economy. Past authoritarian tendencies combined with the potential uses of digital economy technologies may make some potential future paths for many African countries dystopic. These postcolonial processes also reflect widespread inattention to both structure and function of legal systems generally.

This lack of attention has led to a tendency to not undertake commonplace legal reforms and updates to existing laws to reflect changing circumstances, including those related to the digital economy, lack of attention to obligations that bind Nigeria when it signs international treaties and other instruments, lack of remediation of significant weaknesses in judicial systems that are a legacy of colonialism, inadequacies in criminal justice systems, failure to constrain security forces and police, inadequate attention to facilitation of local creativity and innovation, a poor enabling environment for local businesses, limited ability to enforce contracts, inadequate facilitation of robust economic opportunities for most people in Nigeria, failure to constrain widespread corruption, lack of transparency, and lack of accountability for government expenditures. Although legal systems inevitably have points of failure, all of these taken together make Nigeria's legal system particularly ineffective in important respects. Further, successive governments have not sufficiently recognized and have failed to set out a plan for how to rectify these continuing problems.

Postcolonial lawmaking processes in Nigeria reflect significant authoritarian elements that have not been remediated by the presence of civilian regimes because civilian regimes in Nigeria have also had significant authoritarian leanings. Initial Nigerian government and security force responses to the 2020 #EndSARS protests reflect persistent authoritarian tendencies in Nigeria. The Special Anti-Robbery Squad (SARS), which was a focal point for the protests, had a long history of abuse and repression that particularly targeted young people. As Chimamanda Ngozi Adichie notes in an October 2020 *New York Times* opinion piece:

> For years, the name SARS hung in the air here in Nigeria like a putrid fog. SARS, which stood for Special Anti-Robbery Squad, was supposed to be the elite Nigerian police unit dedicated to fighting crime, but it was really

> a moneymaking terror squad with no accountability. SARS was random, vicious, vilely extortionist. SARS officers would raid bars or stop buses on the road and arbitrarily arrest young men for such crimes as wearing their hair in dreadlocks, having tattoos, holding a nice phone or a laptop, driving a nice car. Then they would demand large amounts of money as "bail." . . . . My cousin is one of the fortunate few who could pay an amount large enough for SARS, and who was released. He is not one of the many tortured, or the many disappeared, like Chijioke Iloanya.[97]

Like their colonial predecessors, governments in Nigeria are sensitive to criticism. In August 2019, for example, the Nigerian government detained Omoyele Sowore, publisher of the New York–based news website Sahara Reporters, who ran against President Buhari in the March 2019 elections. Sowore was charged with treason, cybercrime, and money laundering offenses. Sowore was detained because the Department of State Security (DSS) claimed that his call for nationwide protests in August 2019 was an insurrection.[98] Sowore was ordered detained for a renewable forty-five-day period by the Abuja High Court; he remained in detention even after a November 2019 bail order by the Abuja Federal High Court ordered the DSS to release him. The DSS did not comply with the court's order for some time. Sowore was finally released from jail on December 5, 2019, and was rearrested on December 6, when DSS agents stormed the court to arrest Sowore in the Federal High Court in Abuja. The arrest was highly visible with pictures of a fight breaking out in court. The Nigerian government claimed that Sowore sought to overthrow the Nigerian government by calling on citizens to protest against the government. Sowore is one among many journalists, human rights defenders, and activists targeted by federal and state authorities in Nigeria. As a result, in November 2019 Amnesty International to declared three human rights defenders, one of whom was Sowore, prisoners of conscience for having "faced arbitrary detention and unfair trials solely for exercising their right to freedom of expression."[99]

The Sowore arrest is part of a broader pattern of increasing repression of the press in Nigeria. Actions taken against Sowore, and other journalists and activists in Nigeria reflect a long history of authoritarianism in Nigeria. The government's actions also underscore the difficulty of any meaningful legal reform in Nigeria. The refusal to observe a court order is an indication of lack of adherence to rule of law.

The Sowore arrest also reflects the Nigerian government's high level of sensitivity to critical speech and dissent. In addition to reflecting approaches to critical speech under colonial rule, the posture of multiple governments in postcolonial Nigeria is not one that is conducive to problem solving approaches that seek to address problems of poverty, slow growth, pervasive insecurity, dealing with Covid-19, and the many other challenges that Nigeria faces. Addressing Nigeria's continuing challenges will require debate, dialogue, and the identification of consensus within what is likely to be vigorous disagreement, as well as significant criticism and opposition. Repression of opposing viewpoints is detrimental to dealing with clear and present challenges that Nigeria faces. One key challenge is how to constrain the government and government officials.

EXTERNAL RELATIONSHIPS, EXTRACTION, AND POSTCOLONIAL RULE

Authoritarian Rule, Human Rights, and Oil Resources

Experiences of authoritarianism and repression in Nigeria demonstrate that slipping into greater levels of repression may happen quickly and may be difficult to dislodge. Under the regime of General Sani Abacha, which ended in 1999, human rights violations became pervasive in Nigeria. Human rights abuses of the Abacha regime led to the 1995 execution by hanging of nine people (the Ogoni Nine), including Ken Saro-Wiwa, a Nigerian writer, television producer, and environmental activist, who led a movement for the environmental and human rights of the Ogoni people in the Niger Delta in southeastern Nigeria. Saro-Wiwa was president of the Movement for the Survival of Ogoni People (MOSOP), which was formed to campaign for social, economic, and environmental justice in the Niger Delta, which is the primary source of Nigeria's oil exports. For much of the time since independence, Nigeria has been heavily reliant on oil as a source of government revenues, and as Nigeria's primary export. Nigeria has tried to reduce its reliance on oil and gas as a source of government revenue.[100]

Critical data about Nigeria's economy can be scarce, and sources may have different numbers for key statistics relating to government finance.[101] More than 90 percent of Nigeria's foreign exchange earnings come from sale of oil and natural gas.[102] The COVID-19 pandemic has devasted Nigerian government oil revenues, which may further exacerbate existing sources of instability and unrest.[103]

The production and sale of oil in Nigeria also highlights relationships between the external and the internal in Nigeria. Nigeria is a major global exporter of oil and received an estimated $600 billion in oil proceeds between 1960 and 2006.[104] Proceeds from oil production have not benefited the vast majority of people in Nigeria, and robust oil revenues have not stopped Nigeria from being the poverty capital of the world. A 2013 Chatham House report estimated that between $3 billion and $8 billion of oil proceeds is stolen annually in Nigeria.[105] In 2019, *The Economist* noted that Chatham House estimates suggest that $582 billion had been stolen from Nigeria since independence.[106]

Nigerian governments have attempted to recapture stolen funds, including in cases involving funds taken by General Sani Abacha. The Nigerian government also launched a case against Diezani Alison-Madueke, the former Nigerian Oil Minister in the government of former President Goodluck Jonathan. Alison-Madueke is under investigation for money laundering in the United Kingdom and is on trial for corruption in Nigeria where "14 charges bordering on theft and concealment to the tune of $153 million, have been filed against her by the EFCC."[107]

In his discussion of the Second Nigerian Republic under President Shehu Shagari, political scientist Richard Joseph discusses the "mundane reality beneath the rhetoric of party formation" in Nigeria:

> The most successful party in 1979 would not be the one with themes perceptive leaders, or the most innovative proposals for Nigeria, but rather the one most likely to institute an 'I eat, you eat' [I Chop, You Chop] policy between the ethnolinguistic, regional and religious communities, as well as between individuals who managed to push their way to the top rungs of the party's hierarchy.[108]

Joseph refers to this as prebendal politics which "knits together the main features of Nigeria's contemporary socio-political system."[109] The principle of prebendal politics as described by Joseph transcends legal and other institutions: "[I]t is also a principle whose logic eventually undermines the competence and legitimacy of state institutions, and finally saps the authority of those who have successful appropriated its strategic offices."[110]

In addition to enabling the politics described by Joseph, which has facilitated corruption on a vast scale, oil production in Nigeria has devastated the local communities. MOSOP was formed in response to the environment destruction that accompanied oil production, including from oil blowouts, spillages, oil slicks, and pollution, in part from flaring of natural gas.[111] Ken Saro-Wiwa was one of nine people executed by the Nigerian government in 1995. These executions were condemned internationally and led to responses outside of Nigeria, including the imposition of sanctions on Nigeria by the United States and European Union and suspension of Nigeria's membership in the Commonwealth. The United Kingdom did not impose sanctions against Nigeria on account of the executions, even after an appeal from South Africa's President Nelson Mandela, because it sought to protect Shell Oil, which is an Anglo-Dutch company, and its own commercial interests in Nigeria.[112]

Lawsuits, Elite Accumulation, and Michael Jackson Memorabilia

Nigeria is not alone in having vast poverty despite significant natural resources. The Nguema family in Equatorial Guinea (a former Spanish colony), which has been in power since 1979 when the current president Teodoro Obiang Nguema Mbasogo took power in a coup, has accumulated an immense amount of overseas assets. In 2017, a Paris court convicted Teodoro Nguema Obiang Mangue, the second vice president of Equatorial Guinea and son of the current president, in absentia for money laundering and embezzlement of more than €150 million. Nguema Obiang's lifestyle "raised questions about corruption with posts on Instagram (showing him driving luxury cars or riding limited-edition motorcycles … [I]n Paris, where he would spend a few months a year … he displayed a $22 million art collection in his mansion."[113]

Nguema Obiang received a three-year suspended sentence and was fined €30 million, which was also suspended by the trial court. The French government kept more than €150 million of his assets, which had been seized by the police in Paris in 2012.[114] These seized assets included a 6-story, 101-room mansion valued at approximately €150 million with its own hair salon, cinema, gym, and nightclub, decorated with more than €40 million of furniture, and including a garage that contained a fleet of luxury sports cars.[115] Nguema Obiang's conviction was upheld by an appeals court (Cour d'appel de Paris) in early 2020. The appeals court imposed a harsher penalty than the trial court by upholding Nguema Obiang's conviction, but lifting the suspension of the €30 million fine.[116] The legal case was a landmark one led by two anticorruption NGOs, Sherpa and Transparency International,[117] and "[m]arked a turning point in France," which had "long turned a blind eye to the families of corrupt foreign dictators buying up Paris real estate and going on luxury spending sprees."[118]

The French raid and asset seizures have led to further litigation in a case brought by Equatorial Guinea against France at the International Court of Justice (ICJ), the principal judicial organ of the United Nations. Equatorial Guinea instituted proceedings against France at the ICJ, arguing that France had failed to respect the sovereignty of Equatorial Guinea because the Paris mansion was a diplomatic mission. In a December 2016 interim ruling, the ICJ notes that Equatorial Guinea invoked provisions of the Palermo Convention relating to principles of sovereign equality and non-intervention in the internal affairs of another state and the immunity of Nguema Obiang from foreign criminal jurisdiction as vice president of Equatorial Guinea, and provisions of the Optional Protocol to the Vienna Convention concerning the inviolability of premises of diplomatic missions.[119] The 2016 interim ruling ordered France to give the Paris property the same protections as all other diplomatic locations pending a final decision in the case.[120]

In early 2020, some eight years after the raid and seizure in Paris, the ICJ began a series of hearings in the diplomatic immunity case between Equatorial Guinea and France.[121] The arguments made by Equatorial Guinea in these hearings highlight a particular approach to the external and internal in postcolonial contestation between former colonizers and the colonized. The Ambassador from Equatorial Guinea to the Netherlands framed the dispute with France as reflective of a lack of respect for a sovereign and fully independent state,[122] which makes this case an external matter of relations between two sovereigns, one of whom accuses the other of behaving as if it were still a colonial power. This framing makes the spending by the vice president in France a matter of preserving Equatorial Guinea's power as a sovereign government. One commentator has characterized the arguments of Equatorial Guinea as "a modern-day effort to subjugate the government and plunder the riches of Africa dressed up in the language of law."[123] This is, however, a form of argument that may have power in many postcolonial contexts in Africa and elsewhere, particularly given the paternalism that was a core aspect of colonialism. Paternalism has continued to shadow relationships between former colonies and their colonizers, particularly in the case of France, which has been described as having "maintained disproportionate influence over its former African colonies [over the past 60 years, including] control over their military and currencies."[124] In December 2020, the ICJ ruled in favor of France, finding that the building raided by France in 2012 "never acquired the status of 'premises of the mission' of the Republic of Equatorial Guinea in the French Republic within the meaning of Article 1 (*i*) of the Vienna Convention on Diplomatic Relations."[125]

The dispute between Equatorial Guinea and France reflects postcolonial framing from an African perspective as requiring equality in relations between former colonies and their former colonizers. This issue is stark in this case because the recovery of assets would go to France. As a result of this case, a French parliamentary commission drafted a report in 2019 that recommended that funds seized on account of corruption should be returned to local people, the true victims of corruption. This French parliamentary report also recommended that confiscated funds be transferred to the French Development Agency to invest in social projects – including those related to health, education, and access to water – in the country in which the funds originated.[126] In 2018, the French Senate passed a bill dealing with foreign bribery that was not enacted. The provisions of this bill would have created a dedicated fund to organize seized assets for the benefit of victimized populations.[127] Even if France had enacted a law at the time of the Obiang case that required that the seized funds be returned to Equatorial Guinea, where such funds might be sent remains a troublesome question. Nguema Obiang's father is an authoritarian ruler who might seemingly have some say over how the money returned to Equatorial Guinea is spent.

The structure of discourse by Equatorial Guinea at the ICJ ignores the internal impact of uses of funds from sales of raw materials for people inside Equatorial Guinea, many of whom remain poor. This case illustrates patterns of postcolonial relationships between the internal and the external in Africa in which some external actors such as accounting, legal, and public relations firms serve as intermediaries that facilitate internal extraction for external benefit. They thus enable internal elites to exploit internal resources and, with the assistance of such external intermediaries, move internal resources outside of the country for varied purposes, including funding external asset purchases and external bank accounts. Other external actors, particularly governments outside of Africa, but in the Nguema Obiang case NGOs, may take legal action against the internal African extracting person.

The situation in Equatorial Guinea is acute because it has limited oil reserves that will be exhausted by 2035.[128] Nguema Obiang has collected assets in multiple countries. Other cases involving assets collected by Nguema Obiang in other countries have ended in settlements in which proceeds from seized assets were in some instances directed to be used for the benefit of the people of Equatorial

Guinea. In 2019, the Public Prosecutor's Office in Geneva, Switzerland closed proceedings against Nguema Obiang and two other defendants. The Prosecutor's Office confiscated twenty-five automobiles seized during the proceedings and sold the cars at auction for $23 million in late 2019.[129] Equatorial Guinea agreed to pay 1.3 million Swiss francs to the State of Geneva to cover costs of the proceedings.[130] Swiss prosecutors had also requested that Dutch authorities impound Nguema Obiang's super yacht, the $115 million *Ebony Shine*, which features a cinema and contraflow swimming pool, with six staterooms that sleep twelve, as well as eleven staterooms for a crew of twenty-two. The Obiang legal team argued that the yacht belonged to the Ministry of Defense and that the yacht's dive facilities were for training. The Swiss prosecutors closed proceedings against the yacht and returned it to Nguema Obiang.[131]

In October 2014, Nguema Obiang reached a settlement with the US Department of Justice, following a Complaint for Forfeiture in Rem filed in October 2011,[132] which sought forfeiture of a mansion in Malibu, a 2011 Ferrari 599 GTO, and certain Michael Jackson memorabilia. In the settlement agreement, Nguema Obiang was able to keep his Michael Jackson memorabilia and his Gulf Stream jet (which is subject to seizure if it returns to the United States), but forfeited more than $30 million of assets including the mansion and the Ferrari, and the value of the Michael Jackson memorabilia was transferred to the US government. The US government announced that it intended "to utilize the net forfeited assets for the benefit and social welfare of the people of Equatorial Guinea."[133] The US Department of Justice press release notes that through "relentless embezzlement and extortion, Vice President Nguema Obiang shameless looted his government and shook down businesses in his country to support his lavish lifestyle, while many of his fellow citizens lived in extreme poverty . . . . After raking in millions in bribes and kickbacks, Nguema Obiang embarked on a corruption-fueled spending spree in the United States."[134]

These types of external legal cases undertaken in courts outside of Africa, in which people challenge activities within Africa or by African rulers, can take a long time. The asset seizures in France in 2012 were still being litigated in 2020 at the ICJ. External legal cases also require significant external legal and other expertise and are expensive. Litigating these cases internally is, however, not an option, given the authoritarian bent of the government of Equatorial Guinea. In 2019, the government of Equatorial Guinea issued arrest warrants against sixteen people that appeared to be in retaliation for the Paris money laundering trial.[135] Asset seizures from officials of African countries who use public money for private purchases amounting to hundreds of millions, or even billions of dollars, would be better handled by preventing the asset transfers and sales to begin with, rather than litigating about assets purchased overseas after the fact. This is particularly true because funds garnered from internal extraction can be used to bolster the legal resources of those using public money for private uses. Financial systems and intermediaries outside of Africa facilitate external transfers by corrupt and abusive regimes, while internal frameworks fail to constrain governments and government officials throughout Africa.[136] The approaches by Switzerland and the United States emphasize the need to use the seized funds for the benefit of people in the country from which the funds were taken, which is an important recognition in legal remedies for private uses of public funds from African countries.

Uses of public funds for external purposes reflect the external direction of flows of funds and resources that characterized colonialism. Internal legal frameworks did not restrict these flows during colonialism because extraction was a core purpose of colonialism. Internal constraints on such flows have not been robust, if even enforced, since the end of colonialism. External actors often benefit from these flows as well, which has meant that external legal and other infrastructures may also facilitate such flows. These illicit financial flows (IFFs) continue to take advantage of gaps between what people say (evident in the fact that statements expressing opposition to corruption are commonplace) and what people actually do (in engaging in or facilitating corruption) from both internal and external perspectives.

Postcolonial extraction also takes advantage of different jurisdictions in which laws apply. Internal extractors may rule or have close connections with rulers, which makes internal enforcement of laws prohibiting extractive actions that involve conversion of public resources for private benefit unlikely to occur. Extracted funds may be difficult to locate and recover. This difficulty is partly due to various legal frameworks or jurisdictions that might be involved. Reclaiming funds typically requires a long process in each jurisdiction where funds are located. Those who have extracted funds and remain in power may be able to demonstrate that the use of funds was legitimate and may be protected by international law, including instruments protecting diplomatic institutions. The amounts that may be taken make any legal case likely long and protracted. Those who have taken funds, or their families, may end up with significant amounts of money, even if most funds are returned. This structure of incentives is unlikely to avert future extraction.

Natural Resources, External Engagement, and Internal Conflict

As Lord Lugard envisaged almost 100 years ago, African countries remain key sources of raw materials for the world, often with insufficient deployment of funds from sales of raw materials for internal needs for the majority of the population. The continued position of African countries as sources of raw materials is due to decisions of both colonial and postcolonial rulers. People within Africa continue to be victims of institutional structures based on colonial policy design that was intended to facilitate colonial era extraction but continues to be used long after the formal end of colonialism by rulers and other elites.

The €150 million at issue in the Equatorial Guinea asset seizure case is higher than the amount spent in Equatorial Guinea in 2011 on education ($140 million) or health ($92 million).[137] The Nguema family's rule in Equatorial Guinea has been described as a form of "predatory despotism."[138] As a result, the significant funds that have flowed into Equatorial Guinea from oil sales have "only affected macroeconomic indicators but not people's current standard of living" and "many of the benefits of the extractive industry are being accumulated far from the country, not only by the foreign companies but also by individuals who occupy the government."[139] Equatorial Guinea has one of the highest levels of per capita income in Africa but performs poorly by varied measures of social development, including immunization levels, life expectancy, and infant mortality. Half of the population does not have access to potable water. Equatorial Guinea lags "far behind its much poorer neighbors" in part as a result of "the vast personal fortunes that senior government officials have amassed during the oil boom and because of how the country invests-or doesn't invest – in itself."[140]

Rent-seeking and corruption are part of the reasons that so many in Africa are poor. Rent-seeking by public officials in Africa may cause economic harm and stifle investment and growth.[141] Weak institutions mean that internal constraints may not restrain internal rulers who extract. This makes extraction one key continuity between colonialism and independence in Africa. Equatorial Guinea is not an outlier in Africa.[142] Constraining this type of behavior has become more difficult in a world of globalized financial markets where billions of dollars can be moved with the click of a mouse. In African contexts, private individuals who extract funds from resources for which they are merely stewards rather than owners are facilitated by networks of intermediaries, including service professionals such as lawyers, accountants, bankers, and public relations agents that "provide creative mechanisms through which kleptocrats channel their ill-gotten gains."[143] The Mozambique debt corruption case and the complex financial schemes in Angola evident in the Luanda Leaks documents demonstrate how global financial institutions and consulting firms use their expertise to facilitate extraction of public resources in African countries for the private benefit of government officials.

Kleptocracy, or a "society whose leaders make themselves rich and powerful by stealing from the rest of the people,"[144] is difficult to constrain legally in contexts where institutions are weak. Even if kleptocrats behave in a way that is contrary to the written law within the country from which the funds were extracted, they are unlikely to enforce such laws against themselves. Although constraining such behavior before it occurs would minimize internal harm, external enforcement may be the best option at present. This type of external enforcement may take a long time because government officials against whom cases are initiated may have extensive public and private financial resources at their disposal. Other approaches, including sanctions and investigative reports, have not really had a significant impact. Innovative legal and policy approaches are clearly needed in this area. Those who extract from inside also have access to legal and other resources that may make it difficult, expensive, and time-consuming to get funds returned to the source country.

Equatorial Guinea is an example of how elites in too many countries in Africa may spend funds received from sales of raw materials. Equatorial Guinea is a small country with a population of just over 1,000,000 who experienced a transformation since identification of large offshore oil reserves in the 1990s. Prior to the discovery of oil, Equatorial Guinea primarily exported coffee, timber, and cocoa. Oil has led to significant changes in Equatorial Guinea: the country has become "the destination for hundreds of companies and thousands of immigrants near and far" with significant "construction roads, other large infrastructures [and] urban quarters", creating "new social geographies, while cities have grown enormously at the expense of the abandonment of rural habitats."[145] At the same time, continuities exist, including the same president for forty years, "military and police presence at checkpoints all along the roads, [and] strikingly low levels of public services such as health and education."[146] Andres Exono Ondo, Secretary-General of Convergence for Social Democracy, one of only two opposition parties in Equatorial Guinea notes: "We have many many hotels. But no schools. No good hospitals. No water, nothing."[147] In addition, to diverting funds needed for things such as education and healthcare, kleptocrats may have little incentive to invest in anything that might enhance future opportunities and paths that might enable African countries to be more than a source of raw materials.

African countries have long been sources of raw materials for which much of the value chain exists externally. Nigeria, for example, is one of the leading global exporters of petroleum but has little internal fuel refining capacity because the four refineries owned by the Nigerian government are closed or not really functional. Nigeria's refineries are in a poor state due to lack of maintenance after the Nigerian National Petroleum Corporation (NNPC) lost its autonomy in the early 1990s under a military government and began to experience interference and directives from politicians.[148] In October 2019, Nigeria produced an estimated 2 million barrels in daily crude oil production but had refining capacity of only 445,000 barrels per day.[149]

The lack of internal refining capacity has led Nigeria to exchange crude oil for imported fuel, a process that is "often fraught with fraud"[150] and creates opportunities for various forms of arbitrage. In exchange for its high quality, low sulphur *Bonny Light* crude from the Niger Delta, Nigeria imports 900,000 tons per year of low-grade, *dirty* fuel, from external sources, including Dutch, Belgian, and other European refineries.[151] Nigeria also relies on internal refining from small-scale artisanal refineries that produce illegal fuel from oil stolen from pipelines in the Niger Delta. Use of dirty refined petroleum has led to a high level of emissions of particulate matter and sulphur oxides, "which are a major source of visible air pollution" in Nigeria and a potentially serious health hazard.[152] Because internally refined fuel uses Bonny Light crude, it actually contains less sulphur than imported fuels: 152 times more than the European sulphur standards for diesel and 40 times the EU level for gasoline, as compared with 204 times the EU sulphur standards for diesel and 43 times that level for imported gasoline.[153]

Nigeria's current strategy to deal with a lack of internal refining capacity is a large-scale $12 billion refinery in Lagos that will be the largest in Africa. This refinery, which has been delayed, is scheduled to open in 2021.[154] When completed, the refinery will the "largest single train petroleum refinery" in the world.[155] This refinery is being constructed by Aliko Dangote, a billionaire and one of the wealthiest men in Africa with a successful track record in business with Dangote Group, a major industrial conglomerate. The Dangote refinery has been delayed due to port conditions resulting from outdated transport infrastructure that have led to problems importing steel and other equipment. The poor road network has also contributed to port congestion.[156]

In addition to this type of large-scale project, Nigeria might benefit from thinking about smaller scale projects that are more distributed, that can create opportunities that involve less concentrated risk of failure than is likely to be the case with a strategy that concentrates on large-scale projects such as the new refinery being constructed in a free trade zone near Lagos. One starting point for thinking about such opportunities might be to enhance internal capacity and opportunity based on activity that is already internally evident in Nigeria, such as in the Niger Delta, where people are producing illegal fuel in small-scale artisanal refineries that is, in some respects, of higher quality than imported fuel. These small scale artisanal producers participate in an informal economy in Nigeria that is far larger than the formal economy. The *informal* economy is informal in part because formality in Nigeria often involves a host of complications, from slow bureaucratic processes that may require multiple steps and payment of bribes, to a legal and regulatory environment that does not sufficiently facilitate internal economic opportunities for the majority of people in Nigeria. The informal economy also reflects persistent patterns of exclusion. Policies and practices that value the internal would entail seeking out ways to incentivize development of practices and innovations that have been too often left outside of official policy-making and lawmaking processes.

Nigeria and Equatorial Guinea show paths taken by a number of countries with significant natural resources that do not deploy benefits of such resources in ways that give sufficient internal benefit to the majority of the population. Countries with significant endowments of oil, minerals, and other natural resources may suffer from what some refer to as the *resource curse*. Conflict commodities are thought to have financed one-third of armed conflicts since the end of the Cold War.[157] *Blood diamonds*, also referred to as *conflict diamonds*, are diamonds mined in an area of war or conflict with sale proceeds going to fund insurgency or war. Blood diamonds are a prominent example of conflict commodities in Africa. Conflict commodity wars have been devastating in Africa: "[m]ore than three million people died as a result of these wars in the 1990s and early 2000s; many more millions of lives have been damaged, and the existence of entire nations has been called into question."[158] Blood diamonds have been associated with a number of countries in Africa, including Angola, Ivory Coast, Guinea, the Democratic Republic of the Congo (DRC), Liberia, and Sierra Leone. The role of conflict diamonds in wars and other conflicts has led to an international conflict diamonds governance system of which the Kimberley Process Certification Scheme is a primary part.

Conflicts over natural resources in Nigeria are at the core of internal conflicts and instability in the Niger Delta, where much of Nigeria's oil is produced. External responses to the 1995 Ogoni Nine executions underscores continuity and change in external actors that might be involved in Nigeria and other African countries today. Former colonizers and other global powers play a continuing role in the political, economic, and at times, military spheres. Regional and pan-African groups play an increasingly prominent role today, evident in the actions of Nelson Mandela, who condemned the Ogoni Nine executions and attempted to organize broader condemnation by other African leaders. Responses within Africa reflected internal views of external actions that connected external condemnation of a fellow African leader to colonialism:

> Mandela vividly condemned General Abacha's action. He even made vain attempts to win the hearts of other fellow African leaders .... Mandela called for sanctions to be imposed against Nigeria and proposed that the Commonwealth should openly condemn General Abacha's action. To his surprise, his counterparts from other African countries did not share his views, nor did they approve his proposal .... Instead, they blamed Mandela for playing into the hand of former colonial masters by dividing African leaders. The fact that Mandela's actions were triggered by something they all knew was wrong did not seem to matter. Internally, Mandela was reminded by his ANC colleagues of Nigeria's role in the fight against apartheid-a view which was shared by some opposition political parties in South Africa.[159]

Much like the response of Equatorial Guinea to French asset seizures in 2012 in Paris, the collective internal reaction within Africa that Nelson Mandela encountered reflects a legacy of colonial and postcolonial encounters with the external in Africa that have involved paternalism. Discussions about Africans by British colonial officials in archival documents are full of derogatory statements about African people. Derogatory and distorted images of Africa and people of African descent continue to be globally widespread today. These past experiences may contribute to reflexive opposition to actions of external powers that are intended to nudge African leaders to reach a particular decision or support a specified policy. This type of opposition to the external has, however, not typically reached very deep and has at times remained strategic, if not rhetorical in nature. As a result, institutions throughout Africa continue to reflect the external at their roots in ways that have not been disrupted. The legal structures and external relationships that facilitated Abacha's authoritarianism and his looting of billions of dollars reflect long-standing uses of external models and relationships that have continued to be detrimental to the vast majority of people in Nigeria.

Human Rights and "Model" Democracy in Mali

Events in West Africa since the 1995 Ogoni Nine executions may suggest greater willingness of African leaders to criticize other African leaders and even take action, at least in certain cases. Following a coup in Mali in March 2012, ECOWAS, the West African regional political and economic union, suspended Mali, and sent delegations to Mali to mediate a resolution to Mali's political crisis. ECOWAS then imposed economic and diplomatic sanctions on Mali, and ECOWAS member states bordering Mali closed their borders. The African Union (AU) similarly imposed sanctions, asset freezes, and travel bans against coup leaders. The AU also planned to undertake an African-led support mission in Mali. Prior to deployment of the support mission, the Islamist insurgents who held northern Mali launched a military offensive against the government-controlled South that threatened Bamako, the capital city of Mali. This led the interim president of Mali to call on France, Mali's former colonizer, to intervene militarily.[160] France launched Operation Serval in early January 2013. The African support mission was then deployed.

Prior to the 2012 coup, Mali was considered a "model of African democracy."[161] The 2012 Mali coup highlighted the fragility of a Malian state that could not withstand intensified instability in the North resulting from the collapse of the Quaddafi government in Libya.[162] Mali experienced another coup in August 2020. After weeks of protests over a disputed election, the military detained the president, the prime minister, and other government officials. Shortly after being detained, the president announced his resignation on state television.[163] The 2012 and 2020 coups in Mali, the #EndSARS protests in Nigeria, the Arab Spring in Northern Africa, and other events in African countries ranging from small fires to conflagrations also highlight the potential unpredictability of events that might lead to widespread instability. In Nigeria and other countries in Africa, significant known factors that lead to instability exist, including cleavages along ethnic, religious, regional, generational, and other differences.

After the 2012 Mali coup, civilian rule was restored after just one month. The coup leaders were arrested in anticipation of a trial. In January 2020, General Amadou Haya Sanogo, the former junta leader, was granted bail after having been in pretrial detention for more than six years after his arrest in 2013. Sanogo has been awaiting trial over the abduction and murder of twenty-one paratroopers in Mali. Pretrial detention occurs when accused persons are detained before they are tried, which may result from various factors, including their failure to post bail, denial of their release, or an extended process leading up to their trial. Recent criminal justice reform efforts inside and outside of Africa have focused on reforming pretrial detention, which may undermine rule of law and chances for a fair trial and expose detainees to violence and abuse.

Although imprisonment rates in Africa are not high relative to the rest of the world, pretrial detention levels are high. Globally, just under one-third of all prisoners are pretrial detainees; this figure is close to 40 percent in Africa and over 50 percent in Central and West Africa. Nigeria's levels of pretrial detention are high: "[o]f the world's ten prison system[s] with the highest proportion of pretrial detainees, half are in Africa. In places such as the Benin, DRC, Liberia, Libya and Nigeria, 70 percent or more of all prisoners have not been convicted."[164] The release of Mali coup leader Sanogo is consistent with a justice system in which officials and security forces are not constrained:

> Significant human rights issues included: reports of unlawful or arbitrary killings, including extrajudicial killings, by both government and nonstate actors; forced disappearance by government forces; torture by government forces; arbitrary detention by government forces . . . . The government made little or no effort to investigate, prosecute, or punish officials who committed violations, whether in the security forces or elsewhere in the government, and impunity continued to be a problem.[165]

The development of internal frameworks for justice and accountability are critical aspects of democracy or any form of governance for the benefit of the many within Africa. This would give those harmed by governments or their representatives recourse for the harms that they suffer. This is important in the context of Africa, where countries typically have significant diversity along multiple measures, and many people who are poor may lack opportunities for employment, healthcare, housing, food, and other things that improve quality of life. The historical experiences of oppression during colonialism make the need to disrupt continuing patterns of oppression even more urgent. This would entail disruption of legal frameworks and institutions that facilitated oppression during colonialism and that continue to shape treatment of people within former colonies. Such disruption would also require reform of existing legal frameworks in line with key principles that can serve as the basis for future paths in which law guides actions, particularly by governments and those who rule.

In Nigeria and elsewhere in Africa, forests are present with much underbrush that is rarely tended. The roots of the trees do not run very deep. Institutions that are not deeply rooted may be easily toppled. These forests are prone to rapid conflagration in part because sparks have become so commonplace in many places in Africa that they become part of the fabric of everyday living and are largely ignored, leading some to describe less volatile countries as *stable*, particularly where leadership is entrenched or otherwise apparently stable. These sparks are, however, underscore points of tension and contestation in places where many face significant and persistent difficulties in daily life and where opportunities for many are scarce. Sparks in these contexts have potential to erupt in ways that may be difficult to predict. The scope and duration of any conflagrations that might arise are unpredictable. In Mali, the 2012 coup leaders indicated that they did not agree with how Mali's government was handling the Tuareg rebellion in the North that came about in part due to consequences of the Arab Spring. Mali has had two coups in the last decade. The impact of protests such as the #EndSARS protests that began in Nigeria in October 2020 may be difficult to anticipate in terms of specific timing. Any conflagration that might come from such protests may similarly be difficult to predict. In Tunisia, where the Arab Spring protests emerged, a revolution on three continents was started when a fruit and vegetable seller set himself on fire.[166]

The potential for unexpected events to heighten unrest was evident in Ethiopia in late June 2020. Ethiopia erupted in protest over the assassination of Hachalu Hundessa, a singer, songwriter, and civil rights activist. His songs called for greater rights for the Oromo people, the largest ethnic group in Ethiopia, who have long complained about being marginalized. Hachalu was imprisoned for five years at the age of seventeen for his political activities. He developed his musical skills while in prison and had released two albums at the time of his death. Artists have played an important role in protests by ethnic Oromo youth: "[f]ar from being a footnote in the history of the Oromo struggle for freedom and justice, musicians, poets and creators are its centre of gravity – the signature tune and the definitive sound of the Oromo revolution."[167] In the aftermath of Hachalu's murder, protests by Oromo and Amhara, two-thirds of Ethiopia's population, were met with brutal government suppression. In the days following the killing, at least 289 were dead, along with more than 7,000 detentions. The Internet was shut down within hours of the killing and was only restored after four weeks.[168] By late 2020, a military confrontation between the Ethiopian government and rebel forces in the northern Tigray region had arisen that had the potential to have a broader regional impact, including in Eritrea, Djibouti, Sudan, and Egypt.[169]

GOVERNANCE AND ACCOUNTABILITY

Legal Recourse for Internal Harms

Protests in Nigeria, Ethiopia, Cameroon, and elsewhere in Africa attest to contestation and opposition to government policies. This opposition reflects ongoing contributions of individuals and organizations that have opposed some of the most visible elements of poor colonial and postcolonial governance, including authoritarianism, corruption, and human rights violations. In Nigeria, these defenders of have included lawyers, writers, women's rights activists, trade unions, democracy activists, and varied civil society groups, some of whom have faced violence, imprisonment, and even execution. As has been the case elsewhere in Africa, many of these individuals and groups make use of digital technologies that highlight potential ways that digital technologies could facilitate inclusion. These internal actors attempt to counterbalance authoritarian tendencies in Nigeria. A future path in Nigeria that incorporates the insights, knowledge, and energy of these internal groups could be used to develop policies and laws intended to benefit the many and constrain those in power, which is an essential element of the rule of law.

At present, internal legal frameworks may not offer much recourse from within African countries, particularly to those internally victimized by authoritarian rulers. Although internal legal frameworks may not offer recourse to those victimized by their rulers in Nigeria and other countries in Africa, external legal frameworks may offer the possibility of recourse. Today, external actors may turn a blind eye to, or facilitate, internal abuses within countries in Africa. External facilitation of internal abuses is drawing greater scrutiny today. This is evident in the recent cases against Obiang and in instances of IFFs, including in the Luanda Leaks case and the Mozambique debt corruption case,[170] which have involved external facilitation of internal corruption by global consulting firms and banks.[171] Human rights abuses continue to draw scrutiny by human rights groups but may not lead to much other external action.

The role of Shell Oil in the Niger Delta, global banks in Mozambique, and global consulting firms in Angola underscore the presence and actions of multinational businesses, which are a dominant external factor today, not only in Nigeria, but throughout the world. The activities of these and other multinational actors may be difficult to regulate using traditional domestic, foreign, and international legal frameworks. Multinational companies also have an ability to structure themselves in ways that may make them relatively impervious to attempts to regulate them.

In the over twenty years since the execution of Ken Saro-Wiwa in Nigeria, several legal cases have been brought against Shell Oil, which "stands accused of complicity in the unlawful arrest, detention and execution of nine men who were hanged by Nigeria's military government."[172] The aftermath of the execution of the Ogoni Nine, who were executed after an unfair trial, reflects one more example of the interaction between the internal and external in Nigeria. Esther Kiobel and three other women whose husbands were executed in 1995 brought lawsuits in the United States and in the Netherlands to attempt to hold Shell accountable for human rights abuses that they believe led to the murder of their husbands. Although the case in the United States did not reach a trial on the merits,[173] in 2019, a Dutch court agreed to hear their case against Shell.

In 2009, Shell Oil settled a case filed in the United States by Ken Wiwa, the son of Ken Saro-Wiwa, and other relatives of the Ogoni Nine for more than $15 million.[174] The legal cases brought by family members of the Ogoni Nine reflect a trend in which Africans are increasingly litigating outside of Africa on account of acts of external actors within Africa.

Recourse for environment harms has become a more likely possibility following a series of court cases in Nigeria and Europe. In November 2020, the Nigerian

Supreme Court dismissed a request by Shell Oil to vacate a 2019 Court of Appeals decision upholding a 2010 decision by the Federal High Court in Asaba, Delta State awarding close to $45 million in damages against Royal Dutch Shell's Nigerian subsidiary for an oil spill in 1970 in Rivers State.[175] In January 2021, in a case that started in 2008, concerning 2006 and 2007 Niger Delta oil spills, The Hague Court of Appeal requested information about the extent of contamination from the spills and whether remediation of the spills are required.[176] In February 2021, in a case described as "a watershed moment in the accountability of multinational companies," the UK Supreme Court ruled that 50,000 Nigerian farmers and fisherman could bring a case in the High Court against Shell for years of polluting oil spills in the Niger Delta.[177]

The Ogoni Nine legal cases, which also involve Shell Oil, illustrate potential impediments to bringing legal cases outside of Nigeria. Amnesty International has supported and documented allegations in the legal cases by Ogoni Nine relatives against Shell and has called on the governments of Nigeria, the United Kingdom, and the Netherlands to investigate Shell for its role in crimes committed by the Nigerian government in Ogoniland in the 1990s, including murder, rape, and torture.[178]

Attempts to hold Shell accountable for human rights violations in Nigeria reflect something of the limits of law as applied to external actors in particular contexts. Oil has been a dominant source of revenue for Nigeria for decades. Although the existence of oil revenues might seemingly be something to celebrate, oil has been detrimental to institutions in Nigeria. Many in Nigeria have not benefited from the proceeds of oil production in Nigeria. Rather, oil in Nigeria has become part of the contested center and has led to corruption driven by the prospects of personal enrichment from access to even a small piece of money flows from oil production.

Transparency, Accountability, and Fiscal Matters in Nigeria

The presence of oil as a central attraction has also diminished investments in and attention to other potential sources of economic growth and prosperity in Nigeria. Despite government officials speaking about the need to diversify the Nigerian economy, Nigeria's fortunes turn to a significant degree on the price of oil. The risks of Nigeria's heavy reliance on oil became glaringly apparent in 2020 with the COVID-19 pandemic, which contributed to a collapse of oil revenues flowing to the Nigerian government. Like other petrostates, Nigeria must now grapple with COVID-19 and volatile and, at times, low oil prices. Nigeria's gas production may offset some of the collapse in oil prices. Although many will undoubtedly suffer, the collapse of oil revenues may force Nigeria to improve infrastructures around local innovation and creativity and local businesses, which could, with an internal gazing structure that emphasizes governance, improve the lives of many in Nigeria who have remained poor despite Nigeria's oil wealth.

The accumulation of overseas assets by General Abacha make clear why control of government is so contested in Nigeria. The Abacha family looted an estimated

$1 billion to $5 billion during the four years and seven months of Abacha's rule.[179] Nigeria has spent over twenty years recovering funds looted by Abacha. A 2002 settlement with the Nigerian government that returned more than $1 billion to Nigeria enabled the Abacha family to keep $100 million of known looted funds,[180] which is not likely to dissuade others in the future. In May 2020, Nigerian President Buhari published an opinion piece in *Newsweek* in which he implicitly refers to, but does not name, the Abacha regime: "[a]nd we can now move forward with road, rail and power station construction – in part, under own resources – thanks to close to a billion dollars of funds stolen from the people of Nigeria under a previous, undemocratic junta in the 1990s that have now been returned to our country from the U.S., UK and Switzerland."[181]

Although the Abacha case is a perhaps extreme example in its magnitude, looting has not been limited to the Abacha regime.[182] Rather, corruption, including through looting and theft of oil, has become commonplace in Nigeria and "is the single greatest obstacle preventing Nigeria from achieving its enormous potential."[183] The centralization of ownership and operation of Nigeria's oil production at the federal government level has facilitated corruption that may well be unstoppable without radical changes. Looting and asset thefts require attention to both the internal and external. External support is critical to prevent flows of proceeds of corruption outside of Africa and to enable return of looted assets. Significant internal changes will be required to confront theft and looting, including policies that promote greater internal transparency, accountability, and attention to legal and accounting treatment and that minimize opportunities for varied methods of extraction. Recovery of looted assets under President Obasanjo (1999–2007) was "hampered by a lack of transparency, an excessive fixation with the Abacha loot, inadequate legal and accounting skills, the uncooperative attitude of accused persons, and, more importantly, limited external support."[184]

Return of looted Abacha funds to Nigeria illustrates the depth of problems with internal accountability in Nigeria. More than $1 billion has been returned from Abacha bank accounts. Some countries have been reluctant to return funds because of concern over management of returned funds. *The Economist* notes that much of the $500 million of Abacha funds returned by Switzerland disappeared.[185] This has led to imposition of accountability requirements on repatriation of Abacha funds to Nigeria. In February 2020, the US Department of Justice announced that it had entered into a trilateral agreement with Nigeria and Jersey to repatriate over $300 million in assets stolen by Sani Abacha. The United States and Jersey agreed to transfer 100 percent of the net forfeited assets to Nigeria "to support three critical infrastructure projects in Nigeria that were previously authorized . . . and [that] the agreement includes key measures to ensure the transparency and accountability, including . . . financial review by an independent auditor and monitoring by an independent civil society organization with expertise in engineering and other areas."[186]

Abuses of money have infected electoral and political processes in Nigeria. Nigeria's budgeting process and method of fiscal allocation from the federal government to states is an important avenue for corruption.[187] The access of politicians to Nigeria's resources is unfettered: "[d]ue to a high level of corruption and impunity, appointed and elected public officials have almost limitless access to public resources."[188] Nigeria practices fiscal centralism, which has been evaluated by various commissions and committees since as early as 1946. Nigeria's federal government has rejected proposals by lower tiers of government for more decentralized fiscal arrangements.[189] The 1999 Constitution of the Federal Republic of Nigeria grants the federal government ownership of Nigeria's natural resources: "the entire property in and control of all minerals, mineral oils and natural gas in under or upon any land in Nigeria or in, under or upon the territorial waters and the Exclusive Economic Zone of Nigeria shall vest in the Government of the Federation and shall be managed in such manner as may be prescribed by the National Assembly."[190]

The Constitutional, legal, and regulatory structure surrounding fiscal matters in Nigeria give the federal government more power than other levels of government. More importantly, "[s]tates and Local Governments are not given strong fiscal incentives or encourages to generate revenue internally. In view of this, they are weak financially and depend on Federal allocation, whereas for any federation to be sustained, there must be fiscal decentralization and financial autonomy.[191] Nigeria's 36 states and some 774 local government areas rely on monthly budget allocations from the federal government. The financial hegemony enjoyed by the Nigerian federal government "reinforces the structural vulnerability of component units while simultaneously intensifying the pressures for better federal economic patronage."[192]

This system of allocation also creates additional centralization in a system that was already heavily weighted toward the center as a result of colonialism. This has significant implications for innovation: "[t]his arrangement of allocation sharing in Nigeria threatens initiatives, innovation and modern ideas of generating resources, especially money, for sustainable development."[193] This has implications for risk-taking and Nigeria's participation in digital economy trends. The heavily weighted center means that risk-taking is also not decentralized. Decentralization through innovation at the state and local level is one potential path to increased prosperity in Nigeria. This is far less likely to occur given fiscal centralism. This in turn has consequences for Nigeria's ability to leverage its significant capacity to become a more visible digital economy player. Public investment decisions may be disproportionately taken at the federal government level, even when greater competence might exist at other levels of government or in the private sector. The dominance and typical scale of federal government initiatives may also limit the breadth of innovative activities that might otherwise occur in Nigeria with greater decentralization.

Colonial Institutional Design and Governance

Colonial institutional design as adapted today in Nigeria poses significant challenges. The regional division introduced in 1946 during colonialism that divided Nigeria into three regions, combined with the discovery of oil after independence, has led to elite competition for access to control of the revenue allocation, which became "central to Nigerian federalism and struggle for power and resources."[194] The continuation of essential elements of colonial policy design has had significant, and often bad, consequences in Africa, particularly for those who do not exert control over the state or otherwise benefit from such control. Problems in the transition of governance systems from colonialism to independence were recognized in advance. In 1949, the Report of the Drafting Committee on the Constitution discussed goals of the constitutional drafting process and the need to devolve power in Nigeria after independence:

> While recognising this fundamental need we have been impressed by the difficulty of evolving a federal system by devolution of authority from the centre. Indeed the problem which confronts us is unique. The federal governments of the United States of America, Canada and Australia, for instance, have been built on the basis of separate states surrendering to a federal government some of their powers for the benefit of all. The reverse process on which we are engaged – that of the creation of a federal government by devolution – is a political experiment for which, as far as we know, there is no precedent which can guide us and we are very conscious of the dangers inherent in such an experiment.[195]

This devolution discussed long ago has yet to occur in Nigeria. Nigeria has responded in several different ways to problems of governance in ways that reflect patterns of internal relationships within Nigeria, particularly between the federal government and states. Nigeria has had considerable internal volatility in its territorial configuration since independence, which is a reflection of Nigeria's distinctive form of federalism. At independence, Nigeria had three regions, which were dissolved in 1967 when twelve states were created. These twelve states were further divided into nineteen states and a Federal Capital Territory (Abuja) in 1976. These were further divided into twenty-one states in 1987, thirty states in 1991, and the thirty-six state configuration in 1996. The pressure for state formation reflects interwoven factors "distributive pressures, sectional anxieties, partisan conflicts, constitutional controversies and institutional dilemmas."[196]

Nigeria also has horizontal inequality between culturally defined groups.[197] as defined by various factors, including region, ethnicity, religion, and language. Past patterns of state formation are also significant, given current patterns of ethnonationalism in Nigeria. Nigeria has also developed institutions intended to address horizontal inequalities that might exacerbate ethnonationalism. Nigeria has constitutional requirements in its presidential system that mandate that a president receive votes distributed across multiple states. A duly elected president must receive a majority of votes cast (in an election of two people) and "not less than one-quarter of the votes cast at the election in each of at least two-thirds of the States in the Federation and the Federal Capital Territory, Abuja."[198] The Nigerian Constitution also requires that the President appoint at least one minister from each state.[199]

Nigeria has also addressed horizontal inequality with laws and the creation of regulatory bodies. The Nigerian Federal Character Commission (FCC) was established in 1996 and has a mandate to ensure representation in the public service by equitably distributing public service positions.[200] These attempts to redress horizontal inequalities may not change structural inequalities. Studies of the operation of the FCC suggest that the FCC has not redressed longstanding imbalances between the North and South, in part because education levels in the North still lag those in the South.[201]

Ultimately, good governance in Africa will require flexible models that reflect a hybrid blend of the external and internal, the old and the new, and other relevant variables that may apply in specific local or regional contexts. Colonialism was, to a significant degree, an experiment in governance for extraction. African countries must focus on creating new experiments in good governance based on specific guiding principles. Part of this creative process must disrupt existing institutions that reflect the ethos or practices of colonial policy design and postcolonial authoritarianism, and must result in development of tools by which to identify and measure outcomes.

The governance recommendations of the Mo Ibrahim Foundation, AfDB, and AU could be used as a starting point for discussion that could be a basis for building concrete policies intended to seed better governance practices in Africa. Inclusiveness, effectiveness, responsiveness, sustainability, transparency and openness, flexibility, and benchmarks should at a minimum also be assessed and their role in new governance regimes discussed and determined. These governance systems must be concrete with clear strategies to reach achievable and measurable goals. Given the deep diversity in many countries in Africa, inclusive governance should be one key goal. Governance should also be responsive to local aspirations and needs. Given the demographic composition of most countries in Africa, they must protect minority rights. This would mean that successive governments should retain policies that work and refine those that do not.

Governance in African countries should have concrete and specific goals that are measurable and actually measured. This ability to benchmark governance strategies, processes, and goals should be for the purpose of flexibility that would entail making changes when existing strategies and processes do not work. Governments in Africa should also foster a reform environment in which robust internal criticism of policies is a norm. Although some examples exist today of countries celebrated for their reform initiatives, particularly Rwanda under President Paul Kagame, instances of reform that are intended to be models for Africa should be sustainable, transparent, and reflect a government that is responsive to the needs of its citizens and to internal criticism. Rwanda has made a number of significant reforms in recent years that government data suggest have led to high levels of average annual economic growth and poverty reduction. Others contest these figures.[202] Debates about economic data in Rwanda reflect persistent questions about data quality and the reliability of statistics in Africa. The lack of transparency surrounding changes in Rwanda make evaluation of their outcomes difficult. In this instance, accurate measurement is critical because repression in Rwanda is justified by some as an acceptable trade-off for strong economic growth and poverty reduction that has led many to call Rwanda the Singapore of Africa.

It is not clear whether reforms in Rwanda will be sustainable. The Rwanda model has relied to a significant extent on its being a favored recipient of external donor funding, which may have been an initial external response to the 1994 Rwandan genocide.[203] Paul Kagame, the president of Rwanda, has been in power for twenty years. Kagame's Rwanda also has a poor human rights record and has undertaken significant internal repression, including of government critics.[204] Questions have also arisen about the role of Rwanda in continuing conflicts in the eastern part of neighboring DRC, as well as mining of conflict minerals such as coltan (tantalum).[205] Transplantation of the Rwanda reform model might not be easy given issues related to scale (Rwanda is a small country). Rwanda and other models inside and outside of Africa can, however, be used by other countries in Africa as a starting point for considering reform strategies and can be used to determine how to develop models that are scalable, that undertake significant reform under a reasonable projected time line, and that are also transparent, responsive, and meet other criteria that make sense in specific local, national, and even regional contexts. As part of this process, countries can draw on expertise from outside of Africa but with a mindset that the external should serve the internal, not vice versa.

Notes

1. Smith, 1989: 3.
2. Scott, J., 1999: 47.
3. Kwarteng, 2011.
4. Jakub Bartoszewski and Andrew P. Morriss, 2020. "An Archipelago of Contrasts: Blacklists, Caribbean Autonomy and the New Tax Colonialism." *IFC Review*, June 17, 2020, accessed October 24, 2020, www.ifcreview.com/articles/2020/june/an-archipelago-of-contrasts-blacklists-caribbean-autonomy-and-the-new-tax-colonialism/.
5. Lugard, 1922: 203.
6. Sharkey, 2003: 24.
7. Visits of Native Chiefs. TNA CO 583/243/21.
8. Mamdani, 1996.
9. Roberts and Mann, 1991: 4.
10. Larkin, 2008: 21–25.

11. Lugard, 1922: 202.
12. *Adanji* v. *Hunwo* (1908) 1 NLR 74, 78 (Acting Chief Justice Speed).
13. Acemoglu, Chaves, Osafo-Kwaako, and Robinson, 2014: 4.
14. Sen, 2000: 3.
15. Rusalem, 2016.
16. Susan E. Rice, 2002. US Foreign Assistance and Failed States. Brookings Institution Report, www.brookings.edu/research/u-s-foreign-assistance-and-failed-states/.
17. Fragile States Index, powered by The Fund for Peace, https://fragilestatesindex.org/indicators/.
18. Fund for Peace. 2020, Fragile States Index Annual Report, p. 6, accessed October 24, 2020, https://fragilestatesindex.org/wp-content/uploads/2020/05/fsi2020-report.pdf
19. The top fifty countries in the 2020 FSI and their FSI scores are available here: https://fragilestatesindex.org/wp-content/uploads/2020/05/fsi-2020.xlsx.
20. Espeland and Sauder, 2016: 1.
21. Ibid. at 2.
22. Ibid.
23. Davis, Kingsbury, and Merry, 2012: 11, 15.
24. Notshulwana, 2011: 87.
25. Jedwab, Kerby, and Moradi, 2017: 88–90.
26. African Union. Towards the African Integrated High Speed Railway Network (AIHSRN) Development, p. 1. https://au.int/web/sites/default/files/documents/32186-doc-towards_the_african_integrated_high_speed_railway_network_aihsrn_development-e.pdf
27. Transport Department, Republic of South Africa Rail Working Group. Rail Gauge Study Report. August 2009. www.kzntransport.gov.za/reading_room/reports/natmap/NATMAP%20Rail%20Gauge%20Report%20-%20Final.pdf.
28. The three most common rail gauges are 1.067m (Cape) gauge (61.3%), 1.000m (Metric) gauge (19.2%), and 1.432m (Standard) gauge (14.5%). African Union. Towards the African Integrated High Speed Railway Network (AIHSRN) Development, p. 2, accessed October 24, 2020, https://au.int/web/sites/default/files/documents/32186-doc-towards_the_african_integrated_high_speed_railway_network_aihsrn_development-e.pdf
29. Yomi Kazeem. "African Governments Need to Fix Their Problematic Relationship with Data in their Own Countries." QuartzAfrica, October 16, 2019, accessed October 24, 2020,
30. https://nigeria.opendataforafrica.org/ifpbxbd/state-population-2006.
31. Population Reference Bureau. "Objections Surface Over Nigerian Census Results." April 18, 2007, accessed October 24, 2020, www.prb.org/objectionsovernigeriancensus/.
32. https://twitter.com/MBuhari/status/1181933937096044546?ref_src=twsrc%5Etfw%7Ctwcamp%5Etweetembed%7Ctwterm%5E1181933937096044546&ref_url=about%3Asrcdoc.
33. Kazeem, supra note 29.
34. Jerven, 2013.
35. Lequiller and Blades, 2014.
36. Friedman, 2014.

37. Mo Ibrahim Foundation. 2019. Agendas 2063 and 2030: Is Africa on Track? African Governance Report, p. 64, https://mo.ibrahim.foundation/sites/default/files/2019-10/African_Governance_Report_2019.pdf.
38. Erhagbe, 2012.
39. Smith, 1989: 3.
40. Ibid. at 7.
41. Asante et al., 2019: 2.
42. CIA. *The World Factbook – Ghana*, accessed October 24, 2020, www.cia.gov/library/publications/the-world-factbook/geos/gh.html; CIA. The World Factbook – Cote d'Ivoire, accessed October 24, 2020, www.cia.gov/library/publications/the-world-factbook/geos/iv.html.
43. Asante, Ebeheakey, Opoku-Bonsu and Cornah, 2019: 2.
44. Brempong, 2000.
45. Kyerematen, 1969: 1.
46. Ibid.
47. Ukpabi, 1970: 367.
48. Hansard 4/91 349 ff. March 18, 1901.
49. Edgerton, 2010: vi.
50. Adjaye, 1990: 1.
51. As quoted in Smith, 1926: 6.
52. Ukpabi, 1970: 363.
53. Ibid. at 378.
54. Breunig, 2017: 5, 22.
55. Ibid. at 3.
56. Shyllon, 2003: 141.
57. Sarr and Savoy, 2018: 71.
58. Hicks, 2020: 7.
59. In the case of Benin, the Benin Dialogue Group, which was established in 2010, and has been the center of an ongoing dialogue about sharing and restitution. (Shyllon, 2018).
60. German Culture Ministers Pledge to Return Looted Colonial-Era Artifacts, *ArtForum*, March, 15, 2019 at 2:11 pm, accessed October 24, 2020, www.artforum.com/news/german-culture-ministers-pledge-to-return-looted-colonial-era-artifacts-78925.
61. The prosecutor in the case had requested a sentence of four to eight months. Naomi Rea. "A French Court Acquits Four Anti-Colonial Activists Who Removed a Spear From a Museum, Saying the Gesture Counts as Free Speech." Artnet.com, November 19, 2020, accessed December 2, 2020, https://news.artnet.com/art-world/marseille-mwazulu-diyabanza-1924953.
62. Farah Nayeri. "To Protest Colonialism, He Takes Artifacts From Museums." *New York Times*, September 21, 2020, accessed October 24, 2020, www.nytimes.com/2020/09/21/arts/design/france-museum-quai-branly.html.
63. "Five Go on Trial for Seizing 'Pillaged' African Art-Work from Paris Museum." France24.com, September 30, 2020, accessed October 24, 2020, www.france24.com/en/20200930-five-activists-go-on-trial-for-seizing-african-artwork-from-paris-museum. In October 2020, Mr. Diyabanza was fined €1,000 by the court and was not sentenced to serve prison time. Shortly after being released, he went to the Louvre and attempted to exit with an

Indonesian sculpture. He was arrested and sent to jail but was later released to await trial. Kate Brown. "Restitution Activist Mwazulu Diyabanza Was Arrested After He Tried to Remove an Indonesian Sculpture From the Louvre [UPDATED]." artnetnews.com, October 26, 2020, accessed October 30, 2020, https://news.artnet.com/art-world/mwazulu-louvre-action-1918087.

64. En Direct d'Afrika Museum Berg en Dal Hollande (pays-bas) récupération de notre patrimoine, September 10, 2020, www.youtube.com/watch?v=Pnj34Cp-UUw&feature=emb_logo.
65. Sarr and Savoy, 2018: 29.
66. Breunig. 1996.
67. Garba, 1996.
68. Ibid.
69. Breunig, 2017:54.
70. Cooper, 2002: 4.
71. Munslow, 1983: 224.
72. Cranenburgh, 2008: 953.
73. Nigerian Embassy Berlin, Government, Political Structure, https://nigeriaembassygermany.org/Government.htm.
74. Kirk-Greene, 1980: 26.
75. Munslow, 1983: 227.
76. Meredith, 2005: 218.
77. Munslow, 1983: 227.
78. Christopher, 1988: 233
79. Ibid. at 239.
80. Morrock, 1973.
81. Achebe, 2012: iv.
82. Michael T. Kaufman. "NEW CHAPTER IN NIGERIA: THE OBITUARY; Sani Abacha, 54, a Beacon of Brutality In an Era When Brutality Was Standard." *The New York Times*, June 9, 1998, at A11, www.nytimes.com/1998/06/09/world/new-chapter-nigeria-obituary-sani-abacha-54-beacon-brutality-era-when-brutality.html.
83. Siollun, 2013: loc 98 (Amazon Kindle edition).
84. Ibid.
85. LeVan, 2014: 6.
86. Aiyede, 2005: 75.
87. Political scientist Carl LeVan has collected many of the important decrees issued by Nigerian military regimes between 1966 and 1999. http://carllevan.com/data/nigerias-military-decrees/.
88. Elaigwu, 1988: 186; *Aminu* v. *Nigeria* (2000) AHRLR 258 (ACHPR 2000), at ¶¶ 12, 19.
89. Orr, 1966.
90. Tijani, 2012: xi.
91. Imhonopi and Urim, 2011: 236.
92. Tar, 2009: 168.
93. Nigeria Labour Congress (Dissolution of National Executive Council), Decree No. 9 of 1994, August 18, 1994.

94. Federal Military Government (Supremacy and Enforcement of Powers), Decree No. 12 of 1994, August 24, 1994.
95. Ibid.
96. The Constitution of the Federal Republic of Nigeria 1979.
97. Adichie, 2020.
98. Human Rights Watch. Nigeria: Activist's Detention a Sign of Growing Intolerance. August 7, 2019, accessed October 24, 2020, www.hrw.org/news/2019/08/07/nigeria-activists-detention-sign-growing-intolerance.
99. Amnesty International. Nigeria; Sowore, Bakare and Jalingo Declared Prisoners of Conscience. November 20, 2019, accessed October 24, 2020, www.amnesty.org/en/latest/news/2019/11/nigeria-sowore-bakare-and-jalingo-declared-prisoners-of-conscience/.
100. Sarah Burns & Olly Owen. "Nigeria: No Longer an Oil State?" Oxford Martin School Working Paper, August 2019, accessed October 24, 2020, www.oxfordmartin.ox.ac.uk/downloads/academic/Nigeria_Oil_WP_final_130819.pdf.
101. Ibid.
102. William Clowes, Elisha Bala-Gbogbo and Bill Lehane. "Nigeria Stares Into the Abyss of a Life Without Oil Cash." *Bloomberg*, May 6, 2020, accessed October 24, 2020, www.bloomberg.com/amp/news/articles/2020-05-06/nigeria-stares-into-the-abyss-of-a-life-without-oil-revenue?.
103. Ibid.
104. Geert Wurthmann. Ways of Using the African Oil Boom for Sustainable Development. African Development Bank. Economic Research Working Paper No. 84 (March 2006), accessed October 24, 2020, www.afdb.org/fileadmin/uploads/afdb/Documents/Publications/00806226-EN-ERWP-84.PDF.
105. Christina Katsouris and Aaron Mayne. "Nigeria's Criminal Crude: International Options to Combat the Export of Stolen Oil. Chatham House". September 2013, p. 17, accessed October 24, 2020, www.chathamhouse.org/sites/default/files/public/Research/Africa/0913pr_nigeriaoil.pdf.
106. "Catch me if you can; African kleptocrats are finding it tougher to stash cash in the West." *The Economist* October 10, 2019, https://www.economist.com/middle-east-and-africa/2019/10/10/african-kleptocrats-are-finding-it-tougher-to-stash-cash-in-the-west.
107. Jude Egbas. "How Diezani escaped Nigeria and became Commissioner in Dominica." Pulse.ng, June 7, 2020, accessed October 24, 2020, www.pulse.ng/news/local/how-diezani-escaped-nigeria-and-became-commissioner-in-dominica/bbm3rzv.
108. Joseph, 1987: 150.
109. Ibid.
110. Ibid.
111. Nixon, 1996.
112. Phil Miller and Mark Curtis. "REVEALED: Britain Rebuffed Nelson Mandela's Appeal for Oil Sanctions against Nigeria after it Executed Environmentalists." Declassified UK, December 31, 2019, accessed October 24, 2020, www.dailymaverick.co.za/article/2019-12-31-revealed-britain-rebuffed-nelson-mandelas-appeal-for-oil-sanctions-against-nigeria-after-it-executed-environmentalists/#gsc.tab=0.
113. Lucas Olo Fernandes. "Opinion: Oil, Instagram the Plunder of Equatorial Guinea." *The New York Times*, November 27, 2017, accessed October 24, 2020, www.nytimes.com/2017/11/

27/opinion/equatorial-guinea-obiang-vice-president-corruption.html%202017. Nguema Obiang's Instagram is available here: www.instagram.com/teddynguema/channel/?hl=en.
114. Olo, supra note 113.
115. Angelique Chrisafis. "Opinion: France has Finally Got Tough on Corruption by Seizing a Dictator's Paris Mansion." *The Guardian*. August 6, 2012, accessed October 24, 2020, www.theguardian.com/commentisfree/2012/aug/06/france-tough-corruption-dictators-mansion.
116. Sara Brimbeuf. "The Obiang Case: How will France Return the Stolen Assets." Anti-Corruption Resource Centre, March 26, 2020, accessed October 24, 2020, www.u4.no/the-obiang-case-how-will-france-return-stolen-assets.
117. Sherpa. Ill-Gotten Gains – Equatorial Guinea, accessed December 2, 2020, www.asso-sherpa.org/ill-gotten-gains-equatorial-guinea; Transparency International, On Trial for Corruption: Teodoro Obiang, Son of the President of Equatorial Guinea, Obiang Trial Update, July 5, 2017, accessed December 2, 2020, www.transparency.org/en/news/on-trial-for-corruption-teodoro-obiang-son-of-the-president-of-equatorial-g.
118. Angelique Chrisafis. "Son of Equatorial Guinea's President is Convicted of Corruption in France." *Guardian*, October 27, 2017, accessed October 24, 2020, www.theguardian.com/world/2017/oct/27/son-of-equatorial-guineas-president-convicted-of-corruption-in-france.
119. International Court of Justice. Immunities and Criminal Proceedings (Equatorial Guinea v. France). Summary. June 6, 2018, www.courthousenews.com/wp-content/uploads/2020/02/icj-guinea-jurisdiction.pdf.
120. The court unanimously held that: "France shall, pending a final decision in the case, take all measures at its disposal to ensure that the premises presented as housing the diplomatic mission of Equatorial Guinea at 42 Avenue Foch in Paris enjoy treatment equivalent to that required by Article 22 of the Vienna Convention on Diplomatic Relations, in order to ensure their inviolability." International Court of Justice. Immunities and Criminal Proceedings (Equatorial Guinea v. France). Summary, at ¶ 99, June 6, 2018, www.courthousenews.com/wp-content/uploads/2020/02/icj-guinea-jurisdiction.pdf.
121. Proceedings in the case Equatorial Guinea v. France are available here: www.icj-cij.org/en/case/163.
122. Molly Quell. "France Assailed at UN for Prosecuting Equatorial Guinean Leader." Courthouse News Service, February 18, 2020, accessed October 24, 2020, www.courthousenews.com/france-assailed-at-un-for-prosecuting-equatorial-guinean-leader/.
123. Sarah Saadoun. "The Victims of Corruption Deserve Justice." Human Rights Watch, December 17, 2019, accessed October 24, 2020, www.hrw.org/news/2019/12/17/victims-corruption-deserve-justice.
124. Meera Venkatachalam. "Despite the Rhetoric, Macron Isn't about to Loosen France's Paternalistic Grip in Africa." Quartz Africa, June 3, 2017, accessed October 24, 2020, https://qz.com/africa/998126/emmanuel-macron-will-not-change-frances-francafrique-grip-in-africa/.
125. International Court of Justice. Immunities and Criminal Proceedings (*Equatorial Guinea* v. *France*). Judgment. December 11, 2020, ¶ 126(1), accessed December 11, 2020, www.icj-cij.org/public/files/case-related/163/163-20201211-JUD-01-00-EN.pdf.

126. Laurent Saint-Martin and Jean-Luc Warsmann. Investir pour mieux saisir, Confisquer pour mieux sanctionner. Rapport parlementaire. November 2019, pp. 60-62, accessed October 24, 2020, http://web.lexisnexis.fr/LexisActu/rapport_agrasc.pdf.
127. Proposition de loi No. 109 (Affectation des avoirs issus de la corruption transnationale) was passed by the Senate on November 6, 2018 and sent to the National Assembly in May 2019 where the bill did not advance beyond the first reading. www.senat.fr/dossier-legislatif/ppl18-109.html.
128. African Development Bank. Republic of Equatorial Guinea Country Strategy Paper 2013-2017, p. 11, www.afdb.org/fileadmin/uploads/afdb/Documents/Project-and-Operations/Equatorial_Guinea_-_2013-2017_Country_Strategy_Paper.pdf.
129. Guy Margin. "Behind The $23-Million Auction of Teodorin Obiang's Confiscated Supercars In Switzerland." *Forbes*, October 1, 2019, accessed October 24, 2020, www.forbes.com/sites/guymartin/2019/10/01/behind-the-auction-of-teodorin-obiangs-confiscated-multi-million-dollar-supercars-in-switzerland/#24297bac1595.
130. Republique et Canton de Genève, Pouvoir Judiciaire. Communiqué de Press du Ministère Public. Classement de la procédure contre T. Obiang Les véhicules sont confisqués et le navire libéré. February 7, 2019, accessed October 24, 2020, http://ge.ch/justice/sites/default/files/justice/common/actualites/communiques_de_presse/PJ_MP_COMMUNIQUE_OBIANG_20190207.pdf.
131. The prosecutors' press release states the following concerning the yacht: "Au vu de ces éléments, le Ministère public a décidé de classer la procédure et de lever le séquestre du navire Ebony Shine." [In view of these elements, the public prosecutor decided to close the proceedings and to lift the sequestration of the vessel Ebony Shine.] Republique et Canton de Genève, Pouvoir Judiciaire. Communiqué de Press du Ministère Public. Classement de la procédure contre T. Obiang Les véhicules sont confisqués et le navire libéré. February 7, 2019, accessed October 24, 2020, http://ge.ch/justice/sites/default/files/justice/common/actualites/communiques_de_presse/PJ_MP_COMMUNIQUE_OBIANG_20190207.pdf.
132. First Amended Verified Complaint for Forfeiture in Rem, *U.S.* v. *One White Crystal-Covered "Bad Tour" Glove and Other Michael Jackson Memorabilia*; Real Property Located on Sweetwater Mesa Road in Malibu, California; One 2011 Ferrari 599 GTPO. District Court for the Central District of California, No. CV 11-3582-GW, October 13, 2011, accessed October 24, 2020, www.justice.gov/sites/default/files/press-releases/attachments/2014/10/10/obiang_settlement_agreement.pdf.
133. Stipulation and Settlement Agreement, *U.S.* v. *One Michael Jackson Signed Thriller Jacket and Other Michael Jackson Memorabilia*, U.S. District Court for the Central District of California, No. CV 13-9169-GW-SS, October 10, 2014, accessed October 24, 2020, www.justice.gov/sites/default/files/press-releases/attachments/2014/10/10/obiang_settlement_agreement.pdf.
134. The US case was brought under the Kleptocracy Asset Recovery Initiative. Second Vice President of Equatorial Guinea Agrees to Relinquish More Than $30 Million of Assets Purchased with Corruption Proceeds, Press Release, October 10, 2014, accessed October 24, 2020, www.justice.gov/opa/pr/second-vice-president-equatorial-guinea-agrees-relinquish-more-30-million-assets-purchased.

135. Amnesty International "Equatorial Guinea Rights Lawyer Faces Bogus Charges." February 15, 2019, accessed October 24, 2020, www.amnesty.org/en/latest/news/2019/02/equatorial-guinea-rights-lawyer-faces-bogus-charges/.
136. Chris Raggett. Networks of Impunity: Corruption and European Foreign Policy. European Council on Foreign Relations Policy Brief. March 2020, www.ecfr.eu/page/-/networks_of_impunity_corruption_and_european_foreign_policy.pdf.
137. Human Rights Watch "'Manna from Heaven'?: How Health and Education Pay the Price for Self-Dealing in Equatorial Guinea. 2017, accessed October 24, 2020, www.hrw.org/sites/default/files/report_pdf/equatorialguinea0617_web.pdf.
138. Campos-Serrano, 2013: 316.
139. Ibid.
140. Human Rights Watch. Equatorial Guinea: Why Poverty Plagues a High-Income Nation. January 27, 2017, accessed October 24, 2020, www.hrw.org/news/2017/01/27/equatorial-guinea-why-poverty-plagues-high-income-nation.
141. Corruption involves public misuse of private funds, while rent seeking involves acquisition of access or control over opportunities for earning rents or monopoly profits. Jacqueline Coolidge and Susan Rose-Ackerman. High-Level Rent-Seeking and Corruption in African Regimes. World Bank Policy Research Working Paper 1780. June 1997. Washington, DC: World Bank. http://documents1.worldbank.org/curated/en/855031468767966104/pdf/multi-page.pdf.
142. Acemoglu, Verdier and Robinson, 2004.
143. Elsa Peraldi. "Beating Kleptocrats at their Own Game: Learning How to Tackle Kleptocracy more Effectively." Global Integrity Blog, June 13, 2019, accessed October 24, 2020, www.globalintegrity.org/2019/06/13/kleptocracy/.
144. Cambridge Dictionary, https://dictionary.cambridge.org/us/dictionary/english/kleptocracy.
145. Campos-Serrano, 2013: 314.
146. Ibid.
147. Neil Munshi. "Four Decades of Growth, but Equatorial Guinea's People Still Mired in Poverty." *Financial Times*, December 31, 2019, accessed October 24, 2020, www.ft.com/content/f4d0e2d0-1cc9-11ea-97df-cc63de1d73f4.
148. Ogbuigwe, 2018:182.
149. Eromo Egbejule. "Nigeria's Refining Renaissance." *Petroleum Economist*, October 2, 2019, accessed October 24, 2020, www.petroleum-economist.com/articles/midstream-downstream/refining-marketing/2019/nigeria-s-refining-renaissance.
150. Ibid.
151. John Vidal. "Petrol Sold to Nigeria from Europe 'Dirtier' that Black Market 'Bush' Fuel." *The Guardian*. July 1, 2020, accessed October 24, 2020, www.theguardian.com/global-development/2020/jul/01/petrol-sold-to-nigeria-from-europe-dirtier-than-black-market-bush-fuel.
152. Stakeholder Democracy Network. 2020. Dirty Fuel: An Analysis of Official and Unofficial Petroleum Products in the Niger Delta, www.stakeholderdemocracy.org/wp-content/uploads/2020/05/Dirty-fuel.-Report.-2020-DIGITAL.pdf.
153. Ibid.

154. Oluwatosin Adeshokan. "Nigeria's Dangote Still Expects Refinery to be Running early 2021." The Africa Report, June 15, 2020, accessed October 24, 2020, www.theafricareport.com/29913/nigerias-dangote-still-expects-refinery-to-be-running-early-2021/.
155. Egbejule, supra note 149.
156. David Whitehouse. "Dangote Refinery is Held up by Nigeria's Congested Ports." The Africa Report, October 14, 2019, accessed October 24, 2020, www.theafricareport.com/18562/dangote-refinery-is-held-up-by-nigerias-congested-ports/.
157. Le Billion, 2006: 778.
158. Smillie, 2010.
159. Mngomezulu. 2020: 30–31.
160. Simone Haysom. Security and Humanitarian Crisis in Mali: The Role of Regional Organisations. Humanitarian Policy Group. March 2014, accessed October 24, 2020, www.odi.org/sites/odi.org.uk/files/odi-assets/publications-opinion-files/8829.pdf.
161. The Tuareg Revolt and the Mali Coup. Hearing before the Subcommittee on Africa, Global Health, and Human Rights of the Committee on Foreign Affairs. House of Representatives, 112th Congress, Second Session, June 29, 2012, www.govinfo.gov/content/pkg/CHRG-112hhrg74863/html/CHRG-112hhrg74863.htm; Howard W. French. "In One Poor African Nation, Democracy Thrives." *The New York Times*, October 16, 1996, accessed October 24, 2020, https://timesmachine.nytimes.com/timesmachine/1996/10/16/824658.html?pageNumber=3.
162. Adam Nossiter. "Soldiers Overthrow Mali Government in Setback for Democracy in Africa." *The New York Times*, March 22, 2012, accessed February 24, 2021. www.nytimes.com/2012/03/23/world/africa/mali-coup-france-calls-for-elections.html.
163. Eric Nagourney, "Mali Military Coup: Why the World Is Watching." *New York Times*, August 19, 2020, accessed October 24, 2020, www.nytimes.com/2020/08/19/world/africa/Whats-happening-Mali-coup.html.
164. Marina Ilminska and Martin Schoenteich. "Raising the Profile of Pretrial Detention in Africa. Open Society Justice Initiative, April 21, 2016, accessed October 24, 2020, www.justiceinitiative.org/voices/raising-profile-pretrial-detention-africa.
165. US Department of State. Mali 2019 Human Rights Report, accessed October 24, 2020, www.state.gov/wp-content/uploads/2020/02/MALI-2019-HUMAN-RIGHTS-REPORT.pdf.
166. Rand, 2013: 1.
167. Awol Allo. "We are here": The Soundtrack to the Oromo Revolution Gripping Ethiopia. African Arguments, March 30, 2018, accessed October 24, 2020, https://africanarguments.org/2018/03/30/we-are-here-the-soundtrack-to-the-oromo-revolution-gripping-ethiopia/.
168. Ribka Ayana. "How the Murder of an Ethiopian Singer Triggered an Uprising Against a Disintegrating Democracy." *Time*, July 24, 2020, accessed October 24, 2020, https://time.com/5871217/ethiopia-protests-haacaaluu/.
169. Zach Vertin. "Averting Civil War in Ethiopia: It's Time to Propose Elements of a Negotiated Settlement." Brookings Blog, November 16, 2020, accessed December 2, 2020, www.brookings.edu/blog/order-from-chaos/2020/11/16/averting-civil-war-in-ethiopia-its-time-to-propose-elements-of-a-negotiated-settlement/.
170. Sydney P. Freedberg, Scilla Alecci, Will Fitzgibbon, Douglas Dalby and Delphine Reuter. "How Africa's Richest Woman Exploited Family Ties, Shell Companies and Inside Deals to Build An Empire." International Consortium of Investigative Journalists, January 19, 2020,

accessed October 24, 2020, www.icij.org/investigations/luanda-leaks/how-africas-richest-woman-exploited-family-ties-shell-companies-and-inside-deals-to-build-an-empire/?gclid=CjwKCAjwz6_8BRBkEiwA3p02VaMcxFUCEiwk8Drmipk2VJ8dhmsXQZvHjmfmgehY_E8jYwhwMOEr9BoCI-IQAvD_BwE; Yassir Khudayri. "How Mozambicans Shoulder the Burdens of Corruption." Open Society Justice Initiative, February 29, 2020, accessed October 24, 2020, www.justiceinitiative.org/voices/how-mozambicans-shoulder-the-burdens-of-corruption.

171. Michael Forsythe, Kyra Gurney, Scilla Alecci and Ben Hallman. "How U.S. Firms Helped Africa's Richest Woman Exploit Her Country's Wealth." *The New York Times*, January 19, 2020, accessed October 24, 2020, www.nytimes.com/2020/01/19/world/africa/isabel-dos-santos-angola.html.
172. Amnesty International. Nigeria: Shell Complicit in the Arbitrary Executions of Ogoni Nine as Writ Served in Dutch Court. June 29, 2017, accessed October 24, 2020, www.amnesty.org/en/latest/news/2017/06/shell-complicit-arbitrary-executions-ogoni-nine-writ-dutch-court/.
173. This effectively means that US courts would not have subject matter jurisdiction to hear Kiobel's case under the Alien Torts Statute. *Kiobel v. Royal Dutch Petroleum*, 569 US 108 (2013).
174. Settlement Agreement, *Wiwa* v. *Shell Petroleum*, 96 Civ. 8386 (KMW)(HBP), June 8, 2009, accessed October 24, 2020, https://ccrjustice.org/sites/default/files/assets/Wiwa_v._Shell_SETTLEMENT_AGREEMENT.Signed-1.pdf.
175. Ben Eguzozie. "Shell loses N17bn oil spill judgment, as Supreme Court dismisses company's case." Businessa.m.live.com, November 28, 2020, accessed February 24, 2021, www.businessamlive.com/shell-loses-n17bn-oil-spill-judgment-as-supreme-court-dismisses-companys-case/.
176. *The Environmental Defense Association* v. *Royal Dutch Shell and Shell Oil Development Company of Nigeria* v. *Akpan, The Hague Court of Appeal*, Case Nos. 200,126,849 and 200,127,813, January 29, 2021, accessed February 24, 2021, https://uitspraken.rechtspraak.nl/inziendocument?id=ECLI:NL:GHDHA:2021:134; Elian Peltier and Claire Moses. "A Victory for Farmers in a David-and-Goliath Environmental Case." *New York Times*, January 29, 2021, accessed February 24, 2021, www.nytimes.com/2021/01/29/world/europe/shell-nigeria-oil-spills.html.
177. Stanley Reed. "U.K. High Court Says Nigerians Can Sue Shell in Britain Over Oil Spills." *New York Times*, February 12, 2021, accessed February 24, 2021, www.nytimes.com/2021/02/12/business/shell-oil-spills-nigeria-lawsuit-britain.html; Okpabi and others (Appellants) v. Royal Dutch Shell Plc and another (Respondents) [2021] UKSC 3, www.supremecourt.uk/cases/docs/uksc-2018-0068-judgment.pdf.
178. Amnesty International. A Criminal Enterprise? Shell's Involvement in Human Rights Violations in Nigeria in the 1990s. November 2017, accessed October 24, 2020, www.amnesty.org/download/Documents/AFR4473932017ENGLISH.PDF.
179. Enweremadu, 2013: 56.
180. United States Congress. House Committee on Financial Services. Recovering Dictators' Plunder: Hearings Before the House Subcommittee on Financial Institutions and Consumer Credit, p. 79, May 9, 2002, accessed October 24, 2020, www.govinfo.gov/content/pkg/CHRG-107hhrg79943/html/CHRG-107hhrg79943.htm.

181. Muhammadu Buhari. "Post-Coronavirus, Africa's Manufacturing Moment/Opinion." *Newsweek*, May 29, 2020, accessed October 24, 2020, www.newsweek.com/post-coronavirus-africas-manufacturing-moment-opinion-1507155.
182. Nicholas Hildyard. The World Bank, Red Flags and the Looting of Nigeria's Oil Revenues. October 2018, accessed October 24, 2020, www.recommon.org/eng/the-world-bank-red-flags-and-the-looting-of-nigerias-oil-revenues//
183. Matthew T. Page. A New Taxonomy for Corruption in Nigeria. Carnegie Endowment for International Peace, October 2018, accessed October 24, 2020,\https://carnegieendowment.org/files/CP_338_Page_Nigeria_FINAL.pdf.
184. Enweremadu, 2013: 52.
185. African Kleptocrats are Finding it Tougher to Stash Cash in the West. *The Economist* October 10, 2019, accessed October 24, 2020, www.economist.com/middle-east-and-africa/2019/10/10/african-kleptocrats-are-finding-it-tougher-to-stash-cash-in-the-west.
186. Department of Justice, Office of Public Affairs. U.S. Enters into Trilateral Agreement with Nigeria and Jersey to Repatriate Over $300 Million to Nigeria in Assets Stolen by Former Nigerian Dictator General Sani Abacha. February 3, 2020, accessed October 24, 2020, www.justice.gov/opa/pr/us-enters-trilateral-agreement-nigeria-and-jersey-repatriate-over-300-million-nigeria-assets.
187. Egobueze and Ojirika, 2018.
188. Adebowale Olorunmola. 2016. Cost of Politics in Nigeria. Westminster Foundation for Democracy, accessed October 24, 2020, www.wfd.org/wp-content/uploads/2017/09/Cost-of-Politics-Nigeria.pdf.
189. Egobueze and Ojirika, 2018.
190. Nigeria Constitution of 1999, Chapter IV: Fundamental Rights, section 44(3).
191. Egobueze and Ojirika, 2018: 199.
192. Arowolo, 2011.
193. Egobueze and Ojirika, 2018: 199.
194. Ibid. at 200.
195. Report of the Drafting Committee on the Constitution. 1949. The Bodleian Library, University of Oxford. MSS Brit Emp s 332, Boxes 12-13, Papers of Arthur Creech Jones.
196. Suberu, 1991: 499.
197. Demarest, Langer and Ukiwo, 2020: 315.
198. Nigeria Constitution of 1999, Chapter VI: The Executive, Part I: Federal Executive, A. The President of the Federation, section 134.1.
199. Nigeria Constitution of 1999, Chapter VI: The Executive, Part I: Federal Executive, A. The President of the Federation, section 147.1
200. Demarest et al., 2020: 316.
201. Ibid.
202. Himbara, 2016; Anonymous. Rwandan Poverty Statistics: Exposing the 'Donor Darling', Review of African Political Economy Blog, May 31, 2017, accessed October 24, 2020, http://roape.net/2017/05/31/rwandan-poverty-statistics-exposing-donor-darling/; Anonymous. "Faking it: The Rwanda GDP Growth Myth,: Review of African Political Economy Blog," July 26, 2017, accessed October 24, 2020, http://roape.net/2017/07/26/faking-rwandan-gdp-growth-myth/.

203. Desrosiers and Swedlund note that although contrary to assertions that Rwanda is an aid outlier, "aid relations in Rwanda follow a trajectory seen in a group of privileged aid recipients. Rwanda is not exceptional among a group of nonstandard, more favored recipients." Desrosiers and Swedlund, 2018: 463.
204. Human Rights Watch. Rwanda— Events of 2019, www.hrw.org/world-report/2020/country-chapters/rwanda.
205. In 2011, Michael Next noted that "economic networks centered on Rwanda have been pivotal to both the legal and illegal trade in coltan out of the DRC to the international market." Nest, 2001; Prunier, 2009; "On the Trail of Tantalum: Tracking a Conflict Mineral." Mining Technology, April 20, 2016, accessed October 24, 2020, www.mining-technology.com/features/featureon-the-trail-of-tantalum-4831288/.

4

Legal Imperialism and Institutions

In eighteenth-century England, poachers and brigands sometimes put burnt cork on their faces, so that they would not gleam in the moon-light .... More than one African penal code copied British statutes, and accordingly made it a felony to be found wandering about at night with intent to commit a felony with one's face blackened!

Robert B. Seidman (1981)[1]

THE BERLIN CONFERENCE AND THE CARVING UP OF AFRICA

Colonialism in Nigeria and elsewhere was fraught with contradictions and used methods of borrowing that were problematic, which continue to shape reception of the external. Colonial legal systems were often not carefully implemented, which caused particular problems when power was handed over to local elites at independence. A lack of legal and other types of capacity in many former colonies at independence exacerbated these problems. Colonialism also involved creation of countries and economies that were structured to be uncompetitive. These new countries, which external powers created on a map in consultation with one another but not with Africans, have remained enmeshed in political, economic, and cultural relationships with their former colonizers.

The Berlin Conference reflected external intervention with little or no local input, creating problematic states in decisions that continue to reverberate into the present:

> That controversial gathering of the world's leading European powers precipitated what we now call the Scramble for Africa, which created new boundaries that did violence to Africa's ancient societies and resulted in tension-prone modern states. It took place without African consultation or representation, to say the least. Great Britain was handed the area of West Africa that would later become Nigeria, like a piece of chocolate cake at a birthday party."[2]

Colonial governance draws attention to how states and nations are constructed, imagined and "conceptualized and made socially effective through particular imaginative and symbolic devices."[3] Because of the nature of law and ways that new laws often build upon existing enactments and precedents, the state as constructed by law during colonialism has had a continuing and often negative impact in countries such as Nigeria. Practices of colonial officials reinforced existing hierarchies and created new ones marked by "rituals of control" that "established and demonstrated hierarchy."[4] Governance structures refined during colonialism did not end with independence. Instead, such structures have often continued to shape the construction of the state and treatment of those who fall within the authority of such states. In addition, the operation of the state in Africa and elsewhere reflects transnational patterns of governance that have far too often replicated institutionalized patterns of authority and domination refined under conditions of colonialism.[5] These historical patterns have had significant implications for continuing patterns of external determination in African postcolonial contexts that today involve varied actors, including those other than actual states.

Law was a key element of colonial conquest and justifications for colonialism, which presented the rule of law benefits of colonization as an important aspect of bringing civilization to Africa. However, the actions of colonial powers on the ground did little to establish legal frameworks that would truly facilitate the rule of law. Colonial officials and missionaries often had significant authority to make decisions of long-lasting significance. Notably, however, as was far too often the case in colonial contexts, those making decisions often lacked accountability for the consequences of their choices. Chinua Achebe's response to a question about translating his works into his native Igbo language in a 1994 interview in *Paris Review* highlights the potential power of individual missionaries and other colonial-era decision makers:

> No, my work has not been translated. There is a problem with the Igbo language. It suffers from a very serious inheritance, which it received at the beginning of this century from the Anglican mission. They sent out a missionary by the name of Dennis. Archdeacon Dennis. He was a scholar. He had this notion that the Igbo language – which had very many different dialects – should somehow manufacture a uniform dialect that would be used in writing to avoid all these different dialects. Because the missionaries were powerful, what they wanted to do they did. This became the law .... The way he did it was to invite six people from six different dialectal areas. They sat round a table and they took a sentence from the Bible .... And in this way, around the table, they created what is called Standard Igbo, with which the Bible was translated. The result is incredible. I can speak about it because in my family we read the Bible day and night. I know the Bible very well. But the standard version cannot sing. There's nothing you can do with it to make it sing. It's heavy. It's wooden. It doesn't go anywhere.[6]

Events in Chinua Achebe's novel *Things Fall Apart* unfold in Igboland, which is in southeastern Nigeria.[7] The passage from Chinua Achebe's interview highlights the profound impact of missionaries in colonial and postcolonial contexts. He draws particular attention to their role in critical questions related to language, and not just in Africa.[8] Missionaries in African colonial contexts included Europeans, European Americans, freed African slaves, and African Americans. Bishop Samuel Ajayi Crowther of the Church Missionary Society was a freed Yoruba slave and missionary who became the best-known Christian of African descent in the British Empire in the last decades of the nineteenth century.[9] African American missionaries, often sent to Africa by white missionary boards, had a substantial influence in Africa, as verified in missionary journals of the time.[10] Notably, treatment of African American missionaries reflected complexities of the internal and external. Broader external concerns emanated from the racial context in United States, where, after 1900, white mission boards began to oppose black missionaries, reflecting racial trends in the early decades of the twentieth century in the United States. British colonizers in turn feared the impact of African American missionaries in inciting political desires among Africans that could jeopardize the colonial system.[11]

The impact of social context on missionary activities had been apparent in the early nineteenth century when British missionaries converting and educating slaves in the West Indies used altered versions of the Bible that omitted passages that could incite rebellion,[12] including those involving Moses' freeing the Israelites from captivity, while retaining passages that reinforced the institution of slavery. Omitted passages included 90 percent of the Old Testament and 50 percent of the New Testament, which meant that the Slave Bible included only 232 of the 1,189 chapters in the standard Protestant Bible.[13]

The Slave Bible highlights something of the utmost importance in understanding borrowing from external models in colonial and other contexts in Africa. Uses of external models were often distorted, at times intentionally, and in some instances, due to intermediaries' lack of full understanding of the models being used. Problematic uses of external models continue to shape events in former colonies in Africa.

During colonialism, those with authority to make determinations about what models should be used often had underlying agendas and assumptions that shaped choices about uses and modification of external models in African contexts. Borrowings were altered, for example, due to racial assumptions about the underlying nature and capacity of *natives*. Borrowings were also shaped by a *portfolio* approach by British colonial administrators. *Portfolio* approaches meant that decisions about various things within colonies, including for example, choices about which crops should be grown in a colonial possession, were shaped largely by external needs and considerations. These portfolio approaches were most evident in resource allocation decisions among different colonies that were based to a significant extent on British, rather than local, needs and considerations. This made decision-making processes in colonial contexts of domination fundamentally different from decisions that might be made internally by a government with a greater degree of internal orientation. It also meant that patterns of borrowing were often fragmentary and difficult to reconcile with internally driven and coherent decision-making processes.

Manners in which authority was imposed before and during colonialism exacerbated this fragmented approach. Although this book uses the terms *colonial project* and *colonial system*, the reality on the ground was far more complex. The creation of Nigeria as a legal entity illustrates the complexity of types of colonial possessions and sources of authority in colonial contexts. The present-day country of Nigeria is an amalgamation of multiple British possessions that were at one time administered separately, which has important continuing implications for law. Lagos came under British influence in the nineteenth century. At the end of 1851, a British military force deposed the ruler of Lagos, Oba Kosoko, and, at the beginning of 1852, signed a treaty with his successor, Oba Akitoye (who was also Kosoko's predecessor).[14] Akitoye gained British support by allying himself with the British and agreeing to end the slave trade.[15]

The intervention of the British in a power struggle over leadership in Lagos illustrates the reshaping of existing internal struggles by external powers. This intervention in colonial Lagos reflects patterns evident in British colonial Africa. In such interventions, "European observers frequently took sides" in a range of contested and disputed spaces, including in Zambia "during inheritance disputes, backing their favorite candidate with extraordinarily complex historical and anthropological arguments" reflecting a political system "which had been built on a very effective publicity machine which operated through violence, but which had always been unstable at the margins; that the power of its elaborate system of chiefly control was more apparent than real."[16]

Nigeria is an artificial construct comprised of many separate entities that were assembled into a single colony in 1914. In 1955, Lord Hailey described Nigeria as "perhaps the most artificial of the many administrative units created during European occupation of Africa."[17] In 1861, a Treaty of Cession ceded Lagos to the British Crown, who administered the colony.[18] The Royal Nigeria Company (RNC), one of a number of chartered companies that administered territories claimed by European powers, was given a royal charter in 1886 to undertake administration of territory in the lower Niger and Benue River regions. The vaguely designated territory, named the Oil Rivers Protectorate in 1889, became the Niger Coast Protectorate in 1893.[19] This territory was amalgamated with former RNC territories in 1900,[20] forming the Southern Nigeria Protectorate. The Lagos Colony was combined with the Southern Nigeria Protectorate in 1906, forming the Colony and Protectorate of Southern Nigeria. Northern Nigeria was governed as a protectorate from 1900 to 1914. In 1914, the Colony and Protectorate of Southern Nigeria was merged with the Northern Nigeria Protectorate to form Nigeria.

Each of the component entities in Nigeria had its own laws and regulations adopted by those responsible for administering the territory. Laws and regulations were typically carried over at the time territories were combined, which could lead to administrative difficulties in even understanding what prior legal commitments had been made by constituent entities. When the RNC charter was revoked in 1899, the Order in Council[21] provided:

> Subject to the provisions of this Order or of any Proclamation made under this Order, all Statutes, Orders in Council, Rules, Regulations, or Treaties, together with any jurisdiction exercisable thereunder, whether exercisable by Her Majesty or by any person on her behalf, or by any Court within Southern Nigeria, or under any Commission or under any Charter granted by Her Majesty, which at the commencement of this Order are in force within the limits of this Order, or any part of such limits, shall remain in full force, and every suit, action, complaint, matter of thing, civil or criminal, which shall be depending in any Court within Southern Nigeria at the commencement of this Order shall and may be proceeded with such Court in the like manner as if this Order had not been passed.[22]

This manner of incorporation of past laws and legal cases into new administrative structures without scrutiny has led to significant legal overhang that is still evident even today. The fragmented tendency in patterns of lawmaking before the amalgamation of Nigeria in 1914 persisted into the colonial era when colonial administrators at times adopted different legal frameworks in different segments of Nigeria. Thus, even after the formation of Nigeria, colonial laws at times applied differently in Northern Nigeria as compared with the rest of Nigeria. RNC lawmaking processes reflect just one strand of lawmaking in a portion of what later became Nigeria.

Although many divide experiences in African countries into categories such as colonial era and postindependence era, such demarcations are by their nature unspecific, and many times have meanings that extend beyond commonplace understandings of such terms. For example, a legal instrument stating that a country has become independent is not by itself indicative of a fundamental change in internal legal arrangements of the now formally independent place or a modification in dynamics of relationships between former colonizers and the colonized.

Past laws, regulations, and determinations shape current conceptualizations of law in theory and in the application of law in practice in real-world contexts. At the time of independence, insufficient attention was given to the deeply embedded nature of laws enacted during colonialism. A significant legal hangover from the colonial era still exists in relation to a broad range of legal and regulatory frameworks that derive from colonial-era laws, ranging from laws relating to business to laws imposing criminal penalties for homosexuality.[23] As a result of these colonial hangovers, political and economic incumbents in many African countries continue to use the tools, policies, laws, and processes created and deployed during and prior to the colonial era. The pervasive presence of colonial hangover is apparent in the retention of legal traditions such as customary barrister robes and wigs in Africa, where lawyers continue to cloak themselves in colonial dress, although such practices are waning in Britain itself.[24]

The structure of colonial legal institutions and relationships mirrored the extractive goals of colonialism and mechanisms of control that facilitated extraction. The development of functional institutional frameworks is key to Africa's achieving any sustained economic growth in the future. An institution can be defined as "a public system of rules which defines offices and positions with their rights and duties, powers and immunities, and the like[, which] specify certain forms of actions as permissible, others as forbidden."[25] An institution can be also thought of as an abstract object or as "a possible form of conduct expressed by a system of rules."[26]

Even at independence, when British colonial activities were severely criticized, if not condemned, British legal traditions were not seen in as negative a light as other aspects of British domination in Africa. The role of law as a tool of imperialism and domination was often not a point of emphasis. Kalu Ezera, for example, saw British experiments with federal constitutions for its colonies as representing "one of Britain's contributions to the art of government."[27] Even before colonialism, European powers began imposing European legal systems throughout Africa. These legal systems, combined with customary law, are essential elements in the hybrid legal systems that exist throughout Africa today. Countries in Africa colonized by Britain developed legal systems that reflected England's common law heritage. Countries colonized by other European powers, including France, Portugal, Spain, and Germany, developed legal systems based on continental European civil law traditions.

Notably, both civil law and common law developed out of contexts of conquest. Civil and common law systems reflect an enduring legacy of the Roman Empire.[28] As was the case in colonial Africa, received Roman law transcended national borders and replaced or at least supplemented local customary laws.[29] The nostalgia with which the Roman Empire may be viewed in the United States and Europe is a significant contrast to views of colonialism of modern empires.[30] Perceptions of past empires as advancing civilization may, however, contribute to views of colonialism in Africa that emphasize the presumed benefits of colonialism and its *civilizing* effect. Perspectives that emphasize this civilizing effect tend to deemphasize the exploitation of natural resources and human beings, violence, and other destructive effects of empires. Roman law in Europe is often celebrated as having had a unifying effect that "supplied the backbone for a common European legal tradition."[31] Civil law traditions imposed in African countries during colonialism came at a time when civil law was changing with the emergence of nation-states in the eighteenth and nineteenth centuries. These nation-states had begun to create codes that reflected codes of Roman law mixed with local laws. These new codes included the French Civil Code of 1804 and later, the German Civil Code.[32]

Roman law was introduced in England as well. English common law reflects the impact of the Norman invasion in 1066. Some historians consider the Norman kings to have been colonial rulers.[33] The Normans and their successors developed a new court system and a legal system based on standardized forms of legal action (writs) derived from pre-Norman Anglo-Saxon writs, which emerged as instruments of executive administration.[34] In common law systems, court decisions are a means for the development of law, which has led to "a distinctive influence on the law."[35] In common law systems, past court decisions often have precedential value, which means that earlier court decisions are important in common law systems. In England, a judicial precedent is authoritative – "it is not merely evidence of the law but a source of it; and the courts are bound to follow the law that is so established."[36] The strict approach to precedent under English law is not necessarily suitable in the "rapidly changing social and economic conditions" that existed in Africa during colonialism.[37]

Common law developed over time in England and spread with British imperialists and colonialists around the globe to countries such as the United States, Canada, New Zealand, Australia, India, and many countries in Africa, including former British colonies such as Ghana, Kenya, Nigeria, South Africa, and Zambia. Although borrowing is a pervasive aspect of legal systems, legal borrowings in British and other colonial and postcolonial contexts in Africa have often reflected significant reliance on external models with little real customization for local contexts. During the colonial era, laws of the colonial power (or duplicated laws from other colonial possessions of the colonial power) were the primary sources of law in British colonies. Demarcating the end of colonialism is difficult from a legal perspective, particularly with respect to everyday laws, which had significant continuity during and after colonialism. Laws derived from international sources have also been an important source of law on the books in many African countries. Legal and other experts, who continue to play a key role in varied contexts and who may be engaged by donors or others, have reinforced external-facing patterns of lawmaking. Legal education and training also continue to contribute to external-facing patterns of lawmaking. For varied reasons, legal borrowings tend to be sticky in that they may continue to shape law long after their adoption.

Legal borrowings in African contexts have not always been highly effective, in part because of how British colonial administrators and postcolonial legal officials and policymakers have undertaken borrowing. Further, lawyers as part of the postcolonial elite, have been trained in ways that may hinder effective legal reform of and development of new approaches to legal frameworks within Africa. In addition to controlling internal legal systems within their colonies, colonizing powers also played a key role in the development of international law, which was used to provide legal justifications for varied acts by colonial powers. International law has typically been written thus far as a "history of rules developed in the European state system since the 16th century which then were spread to other continents and eventually the entire globe," which reflects an incomplete and Eurocentric story of international law that

> generally ignore[s] the violence, ruthlessness, and arrogance which accompanied the dissemination of Western rules, and the destruction of other legal cultures in which that dissemination resulted ... this history of international law was a history of conquerors and victors, not of the victims ... the conventional story ignores too many other experiences and forms of legal relations between autonomous communities developed in the course of history ... [and] discards such extra-European experiences and forms which were discontinued as a result of domination and colonization by European Powers as irrelevant to a (continuing) history of international law.[38]

Law was central to colonialism,[39] which was facilitated by international law.[40] Contradictions were at the core of the colonial endeavor itself and evident in competing conceptions of colonialism and its legal bases, which were used to justify colonialism in general and specific acts such as the invasion and ransacking of Benin. The Berlin Conference of 1884–1885 contributed to the formalization of colonial spheres of interest in Africa. The Berlin Conference led to the General Act of 1885 (Berlin Act) that was signed by representatives of the United Kingdom, France, Germany, Austria, Belgium, Denmark, Spain, the United States (who signed but which did not ratify the Berlin Act), Italy, the Netherlands, Portugal, Russia, Sweden-Norway, and Turkey (Ottoman Empire).[41] European division of Africa also highlights the impact of cooperation and competition among European powers in colonial African contexts.

The Berlin Act, which reflected little or no input from Africans, became a key basis for the establishment of European colonial possessions in Africa. Although the Berlin Act contemplated a governance regime in Africa based on free trade, it led to highly monopolistic colonial possessions in Africa that were enforced with coercion and violence.[42] For example, the imposition of colonialism in southeastern Nigeria during the time of the warrant chiefs involved various types of coercion and violence:

> Another important factor which helps to account for the way the choice of the early Warrant Chiefs was made is to be found in indigenous reaction to the high-handed procedure of the colonial government in the days of military conquest and subjugation .... It was the policy of the Protectorate Government to disarm any community its forces over-ran as a means of ensuring its future good behaviour. During the Aro Expedition the policy was to demand guns from a village at the rate of one gun for every four houses. If the villagers failed to surrender guns to the satisfaction of the political officer accompanying the column, the soldiers either burnt the town or lived off it until the demands of the government were fully met. The effect of this policy on the people was often heightened recalcitrance and increased distrust of the government .... It was also official policy to seize local leaders and keep them as hostages to be released only if government demands were met by their people ... the Officer Commanding the Aro Field Force, ordered his officers to treat as 'hostile' any village in which the leaders did not surrender as soon

as the military patrol entered it, and to keep any leaders who surrendered until guns had been handed in, food provided for the troops and roads made.[43]

The warrant chief system was reformed after a massive and coordinated uprising of Igbo women that is referred to as Ogu Umunwaanyi (Women's War).[44] In 1929, women, who had suffered under the warrant chief system, led protests against the warrant chiefs. Warrant chiefs "were reported as having taken women to marry without conforming to the customary process, which included the woman's right to refuse a particular suitor [and having] also helped themselves to the women's agricultural produce, and to their domestic animals."[45] Igbo women were rendered invisible by decisions of the colonial administration and excluded from political participation to a significant degree during colonialism because of assumptions made by colonial authorities about gender. They protested in response to implementation of a new system of taxation. The Women's War demonstrates the roles played by women in resistance to colonialism. Other women's groups, including the Abeokuta Women's Union, also played a role in the resistance to colonialism in Nigeria.[46]

The Berlin Act had a seemingly humanitarian goal of suppressing the slave trade along with a worldview that accepts without question the subjugation of "subject" or "native" populations in Africa,[47] as well as various forms of compulsory labor. Within this worldview, the Berlin Act positions Europeans as protectors of local populations in Africa.[48] British governance systems in Africa during the precolonial period were based, in some instances, on treaties of protection of the sort entered into by the RNC in what later became Nigeria.

In 1886, the RNC, which was given a royal charter to undertake administration of territory in part of what later became Nigeria, entered into similar, and often identical, treaties of protection with various indigenous rulers.[49] The RNC enacted a broad range of regulations that dealt with business, commercial, and other legal matters,[50] including regulations relating to import, export, and customs duties, license duties, fiscal and administrative matters, judicial frameworks and courts, registration of foreigners, and policing and military force. Precolonial lawmaking by the RNC was not the product of any sustained engagement with local representatives or authorities. Further, such lawmaking reflected an overriding focus on the promotion of British commercial and other interests and policies intended to give the company both political control and commercial domination over territories under the company's administration. The company sought to impose a monopoly over commercial relations in the territory under its administration,[51] which had a negative impact on German and other European traders and local Nigerian traders, some of whom took up arms against the company.[52]

Potential shortcomings in legal frameworks were apparent from the earliest days of British intervention in Nigeria. In Nigeria, formal legal engagement in the lower

Niger River region was evident in RNC treaties, which were fill-in-the-blank documents signed by rulers who likely did not read or speak English, were not literate, and were unlikely to have understood the entirety of what they were signing. These treaties typically granted the RNC "powers vested in them by the native Chiefs, and under the supervision and control of Her Majesty's Government."[53] The powers vested in the RNC by the "native Chiefs" reflected legal fiction: although each of the "native Chiefs" signed a treaty granting the RNC rights of ownership, supervision, and control, each such treaty was virtually identical, which suggests that the "native Chiefs" had little actual power to negotiate terms of engagement with the RNC.[54]

These treaties became a basis for colonial property claims that underlay indirect rule. Although the RNC was successful in monopolizing the palm oil trade and was profitable, the RNC was unpopular among German and French merchants, local Nigerian merchants (who could only exchange goods on an extremely unequal basis with the company), and Liverpool merchants. The advantages the RNC received during the time of its charter continued to give it significant advantages during the colonial era in Nigeria.[55] The RNC reverted to its original name, United Africa Company,[56] after it lost its charter, becoming a major commercial force throughout West Africa and eventually a wholly owned subsidiary of the multinational firm, Unilever.[57]

The RNC illustrates important aspects of European imperialism and colonialism that continue to resonate today. Imperialism and colonialism included significant commercial aspects, which were often predominant, and which typically focused on extractive activities.[58] In addition to chartered trading companies, merchants, including those based in Liverpool, and smaller European, Syrian, and indigenous African merchants also participated in commercial activities in British colonial possessions in West Africa.[59] The operation of colonial commercial interests in Africa can be tied directly to persistent continuing economic and political weaknesses.[60]

European demands typically drove precolonial and colonial trading relationships between Africa and Europe.[61] Furthermore, the external entities that operated in Africa did not operate for the benefit of the colonized, but rather for external commercial interests.[62] Although decolonization brought independence to former colonies, "it did not, as a rule, change the underlying social and economic structures of their societies."[63] Consequently, although authoritarian in nature, the colonial state, as a legally constituted and administered state, became a basis for postindependence legal structures.[64] Colonial rule and law-making in Africa did not provide a good basis for the emergence of postindependence democratic states.[65]

RNC correspondence makes clear that the treaties entered into with such "native Chiefs" were intended to preclude foreign interference from other European powers.[66] The Treaty with the King and Chiefs of Opobo strikes out one paragraph from the form - the paragraph that relates to free trade.[67] RNC treaties typically granted it fairly identical powers: they cede the "whole of the territory" to the RNC in perpetuity, the RNC agrees to not interfere with native laws or encroach upon private property rights or interfere with land now occupied by the natives. The treaties give the RNC exclusive right to exclude foreigners, and the RNC typically agrees not to take possession of natives' land without compensation. In some instances, the African treaty signatories agree to significant restrictions on commerce: the King and Chiefs of Gandy agreed that no one should have the right to mine or trade in their territory without the sanction of the Company,[68] while the King and Chiefs of Bapassa gave the RNC sole power to mine, farm or build.[69]

When the RNC's charter was revoked in 1899,[70] its territories were transferred to the British Crown for a sum not to exceed £865,000.[71] The act governing transfer of RNC administrative powers to the Crown provided:

> And whereas it is proposed to transfer to the Crown the administrative powers of the said Company, and the benefit of the treaties made by the Company, and the land, property, and mining and other rights acquired by the Company, but to reserve to them, subject to certain exceptions, their plant and trade assets and their stations, buildings, wharves, and workshops, and the sites thereof, and to revoke the charter of the Company, and to make certain payments in consideration of the said transfer, and for meeting liabilities attaching to the territories administered by the Company.[72]

RNC's activities and treaties were questioned in the House of Commons debate in Committee about the Royal Niger Company Bill, which revoked the RNC royal charter. In this debate, Committee members expressed a view that the amount to be paid to the RNC was excessive.[73] One committee member also noted the restrictive nature of the Company's treaties:

> I find twenty-five of these treaties have been signed since 1886, and consequently came under the company's charter. In them the signatory chiefs bind themselves 'not to have intercourse with any strangers or persons except through the Royal Niger Company.' Again, in Form X, No. 35, we have other treaties containing a similar clause. Everyone of these was signed in and after 1890, some of them so recently as 1892, and it is obvious that the company during the period of its existence as a chartered company has signed treaties pledging itself to do certain things for the native chiefs and exacting from them in return an undertaking not to allow any strangers or foreigners to come into their territory. Never was a more monstrous engagement entered into under any charter than this. This is bad enough, but the reigning chief is not to admit any stranger, Englishman included, who is not connected with the company. That is not all. There are fifty of these treaties for which absolutely nothing has been paid. The company have agreed to pay a certain sum per annum, and now the Government are taking upon their own shoulders these very obligations. The right hon. Gentleman buys certain land of the company, which alleges that it has acquired a wide strip of territory along the banks of the Niger for a distance of 500 miles. How did they acquire it?[74]

CUSTOMARY LAW, ENGLISH LAW, AND COLONIAL CONQUEST

Confronting the centrality of the external in African legal systems would involve disruption and reconstruction, not intended to eliminate the external, but rather its exposure, understanding, control, and containment. In colonial contexts in Africa, various forms of borrowing, including of laws, were part of flows of knowledge that occurred in contexts of pervasive power asymmetries that shaped both external flows of knowledge and the internal itself. African legal systems contain elements from both external colonizer legal systems and internal legal systems. *Customary* law, a pervasive aspect of legal systems, grows out of social practices within a community and is of particular importance in international law.[75]

Customary law as it developed in colonial contexts was often not the traditional, immutable category imagined by colonizing powers. Instead, customary law also had reactive elements that were a product of the colonial encounter.[76] In some instances, customary law became a field of contestation. In the criminal and family law areas, for example, Martin Chanock notes:

> African law represents the reaction of older men to a loss of control over wrongdoing generally and, more acutely felt, to a loosening of control over women. This reaction grew in strength during the first thirty or forty years of the colonial period . . . with the policy of indirect rule, a large portion of the administration of justice was turned over to precisely those people who had reason to define and, more importantly, to administer the law in a restrictive and authoritarian way.[77]

The development of customary law that forms a part of African legal systems also involved the invention of tradition in at least some instances. From the perspective of colonizing powers, the notion of customary law "belonged to an ideology that generally accompanied and formed part of colonial domination."[78] African law was both disdained and treated as a convenient tool for colonial conquest. British administrators "did not think much of African law, or of anything else African, and were determined to bring law and order, and above all what they saw as equitable justice, to the savages they had just rescued from chaos."[79] The combination of reaction, domination, and invention may make it challenging to understand the shape of customary law prior to colonialism. This is important because appeals to the past, including recourse to tradition or custom, have long been used in later debates that seek to use notions of the past, which may be invented, to bolster positions in current-day controversies: "[a]ppeals to the past are among the commonest of strategies in interpretations of the present."[80] In debates about criminal justice reform in postindependence Malawi in the mid-1960s, reformers evinced "hostility to technicalities in criminal justice" such as lawyers and British rules of evidence, and "nostalgia for a traditional justice that was supposedly free of those."[81]

Various forms of customary law were present in precolonial African legal systems. In Nigeria, for example, prior to the coming of the British, "Nigerian societies and communities at varying levels of political sophistication were governed by customary laws. The machinery for the administration of these laws consisted entirely of customary tribunals or institutions."[82] This machinery varied by group, and some in Nigeria, including the Edo, Hausa, and Yoruba peoples, had something similar to formal courts, while other groups did not. The presence of multiple sources of law in many African countries underscores the high degree of legal pluralism that exists in African legal systems evident in the widespread and fundamental presence of "two or more legal systems [that] exist in the same social field."[83] Colonial authorities' approaches to customary law were based on an association of ethno-religious customary practices with law.

In southern Nigeria, customary law "was unwritten; its principles are sometimes expressed in proverbs; it might even be said to be latent in the breast of the community's ruling elite or of the court remembrancers, and given expression only when expression was called for; but it was no less real than the written codes of continental Europe as a vital instrument for regulating the society."[84] Proverbs have been an important source of juristic thought in many African cultures,[85] and proverbs continue to be a "vital aid to judicial administration in matters of law and justice as well as traditional and socio-political systems in Africa."[86] Proverbs reflect a "grammar of values ... [c]omment on behavior, whether in commendation or criticism, and whether in the household, in the market-place, or in the law court, is interspersed with the proverb."[87]

Islamic law was the law of the state in northern Nigeria at the time of colonialism. Islam came to West Africa in the eleventh century along trade routes through Arab and Berber traders, the Almoravids, and itinerant Islamic scholars. They brought with them the Maliki School of Islam, which became predominant in West Africa, including in Nigeria. Islamic law judges have enforced Maliki Code in northern Nigeria for over 500 years, contributing to a "distinguished tradition of Islamic learning famous through the Islamic world [that] produced two great Islamic States, the Sokoto and Kanem-Bornu Caliphates in the western and eastern parts."[88] The Nupe, an ethnic group in the Middle Belt region of Nigeria that converted to Islam prior to the Sokoto Jihad, have preserved Arabic manuscripts of early Muslim scholars in Nupeland on topics that include Islamic jurisprudence, which gives evidence of the presence of Islamic law in Nigeria as early as the fifteenth century.[89]

At the time of colonialism, northern Nigeria and other parts of Nigeria had been radically reshaped following a jihad launched between 1804 and 1809 by Fulani Muslim scholar and leader Usman dan Fodio. Dan Fodio, who founded the Sultanate of Sokoto, was "the outstanding personality in the history of Northern Nigeria during the late eighteenth and early nineteenth centuries."[90] This jihad brought most Hausa Emirates under control of Usman dan Fodio's followers and created the biggest Islamic empire in the West African subregion in the nineteenth century.[91] Hausa-Fulani is an ethnic designation given to the dominant ethnic group in northern Nigeria. The Fulani are a widely dispersed ethnic group that form one of the largest ethnic groups in West Africa. Hausa remained the dominant language of administration following Usman dan Fodio's jihad, and intermarriage between the Hausa and Fulani was frequent. In Nigeria, Islamic law was typically classified as customary law during colonialism. British colonial authorities introduced English law in northern Nigeria but permitted Islamic law to apply in specific limited contexts: Islamic criminal law was "largely abolished and the Islamic civil justice system was also tampered with."[92] English law typically took precedence over Islamic law in instances of conflict.

Treatment of Islamic law during colonialism led to contestation that did not end with independence. Beginning in 1999, Zamfara State in northern Nigeria introduced sharia courts and changed the status of existing sharia courts, leading to local and international debates.[93] As a result of the Zamfara State reform, for the first time in Nigeria's history since imposition of English law, sharia courts gained authority over civil and criminal cases in Nigeria.[94] Within two years, twelve states in northern Nigeria had enacted legislation establishing expanded sharia courts, which some opponents stated was contrary to secular principles in the Nigerian Constitution. These new legal and judicial frameworks reflected a longstanding feeling, particularly in the northern Muslim political class about an "unjustifiable dominance of common law in Nigeria's legal system" that was not "normatively neutral" because it derived from Christian traditions.[95] The expansion of sharia was popular among northern Muslims and was intended to address disaffected Muslim youths, but had strong opposition in the South and majority Christian Middle Belt region of the North.

Debates about expanded sharia highlight divisions between northern and southern Nigeria and Islam and Christianity and the role of the Middle Belt region as a diverse and liminal area between north and south that has a predominantly Christian population. The Middle Belt today is the location of ongoing ethnic and religious strife.[96] Nigeria is the most populous country in the world where the population is roughly split evenly between Christians and Muslims. Debates about sharia law in northern Nigeria, which were accompanied by riots in some communities, underscored the potential explosiveness underlying this contestation. External actors from the broader Islamic world also played an important role, with Muslim countries lobbying the Nigerian government to promote sharia and pledging to train Islamic judges and provide resources, and Nigerian judges receiving training in Saudi Arabia.[97]

Notably, the Sokoto Sultanate military jihad had a significant impact in southwestern Nigeria, which had experienced widespread intra-Yoruba conflict and war during the nineteenth century, leading to significant movement of people. A significant proportion of Yoruba people in southwestern Nigeria is Muslim.[98] In 1894, Muslims, who constituted half or more of the population of Lagos, unsuccessfully petitioned British authorities to establish sharia courts in Lagos for the use of Muslims.[99]

This case regarding sharia law in nineteenth-century Lagos highlights the impact of British choices about which laws would apply that continue to have relevance in Nigeria over 100 years later. These choices about how to deal with legal hybridity in Nigeria have shaped a broad range of legal and other institutions in ways that have not been fundamentally altered. This raises questions about legal education, which has incorporated hybridity to some extent, and the practice of law, where English law remains deeply influential. Appearances by legal practitioners in English law–based courts in Nigeria "have always been conditioned upon proper professional dress . . . [in] magistrates courts, the dress is a dark suit comprising trousers, coat and a white shirt worn inside, with black socks . . . [f]or State and Federal High Courts and the two federal appellate courts, the English lawyer's black gown, wig and white bibs must be added . . . judges often insist on the observance of the dress code whenever they see a barrister not fully professionally dressed."[100]

The impact of sharia law in northern Nigeria and unaddressed conflicts between sharia law and the Nigerian Constitution gained international visibility in 2020 because of sentences handed down by sharia courts. In August 2020, Yahaya Sharif-Aminu, a twenty-two-year-old singer was sentenced to death by hanging by a court in Kano, Nigeria for blasphemy against the Prophet Muhammad because of a song that he composed and circulated on WhatsApp. The song praised the founder of the Tijaniya Muslim sect that some thought projected the sect founder above the Prophet Muhammad. This led a mob to storm Sharif-Aminu's family home and burn it down, "while the singer was in hiding after the frenzy that followed his song . . . [t]he mob later [went] to the headquarters of the Islamic police to demand the arrest and prosecution of the singer."[101] This same court in Kano sentenced a thirteen-year-old boy to ten years in prison, also for blasphemy, after Omar Farouk, was "accused of using foul language towards Allah."[102] This sentence received widespread criticism internationally – UNICEF condemned the sentence, Farouq's lawyer noted that the conviction is incompatible with the Nigerian Constitution,[103] and Piotr Cywińsk, the director of the Auschwitz-Birkenau Museum in Poland wrote a letter asking President Buhari to pardon Omar Farouq, offering to share a part of his sentence. Cywińsk assembled a group of 120 adult volunteers, each of whom offered to serve a month in a Nigerian prison in Omar Farouq's stead.

The Nigerian Constitution guarantees freedom of religion, freedom of expression, as well as freedom from torture and inhumane or degrading treatment, and reflects other values that are incompatible with the August 2020 Kano sharia court rulings. The incompatibility between different legal regimes is a characteristic feature of the Nigerian legal system that reflects types of conflicts that were apparent during colonialism and that remain largely unaddressed. Little has been done from a legal perspective to address such incompatibilities for reasons related to politics and state fragility.

Precolonial legal systems in Nigeria and elsewhere in Africa encompassed a broad array of relationships and transactions, including marriage, family, and inheritance matters, land matters, crime and punishment, and commercial transactions. A range of credit transactions were present in precolonial Nigeria.[104] "[C]redit transactions were a common feature of commerce" during the slave trade era in Yorubaland.[105] Traders came from different ethnic and cultural backgrounds, and creditors had varied means for collecting debts.[106]

On occasions when debts were not settled, the most punitive form of credit enforcement was èmú or seizure for debt, also referred to as panyarring, which permitted creditors to seize debtors or their associates, effectively holding a community collectively responsible for liabilities of a community member.[107] Panyarring was a point of tension in African–European and intra-African relations.[108] In Ghana, Gareth Austin found no evidence of panyarring after 1903 and notes the availability of English law remedies: "a new alternative remedy was available to the frustrated creditor: the presentation of a promissory note at the commissioner's court."[109]

Pawnship was a credit institution in the precolonial period that survived well into colonialism. In pawnship, individuals served as collateral and interest payment on loans. In Igboland between 1900 and 1936, pawnship (*igbo ibe*) was one of four means of marriage identified by Olatunji Ojo.[110] Pawnship, which enabled forced marriages and existed alongside slavery, feeding victims into the slave system, was "widely considered relatively benign, since most pawns remained in their own community . . . [serving] creditors until the debt was liquidated."[111]

Practices such as pawnship and child marriage offer examples of the multifaceted nature of contacts with British-related institutions and representatives, as well as how such contacts affected customary practices. Changes were driven not only by formal colonial administrative and legal actions. For example, colonial economic transformation, which introduced new markets and improved transportation, gave women more economic opportunities outside of Igboland. These trading opportunities enabled women from Asaba, a major trading center in eastern Nigeria, to trade in textiles, palm oil, and foodstuffs as far as Lagos, Calabar, Benin City, and beyond. This gave women "greater access to and control of independent sources of income."[112] Christian missionaries also trained female teachers, nuns, and nurses with curricula that included "topics on domestic science and the virtues of womanhood . . . educated and Christian girls led the protest against forced marriage."[113] As was the case with pawnship, panyarring appears to have had a more deleterious impact on women than on men.[114]

British imperialists and colonialists did not see precolonial African systems as *true* sources of law. Customary law was studied and cataloged,[115] in part to assist with colonial conquest. In contrast to English law, which was placed at the apex of an assumed evolutionary progression of law, customary law was delegated to the realm of anthropology: "As a body of habits, conventions, or moral standards . . . customary law was not fit for legal analysis. Rather, it was consigned to the discipline of anthropology."[116]

Anthropologists played a key role in colonial projects:

> Anthropology in British colonial Africa . . . was basically very 'relevant' to the colonial governments and to the imperialist systems of which they were part. Anthropologists helped gather the intelligence about native people which allowed these people to be efficiently ruled and exploited in the colonial interest – that is, in the interests of the white settlers, the colonial administrators, the government of the metropolitan country, and the Western capitalist enterprises in Africa.[117]

The consignment of customary law to the anthropological realm was evident in the study of African law as an academic discipline.[118] After World War II, the School of Oriental and African Studies (SOAS) undertook a project to systematize customary law. This Restatement of Law Project was a research initiative based at the Department of Law at SOAS active from the 1950s to the 1970s. Although this project reflects the transition of the study of African law to areas outside of anthropology, the approach of the Restatement project was decidedly anthropological. Informants were used, and information was collected about the laws of such things as marriage and divorce, organized by ethnic group.[119] A group of American law professors in the 1960s and 1970s also undertook to prepare restatements of customary law in Ethiopia.[120]

British officials restricted application of customary law to designated courts and put in place what they saw as authentic legal systems that superseded customary law, particularly in key areas of concern for them, including economic and other forms of control. British commercial and political interests were present long before the establishment of formal colonial territorial possessions in what later became Nigeria.

Implementation of English legal frameworks and institutions came before formal colonial rule. In Nigeria and elsewhere, Britain's colonial rule included a diverse range of formally designated relationships, including territories granted to chartered companies such as the RNC. Some British colonies were self-governing and semi-autonomous "Dominions."[121] This status was typically reserved for colonies with British settlers, and included Australia, New Zealand, South Africa, Canada, and Ireland. British possessions in Africa included territories referred to as protectorates, over which the British had full control. "Crown Colonies," where "control of the executive government remained in the hands of the Crown acting through the Imperial Government" were also referred to as "Colonies not possessing responsible government," in contrast to "Colonies possessing responsible government," but which were not "Dominions," including Malta and Rhodesia.[122] This topography was complex and at times random. The category that a British possession fell into was largely determined by "historical accident, and not regulated by any definite theory."[123] Dominions were permitted greater local autonomy and had greater ability to adapt British legal frameworks to local contexts. Furthermore, in such colonies, the British "seriously entertained the possibility of creating a new and perhaps better England,"[124] which had significant implications for the construction of legal and other institutions in Dominions. The expansion of English law in Southern Nigeria reflected both administrative and economic requirements of the British.[125] This expansion of law paved the way for British domination during colonialism.

The Nigerian legal system developed from four main sources of law: English law, Nigerian customary law, local legislation, and local court decisions. English law, which has been a predominant influence on the Nigerian legal system, is itself made up of distinct strands of law, including English common law, doctrines of equity, and statutes of general application that were in force in England on January 1, 1900.[126] English law is said to have been received in Nigeria, although *imposed* is more accurate terminology. Nigerians did not have a choice about the reception of English law in Nigeria. Local or indigenous customary law was subordinated to English law, and "treated as a foreign law in the higher courts."[127]

In Nigeria, the presence of multiple sources of law has contributed to continuing difficulties in the application of law even today. The part of the Nigerian legal system that comes from English law is thought by many to not function well:

> an attempt to foist the received English legal system on the nation has been problematic. The English legal system, particularly the official judiciary, is viewed by a great majority of the people as an elitist institution. Because of the many problems of the English legal system, such as prolonged delay in adjudication of disputes, high cost of litigation, corruption, and the bitterness and rancour that follow court judgments, a large chunk of the population feel alienated from this foreign and in most cases, strange legal system. They would rather resort to their more familiar customary laws to settle disputes and determine regular issues such as marriage and inheritance rights. Since these customary laws belong to the people, they are more able to understand the system and to accept a settlement or determination that emanates from it.[128]

Customary law existed under "several disabilities," the most important of which were its primary application to interpersonal relationships (land transactions, inheritance and succession, marriage and divorce) between "natives," applicable only "where in the opinion of the court it was not contrary to equity and good conscience" "where it was not contrary to an existing imperial enactment," and "where it was provable by evidence as a fact."[129] English law, as adopted in British colonial Africa, thus subjected customary law to several tests that limited the applicability of customary law. These tests included the *repugnancy test*, *incompatibility test*, and *public policy test*, which "were open-ended in order to give latitude for muzzling incongruous laws and in a number of cases they were employed to invalidate aspects of Islamic law."[130]

African countries continue to use repugnancy and incompatibility tests to limit the application of customary laws. The Kenyan Judicature Act, which deals with jurisdiction of courts, provides: "The High Court, the Court of Appeal and all subordinate courts shall be guided by African customary law in civil cases in which one or more of the parties is subject to it or affected by it, so far as it is applicable and is not repugnant to justice and morality or inconsistent with any written law, and shall decide all such cases according to substantial justice without undue regard to technicalities of procedure and without undue delay."[131] The application of these tests, which when enacted gave English courts tremendous discretion, continues to be inconsistent and subjective, which the Nigerian Supreme Court acknowledged in the 1995 case *Lawal-Osula v. Lawal Osula*.[132]

Repugnancy, incompatibility, and public policy tests raise continuing issues, including presentation of evidence of customary law, treatment of internal contestation, and how law is conceptualized in relation to social change. The conceptualization of customary law by British colonizers was exceedingly static, despite that fact that customary law could be a reactive force that reflected an ongoing response to changes that came with the advent of the British. The static conceptualization of customary law continues to have force. What is accepted as customary law will depend on what evidence a court accepts as demonstrating the existence of the law. The Nigeria Evidence Act 2011 provides that opinions of "persons who would be likely to know of its existence if it existed are admissible" as evidence of customary law, which would seem to permit any member of a particular group out with knowledge about the group to give evidence about customary law.[133] This may be difficult in contexts in which customary law is asserted in ways that are arbitrary, discriminatory, misogynistic or otherwise contrary to stated goals and specific legal arrangements in other legal arenas.

Postcolonial African legal systems continue British approaches to customary law that tend to adhere to past conceptions of relationships and past power dynamics. This may cause significant legal issues in some contexts, including in relation to conflict of laws. Conflict of laws also exist between the concept of wills under Islamic law and Nigerian common law.[134]

Legal treatment of customary practices raises issues concerning internal contestation and legal transition and change. This is obviously an issue with any type of law, but is a particular point of tension with customary law because of its asserted connection to traditional practices that are thought by some to be age-old and immutable. In addition to certain mistaken assumptions about the nature of customary law, the adoption of English law in Central Africa reflected inaccurate assumptions about the nature of English law. British officials implementing colonial legal systems did not necessarily understand how their own legal processes actually functioned:

> Yet the ways open to Africans pursuing legalization were curiously fashioned, affected by the determination of British legal administrators not to commit customary law to writing for fear that this would freeze it and arrest its development. At the bottom of this was the British lawyers' misunderstanding of their own legal processes. They thought of judges as essentially applying rules and precedents rather than as adapting them to fit new situations. They thought therefore that the absence of definition and precedent would make change in Africa easier. But it made it harder, freezing the law in a reactionary stance rather than allowing it flexibility.[135]

British administrators may also have lacked awareness of the impact of legal interventions on internal contestation. As Britain implemented indirect rule, disputes arose about the status of women and how men used customary law to contain women and push back on ongoing societal changes. Muna Ndulo notes that broad agreement exists that customary law in its present form is "distorted" in that customary law has been "influenced by the recent interaction between African custom and colonial rule" and that the "sources of customary law that are historically and presently accepted as authoritative are a product of social conditions and political motivations."[136] He also notes changes in customary law connected to increased urbanization in Africa and raises the fundamental question of "whether the continued application of customary norms that discriminate against women can be justified with reference to any set of prevailing social norms or traditions or cultural standards."[137]

COLONIAL COURTS, LEGISLATIVE COUNCILS, AND SEPARATION OF POWERS

Implementation of English legal frameworks and institutions often came before formal colonial rule. The British consulate for the Bights of Benin and Biafra, headquartered on the island Fernando Po, brought early elements of English law to what later became Nigeria in 1849 in response to British traders who "were dissatisfied with the quality of justice available at the indigenous tribunals."[138] Fernando Po is today called Bioko, and is part of Equatorial Guinea, a former Spanish colony. The establishment of courts that applied English law to disputes involving Westerners was a critical part of British domination of Nigeria. This use of English courts meant that commercial disputes involving British interests would use courts that were favorable to British interests.

Consular and other courts, including Courts of Equity, were a form of legal imperialism that reflected the extraterritorial reach of Britain prior to formal colonialism. Extraterritorial courts were used by Western states in Japan, the Ottoman Empire, and China. These exterritorial courts, not local courts, had jurisdiction over disputes or cases involving Westerners.[139] In Japan, the Ottoman Empire, and China, Western states "limited, and eventually eliminated in collaboration with groups in the local elite, the authority of indigenous legal systems."[140] These extraterritorial courts replaced indigenous legal categories and practices with Western ones, which had significant implications for the operation of local legal systems.

Early colonial courts in Africa often did not function well for various reasons. The colonial administration, which effectively controlled courts, was often ignorant of local languages and at the mercy of varied intermediaries, including interpreters; in Malawi, "justice was often administered in an atmosphere of scorn, impatience, and cruel schoolboy humor . . . [t]he role of the new courts made it inevitable that they would become unpopular . . .far from bringing a new justice, they settled down to a daily routine of punishing tax offenders and offenders against the employment laws and the host of other new ordinances . . . as, the arms of colonial discipline."[141]

Despite this, Martin Chanock notes that people in Malawi sought out these new courts, which were flooded with women seeking divorce or in their words, "release from slavery." Colonial courts in this context were a forum of contestation surrounding competing views within Malawi about women that reflected notions by men of a precolonial world where women "had occupied themselves with 'cooking and pounding . . . helping their husbands and fathers . . . [they] are loving and amiable in their homes . . . divorce was rare . . . Where the authority of parents or chiefs is obeyed implicitly . . . there could be no common divorces.'"[142] In Malawi, officers in the colonial administration came to agree with the men that "women were getting out of control." The loss of control of men during early colonialism was rectified with the coming of indirect rule, and the loss of authority in early colonialism was felt in "'legal' fields over which these men were again given power in the early 1930s."[143]

In Nigeria between the early 1850s and 1915, English style courts were an important part of British domination. Although the precise dates are unclear, the earliest courts in Nigeria were Courts of Equity established in the Niger Delta between 1850 and 1854.[144] The establishment of these courts reflected more interventionist British policies to replace prior accommodations "to local customs for settling disputes and facilitating trade" and to "take-over this indigenous tradition by grafting on European concepts of law and jurisprudence in the interests of British traders."[145] These courts likely had little impact and were ad hoc: "sat infrequently, followed no formal procedures, and administered no fixed body of law."[146]

More comprehensive efforts to introduce English law came with the annexation of territories in Nigeria, when English law and courts to enforce English law were established. After Lagos was annexed in 1861, courts based on British judicial administration were established, including the Commercial Court, the Petty Debt Court, and the Vice-Admiralty Court in 1863; the Court of Requests in 1871 and the Court of Divorce and Matrimonial Causes in 1872.[147] In 1866, the administration of Lagos was merged with Sierra Leone, and was then transferred to the Gold Coast in 1874. Lagos became an autonomous colony again in 1886. In 1876, the courts established by the British were abolished (except for the Vice-Admiralty Court) and replaced by a single Supreme Court with unlimited jurisdiction. The Supreme Court was the equivalent of the High Court of Justice in England.[148] The Supreme Court Ordinance 1876 established the full Supreme Court as a court of appeal.[149]

The Supreme Court Ordinance 1876 directly copies and pastes concepts and structures derived from English law. This ordinance provides that "The Common Law, the doctrines of Equity, and the Statutes of general application which were in force in England at the date when the Colony obtained a local Legislature, that is to say, on the 24th day of July 1874, shall be in force within the jurisdiction of the Court", and extends all Imperial Laws, but "only as the limits of the local jurisdiction and local circumstances permit."[150] The Supreme Court is also given jurisdiction over customary law, and the Ordinance makes clear that such laws and customs "shall be deemed applicable in causes and matters where the parties thereto are natives of the said Colony or Territories, and particularly ... in causes and matters related to marriage and to the tenure and transfer of real and personal property, and to inheritance and testamentary dispositions."[151] These laws and customs are secondary to English law, and existing local laws and customs must not be "repugnant to natural justice, equity, and good conscience, nor incompatible either directly or by necessary implication with any enactment of the Colonial Legislature."[152] The court is also authorized to apply customary law in mixed cases involving natives and Europeans "where it may appear to the Court that substantial injustice would be done to either party by a strict adherence to the rules of English law."[153] The ordinance also provides that customary law should not apply if it appears that the transaction "should be regulated exclusively by English law." Under the structure established in the ordinance, rules of equity take precedence over common law, which takes precedence over customary law.

The Supreme Court Ordinance 1876 establishes that courts in the Gold Coast Colony (which for a time included Lagos) should follow English courts to a significant degree in form, operation, and structure. The ordinance establishes a complex and formal architecture for courts rooted in the external that brings a long history of English courts to a markedly different context where at the time few local people spoke English, let alone had the training to navigate the requirements created by this new court system.

Over time, various parts of what became the Protectorate of Southern Nigeria became subject to jurisdiction of English courts. Yorubaland, parts of which had been excluded from the jurisdiction of English courts, became subject to jurisdiction of English courts by 1915. In the Oil Rivers Protectorate, which contained the territories for which the Royal Niger Company had received a charter, a supreme court and statutory native courts replaced previous arrangements of consular courts, courts of equity, and courts of the Royal Niger Company. In the Protectorate of Northern Nigeria, the Protectorate Courts Proclamation 1900 established several courts, including a Supreme Court, provisional courts, and statutory native courts.[154] The 1900 ordinance limits those authorized to practice as barristers and solicitors in the court to persons admitted as barristers or advocates in Great Britain or Ireland or those otherwise deemed fit, who might be admitted temporarily.[155]

These early courts in Nigeria laid down structures of governance that continue to have an impact, particularly as they relate to legal institutions. Colonial legal institutions and postcolonial constitutions adopted throughout Africa have incorporated structures that reflect separation of powers in form, but notably typically not in function. John Locke and Baron de Montesquieu have been influential in shaping ideas about separation of powers. Montesquieu's ideas about separation of powers were significantly influenced by time spent in England. Constraint of executive power and an independent judiciary have been considered essential features of the British Constitution,[156] which is notably not a single codified document, but rather, is set forth in Acts of Parliament, court judgments, and convention.[157] British constitutional forms typically extended to its colonies, particularly its settler colonies.[158]

The essential features of this uncodified British Constitution were incorporated into constitutional structures in self-governing settler colonies, including the United States, which went further in ensuring judicial independence. In the British constitutional order, courts constrained executive power.[159] However, the British Constitutional structure did not until recently include strict separation of powers.[160] Iyer notes Blackstone's view that "constitutional formalism is less important than conventions and social structures with a strong disposition towards the common weal,"[161] which makes borrowings based on copying the British model potentially problematic in new contexts that do not have the same conventions and social structures. When structures were based on English law models were copied in colonies in Africa, constraints on the arbitrary exercise of executive power, which had developed over centuries in England, did not accompany these imposed structures. Thus, the substance and function of forms of governmental organization in England did not effectively translate in contexts of imposed legal structures during colonialism. This was not an accident because the colonial government was authoritarian and had little reason or likely desire to constrain itself. The historical evolution of constraint of the executive power in England was typically not because the executive desired to be constrained. Rather, other institutions developed that constrained executive power. The failure to constrain the executive power in governance structures in former British colonies during and after colonialism is a critical governance failure that came to pass during colonialism, with continuing effects today.

Separation of powers is important for the rule of law. Law must "effectively restrain power," which requires that government officials "obey the rules which Parliament has enacted"; law's ability to restrain government officials "can only be ensured if the courts have the jurisdiction to enforce legal limits which govern the exercise of executive power."[162] As John Locke notes, "[w]here-ever law ends, tyranny begins."[163] Ideas about rule of law and separation of powers may reflect significant gaps between theory and practice. Misunderstanding may also exist concerning what these concepts mean. What constitutes rule of law and how rule of law can be implemented in postcolonial contexts in Africa remains a continuing question.

British ideas about separation of powers shaped government structures established throughout British colonial possessions in Africa. During colonialism, the colonial administration in Nigeria established the same branches of government present in Britain, at times from verbatim borrowings. However, differences of context and timing made the functioning of these branches of government different from and often ineffective in African colonial contexts, in part because the substance and meaning of these structures did not accompany this transplantation. These transplants were thus akin to transplanting organs with no blood flowing between them. Legal transplants in Africa therefore reflect a triumph of anatomy with insufficient concern for physiology or context. As a result, transplants in non-Dominion colonies in Africa have often not led to effective and fully functioning legal systems.

Ideas about separation of powers reflect a long discussion in the West driven by a central purpose of averting tyranny.[164] The branches of government developed in British colonial contexts were not established to avert tyranny, but rather, to advance it in the form of authoritarian colonial rule. The colonial administration exemplifies the unchecked executive power that is the antithesis of a monarchy with limited powers evident in Locke's theories about executive power.

In Nigeria, the first courts were consular courts that existed before formal colonial administrative structures were established. After colonial administrations were established, a legislative sphere was typically also put in place as is evident in the legislative council established in Nigeria and other British colonies. The establishment of these spheres of governance reflected elements of the structure, but not the function, of governance categories in Britain. Notably, Britain did not at the time have strict separation of powers between the legislative, the executive, and the judiciary, although these spheres were distinct.

Although many postindependence constitutions in Africa borrow from British, American, and other models to provide for separation of powers, imperial presidential patterns are common.[165] Power relations in African countries often do not follow constitutional structures as laid out. As a result, despite "the existence of written constitutions, insufficient government accountability led to the inability to prevent abuses of power ... [o]ne of the major reasons for Africa's dismal record of constitutionalism is the ease with which African leaders have managed to adopt imperial tendencies, enabling them to rule largely without legislative or judicial interference."[166] This is even the case in Botswana, which is considered by many as "Africa's most successful example of an open, transparent, and democratic government."[167]

The imperial presidency pattern in multiple countries in Africa today also reflects colonial legacies of strong executive power. Colonial governance was authoritarian in many respects. The authoritarian colonial state became a basis for postindependence legal and governance structures.[168] Patterns of governance established in colonial Nigeria continue to be problematic in postcolonial Nigeria.

Challenges facing the judiciary in Nigeria today reflect the institutional structure established during colonialism that has led to issues of concern with the form and function of the judiciary. In October 2016, the Nigerian Department of State Service (DSS) raided the homes of seven senior judges, including two Supreme Court justices, and arrested judges on charges of corruption. This was unprecedented in Nigeria, despite "long-standing perceptions of a questionable credibility of Nigeria's judiciary and of the commercialisation of justice in the country."[169] The raids recovered large amounts of cash, including Nigerian and foreign currencies (US dollars, euros, British pounds), totaling some $800,000 that was recovered from just three judges.[170] This raid draws attention to multiple points of institutional failure in Nigeria. The first institutional failure relates to judicial corruption and the perception in Nigeria that judges are corrupt. A second point of failure concerns the dominance of the executive in Nigeria in practice, even in instances when law on the books may not support the actions of the executive. The National Judicial Council is empowered under the 1999 Nigerian Constitution to "recommend to the President the removal from office of the judicial officers" such as Supreme Court justices and to "exercise disciplinary control over such officers."[171] This DSS raids may reflect the fact that the "NJC [Nigerian Judicial Council] does not appear to have been especially vigilant with respect to judicial corruption."[172] Courts in Nigeria may also experience challenges from lack of security and operational difficulties related to lack of infrastructure.[173] The dominance of the executive over the judiciary in Nigeria reflects a long history of executive dominance that became normalized during colonialism.

Tensions between the executive and the judiciary were apparent from the early days of the British colonial administration in Nigeria. The Hon. Justice Willoughby Osborne, the chief justice of Southern Nigeria from 1906 to 1913, had a strained relationship with the executive branch of the colonial administration about "undue executive interference in purely judicial matters such as the transfer of judicial officers to the legal department by the governor."[174] The chief justice attempted to maintain an independent judiciary. He believed that because he was head of the judicial department, the colonial governor was legally required to consult him before making staff appointments in the judicial department. The Colonial Office determined on a course that did not maintain an independent judiciary: "the Colonial Office upheld the governor's right to appoint judicial officers. The governor was, however, directed that 'as a matter of propriety, and for the better conduct of business, the Chief Justice should be consulted whenever it is possible to do so'."[175] As a result, by 1914 "the judiciary was organized to provide judicial back-up to the colonial executive and administrative control of the Nigerian state," and the so-called 1914 reforms "disproportionately increased the powers exercisable by political administrative officers in exclusively judicial matters and concentrated power in the hands of the executive to the detriment of the people who were at the receiving end of executive justice."[176]

Significant judicial reforms were undertaken in Nigeria in 1933. These reforms introduced a high court with coextensive jurisdiction with that of the Supreme Court, magistrate's courts and a new system of appeals. These structural reforms did not, however, end executive dominance or political officers' exercising influence in judicial matters:

> The executive continued to make the discharge of the duties of judges and magistrates unnecessarily burdensome and loathsome . . . .The actions and sometimes inaction of the executive destroyed the confidence of the people in the ability of the court to dispense justice and, as such, many of them had the impression that the judge was biased or incompetent . . . .However, despite the provisions of the new ordinances and the attempts to refine the process and machinery of justice in colonial Nigeria, the on-the-spot agents of colonial administration still believed in the supremacy of the executive over the judiciary.[177]

Courts in Nigerian and other colonial contexts were not only different in form but also in function. Courts often did not operate primarily based on principles related to justice or fairness, but rather on those related to expediency:

> It has been demonstrated that the judiciary during colonial rule was intended to be a state institution created and financed by the colonial overlord as an effective agency of social control. All the reforms were put in place to enhance the performance of their duties in promoting the interest of Britain in the country . . . . Britain was never interested in the development of Nigeria into a viable, democratic, self-administering state. Colonial designs, including judicial reforms were meant to protect the mercantile an imperial interests of Britain, and not to institute any system that would ensure justice. Colonial judicial reforms . . . emphasized executive justice rather than social justice.[178]

The executive also exercised significant control over the legislative function in British colonies in Africa. Colonial legislative bodies were also not representative. Executive and legislative functions were typically mixed in British colonies. The colonial governor, in whom significant power was concentrated, typically headed an Executive Council and Legislative Council.[179] The governor was President and official spokesperson in the Legislative Council. In Zambia (then called Northern Rhodesia) and Kenya, both of which were settler colonies, the legislative council included a mixed membership of *official* representatives appointed from colonial senior executive officers and *unofficial* members from the civilian population. *Official* representatives represented British government interests, while *unofficial* ones represented the interests of European immigrants.[180] Colonial legislative councils, however, had little effective power. The Colonial Office could veto any legislation enacted by a legislative council. Further, the British Parliament in London kept ultimate legislative power over both colonies. In Nigeria, the first legislative council was formed in Lagos in 1862, but began to have more consistent relevance after 1886.[181] As was the case in Kenya and Zambia, the Nigerian legislative council had an *official* majority. The Lagos Legislative Council, first legislative council in Nigeria, was an advisory body that did not perform any lawmaking functions. After the amalgamation of Nigeria in 1914, a new legislative entity, the Nigerian Council, was formed. This body also had no legislative power and performed no legislative functions.[182]

In addition to being controlled by the colonial executive, legislative councils were not representative bodies. Legislative councils had limited African representation. In Kenya, where settlers were 0.5 percent of the population, the first African was not appointed until 1944. Prior to that time "various appointed European members – many of them missionaries – represented African interests in the council."[183] In Zambia, where settlers were 3 percent of the population, the first African members were appointed to the legislative council in 1948.[184] Substantive African representation in Kenya and Zambia occurred through elections in 1957 and 1954, respectively. Although Nigeria had representatives appointed far earlier, the representation gap was similarly stark. In 1914, the Nigerian Council had thirty-six members, six of whom were Nigerian. In 1922, the Clifford Constitution provided for the election of four Nigerians of a total of forty-six council members.[185] The Colonial Governor chose the other forty-two members, who represented private and business interests.

Extremists could capture legislative councils. In Zambia, representatives of European immigrants who founded the Northern Rhodesia Labor Party (NRLP) elected to the legislative counsel beginning in 1938, "took an overtly racist path, and pushed for greater pay and working conditions for European industrial and mine-workers at the expense of Africans ... the NRLP's singular hostility to African interests irreparably poisoned interracial politics in the colony."[186] Limited African representation in legislative councils appears to have had an impact on their responsiveness to issues of concern to local people. Proceedings of legislative council meetings in Nigeria were not always responsive to grievances of Africans, and the local press and native councils were more feasible avenues for Africans to express grievances.[187] The structure of precolonial legislative structures did not provide a good basis for postcolonial Nigerian legislatures.

The British Parliament played a role in preparing legislatures in Nigeria for independence. Correspondence with legislative bodies in Nigeria reflects guidance offered by representatives of the British Parliament. This guidance tended to reflect an underlying assumption of direct borrowing from British models:

> The House of Commons has indeed been generous to us and to the other Legislatures in Nigeria, in affording opportunities for our Clerks and some of our

> presiding Officers and their Deputies to gain experience of what is done at Westminster and how it is done.[188]

Correspondence about legislative matters between representatives in Nigeria and at the Parliament in London also reflected a focus on the form of what a parliament should look like rather than on the substance of what parliaments actually do.[189] For example, in May 1955, the governor of the Western Region of Nigeria raised questions about the "propriety of the use of a mace by the Upper Chamber, the House of Chiefs."[190] The mace in the British Parliament is the symbol of royal authority. Neither House of Parliament can meet or pass laws without this mace.[191] Whether this symbol should be used in Nigeria and its meaning in Nigerian contexts does not appear to have been questioned, which highlights the tendency to cut-and-paste borrowing of British legal structures, laws, and symbols in colonial legal contexts in Nigeria and elsewhere.

Other correspondence in anticipation of Nigeria's becoming independent reflected outreach on behalf of Nigerian legislators to other Commonwealth legislatures – including in India, the West Indies, Northern Ireland, and Australia – about membership in upper and lower houses, the size of the upper house chamber in relation to the lower house chamber, and details about Parliament opening ceremonies.[192] These topics reflect the extent to which legislative practice in the process leading up to independence in Nigeria sought to copy what was present in Britain and other former colonies. This reflects a cut-and-paste approach to governmental design that has been far too prevalent in Nigeria and elsewhere in Africa.

Although the National Assembly in Nigeria is structurally positioned in the Nigerian Constitution to play an important role in Nigeria, the legislature has not functioned in line with the expectations embedded in Nigeria's constitutional structure. A 1987 report notes:

> It is a well known fact that up till 1979, legislatures were the weakest link in the making of public policies in Nigeria. Between the establishment of the Nigerian Council by Lugard soon after the amalgamation of the Southern and Northern Protectorates of Nigeria in 1914 and the end of the first thirteen years of military rule, public policy making was dominated by the executive. Indeed, a national daily newspaper in 1963 referred to the Federal Legislature as an 'expensive and irrelevant talking shop'.[193]

The 1999 Constitution of the Fourth Republic of Nigeria provides for an upper and lower legislative house, with 360 legislators in the National Assembly and 109 members in the Senate, the upper house. In the first term of the Fourth Republic, management of relations between the executive and legislature was "the single most problematic issue since the return to democratic rule in 1999."[194] Rotimi Suberu notes that the current National Assembly is both ambivalent and contradictory. The legislature has "passed significant constitutional amendments and electoral reforms, curbed executive abuses, and functioned as a veritable platform for interethnic negotiation and conciliation."[195] At the same time, the legislature has "often abused or underperformed its core functions of legislation, oversight, representation, and constituency engagement, thereby attracting widespread opprobrium for its ineffectiveness, obstructiveness, venality, and impunity."[196] Further, prebendal aspects of the Nigerian political economy, "defined by the appropriation of public institutions for personal and group enrichment, have powerfully shaped legislative functions and processes, leading to legislative corruption, dysfunction, and decadence."[197] From the perspective of actually passing legislation, which is critical to both addressing colonial legal legacies and creating new laws that address local interests and needs, the Nigerian legislature is not generally thought to be highly effective.[198]

PETITIONS AND THE POWER OF THE COLONIAL STATE

In Nigeria, courts were the first element of English law to be introduced. Courts, including those based on consular jurisdiction, were established with an intent to privilege British commerce by ensuring that English law would be the law that was used to settle disputes: "[t]he survival of British enterprise in Nigeria depended on the ability of the administration to exercise undisputed power in the settlement of disputes and to punish what it regarded 'as deviant patterns of behavior.' The British legal system was also considered appropriate for use in the introduction, retention, and protection of the exploitative British fiscal and financial policies in Nigeria."[199]

The executive branch in colonial Nigeria controlled and directed the other branches of government. The colonial era vision of government within this branch involved inattention to local concerns, paternalism, and authoritarianism. Colonial records also illustrate the negative and derogatory views that colonial administrators had of many Africans. These derogatory views of Africans often translated into paternalism in the implementation of policies, particularly for Africans who were not educated under the British system. Lord Lugard, for example, had negative images of Africans, stating "the typical African ... is a happy, thriftless, excitable person, lacking in self control, discipline and foresight, naturally courageous, courteous and polite, full of personal vanity, with little of veracity; in brief, the virtues and defects of this race-type are those of attractive children."[200] Some Africans, particularly educated elites, were ascribed a higher status and served as intermediaries between the masses and colonial rulers.

The colonial state formed a poor basis for postcolonial rule for many reasons, including its lack of accountability to those over whom it ruled. The structure of colonial governance and dominance of the executive branch led to limited representation for local people within government as a matter of structure and process. Colonial administration responses to petitions are revealing. Colonial archives contain a wide range of petitions submitted to colonial administrators. These petitions covered a range of things, from disputes about "native" chiefs, to land disputes to complaints about colonial administration decisions and other matters.

Colonial officials clearly did not like these petitions or complaints, particularly when they came from Africans. Colonial officials also typically responded to those complaining without reflecting upon or changing the policies or decisions at issue.

An examination of treatment of petitions submitted by Edema Arubi, a Nigerian retired civil servant, and Sir William Geary, an English lawyer, illuminates how colonial administrators in Nigeria responded to petitions. These petitions also highlight the advantages of having an English voice in support of a petition. Petitions by Edema Arubi are thought to have contributed to his criminal prosecution on charges of extortion. He was found guilty on three counts of offenses under the Illiterate Protection Ordinance and sentenced to a fine of £5 or one-month imprisonment for each of three counts, with the sentences to run concurrently.[201] Although Edema Arubi was well known with significant clout, his light sentence "should be seen as an attempt by the colonial administration to underscore the point that it was capable of dealing decisively with any opposition to its preferred course of action and administrative style."[202]

Edema Arubi was a renowned letter writer. The letterhead on his petitions indicated that he was a journalist and public writer who was retired from Nigeria Civil Service. He describes his services as the Arubi Independent Defense Service.[203] On March 27, 1940, he wrote a petition to Malcolm MacDonald, Secretary of State for the Colonies. This petition relates to earlier petitions he had submitted concerning rents paid by the Itsekiri people on Crown lands in Warri Province.[204] Colonial officials were frustrated by the volume of petitions submitted by Arubi and raised questions about the extent to which the Itsekiri council had authorized petitions by Arubi on behalf of the Olu Itsekiri.[205] In internal notes concerning an Arubi petition, colonial officials state that it "is necessary for Mr. Arubi to realize that in war time either he must curtail his output as a petition writer or he must expect inevitable delays, especially on matters which require considerable investigation."[206]

A number of Edema Arubi's petitions related to payments due to local leaders based on past agreements that such rulers be paid subsidies.[207] The colonial administration in Nigeria attempted to put in place new rules for petitions that would limit the activities of petition writers such as Arubi.[208] In response to the new rules, Arubi wrote a petition protesting the new requirements for petitions. A colonial administrator noted that "it is intolerable that they [colonial officers] should be burdened by extra work caused by an unbalanced agitator such as this man."[209]

Sir William Geary went to Sierra Leone in the 1890s and served in various legal capacities in West Africa, eventually becoming Attorney General to the Gold Coast Colony from 1895 to 1897.[210] He was educated at Eton and Christ Church, Oxford and called to the Bar at the Inner Temple in 1884. He was a barrister-at-law in England and a barrister-at-law and solicitor in Nigeria. He represented multiple African clients in Nigeria. Geary was the author of a number of books, including *Nigeria under British Rule* (1927). Geary's experience and status as a baronet meant that his petitions were heard by colonial administrators. His experience as an insider and attorney general within a colonial administration gave him an understanding of internal operations, dynamics, and assumptions within colonial administrations. This enabled Geary to raise issues related to practices of the colonial administration in the course of his representation of African clients who might otherwise have lacked voice in colonial archival legal records. Colonial officers were clearly annoyed by Geary, often dismissed or even denigrated the issues that he raised, and generally considered him to be a nuisance and a pest, but nonetheless responded to his inquiries. For example, in a notation to a colonial administration file involving a letter written by Geary in 1940 concerning compensation for killed and injured railway employees, a colonial officer notes that "Sir W. Geary is a great nuisance but occasionally . . . his persistence is in a good cause."[211]

In response to another Geary petition, comments in colonial administration files note that it "is quite impossible to convince this troublesome old man that in time of war, with the consequent shortage of staff and much additional work, there are more important matters than his representations."[212] However, unlike Edema Arubi, the colonial administration could not really put him in jail or simply ignore or dismiss his complaints on behalf of his clients. His status also gave him access to senior officials in the British government, including Secretary of State for the Colonies Arthur Creech Jones, with whom he corresponded concerning at least one case.

In his correspondence with colonial officials, Geary depicted himself as a "friend of the African." Colonial officers remarked on a number of occasions that he appeared to be well compensated for his work. Notably, Geary was not a friend of African women. The legal sphere in Nigeria and Britain has long been heavily male-dominated. Although cases involving women are evident in colonial archival records, women's voices are less frequently heard in archival records related to law. In a case in which he represented a Nigerian man accused of seducing a young woman, Geary notes:

> As to the first that he seduced Amdat, it now appears that when they began living together (which is admitted) she was 18 years old; Now with a long experience of Lagos, I can affirm that an African woman begins her sexual life at 14 usually or thereabouts, and it is against all probabilities, that a Lagos woman of 18 years old who has been living in Lagos should have remained up till that age without sexual intercourse.[213]

Geary's representation of African clients is, however, instructive because he was at one time an insider in the legal infrastructure of colonialism. Even after he started representing Africans in disputes with the colonial government, his status as an Englishman and a baronet gave him access to colonial officials that was not possible for most Nigerians during this time period. In several cases, Geary criticized colonial administrators and used varied legal approaches to advocate for better treatment for his clients. Geary was not alone in doing this. The Anti-Slavery Society and the

Aborigines Protection Society also wrote letters to colonial officials concerning treatment of Africans. Geary's representation of individual clients in Nigeria and Sierra Leone give evidence as to the dynamics of individual disputes between local people and colonial administrations. These disputes also demonstrate the authoritarian tendencies of colonial administrations, particularly as they relate to any type of criticism, as well as core attributes of colonial governance. These disputes also reveal the ad hoc nature of colonial administrative processes, as well as the systematic way in which Africans were denied a voice in their own countries in an administration that was run to a significant degree by and for foreigners.

In an April 1939 letter to the secretary of state for the colonies, Geary asked that the Colonial Office accept the proposition of "Administrative Responsibility" in a land dispute involving a petition by a Mr. I. E. Davies in relation to the termination by the colonial government of his lease of Crown land in Sierra Leone:

> If a Governor or Acting Governor of the Responsible Head of a Department in regard to matters within his department make a reasonable representation to a Native (or European) which is acted upon by the person to whom the representation is made the Government must honor such representation and accept liability therefor.[214]

The client in this case, Isaac E. Davis wrote multiple letters to colonial administrators attempting to obtain a long term lease of fifty years for the farm land that he occupied that was the subject of the dispute.

As was the case with most of the disputes in which Geary represented clients, the colonial administration responded to the issues he raised, but typically did not alter its position. In the Davies case, the Governor of Sierra Leone, Sir Douglas James Jardine, indicated in a letter to Malcolm MacDonald, the Secretary of State for the Colonies that "neither in law nor in equity is Mr. Davies entitled to any compensation whatsoever for the termination of his year-to-year tenancy",[215] which is exactly the same position taken by the colonial administration at the beginning of the dispute in 1937.[216] The Governor did, however, indicate that suitable Crown land was available near Freetown that could be leased to Davies. Notably, the colonial administration did not respond in any robust way to the legal arguments that Geary made in his communications with them, but rather, focused on disputes of fact and the sentiment that even illiterate people should have known that what Davies had requested was simply not possible.[217] The Davies dispute and others document in colonial records reflect significant inattention to questions of legal process. Geary's assertion that administrative responsibility should apply in this case is not really addressed. Sir William Geary represented African clients on a range of matters. Land issues that were the subject of the Davies case were one area of representation for Geary.

In land matters, in addition to issues related to applicable laws, Geary consistently raised issues related to process and consistently drew attention to failures of process. In a land dispute in which the Nigerian Government refused a Petition of Right,

Geary states: "I humbly submit that the refusal of a Fiat is not the act of a civilised Government and that it is a denial of justice . . . . It results that there is no security of property in Nigeria."[218]

Disputes about chiefs were another major area in which Geary represented clients. Correspondence with colonial administrators in Nigeria and the Colonial Office in London reveal much about how African leaders were selected and deposed during colonialism. Although the British claimed that indirect rule preserved traditional principles and institutions, petitions and discussions regarding chieftaincy disputes also illuminate how *traditional* institutions were reshaped by British colonial intervention and manipulation.[219] The politicization and manipulation of traditional chieftaincy titles by Nigerian elites continues to the present day. Shortly after colonialism, the *Owo Crisis* emerged from a political dispute between leaders of the Action Group, the leading party in southwestern Nigeria. This political dispute led to contention over candidates for the position of the Olowo (oba) of Owo that continued into the early 2000s. As one commentator notes, the "Olowo crisis was more or less a case of elite fragmentation and manipulation rather than a serious grassroots problem. The conflict had, however, claimed several hundred lives and invaluable loss of property" before being laid to rest in 2003.[220] In March 2020, Lamido Sanusi, the Emir of Kano and former governor of Nigeria's Central Bank, was removed from his position by the governor of Kano state. Sanusi has criticized corruption within the Nigerian federal government and on the part of the governor that removed him.[221] Sanusi was also banished from the state.

Geary was persistent in the pursuit of his cases, which he acknowledged may have had a negative impact. In 1940, he represented the Elewu of Ewu in a dispute that involved his client's right to wear a crown, which his client would supply at his own cost. A crown was allegedly seized from the father of the present Elewu of Ewu by the late Captain Ambrose. According to Geary, Captain Ambrose did not take the crown "wantonly or for himself, but from a sense of duty (though mistaken) . . . It is suggested that my client's predecessor was not entitled to war a crown . . . . I am told that though the present Oni of Ife has not done anything personally, he thinks his grandfather did give a staff to my clients predecessor."[222] Again, drawing attention to legal process or the lack thereof, Geary notes that:

> There may be a prejudice against my client both at the Colonial Office and in the mind of the Nigerian Government from the length of this file and perhaps the persistence of myself his Solicitor. But this is a matter of justice, like that of the claimant to a Peerage before the Committee of Privileges, the claimant may be a rogue or a fool, (my client is neither), he may be a man of color like Lord Sinka, but if he proves his case, he has a right to set in the House of Lords.[223]

Colonial officials typically did not address questions raised by Geary about legal process in cases involving Geary clients. In a 1937 case, the Colonial office responded to Geary's request for an interview: "Mr. Ormsby Gore [Secretary of

State for the Colonies between 1936 and 1938] has considered your proposals but sees no reason to differ from the views expressed to you by the Governor, and in these circumstances it is not considered that any useful purpose would be served by the interview which you desire."[224] In a January 1937 letter to Ormsby Gore, the Nigerian colonial administration discussed the manner of selection of the Awujale, the royal title associated with the Ijebu kingdom of southwestern Nigeria. The Ajuwale is one of several Yoruba obas (kings). Yoruba have traditionally lived in towns, likely for centuries prior to colonialism. At the center of each town dwelt an oba in a palace. Yoruba obas were traditionally powerful. The office and person of the oba were sacred, and the oba was "the priest and protector of his people, and they naturally wished to live in his shadow."[225] As was the case in Ghana, where the British Governor wished to sit on the sacred Asante Golden Stool, British colonizers demystified traditional rulers to give legitimacy to their own rule.[226]

Deposing and replacing existing traditional rulers was one way that these rulers were demystified by clearly establishing who was really in charge. British were repeatedly unimpressed with the Ajuwales. In discussing the appointment of one potential candidate for the Awujale, a colonial officer notes that Ademolu of the Ogbagba family was appointed Awujale and "was recognized on probation for one year by Mr. Young, Commissioner of the Abeokuta Province in which Ijebu Ode was then included . . .Before the expiration of the year Mr. Young had changed his mind as to the suitability of Ademolu describing him as 'an exceptionally weak man who has been elected by the Odis on that account', and "with the consent of the Governor's Deputy, Mr. Temple, Ademolu was therefore deposed, and one Adekoya of the Tunwashe house was installed in his place."[227] The colonial administration was unhappy with Adekoya because "[c]onsiderable unrest in Ijebu resulted from his appointment." Adekoya was then "removed and given a pension, and Ademolu was reinstated and reigned quietly until he died in 1925."[228] Adenuga of the Tunwashe family was then appointed.

Geary also represented clients in disputes about compensation owed to chiefs. He sent a printed document entitled "Bilking the Black Men" to all members of Parliament concerning amounts owed to the Chiefs of Opobo, for which he asserted the government had been in default since 1939.[229] The debts related to deferred compensation obligations from the 1890s that had not been paid. In his letter to Parliament, Geary states that the compensation was due on account of canoes and other property belonging to Ja Ja and other Opobo chiefs for canoes and other property that had been confiscated in naval operations following the kidnapping of Ja Ja of Opobo, who died in 1891 in Tenerife, Spain after having been deported from Nigeria and then sent to St. Vincent.[230] Geary notes that the original document certified in 1892 was presented to the Nigerian government in 1939. These claims were not paid. Geary goes on to note that in August 1943, the Opobo chiefs "retained the undersigned, a Nigerian solicitor, who was in England to take up the case with the Colonial Office. The African thinks that, though there may be color prejudice locally, he may get impartial justice and consideration from H.M.'s Secretary of State."[231]

The colonial administration in Nigeria and Colonial Office in London did not like Geary's undertaking this case and indicated that they were busy with other activities related to World War II. Resident officers in Nigeria appeared to consider Geary a nuisance, noting that Sir William Geary "continues to bombard us with letters about the claim of the Opopo [sic] chiefs,"[232] They also noted a lack of clarity surrounding the early treaties with "native" chiefs. Because of this lack of clarity, it appears that they could not easily determine who was actually entitled to receive the sums in question:

> Unfortunately, the business of determining now who should receive this money is proving very intractable. Under the 1892 Bond, the money was to be paid to the Chiefs of Opobo, 'their heirs or successors', and it does not need much imagination to appreciate how extremely difficult it is, more than fifty years later, to decide who are the rightful heirs or successors.[233]
>
> In order to settle the question as quickly as possible once the claim had been admitted by His Majesty's Government, the Nigeria Government had proposed to the Opobo Chiefs that a special tribunal should be established under a special ordinance for the purpose of investigating the proper payees . . . the Chiefs were unwilling to accept a special tribunal . . . . Sir William Geary suggested that payment should be made immediately to the list of heirs and/or successors appended to the letter to him of the 8th February, of which he had sent a copy to the Colonial Office, the payees giving the Government an indemnity against any other claims.[234]

Because of the administrative history of colonial rule in Nigeria, uncertainty also existed concerning who was actually responsible for the payment. The Colonial Office was also concerned about setting a precedent concerning payment obligations:

> It has not been easy to decide how these claims should be dealt with in the absence on the one hand of any records relating to them and on the other hand of any arrangement for dealing with outstanding liabilities of His Majesty's Government when the Nigerian Coast Protectorate was taken over by the Secretary of State for the Colonies in 1899, or of any general custom for dealing with outstanding or belated claims against Government when there has been a transfer of administration from His Majesty's Government to a Colonial Government. On the one hand had the money been paid immediately to the Chiefs in 1892 it would probably have been found from the revenues of the Protectorate . . . . It may be that the term. "His Britannic Majesty's Government" was meant to represent the Government of the Protectorate and if this is so it might be argued that it is for the Nigerian Government to meet the claim as the successor, as far as Opobo is concerned, to the Government of the Niger Coast Protectorate . . . but it has been felt that, if the Nigeria Government were now to be asked by His Majesty's Government to meet these claims from their own revenues, this request might be misunderstood locally,

in view of the fact that the agreements on which the claims were based were issued on behalf of His Majesty's Government, and that a very unfortunate impression might thereby be created. In all circumstances the Lords Commissioners of the Treasury have agreed to meet these claims from the Exchequer as an act of grace, on the understanding that this is not to be regarded as in any sense constituting a precedent.[235]

Geary's clients were highly appreciative of his work in getting payment for their claims:

We endorse your pressure on the Government for payment with interest as from March, 1939. As a celebrated lawyer you must be convinced of the legality of the point you submit to convince Government of the necessity, the reasonableness, and the legality of payment with interest. We pray that unrelentlessly you should prosecute the cause .... It is evident that your labors are bearing fruit. But all that we anxiously await to hear is the date of payment .... Now that the Government has signified its intention to pay, you would please press so unrelentlessly that payment is no longer delayed.[236]

This episode highlights an ongoing lack of attention and care about matters of law in colonial legal administration. Colonial administrators tended to be dismissive of petitions by Africans. Their file comments also indicate that they also did not like petitions made by Geary, but were typically responsive to his questions. Colonial administrators expressed concerns in this case about Sir William Geary's compensation arrangements with his clients:

Sir William Geary has meanwhile been giving us a good deal of trouble at this end .... You will notice that according to the 8th February Sir William Gary seems to be very much financially interested in the matter. We are going separately into the question of the propriety of the arrangement apparently proposed between him and the Chiefs. I do not know whether your Legal Advisers would have any view on this aspect of the matter.[237]

.Geary's clients also raise questions about his fees:

With reference to your charge we add to the £1000 already offered, 20% of the interest secured. Opobo Chiefs of today are not those you used to know or hear about. In fact, the depredations during the naval blockade between 1888 and 1889 adversely affected the wealth of the town. Some of the Houses are in a decrepit condition as a result of the pillages. It is almost impossible for some of the Houses claiming the compensation to subscribe to the £300 fee. We earnestly request you to prosecute the matter with all the fervor and zeal. If you succeed, as we believe you could succeed, £1000 with 20% of the interest would don't be an unreasonable offer.[238]

Geary was involved in other petitions concerning compensation for local rulers based on nineteenth-century treaties, including the Akarigbo of Ijebu-Remo, with the Fabian Colonial Bureau requesting information about this case in a letter to the Colonial Office in 1946, some two years after Geary's death.[239]

Geary also raised issues related to racial discrimination against Africans in a number of cases. In a land case where Geary represented a client, Chiffons Idugu, whose rents had been detained by the Nigerian Government, Geary raises questions about the Government's actions:

> The reason given, hostile feeling between the parties, seems wholly inadequate why the government should retain money belonging to one party, accruing rents from his lessees. It may well be that an unsuccessful Plaintiff litigant is disgruntled, but is that any reason why the successful defendant should be penalized? If A sues B, and fails, why should C detain in his hands money accruing from D, lessees of B? This seems not only irrational but contrary to natural justice and is all the worse when done by a European official to a native.[240]

Inadequacies of colonial Nigerian government processes are evident in general administrative approaches and decisions in response to petitions and complaints. In colonial Nigeria, licensing requirements were put in place that gave the colonial governor authority over all mineral oil activity on all colonial lands.[241] The government ownership of natural resources established during colonialism, carried over into postcolonial governments.

Colonial administrators often had absolute discretion over determinations of compliance with regulatory requirements. This gave officials significant ability to block activities on substantive or non-substantive bases. Those blocked by colonial officials had little recourse for challenging these decisions. Laws and regulations that facilitate administrative blocking of activities remain a legacy of colonialism and facilitate corruption today by providing corrupt officials with multiple avenues for extraction of rent, often with little transparency into the bases of decisions.

In one case in which Geary represented a local Nigerian client, Adebamibo Koku, colonial authorities were vehement in denying that race was involved in the denial of a prospecting license when Koku sought to register under the Minerals Ordinance. At the same time, however, these authorities did not really offer any robust rationale for their denial of the prospecting license, particularly because they had in the past apparently given licenses to European applicants with similar profiles to Koku.[242] Colonial officials note that the governor had discretion in such matters and that the secretary of state was not prepared to interfere with the governor's discretion but was satisfied that Geary's "implied suggestion of racial discrimination is without justification."[243]

The government's approach to the mining ordinance licensing matter reflects an important aspect of government administration in colonial Africa that continues to have relevance. Rather than seeing licenses as something to be granted as a matter of course, which would reflect and enabling approach to economic regulation, the colonial government sees the granting of the license as a matter of arbitrary Nigerian government discretion. Furthermore, the government's actions reflect an approach that does not require transparency as to the reasons that the license was denied, or recourse upon which to challenge or request review of the government's denial.

In Koku's interview for a mining license, the interviewer agreed with Koku's statement that licenses have been granted in the past to those without the qualifications they required of Koku and acknowledged Koku's previous study and willingness to undertake future study about mining. The Chief Inspector of Mines said to Koku: "Yes, I agree Mr Koku, that many of those who have got licensed know nothing about mining business and now Government is not prepared to grant licenses to others who have not the knowledge."[244] The Chief Inspector of Mines also indicated in response to a question from Koku that the government did not intend to withdraw any licenses issued to miners with a similar profile to Koku. The Governor is said to have made the decision about the Koku license because "Mr. Koku's ignorance of prospecting and mining operations rendered him incapable of understanding the Minerals Ordinance in such a way as to form a reasonable guide to and restriction on his actions."[245]

Geary and Koku both felt that this rationale was a pretext for denying Koku a license based on race. Geary notes that "[i]s it not the fact that most persons are grantees of concession without previous experience e.g. the late Mr. Rhodes. I would respectfully submit that an African has an equal if no not preferential right to share in the Mineral riches of his country."[246] In correspondence with the Under Secretary of State for the Colonies, Geary also indicates that he believes that the treatment is discriminatory: "If rights so granted to others, why not to my client. It may be that there is some prejudice against my client either because he is African or because he was assaulted by an official and ventured to complain thereof."[247]

Koku noted that although the Chief Inspector of Mines continued to refuse to grant him a prospecting right, his case had assisted two African applicants who applied for mining licenses after he questioned his denial of a prospecting right, noting that the Chief Inspector of Mines appeared to be handling these cases differently from his case. Koku also notes that the departure of the former Chief Inspector of Mines had made things better for African applicants for licenses: "the tide has changed for the better and Africans who have been refused of Prospecting rights have been written to, to fill Forms, and this is a result of your appeal on my behalf, that Africans should have a right to exploit the Mineral resources of their country."[248]

As part of his strategy in appealing the denial of the Koku license, Geary approached Arthur Creech Jones, a Member of Parliament from the Labour Party (and later colonial secretary), concerning the grounds for the denial of Koku's application. Creech Jones wrote a letter to the colonial secretary asking for information concerning the grounds for denial of the application and asking "can I be assured that there was no discrimination against this man for any reason at all?"[249] The colonial secretary wrote back several months later relating the explanations offered by the colonial administration in Nigeria, who assured Creech Jones that Koku's denial was based on his "ignorance of prospecting and mining operations [that] rendered him incapable of understanding the Minerals Ordinance in such a way as to form a reasonable guide to and restriction on his actions."[250] In a letter to Geary, Creech Jones indicated that he received a response from the Colonial Office "in respect of mining prospecting rights to Africans ... I need not say that I am skeptical as to the explanation offered."[251]

The Koku case represents an individual example of a broader phenomenon during colonialism in which opportunities within Nigeria were mediated by foreigners who represented external interests but whose decisions had tremendous internal impact. This internal impact led to systematic prioritization of British interests and exclusion of Africans in key spheres of the economy. The registration requirements under the Minerals Ordinance were not intended to facilitate economic opportunity for locals in Nigeria, but rather, were targeted at external commercial interests. Legal frameworks that were put in place during colonialism underscore how colonial legal institutions, which have persisted after independence, have limited essential economic opportunities for local people in Nigeria and other former colonies.

Notes

1. Seidman, 1981: 152.
2. Achebe, 2012: iv.
3. Ferguson and Gupta, 1978: 981.
4. Ibid.
5. Ibid. at 991–992; Anghie, 2005.
6. Achebe, 1994. The missionary involved in creating "Union Igbo" was Archbishop T.J. Dennis who served as a missionary in Africa under the Church Missionary Society. Ekechi, 1978.
7. Nwagbara, 2007.
8. Pennycook and Makoni, 2005.
9. Barnes, Andrew, 2018.
10. Seraile, 1972.
11. Ibid. at 201.
12. *Of the Holy Bible for the Use of the Negro Slaves in the British West-India Islands*, 1807.
13. Michel Martin. "Slave Bible From the 1800s Omitted Key Passages That Could Incite Rebellion." NPR.com, December 9, 2018, accessed October 24, 2020, https://www.npr.org/2018/12/09/674995075/slave-bible-from-the-1800s-omitted-key-passages-that-could-incite-rebellion.
14. Smith, Robert, 1979: Appendix A.
15. Kopytoff, 1965: 73.
16. Moore and Vaughn, 1994: 4.
17. Wolton, 2000: 3.

18. Smith, Robert, 1979: Appendix C.
19. Afigbo, 1972: 8.
20. The RNC's charter was revoked in 1899. Foreign Jurisdiction Act 1890 Order in Council, 27th day of December 1899. The Southern Nigeria Order. TPA HC/CL/JO/10/197/26.
21. An Order in Council is a type of legislation made by the monarch acting on the advice of Privy Council that is approved in person by the monarch. Orders in Council are a legal means by which the United Kingdom makes laws for its colonies and dependencies. Understanding Legislation, www.legislation.gov.uk/understanding-legislation.
22. Foreign Jurisdiction Act 1890 Order in Council, 27th day of December 1899. "The Southern Nigeria Order in Council 1899." TPA HC/CL/JO/10/197/26.
23. This book discusses a number of colonial hangovers in the commercial law sphere. Laws criminalizing homosexuality introduced during colonialism have been upheld in a number of countries in Africa, including Kenya, despite having been overturned in the United Kingdom, but notably overturned in Botswana. Jacob Kushner. "The British Empire's Homophobia Lives On in Former Colonies." *Atlantic*, May 24, 2019, accessed December 2, 2020, www.theatlantic.com/international/archive/2019/05/kenya-supreme-court-lgbtq/590014/; Alan Yuhas. "A Win for Gay Rights in Botswana Is a 'Step Against the Current' in Africa." *New York Times*, June 11, 2019, accessed December 2, 2020, www.nytimes.com/2019/06/11/world/africa/botswana-gay-homosexuality.html; Human Rights Watch. 2008. *This Alien Legacy: The Origins of "Sodomy" Laws in British Colonialism*. New York: Human Rights Watch, accessed December 2, 2020, https://www.hrw.org/sites/default/files/reports/lgbt1208_web.pdf; The Law Library of Congress, Global Legal Research Center Laws on Homosexuality in African Nations, February 2014, accessed December 2, 2020, www.loc.gov/law/help/criminal-laws-on-homosexuality/homosexuality-laws-in-african-nations.pdf.
24. McQueen, 1999.
25. Rawls, 1999: 55.
26. Ibid.
27. Ezera, 1964: xi.
28. Herzog, 2018: 13.
29. Siems, 2018: 51.
30. Mattingly, 2013: 3–4.
31. Herzog, 2018: 7.
32. Siems, 2018: 51–52.
33. West, 1999.
34. Barraclough, 1954: 193.
35. Siems, 2018: 55.
36. Goodhart, 1930: 175.
37. Goodhart makes this argument with respect to the United States. Ibid. at 188.
38. Fassbender and Peters, 2012: 1–2.
39. Birnhack, 2012: 26–28; Roberts and Mann, 1991; ; Adewoye, 1977.
40. Anghie, 2005.
41. Preamble, General Act of the Conference of Berlin Concerning the Congo, Signed at Berlin, February 26, 1885, *American Journal of International Law* 3 (1909): 7–25 (hereinafter "Berlin Act").

42. Craven, 2015: 31, 38, 50–51, 57; Berlin Act, arts. 1, 11, 12, 26, 35.
43. Afigbo, 1972: 67–68.
44. Matera, Bastian and Kent, 2011.
45. Allen, 1972: 172.
46. Johnson-Odim and Mba, 1997: 72–77.
47. Shepperson, 1985: 39.
48. Berlin Act, *supra* note 41, art. 6.
49. The RNC to Sir J. Pauncefote (December 20, 1886). TNA FO 403.
50. The National Africa Company Ltd. to the Earl of Iddelsleigh (October 28, 1886). TNA FO 403; The National Africa Company Ltd. to the Earl of Iddelsleigh (November 8, 1886). TNA FO 403.
51. The Company exercised monopoly power despite the fact that the Company Charter indicated that it would not impose such a monopoly. Extract from the "London Gazette" of Tuesday, July 13, 1886, Article 14 – Prohibition of Monopoly (July 12, 1886). TNA FO 403.
52. Akinwumi, 2002.
53. The National African Company (Limited) (later Royal Niger Company) Charter was based on the North Borneo Charter. Foreign Office to Law Officers and the Crown and Sir J. Deane (March 13, 1886). TNA FO 403.
54. Treaties were signed, for example, by the King and Chiefs of Kolama, Sengana, Akassa, Alenso, Ojormah, Gandy, Bapassa, Achiagi, and Gandu. The RNC to Sir J. Pauncefote (December 20, 1886). TNA FO 403.
55. Pearson, 1971: 69, 85.
56. Pedler, 1974: 117–124.
57. Fieldhouse, 1994: 3.
58. Mulligan, 2009; Lynn, 2006; Hopkins, 1968; Hopkins, 1976a; Mathew, 1968: 274–278.
59. Lynn, 1992.
60. Vail, 1976.
61. Noah, 1989: 25–27.
62. Dike, 1956: 203–206.
63. Ghai, 1991: 8.
64. Read, 1979: 6.
65. Munslow, 1983: 224.
66. The National Africa Company Ltd. to the Earl of Iddelsleigh (August 18, 1886). TNA FO 403.
67. Article VI of the form treaty is struck through. This Article provided: "The subjects and citizens of all countries may freely carry on trade in every part of the territories of the Kings and Chiefs parties hereto, and may have houses and factories therein." Treaty. King and Chiefs of Opobo. December 19, 1884. TNA FO 93/6/16.
68. The RNC to Sir J. Pauncefote, Inclosure 7 in No. 18 (December 20, 1886). TNA FO 403.
69. The RNC to Sir J. Pauncefote, Inclosure 8 in No. 18 (December 20, 1886). TNA FO 403.
70. Revocation of RNC's Charter (L.G., Dec. 29, 1899). TNA FO 881/7225X.
71. Royal Niger Company Act 1899. 62 & 63 Vict. c. 43, § 1(1). August 9, 1899. TNA CO 583/199/16.
72. Ibid.

73. Hansard HC Deb 26 July 1899 vol 75 cc370-426. Statements of Mr. Dillon and Mr. Labouchere.
74. Hansard HC Deb 26 July 1899 vol 75 cc370-426. Statement of Mr. Labouchere.
75. Postema, 2007.
76. Merry, 1988: 875.
77. Chanock, 1978: 80.
78. Snyder, 1981: 49.
79. Chanock, 1978: 86.
80. Said, 1993: 3.
81. Chanock, 1978: 82, 86.
82. Alao, 2003: 201.
83. Merry, 1988: 870.
84. Adewoye, 1977: 2–3.
85. Adewoye, 1987: 1–17.
86. Kuwali, 2014: 81–82.
87. Herskovits and Herskovits, 1998: 56–57.
88. Oba, 2002: 823.
89. Ibrahim, 1988.
90. Bivar, 1961.
91. Munir and Odeh, 2014.
92. Lawan, 2014: 303.
93. Ibid. at 311.
94. Vaughan, 2018: 239–240.
95. Ibid. at 242.
96. Higazi. 2011. *The Jos Crisis: A Recurrent Nigerian Tragedy*. Discussion Paper No. 2, accessed October 23, 2020, Friedrich-Ebert Stiftung, http://library.fes.de/pdf-files/bueros/nigeria/07812.pdf.
97. Vaughan, 2018: 251.
98. Religious identification appears to have shifted over time among the Yoruba with a slow shift from Islam to Christianity since 1963. The 1952 census indicated a slightly larger Muslim than Christian population (43.3 percent Muslim to 38 percent Christian). The 1963 census figures suggested roughly equal numbers of Yoruba Muslims and Christians (46.3 percent Muslim and 45.5 percent Christian). More recent survey data indicate a Christian majority among the Yoruba of 67.1 percent, with 31.6 identifying as Muslims, and 1.3 percent identifying as traditionalists. Nolte, Jones, Taiyari and Occhiali, 2016: 546, 551.
99. Makinde and Ostien, 2012: 51.
100. Lawan, 2014: 324–325.
101. Court Sentences Singer to Death for Blasphemy, Media Foundation for West Africa, August 12, 2020, accessed October 23, 2020, https://www.mfwa.org/country-highlights/court-sentences-singer-to-death-for-blasphemy/.
102. Mili Godio. "Auschwitz Museum Director Asks President of Nigeria to Pardon 13-Year-Old Boy Jailed for 'Blasphemy'." *Newsweek*, October 6, 2020, accessed October 23, 2020, www.newsweek.com/auschwitz-museum-director-asks-president-nigeria-pardon-13-year-old-boy-jailed-blasphemy-1534310.

103. 1999 Nigerian Constitution, arts. 10, 38, and 39.
104. Austin, 1993.
105. Ojo, 2007: 32–33.
106. Ibid. at 34–35.
107. Ibid. at 35.
108. Ibid. at 36.
109. Austin, 2005: 220.
110. Ojo, 2016.
111. Ibid.
112. Ibid.
113. Ibid.
114. Ojo, 2007: 47–48.
115. Partridge, 1911.
116. Bennett, 2019: 652, 656.
117. Stauder, 1974: 43.
118. Harrington and Manji, 2003.
119. For example, in a series of documents, marriage and divorce practices for the Nankani, Kanuri, and other groups were collected and documents. Restatement of the Laws of Marriage and Divorce, by Arthur Nylander, Ph.D. (Research Officer, School of Oriental & African Studies), London. SOAS Archive PP MS 74, Restatement of African Law, Box 10.
120. Tuori, 2010.
121. Scott, F., 1944.
122. Keith, 1924: xvii.
123. Ibid. at 265.
124. McQueen and Pue, 1999: 5.
125. Alao, 2003: 201.
126. Adewoye, 1973: 149.
127. Ibid.
128. Nwocha, 2016: 431.
129. Amankwah, 1970: 40.
130. Lawan, 2014: 306.
131. Judicature Act of 1967, § 3, 2 Laws of Kenya, Cap. 8 (rev. ed. 2012), available at http://kenyalaw.org/kl/fileadmin/pdfdownloads/Acts/JudicatureAct_Cap8.pdf.
132. Janet Babajide. *Lawal-Osula* v. *Lawal-Osula*, (1995) 10 SCNJ 84; An Overview, oniguguru.com, April 14, 2014, accessed March 6, 2021, http://oniguguru.blogspot.com/2014/04/lawal-osula-v-lawal-osula-1995-10-scnj.html.
133. Nigeria Evidence Act 2011, Section 73.
134. Chiroma, 1993.
135. Chanock, 1998: 237.
136. Ndulo, 2011: 88.
137. Ibid. at 92.
138. Ibid.
139. Kayaoglu, 2010.
140. Ibid.

141. Chanock, 1978: 87.
142. Ibid. at 87.
143. Ibid. at 88.
144. Lynn, 1995: 56–57.
145. Ibid. at 58.
146. Roberts and Mann, 1991: 11.
147. Alao, 2003: 202.
148. Ibid.
149. Ordinance No. 4.—1876. An Ordinance for the Constitution of a Supreme Court, and for other purposes relating to the Administration of Justice. March 31, 1876 ("Supreme Court Ordinance"). Section 7. Ordinances, and Orders, and Rules Thereunder, in Force in the Colony of Lagos, December 31, 1893. Google Books Edition, pp. 33-35
150. Ibid. at Section 14, Section 17.
151. Ibid. at Section 19.
152. Ibid. at Section 19.
153. Ibid. at Section 19.
154. Alao, 2003: 202–203.
155. Supreme Court Ordinance, 1900, Section 71, Section 74.
156. Vile, 1998: 111–113.
157. Bogdanor, Khaitan, and Vogenauer, 2007.
158. Perham, 1950: vi.
159. Reinstein, 2009: 284.
160. Iyer, 2018: 507.
161. Ibid. at 509.
162. Meyerson, 2004: 2.
163. Locke, 1689.
164. Fombad, 2005: 309.
165. Ibid. at 318.
166. Ibid. at 319.
167. Ibid. at 302–303.
168. Read, 1979: 7.
169. Okenyodo, 2018: 1.
170. Sylvester Ugwuanyi. "Why We Arrested High Ranking Judges – DSS Releases Official Statement." DailyPost, October 8, 2016, accessed October 23, 2020, https://dailypost.ng/2016/10/08/arrested-high-ranking-judges-dss-releases-official-statement/.
171. 1999 Nigerian Constitution, Schedule II, I, section 21(a)–(b).
172. John Campbell. "Fallout Continues in Nigeria from Judges' Arrest for Corruption." Council on foreign Relations Blog, October 19, 2016, accessed October 23, 2020, www.cfr.org/blog/fallout-continues-nigeria-judges-arrest-alleged-corruption.
173. Okenyodo, 2018: 8–9.
174. Alao, 2003: 204.
175. Ibid. at 204.
176. Ibid. at 204–205.
177. Ibid. at 208–209, 211.
178. Ibid. at 213.

179. Ochieng'Opalo, 2020: 101.
180. Ibid. at 102.
181. Tamuno, 1969: 556.
182. Tom and Attai, 2014: 67.
183. Ochieng'Opalo, 2020: 102, 104.
184. Ibid..
185. Tom and Attai, 2014: 67:.
186. Ochieng'Opalo, 2020: 105.
187. Tamuno, 1969: 560–563.
188. Remarks of the Chief Secretary of the Federation (Sir Ralph Grey), House of Representatives Debate, March 5, 1957, p. 216. TPA HC/CL/DO/1/60, Box 26.
189. Northern Nigeria. Letter to Members of the House Assembly on Procedure. TPA HC/CL/DO/1/62, Box 24.
190. TPA HC/CL/DO/1/60, Box 26.
191. The mace of the House of Commons dates from the reign of Charles II. The House of Lords used two maces, one dating from Charles II and the other from the reign of William III. Mace (The), UK Parliament Glossary, accessed October 23, 2020, www.parliament.uk/site-information/glossary/mace/.
192. Responses to inquiry from Mr. R.D. Barlas, fourth Clerk at the Table, House of Commons from India, Northern Ireland, the West Indies, Australia, and Canada. TPA HC/CL/OO/1/63, Box 27.
193. Report of the Political Bureau. 1987. Lagos: Federal Government of Nigeria, p. 94. As quoted in Tom and Attai, 2014: 68.
194. Aiyede, 2005: 65.
195. Suberu, 2018: 221.
196. Ibid. at 222.
197. Ibid.
198. Tom and Attai, 2014: 70–72.
199. Alao, 2003: 201.
200. Gann and Duignan, 1978: 340.
201. Alao, 2003: 201.
202. Ibid.
203. A number of Arubi's petitions were on behalf the Olu of the Itsekiri. *See* TNA CO 583/254/8.
204. Petitions. Edema Arubi (On Behalf of the Itsekiri People: Crown Lands at Warri). TNA CO 583/245/10.
205. Ekeh, 2005: 100–102.
206. Petitions. Edema Arubi (For Chief Lori of Aja Igba). TNA CO 583/245/9.
207. The Petition of Edema Arubi to the Secretary of State for the Colonies and the Officer Administering the Colony and Protectorate of Nigeria. TNA CO 583/254/8. Some petitions relating to payments of subsidies to rulers in the Niger Delta involved payments of comey, which was a "payment for permission to trade, paid by the British trader to the King and/or his major trading chiefs, as well as for the other charges, including payment for pilots, the 'shakehands' to be paid on making an agreement, and the numerous 'dashes' to maintain goodwill and contacts." Lynn, 1981: 333.

208. Extract from Nigeria Gazette of May 21, 1942, Government Notice No. 604. Petitions. TNA CO 583/254/8.
209. Nigeria No. 224 from Officer Administering the Government to Oliver Stanley Secretary of State for the Colonies dated May 21, 1943. TNA CO 583/254/8.
210. Lawrence, 1993: 261.
211. TNA CO 583/245/7.
212. CO 583/254/11.
213. TNA CO 583/214/11.
214. Petitions. Sir. W.N.M. Geary on Behalf of I.E. Davies. Sierra Leone. TNA CO 267/668/11.
215. Letter from Douglas Jardine to Malcolm MacDonald dated December 7, 1939. TNA CO 267/668/11.
216. Petitions. Sir. W.N.M. Geary on Behalf of I.E. Davies. Sierra Leone. TNA CO 267/668/11.
217. In a letter to the Director of Surveys & Land, Geary makes arguments under the Agricultural Holdings Act 1923 concerning how compensation should be calculated for his client. TNA CO 267/668/11.
218. TNA CO 583/254/11.
219. Albert, 2008: 47.
220. Ibid. at 49–51.
221. John Campbell. Lamido Sanusi: A Man of Nigeria's Past and Possibly Its Future. Council on Foreign Relations Blog, March 31, 2020, accessed October 23, 2020, www.cfr.org/blog/lamido-sanusi-man-nigerias-past-and-possibly-its-future.
222. Letter dated March 26, 1940 from William Nevil M. Geary to The Under Secretary of State concerning the Elewu of Ewu. TNA CO 583/245/5. The Oni of Ifẹ̀ is the spiritual head among the Yoruba. The city of Ilé-Ifẹ̀ in Nigeria has primacy among the Yoruba in government, history, religion, and art. The type of crown in evolved in this case appears to be a beaded and fringed crown of a type deriving from Ifẹ̀. Smith, 1988: 13.
223. Letter dated May 28, 1940 from William Nevil M. Geary to The Under Secretary of State concerning the Elewu of Ewu. TNA CO 583/245/5.
224. Letter from Williams to Sir William Geary, Bart., May 24, 1937. TNA CO 583/214/2.
225. Smith, 1988: 87.
226. Albert, 2008: 48.
227. Enclosure to Nigeria dispatch No. ___ of the ___ January 1937. TNA CO 583/214/2.
228. Enclosure to Nigeria dispatch No. ___ of the ___ January 1937. TNA CO 583/214/2.
229. Letter from William N.M. Geary to Members of Parliament. Petition. Claims of Money by the Chiefs of Opobo. TNA CO 583/264/2.
230. "King Ja Ja of Opobo Dead." *The New York Times*, August 9, 1891, accessed October 23, 2020, https://timesmachine.nytimes.com/timesmachine/1891/08/09/103327868.html?pageNumber=6.
231. Letter from William N.M. Geary to Members of Parliament. Petition. Claims of Money by the Chiefs of Opobo. TNA CO 583/264/2.
232. Letter from Foreign Office to Colonial Office, dated January 8, 1944. Petition. Claims of Money by the Chiefs of Opobo. TNA CO 583/264/2.

233. Comments of Sir George Gater. Petition. Claims of Money by the Chiefs of Opobo. TNA CO 583/264/2.
234. Note of Discussion on Opobo. Claims on the 5th of May, 1944. Petition. Claims of Money by the Chiefs of Opobo. TNA CO 583/264/2.
235. Letter from Oliver Stanley, Colonial Office, to Arthur Richards, Governor. February 8, 1944. Petition. Claims of Money by the Chiefs of Opobo. TNA CO 583/264/2.
236. Letter from Opobo Town to Sir William Geary dated February 8, 1944. Petition. Claims of Money by the Chiefs of Opobo. TNA CO 583/264/2.
237. Letter to H.M. Wilcox, Esq. dated June 15, 1944. Petition. Claims of Money by the Chiefs of Opobo. TNA CO 583/264/2.
238. Letter from Opobo Town to Sir William Geary dated February 8, 1944. Petition. Claims of Money by the Chiefs of Opobo. TNA CO 583/264/2.
239. Letter from the Fabian Colonial Bureau to the Under Secretary of State, Colonial Office concerning the Claim of Akarigbo of Ijebu-Remo dated October 21, 1946. Petition. The Akarigbo of Ijebu-Remo. TNA CO 583/264/6.
240. Letter concerning the Otis Ocha Land from Sir William N.M. Geary to the Under-Secretary of State, Colonial Office, November 8, 1934. TNA CO 583/199.
241. For example, Section 5 of the Southern Nigeria Mining Regulation (Oil) Ordinance 1907 (No. XII of 1907) as amended. TNA CO 879/93/18 states: ""It shall not be lawful to drill for or work mineral oils within or under any lands in the Colony or Protectorate other than such lands as may from time to time be notified by the Governor by proclamation in the Gazette."
242. TNA CO 583/227/13.
243. Ibid.
244. Notes of interview with the Chief Inspector of Mines at Jos by Mr Koku. TNA CO 583/227/13.
245. Letter from the Officer Administering the Government to Malcolm MacDonald, Secretary of State for the Colonies dated September 10, 1938. TNA CO 583/227/13.
246. Letter for William Geary to the Secretary of State for the Colonies dated March 14, 1938. TNA CO 583/227/13.
247. Letter from William Geary to the Under Secretary of State dated May 17, 1938. TNA CO 583/227/13.
248. Letter from Adebamibo Koku to William Geary dated May 25, 1938. Bodleian MSS Brit Emp s 332, Box 18, File 5. Papers of Arthur Creech Jones.
249. Letter from Arthur Creech Jones to Malcolm MacDonald dated July 16, 1938. Bodleian MSS Brit Emp s 332, Box 18, File 5. Papers of Arthur Creech Jones
250. Letter from Malcolm MacDonald to Arthur Creech Jones dated November 1938. Bodleian MSS Brit Emp s 332, Box 18, File 5. Papers of Arthur Creech Jones
251. Letter from Arthur Creech Jones to William Geary dated November 17, 1938. Bodleian MSS Brit Emp s 332, Box 18, File 5. Papers of Arthur Creech Jones

5

Language, Authority, and Law

The Efik chiefs – like many of our rulers of today – didn't bother to learn the technologies that created these foreign products . . .Many Efiks became literate . . . .

Noo Saro-Wiwa *Looking for Transwonderland: Travels in Nigeria* (2012)

COLONIALISM AND LANGUAGE

The operation of the internal and external in colonial contexts has been evident in Africa in the language realm. Missionaries and colonial administrators played a significant role in developing written languages throughout Africa and in decisions about language policy, language construction, and language use. In addition to playing a critical role in the development of local languages in Africa, the decisions of missionaries and colonial administrators about European languages and local languages, particularly in educational contexts, have also had a sustained and continuing impact. Languages in Africa today reflect a continued reckoning between the internal and external throughout Africa evident even in shifting terrains of the global and the local. Despite shifting contexts, the external imprint in Africa has far too often been unmediated by local considerations and local needs, seemingly impervious to continual changes in surrounding environments.

As Zimbabwean writer Dambudzo Marechera notes in his novella/short story collection *The House of Hunger*, language is an essential part of humanity: "[l]anguage is indissolubly connected with what is that constitutes humanity in human beings and also, of course with inhumanity. Everything about language, the obscene, the sublime, the gibberish, the pontificator, the purely narrative, the verbally threatening, the adjectivally nauseating – they are all part of the chiselling art at the heart of my art, the still sad music."[1] Language in African contexts both illustrates and underscores the impact of disruption in varied times and places. The map of languages in Africa today attests to past human migrations by Africans, Europeans, and others, as well as past and present policies that have promoted particular languages and thus have had a profound impact on the landscape of language use and available opportunities. Language used in colonial-era legal documents and laws often reflect a view of Africans as inferior and lacking in capacity relative to people of European descent.

Official and individual choices about language have shaped the language map and have also contributed to hierarchies. Language has played a critical role in the colonization of the mind that is interconnected with conceptions of success and elite status in many colonial and postcolonial contexts. As Dambudzo Marechera observes in an "Interview with Himself," discussing why he did not think about writing in his native Shona language: "[it] never occurred to me. Shona was part of the ghetto daemon I was trying to escape. Shona had been placed within the context of a degraded, mind wrenching experience from which apparently the only escape was into the English language and education .... I was therefore a keen accomplice and student in my own mental colonisation."[2] Marechera's recognition of his own mental colonization demonstrates a point about language and status in African contexts made by Franz Fanon who notes that "[a]ll colonized people – in other words, people in whom an inferiority complex has taken root, whose local cultural originality has been committed to the grave – position themselves in relation to the civilizing language ... In the colonial army, and particularly in the regiments of Senegalese soldiers, the 'native' officers are mainly interpreters. They serve to convey to their fellow soldiers the master's orders, and they themselves enjoy a certain status."[3]

In *Decolonising the Mind*, Kenyan writer Ngũgĩ wa Thiong'o discusses how imperialism continues to control the economy, politics, and cultures in Africa. He puts language at the center of the struggles of African people to "seize back their creative initiative in history through a real control of all the means of communal self-definition in time and space." For him, the "choice of language and the use to which language is put is central to a people's definition of themselves in relation to their natural and social environment, indeed in relation to the entire universe."[4] Ngũgĩ writes in his mother tongue of Gĩkũyũ:

> I believe that my writing in Gĩkũyũ language, a Kenyan language, an African language, is part and parcel of the anti-imperialist struggles of Kenyan and African peoples .... I do not want to see Kenyan children growing up in that imperialist-imposed tradition of contempt for the tools of communication developed by their communities and their history. I want them to transcend colonial alienation.[5]

Ngũgĩ notes that language has a dual character. It is not just a means of communication. It is also a "carrier of culture."[6] Attitudes about language reflect broader conceptions of culture that incorporate hierarchies of cultures that impact borrowing. Uses of language may incorporate significant cultural value from its source. Views of culture play a role in determinations in Africa about how to filter the external when borrowing. Practices of borrowing based on these worldviews are important reasons that lawmaking processes during colonialism that imposed the external with insufficient consideration of internal needs and priorities have continued to a significant degree long after the end of formal colonialism. Hierarchies of language are one example of a broader internalization of colonial hierarchies that has resulted in widespread valorization of the external, which in the case of law and other things, has tended to lead to greater receptivity to the externally generated than internal innovations and creations.

The topography of language in Africa today is often complex, and at times politicized, with an estimated 2,000 languages present. This language map, which reflects continuing changes, was developed by formal and informal means. The language map of Africa bears the imprint of Africa's colonial legacy, whether mediated by missionaries and colonial administrators in formal and official contexts and pronouncements or through myriad interactions among individuals who have needed to establish modes of communication in contact situations. Although local lingua francas exist, including Swahili in East Africa, the designation of local languages as official languages can be an area of tension within African countries, which typically have multiple ethnic and linguistic groups within each country, another important legacy of colonialism.

The politics of language in Africa was evident in early 2020 in Ethiopia, located in the Horn region of East Africa, which added four more official languages to Amharic, formerly the only official language. Amharic, which is spoken by an estimated 45 percent of the Ethiopian population as a first or second language, was the language of the royal court for several centuries.[7] In early 2020, during a period of mounting internal instability in Ethiopia, four additional local languages were added as official languages in an attempt to reduce political instability.[8] The rationales for the addition of new official languages in Ethiopia were not consistent with a military offensive against the Tigray region undertaken in 2020 by the same federal government that added the new official languages.[9] Notably, Ethiopia is unusual among African countries in not having a European language as an official language.

Choices about language have significant implications, not only for law, but for cultural connectivity and the functioning of society, including the operation of political and economic systems. The digital economy highlights the importance of knowledge and information flows in relation to technology, culture, business, the economy, and myriad aspects of societies. How we create, use, and disseminate knowledge and information have thus become of critical importance in the digital economy era. The ubiquity and importance of knowledge and information today may obscure the importance of knowledge systems not driven by digital economy technological and other changes. Language is a knowledge system that shapes our understanding of the world.[10] Choices about language and how such choices are implemented thus have profound sociocultural consequences.

Examination of language policy illuminates tensions and problems in managing the internal and external in African contexts. Language policy has been an issue of concern and at times contention in varied colonial and postcolonial contexts in Africa,[11] which has led to widespread use of languages of former colonial powers as lingua francas in sub-Saharan Africa (SSA) in educational and other contexts. Languages of former colonial powers, including English, French, and Portuguese, were imposed during colonialism with little or no input from local people. Decisions about local and European languages have a continuing and sustained impact. The legacy of colonialism as evident in language is complex and paradoxical. In late 2019, the Academy Awards became a site of contestation about the impact of colonial language policy. Nigeria has become a major global producer of movies, evident in what many refer to as Nollywood. Nollywood began as a video film industry in the early 1990s and now has wide global distribution. Nollywood films are produced in various languages and include English language films, as well as film productions in local languages in whole or in part, including Hausa, Igbo, and Yoruba, three languages with national legal recognition in Nigeria.

The role of English as a lingua franca in Nigeria emerged as an issue in the cultural arena in late 2019 when the Nigerian film *Lionheart*, Nigeria's first Oscar submission, was disqualified from consideration for the International Film Oscar because it was filmed primarily in English. Some 16 percent of *Lionheart* is in the Igbo language with much of the balance in English. In a Twitter thread, *Lionheart* director and Nollywood star Genevieve Nnaji touched on the role of the English language something imposed by British colonialists yet paradoxically serving as a unifying force in a country with hundreds of local languages:

> This movie represents the way we speak as Nigerians. This includes English, which acts as a bridge between the 500+ languages spoken in our country; thereby making us #OneNigeria. It's no different to how French connects communities in former French colonies. We did not choose who colonized us. As ever, this film and many like it, is proudly Nigerian.[12]

In January 2020, the *Oxford English Dictionary*, in recognition of ways in which Nigerian English has shaped the English language, added a number of Nigerian English words for the first time. These new additional words came from borrowings from Nigerian languages or words coined in Nigeria during the second half of the twentieth century, mostly in the 1970s and 1980s. Sources of these words include Hausa, Yoruba, and Nigerian Pidgin.[13] Words added included *buka* (first attested 1972), borrowed from Hausa and Yoruba, referring to a "roadside restaurant or street stall that sells local fare at low prices;" *okada* (first attested 1993), referring to Okada Airlines, a business established by a businessman from Edo state in southern Nigerian and a "term for a motorcycle that passengers can use as a taxi service;" and *guber* (earliest quotation 1989), a borrowing from English that is short for gubernatorial. Borrowings from Nigerian Pidgin include *chop*, a common colloquial word in Ghana and Nigeria meaning to eat but from the 1970s having developed the "sense of acquiring money quickly and easily, and often dishonestly."

The addition of Nigerian English words to the English language lexicon reflect just a small part of the broader contribution of African creativity and innovation to global flows of knowledge. Nollywood similarly reflects cultural vibrancy in Nigeria that is present throughout Africa. However, the valorization of the external remains a powerful colonial remnant that shapes perceptions and conceptions of the value of local innovations and local creations. Disrupting the valorization of the external will be an important element in facilitating future paths for African countries in which the value and importance of local creations and innovations become more broadly recognized and rewarded within Africa before external validation leads to improved internal status. Part of this recognition and reward should include creation of a legal and policy environment that truly supports internal creativity and innovation to a greater extent than at present in Nigeria.

The valorization of the external is widespread throughout Africa, including in the language policy arena. Nigeria is the most multilingual country in Africa, with well over 450 indigenous languages spoken. This diversity of language makes effective language policy imperative. As is the case with other African countries, languages spoken in Nigeria are also spoken in neighboring countries. Hausa, spoken in northern Nigeria, is also spoken in Chad, while Yoruba, spoken in southwestern Nigeria, is spoken in Benin.[14] Overlaps in language among neighboring countries are present throughout Africa and are a legacy of maps drawn by external powers who did not know and likely did not care overly much about the internal impact of where boundary lines were drawn. Languages spoken in the Ivory Coast, a former French colony, are shared with Ghana, Liberia, Guinea, Mali, and Burkina Faso; the first two of these have English as an official language, the latter three of these have French as an official language. Although a number of countries in Africa have recently added or changed their official languages,[15] many countries in Africa today have the language of former colonial powers as an official language, which is far more problematic than it might seem on the surface. Even local languages in Africa bear a strong external imprint from the actions of missionaries such as that of Archdeacon Dennis regarding Igbo in Nigeria. Missionaries have made decisions about standardized versions of languages, orthography, and other matters that have shaped the contours of local languages throughout Africa.[16]

Nigeria currently has two official languages, English and French.[17] French, which is not widely recognized within Nigeria as an official language, was added by General Sani Abacha in 1996 in a surprise announcement that noted that the new official language was intended to permit Nigeria to "become thoroughly bilingual."[18] Three local languages, Hausa, Igbo, and Yoruba are also mentioned in the Nigerian National Language Policy as languages that every Nigerian child should be required to learn in the "interest of national unity."[19] The view that French is needed for Nigerians to be bilingual demonstrates a high degree of external orientation that seems to see bilingualism only in terms of European languages. Most Nigerians who speak English also speak one of hundreds of local languages. The perspective that appears to underlie the announcement of French as an official language reflects an external take on language policy that came to Nigeria with British colonizers and needs to be disrupted.

The adoption of English as the official language in Nigeria is a colonial legacy inherited from British colonizers, who in 1882 undertook an externally oriented education policy that created standards for examining teachers in schools receiving government support based on "reading and writing English, arithmetic, English history, English grammar, geography, especially of the British Empire, and school management, including practical teaching."[20] The 1882 Education Ordinance "deliberately made no provision for the teaching of vernacular [local languages]."[21] Colonial officials even opposed efforts to reduce local languages to writing and generally implemented a policy that did not give government support to instruction in local languages.[22] In contrast, many missionaries preferred vernacular languages, which they believed should take precedence over English and should be a basis for further education in English.[23]

The adoption of English as an official language in Nigeria followed from earlier decisions by external actors based on external interests and needs. The decision to add French as a second language might reflect regional considerations, given that the West African region where Nigeria is located has many former French colonies. It might also reflect an attempt to enhance opportunities for Nigerians who speak English in interactions with international organizations and entities.[24] From a policy perspective, disrupting colonial-era processes of decision-making requires filtering these types of decisions through an internal lens that considers the impact of such decisions on all Nigerians, and evaluates and marshals the resources to support such decisions in a sustainable way. This might well lead to a decision that French be added as an official language in Nigeria but could also mean that other languages might also be added instead of French. Why not Nigerian Pidgin, Swahili, or Chinese, to name just three possibilities? Language policy should be driven by inclusive governance practices that reflect reasonable and realistic policy rationales that chart out feasible and sustainable future paths for policy decisions and that more importantly reflect an internal view of what Nigeria could be.

British colonial administrators would likely not have even questioned selection of English as an official language in Nigeria and other British colonial possessions. The selective introduction of English in Nigeria without universal English language education enabled British colonizers to suppress mechanisms that might facilitate unification across language and other boundaries within Nigeria, and was thus consistent with colonial divide-and-rule tactics.

Decisions concerning language policy that reflect a greater internal orientation would begin with an assessment of the importance of language as a mode of communication in a country that is multilingual with several hundred languages, and multiethnic with significant religious diversity. Finding ways to facilitate communication across existing divides would be an obvious consideration for this hypothetical local decision maker. This could mean several potential paths for language policy. One might be selection of English as an official language, which many consider to be a unifying force in a country with so many languages. This might well be the case. However, if this internal decision maker were to undertake this policy of English as an official language, it would then need to consider ways to implement universal English language education to ensure that all people within the country would be able to actually benefit from this language policy.

A language policymaking English an official language should require substantial investment, and access to opportunities to learn English should be available to all. Another alternative might be selection of a local language to serve as a unifying force, perhaps with English as a secondary official language, which might be important for dealing with necessary interactions with people outside of Nigeria. None of these or other clear paths has been followed in Nigeria during or after colonialism, which has had significant consequences. English was kept as Nigeria's official language after colonialism in part because selection of a local language would likely raise ethnic tensions. Although many Nigerians do not actually speak English, Nigerian urban elites speak English and have no reason to change.[25]

Evaluations of policy paths would also depend on the ability define and measure what constitutes success. By certain measures, the selection of English as an official language has been enormously successful, particularly for those who already have access to opportunities. Nigeria has produced many remarkable writers in English, including authors with significant international recognition. These accomplishments should not, of course, be discounted. However, by measures that consider the entire population, Nigeria's continuation of colonial language policy approaches would likely benefit from reconsideration.

The choice of English, an external language, as the primary official language in Nigeria has significant internal implications, particularly for indigenous languages, some of which are declining in use or even disappearing. During the colonial era, the operation of the colonial administration was facilitated by having local people who could speak English. As a result, at least limited English language education was an important component of colonialism.

Many Nigerians who learned to speak English during the colonial period were educated at missionary schools. Colonial administrators emphasized language education in English from the primary school level. In 1926, however, the colonial government, which depended on African clerks and messengers who were fluent in English, decided to encourage vernacular language education: "the administration or commercial firms could not employ all school leavers who had some knowledge of English. The Colonial Government, therefore, became concerned that education in English was creating expectations of employment and status that could not be realized. This line of thinking governed the decision to develop vernacular education."[26]

During colonialism English language education gave people access to potential opportunities, including to become part of an educated elite that assisted the colonial administration. The vast majority of people in Nigeria did not have these educational and other opportunities. The British colonial administration did not need for all Nigerians to learn to speak English. This would have required significant investment, which was not consistent with the cost containment emphasis and extractive goals of colonialism. Colonial officials also had divergent views of English speaking elites. On the one hand, such elites served as intermediaries in implementing colonialism, including through employment in the colonial administration. British colonial administrators also disdained such elites because, as was the case in India, educated elites could effectively dispute colonial policy and create petitions demanding rights and equitable treatment, which colonial officials clearly did not like. The imposition of new legal, economic, and political systems during colonialism in Nigeria and elsewhere in Africa was facilitated by educated elites who gained a fluency in not only the English language but also in British laws, policies and ways of doing things, which could enable them to become important colonial intermediaries.

As James Scott notes in relation to Vietnam:

> Those in the colonies who first plumbed the mysteries of the new [land] tenure administration enjoyed unique opportunities … the Vietnamese *secrétaires* and *interprètes* who served as intermediaries between the French officials in the Mekong Delta and their Vietnamese subjects were in a position to make great fortunes. By concentrating on the legal paperwork, such as title deeds, and the appropriate fees, they occasionally became landlords to whole villages of cultivators who had imagined they had opened common land free for the taking. The new intermediaries, of course, might occasionally use their knowledge to see their compatriots safely through the new legal thicket. Whatever their conduct, their fluency in a language of tenure specifically designed to be legible and transparent to administrators, coupled with the illiteracy of the rural population to whom the new tenure was indecipherable, brought about a momentous shift in power relations.[27]

Similar patterns were evident in colonial Africa. Ngũgĩ wa Thiong'o notes that "English was the official vehicle and the magic formula to colonial elitedom."[28] The English-speaking educated elite that became prominent during colonialism eventually became an important part of anticolonial movements all over Africa and an important element of postcolonial elites. English remains Nigeria's primary official language and is unlikely to be displaced because of problems related to multilingualism and ethnicity. English also has high prestige in Nigeria: "[e]ducated Nigerians seem to be enjoying the privileges which the use of English accords them. In fact, in the homes of many educated persons, the children are first introduced to English before they are introduced to their parents' mother tongue(s)."[29] Nigerians who are not literate in English "often have a higher competence in their native languages, at least when speaking them, than the educated bilinguals."[30] The presence and uses of

English in Nigeria has an impact on local languages and contributes to the marginalization of those who are not literate in English:

> A major disadvantage with the continued use of English as the sole official language is the alienation of the non-literate persons. Their inability to use English separates them from the rest of society and blurs their relevance in society. Whatever gains society stands to make from the intelligence and wisdom of some of these persons is lost because they are denied opportunities in national debate or discourse. The emphasis on Western educational attainment, which in itself is synonymous with a matter of English, prevents the non-literate from participation in the politics of the nation.[31]

According to UNESCO estimates, female literacy rates in Nigeria for ages 15 and older are just over 50 percent .[32] Nigerian local languages are used as languages of instruction in some primary school contexts. No single language is predominant throughout the country and no single language is spoken by more than 50 percent of the population as a first language. Language issues in Nigeria "are often quite explosive and conflict ridden," as a result, "census never have items or questions on languages," which makes reliable statistics difficult.[33] English is the predominant language of education, media, judiciary, official transactions, the legislature, and international diplomacy.[34]

Nigerian Pidgin is a contact language that initially developed as a language of commerce during the slave trade in the seventeenth and eighteenth centuries in coastal and delta regions in Nigeria. Nigerian Pidgin may be the most widely spoken language in Nigeria and has the potential to become the most widely spoken language in Africa.[35] Nigerian Pidgin has received no official recognition has in the past been stigmatized as a result of its association with people of low status: "[it] lacks prestige because it is often perceived as a bad form of English and associated with non-literate persons and a socioeconomically deprived group."[36] Nigerian Pidgin is, however, a major cultural force and is increasingly visible globally with use among a broad range of Nigerians, including writers.[37] Prince Charles used Pidgin phrases in speeches he gave during a November 2018 trip to West Africa.[38] Given past patterns, this type of external validation is likely to improve internal perceptions of Nigerian Pidgin.

LANGUAGE AND THE LAW

Nigerian language policy has significant implications for the language of law. The language of the law is reflected on multiple levels, including in choices about what languages are used in legal and other settings with legal significance. Language policy in the legal arena does not reflect Nigeria's actual language uses or literacy profile but rather reflects the same language choices made during colonialism. Although language statistics are not always readily accessible in Nigeria, many

Nigerians do not speak English. English is said to spoken by more than 50 percent of Nigerians or an estimated 79 million people,[39] which is more than the number of people in the United Kingdom.

At independence in 1960, Nigeria continued the colonial-era treatment of English as the language of law. Legal business is conducted and documented in English in Nigeria, which has implications for the executive, legislative, and judicial branches. Law reports containing common law precedents are maintained in English. Treatment of English in legal contexts in British colonies reflect the British portfolio approach to management of its colonies. The British sought to establish some degree of uniformity in legal systems in Anglophone Africa. As a result, even the legislation introducing the common law was identical across colonies.[40] When English law was first introduced in Africa, no local precedents were considered available and courts administered English law and relied in English precedents.[41] The focus on precedent in common law systems can lead to logistical difficulties that result from the ever-increasing volume of precedent over time. Courts in common law jurisdictions do not typically report all cases. Even with selective reporting of decided cases, the volume of precedent over time may become difficult to manage.

Courts in Africa confronting these changing conditions would have possessed limited ability to access local precedents because most colonial territories had no permanent official or private mechanisms for the preparation of law reports. The lack of reported cases in some African colonies led to the establishment of African Law Reports at Oxford University in 1966, which prepared reports of African cases.[42] Nigeria, however, has had a long history of published reports, including Nigeria Law Reports, which includes cases from 1881 to 1942 and were official reports printed by the Government Printer in Lagos.[43]

In addition being important in court administration, language is of critical importance in court proceedings. English is the primary language in court proceedings in federal and state courts in Nigeria whether litigants are literate in English or not.[44] Local languages may be spoken in some local courts, including sharia courts in northern Nigeria where Hausa or Arabic is spoken and Customary Courts in southern Nigeria where local languages are spoken.[45] The Nigerian Supreme Court has reaffirmed the status of English as the language of the law in Nigeria: "There can be no doubt that the official language of superior courts of record in Nigeria is English and that if documents written in an language other than English are to be tendered and properly used in evidence, they must be duly translated into English either by competent witnesses called by the party to the proceedings who needs them to prove his case or by the official interpreter of the court."[46]

Legal language is a distinct type of discourse.[47] Given Nigeria's linguistic profile, the role of English in the Nigerian system has significant implications for access to justice. Discourse analysis studies of courtroom exchanges in Nigerian courtrooms illustrate the difficulty that lay participants in court proceedings may face given the use of specialized uses of English legal language in such settings.[48]

The language of the law has implications for legal and other reform efforts, as well as for conflict resolution. The inability of a significant portion of the population to speak the language of the law has implications for the justice system as well. Of notable concern is the criminal justice context in which the language profile of Nigeria would suggest that a significant number those accused might need an interpreter. The Nigerian Constitution provides that every person charged with a criminal offense is entitled to "have, without payment, the assistance of an interpreter if he cannot understand the language used at the trial of the offense."[49] The ability of accused persons in Nigeria to received interpreting services is hindered by "the lack of any policy or central regulation of interpreting services."[50] Failure to supply an interpreter is treated as a matter of procedure if the accused does not ask for an interpreter and a conviction set aside only if failure to supply the interpreter led to a miscarriage of justice.[51]

Communication is a core aspect of any state. The current structure of internal communication within Nigeria, as well as language policies that have led to this situation, are not compatible with effective governance, which at a minimum, requires varied kinds of communication. People within a society should be able to communicate with one another and should be able to communicate effectively with functions of the state, and the state should be able to communicate with its citizens.

Language often plays an important role in building an integrated society that gives its citizens broad access to a wide range of opportunities. Language is also a "means by which citizens access institutions, processes and entitlements which are essential features of a modern state. A state's preference in respect to the official use of a particular language affects the level of enjoyment of services and access to public sector jobs and may even give rise to ethnic tensions."[52] Language is also important for effective political participation, and language policy is of critical importance for the effective functioning of government, including laws and legal institutions.

Language and the law can be an issue of concern even in contexts with language policies that give indigenous languages official status. Tanzania became a British colony after being colonized by Germany, which lost its colonies after World War I.[53] Swahili, which was spoken on the East African coast prior to the colonial period, is a national language in Tanzania and a lingua franca in East and Central Africa that is spoken in Burundi, the DRC, Kenya, Rwanda, Tanzania, and Uganda.[54] In addition to their mother tongues, nearly everyone in Tanzania speaks Swahili.[55]

The Tanzanian parliament exemplifies issues of language use in legislative contexts. From just before independence, Swahili has been the medium of communication in the Tanzanian parliament. In parliamentary debates and submissions, Swahili is the language of choice, although members of parliament may alternate between English and Swahili. Despite a strong pro-local language policy in parliament, various documentation in parliament is drafted in English.[56] As is the case in Tanzania, legislatures in former British colonies throughout Africa use the traditional name used for transcripts of Parliamentary debates in the United

Kingdom. These transcripts are name Hansard, after the first official printer to the Parliament at Westminster.

Courts in South Africa illustrate complexities of language use in a context with multiple official African languages. Language use in South Africa reflects historical legacies of colonialism and Apartheid. South Africa was a settler colony that had significant migration of settlers from Europe after 1652, when the Dutch East India Company established a trading post in Cape Town.[57] The area around the Cape was settled by European workers who established farms in what became the Dutch Cape Colony. South Africa was later colonized by the British. South Africa has a mixed legal system that includes a hybrid Roman-Dutch civilian law, English common law, customary law, and religious personal law.[58]

South Africa has adopted a multilingual language policy within a constitutional framework that specifically addresses the protection of languages and language rights.[59] South Africa has eleven official languages, including nine indigenous African languages. The recognition of language in the South African Constitution reflects an understanding of the general importance of language in society. Prior to its transition to full democracy in 1994, English and Afrikaans were official languages used in governmental matters in South Africa, which effectively excluded the majority of people in South Africa from full access to institutions, processes, and entitlements.[60]

The South African constitutional framework puts the government under a duty to treat indigenous languages equitably. The Section 29 of the South African Bill of Rights prohibits discrimination based on language,[61] while Section 35 of the Bill of Rights provides language rights related to the criminal justice system.[62] Despite this broader language policy, following the March 2017 Heads of Court meeting, "it was decided that the recommendation that English be the language of record at the Superior Courts must be implemented in the absence of a policy decision from the Executive in this regard."[63] Although this decision was made in part in the interests of practicality, it has serious implications for access to justice, given levels of English language competence and use in South Africa. Only 8.1 percent of South Africans speak English at home, "only 27 percent of state aid applicants in criminal cases speak, read, and write English at a satisfactory level," and an "average of 54.21 percent of applicants in criminal cases were found to have little or no knowledge of English as a medium of communication," which means that "most South Africans cannot access justice in their own languages."[64] Treatment of English as a legal language in Nigeria and South Africa reflects ways in which law and the legal profession may not take sufficient account of the impact of legal administration in contexts of linguistic and other forms of diversity.[65]

Missionaries and colonial officials made decisions about language that have had long-lasting, if not permanent effects, throughout Africa. Many making such decisions were not accountable for the consequences of their choices. Those making decisions also typically relied on external sources of authority that typically took little or no account of local needs, local priorities, and local people.

Colonial legal relics are evident in laws, legal approaches, and legal interpretations that might arise in contexts where customary law and English law conflict. Colonial legal relics are not just relevant to the past but also have significant implications for digital-era participation, particularly because digital economy policies and laws relating to business, entrepreneurship, and innovation in many countries in Africa continue to lag behind those of other areas of the world.

Questions of authority and accountability of external actors continue to be critically important throughout Africa. In Africa and elsewhere, the role of technology companies has become increasingly scrutinized in relation to questions of accountability. Some technology entrepreneurs today have unparalleled power today to make decisions that might impact millions, if not billions, of people. These private individuals are not significantly more accountable than their colonial and imperial predecessors. Actor, director, comedian, and screenwriter Sacha Baron Cohen has discussed the role of what he calls the *Silicon Six*:

> These super-rich "Silicon Six" care more about boosting their share price than about protecting democracy. This is ideological imperialism – six unelected individuals in Silicon Valley imposing their vision on the rest of the world, unaccountable to any government and acting like they're above the reach of law.[66]

Notes

1. Marechera, 1978: 7.
2. Ibid. at 6–7.
3. Fanon, 1967: 3.
4. Ngũgĩ, 1986: 4.
5. Ibid. at 28.
6. Ibid. at 13.
7. Teferra, 2008: 166. The status of Amharic in Ethiopia reflects a long period of rule by Amharic-speaking rulers. The four added languages were Oromo, the most widely spoken language in Ethiopia, Afar, Somali, and Tigrigna.
8. Samuel Getachew, "Ethiopia is adding Four More Official Languages to Amharic as Political Instability Mounts." Quartz Africa, March 3, 2020, accessed October 23, 2020, https://qz.com/africa/1812085/ethiopia-adds-afan-oromo-somali-afar-tigrigna-languages-to-amharic/.
9. Ibid. Declan Walsh and Abdi Latif Dahir. "Why Is Ethiopia at War With Itself?" *New York Times*, November 5, 2020 (updated February 12, 2021), accessed March 6, 2021, www.nytimes.com/2020/11/05/world/africa/ethiopia-tigray-conflict-explained.html.
10. Everett, 2013.
11. Mazrui and Mazrui, 1998.

12. Vanessa Nordzi, "Genevieve Nnaji Responds After Her Movie 'Lion Heart' Was Disqualified From The Oscar Awards." ghbase.com, November 5, 2019, www.ghbase.com/genevieve-nnaji-responds-after-her-movie-lion-heart-was-disqualified-from-the-oscar-academy-award/.
13. *Oxford English Dictionary*. Release notes: Nigerian English, January 13, 2020, https://public.oed.com/blog/nigerian-english-release-notes/.
14. Adegbija, 2007: fn 1.
15. In addition to the 2020 changes in Ethiopia, for example, in 2014, Burundi added English and Swahili to join Kirundi and French as official languages (Loi n°1/30 du 3 Novembre 2014 Portant statut des langues au Burundi).
16. Lara-Stephanie Krause. "For Too Long, African Languages Have Been Defined by the European Colonialists Who Wrote Them." QuartzAfrica, May 17. 2018, accessed October 23, 2020 https://qz.com/africa/1279484/languages-in-africa-are-still-defined-by-white-european-colonialists/.
17. Section 1, No. 10, Federal Republic of Nigeria. 2004. Nigerian National Policy on Education. 4th edition, http://wbgfiles.worldbank.org/documents/hdn/ed/saber/supporting_doc/AFR/Nigeria/TCH/National%20Policy%20on%20Education.pdf.
18. Igboanusi and Pütz. 2008.
19. Nigerian National Policy on Education, supra note 17.
20. Section 7, Education Ordinance No. 4.—1882. Ordinances of the Settlements on the Gold Coast and of the Gold Coast Colony, in Force April 7th, 1887 With an Appendix Containing the Rules, Orders in Council, and Proclamations of Practical Utility, and an Index. Google Books Edition, pp. 714-719.
21. Fajana, 1972: 323.
22. Omenka, 1986.
23. Fajana, 1972: 324.
24. Igboanusi and Pütz. 2008: 239–241.
25. Mann, 1990.
26. Adegbija, 2007: 217.
27. Scott, 1999: 48.
28. Ngũgĩ wa Thiong'o, 1986: 12
29. Igboanusi and Lothar, 2005: 17.
30. Ibid. at 17.
31. Ibid. at 18–19.
32. 2018 UNESCO estimates overall literacy rates in Nigeria of 75 percent for ages 15–24 (with rates of 81.6 percent for males and 68.3 percent for females), 28.3 percent for ages 65 years and older (with rates of 40.1 percent for males and 17.6 percent for females), and 62 percent for ages 15 years and older (with rates of 71.3 percent for males and 52.7 percent for females), http://uis.unesco.org/en/country/ng.
33. Adegbija, 2007: 190.
34. Ibid. at 192.
35. Igboanusi and Lothar, 2005: 17.
36. Igboanusi, 2008: 61.
37. Okoye, 2020.

38. Malaka Gharib. "Why Prince Charles Said 'God Don Betta My Bread!' In Nigeria. National Public Radio, November 20, 2018, accessed October 24, 2020, www.npr.org/sections/goatsandsoda/2018/11/20/668604714/why-prince-charles-said-god-don-butta-my-bread-in-nigeria.
39. https://k-international.com/blog/countries-with-the-most-english-speakers/; Euromonitor International.2010. *The Benefits of the English Language for Individuals and Societies: Quantitative Indicators from Cameroon, Nigeria, Rwanda, Bangladesh and Pakistan* (a report compiled for the British Council), www.teachingenglish.org.uk/sites/teacheng/files/Euromonitor%20Report%20A4.pdf.
40. Tetteh, 1971: 89.
41. Ibid.
42. Ibid. at 94.
43. Cottrell, 1972: 63.
44. Igboanusi and Lothar 2005: 14.
45. Opeibi, 2012a: 282.
46. Mohammed Oladapo Ojengbede v. M. O. Esan (Loja-Oke) (S.C. 132/1991) [2001] NGSC 58 (14 December 2001), https://nigerialii.org/ng/judgment/supreme-court/2001/58.
47. Richard and Nwizug, 2017.
48. Opeibi, 2012b.
49. Section 36(6)(e), Nigerian Constitution of 1999.
50. Michael, 2016: 230.
51. Ibid. at 227.
52. Sacks, 2000: 345.
53. Germany's colonial territories in Africa were Togo, Cameroon, Namibia and Tanganyika (later Tanzania). In 1919, Germany's colonial empire was dissolved under the Treaty of Versailles, which ended German colonial rule. Conrad, 2012: 186.
54. Kiango, 2005.
55. Petzell, 2012.
56. Dzahene-Quarshie, 2011: 27.
57. Ross, 2014.
58. Rautenbach, 2010: 144.
59. Section 6 of South Africa's Constitution reflects a treatment of language rights as fundamental rights.
60. Sacks, 2000: 345–347.
61. Section 29 (Education) of the South African Bill of Rights provides "Everyone has the right to receive education in the official language or languages of their choice in public educational institutions where that education is reasonably practicable. In order to ensure the effective access to, and implementation of, this right, the state must consider all reasonable educational alternatives, including single medium institutions, taking into account: (a) equity; (b) practicability; and (c) the need to redress the results of past racially discriminatory laws and practices."
62. Section 35 (Arrested, detained and accused persons) of the South African Bill of Rights provides that Every accused person has a right to a fair trial, which includes the right . . .(k) to be tried in a language that the accused person understands or, if that is not practicable, to have the proceedings interpreted in that language.

63. Heads of Court Resolution on the Language of Record in South African Courts, www.judiciary.org.za/images/news/2019/Heads_of_Court_resolution_on_the_language_of_record.pdf.
64. Annelis de Vries, Russell H. Kaschula, and Zakeer Docrat. "Why Using Just One Language in South Africa's Courts is a Problem." The Conversation, April 16, 2020, accessed October 23, 2020, https://theconversation.com/why-using-just-one-language-in-south-africas-courts-is-a-problem-134911.
65. Niekerk, 2015.
66. Sacha Baron Cohen, "The 'Silicon Six' spread propaganda. It's time to regulate social media sites." Opinion. *Washington Post*, November 25, 2019, accessed October 23, 2020, www.washingtonpost.com/outlook/2019/11/25/silicon-six-spread-propaganda-its-time-regulate-social-media-sites/.

6

Technology Disruption and Digital Colonialism

Facebook's CEO has come to Lagos . . . to seek out software developers and startup founders . . . To see Zuckerberg . . . was at once thrilling and disorienting for these techies.[1]

TECHNOLOGY, PROGRESS, AND LAW

In 2018, South Africa's Vodacom, which is controlled by Vodafone, a British multinational telecommunications company, launched the first commercial 5G service in Africa in Lesotho. Lesotho, which is a tiny landlocked kingdom that is entirely surrounded by South Africa, thus came to be an early participant in a small-scale test of 5G technology.[2] 5G is the next, fifth-generation wireless telecommunications standard that will offer significantly faster connections and "huge data flows that will enable driverless vehicles, smart appliances and Internet-of-Things networks that could eventually connect consumers to factories manufacturing custom-designed products on demand."[3] GSMA, an industry group that represents the interests of mobile operators worldwide, estimates that 5G will account for 20 percent of global connections by 2025.[4] While 5G connections by 2025 are projected to be 50 percent, 48 percent, and 34 percent of connections in Developed Asia, North America, and Europe, respectively, GSMA estimates that 5G connections will be 3 percent of connections in SSA.[5]

The early introduction of 5G in Lesotho is part of a technology revolution that has swept across countries in Africa in recent years. This revolution is evident with technologies related to mobile devices and reflects a wide range of disruptive and other technologies. The list of such technologies is long and varied, and in addition to mobile phones, might include social media and messaging platforms such as Facebook, Twitter, Instagram, and WhatsApp; internet and e-commerce applications; Internet of Things (IoT) devices; drones and robots; technologies that facilitate automation; cloud computing; artificial intelligence (AI); biometrics; biotechnology/genetic engineering; agrotechnology; and peer-to-peer technologies, including file sharing, blockchain, and cryptocurrencies such as Bitcoin. Many implicitly assume that the impact of such technologies will be positive. Although the ultimate effects of these technologies may be uncertain, existing governance practices and institutions in many African countries may give pause to optimistic assumptions.

Consideration of digital-era technologies in African contexts draws attention to patterns of lawmaking within Africa, particularly in the commercial law arena. New technologies in Africa raise significant questions related to legal reform that are both like and unlike those present elsewhere in the world. New technologies in Africa and elsewhere often lead to debates about how laws and regulations should apply to such technologies. These are essentially questions about the legal and regulatory mismatch that might be one consequence of introduction of new technologies. Thus, mobile phones, mobile phone apps, Uber, and various other new technologies and services have required reassessment and varying degrees of reform of legal and regulatory approaches that might have been put in place well before the advent of such technologies.

Recognition of the need for legal changes in response to new technologies have also had an impact on a broad range of legal arenas, including legal education, the administration of law, evidence rules, and e-discovery practices, to name just a few. In Nigeria, for example, evidence laws were reformed in 2011 and civil procedure rules were reformed in 2012 to recognize the reality of the impact of new technologies on the administration of law.[6] Similarly, emerging and new uses of technologies will continue to present challenges for existing laws that may need reconsideration in light of new technologies. Crafting suitable laws and regulations in the context of new technologies is a global issue.

In addition to such acknowledged problems related to digital economy legal and regulatory mismatch, the dissemination of new technologies in Africa also highlights a range of legal concerns that are less familiar, at least in many developed countries. This second set of concerns relates to ongoing colonial legacies, which are by no means limited to law. Legacies of colonialism raise questions about the influence of external forces in Africa in the digital era and the extent to which technology disruption has come with new patterns of digital colonialism. Approaches to lawmaking and regulation in the context of new technologies may be of assistance in dealing with colonial-era legal and policy overhangs. As Lawrence Lessig has noted: "[c]yberspace demands a new understanding of how regulation works. It compels us to look beyond the traditional lawyer's scope – beyond laws, or even norms. It requires a broader account of 'regulation,' and most importantly, the regulation of a newly salient regulator."[7]

The digital economy also highlights the role of technology as a continuing global force that changes, sometimes rapidly, which requires that laws and regulations be flexible to adapt to changing technological and societal conditions. Varied external technologies have long had an impact in African countries. Technology enabled colonialism, providing tools for the initial exploration by European travelers and later territorial conquest. Colonial conquest "depended heavily on rapid-firing rifles and machine guns. In the phase of consolidation, the links that tied the colonies to

Europe and promoted their economic exploitation included steamship lines, the Suez Canal, submarine telegraph cables, and the colonial railroads."[8] Science and technology played a pivotal role in "European expansion, conquest, governance, and resource extraction in colonized areas."[9]

Technological disparities in weaponry led to devastating African casualties in early military engagements with Europeans. In the Battle of Karari (Omdurman) in Sudan in 1898, Anglo-Egyptian forces defeated Mahdist forces with 11,000 dead and 16,000 wounded on the Mahdist side and 49 dead and 382 wounded on the Anglo-Egyptian side. Winston Churchill, then a war correspondent, saw this battle as "the most signal triumph ever gained by the arms of science over barbarians."[10] British colonial policies as reflected in recommendations of the *African Survey*,[11] published in 1938, were "designed to master Africa's environments and its human inhabitants through scientific management and planning."[12] Survey leaders also advocated use of "cultural technologies, such as film and radio, to infiltrate more efficiently the heterogeneous cultures of the continent."[13]

Assumptions about science and progress in the *African Survey* reflect longstanding external visions of African progress and improvement: "[d]uring the last third of the nineteenth century, a number of individuals began explicitly to link the idea of improving the African continent with developing it through science."[14] Attitudes about science and technology and African capacity have shaped conceptions of what future paths for Africa should be.[15]

The industrial economy highlighted the relative technological advancement of European countries and the United States as compared to the rest of the world, and was used as a justification for political subjugation. Widely accepted evolutionary hierarchies have reflected views of human history "as a single evolutionary development through a series of stages which were often loosely referred to as savagery, barbarism, and civilization."[16] Evolutionary assumptions have played an important role in shaping policy prescriptions and assumed future paths. In his 1963 study of West African trade, development economist P. T. Bauer notes that

> certain sectors of the economies have reached an advanced and, in some cases, even a sophisticated stage, while others are only a few decades removed from a barbarous and savage state, or have not yet fully emerged from it. The factors underlying these contrasts and extremes themselves present difficult problems for economic policy and its administration.[17]

Evolutionary approaches also imbued thinking about the development of legal systems. Henry Sumner Maine envisaged an evolution of law from status to contract that accompanied the progress of societies from savagery to barbarism to civilization.[18] Hierarchies of race and status based on evolutionary assumptions played a role in determinations of legal rights in colonial contexts. In British colonial possessions, educated Africans could be placed into a higher category than the masses, with entitlements to opportunities and treatment under colonial legal systems that most local people did not have.[19]

Indigenous peoples in colonial contexts such as in Australia were often placed at the bottom of such hierarchies: "[t]he impression formed by the British [of indigenous peoples of New Holland (an early name given by Dutch navigators to what later became Australia)], was of a people without order, society, or government .... In short, the language of these early accounts, while often broadly sympathetic, was informed by the very firm conviction that the indigenous inhabitants were thoroughly uncivilized."[20] As was the case in Africa, where supposed local failures to exploit raw materials were used to justify colonialism, uses of land by indigenous Australians became a justification for legal frameworks that deprived them of rights to land. In Australia, indigenous land rights were not recognized due to legal fabrications that treated the land as occupied but "'unowned' and therefore 'vacant'."[21] This process in Australia reflected patterns of linguistic and conceptual representation that were used to determine legal rights.[22] Legal treatment of Australian aborigines was based in part on the "absence of aboriginal farms ... because the British were heirs to a long tradition of thought associating the development of property rights with a society's passage through specific stages of civilization."[23]

Determinations of legal rights in colonial Australia and other British colonial contexts were shaped by an assumption of innate British superiority combined with a selective filtering of information in ways that supported particular representations of reality.[24] In Australia, for example, records of early European occupation ignored or obscured evidence of aboriginal agricultural production and farms. In his review of journal and diaries of explorers and colonists in Australia, Bruce Pascoe found "repeated references to [Aboriginal] people building dams and wells; planting, irrigating, and harvesting seed; preserving the surplus and storing it in houses, sheds, or secure vessels, and creating elaborate cemeteries and manipulating the landscape."[25] Archeological evidence demonstrates cultivation and plant management dating back more than 2,000 years in Australia.[26]

Discussions of development often imbed evolutionary assumptions about the trajectory of development of societies thought to fall into the category of *developing*. This is particularly true given the at least implicit assumption of development or progress as following a single unfolding map of predictable development. In a report to the General Assembly of the United Nations by British colonial authorities in Togoland, a former German colony administered by Britain after World War I under a League of Nations mandate, the report writers note: "[l]ocal industries are negligible. They consist of the usual types found among all people of a similar state of civilization. Pottery, of the crudest, mat weaving, and rough baskets are the principal."[27]

Borrowing practices in law and policy reflect assumptions about how the local might achieve projected future outcomes. These practices assume that past historical paths in one location can be used to shape future paths, at times in radically different times and spaces. These assumptions are problematic and may be of limited use in real-world contexts, in part due to the changing topography of both the local and the global in African and other contexts. This is particularly true given the rapidly evolving technologies that have become characteristic digital economy features. A 2019 report by the Tony Blair Institute for Global Change notes that automation may limit the ability of African countries, and developing countries more generally, to follow earlier development paths of countries such as China:

> Rapidly evolving technologies and the astronomical proliferation of smartphones across Africa have already changed lives on the continent and increased aspirations, but they are also altering the development pathways available to these countries ... the labour substitution-substitution effect of automation threatens African economies' ability to leverage manufacturing for job creation, as the emerging Asian economies did in the second half of the twentieth century. This will drastically change the process of development, although how is anyone's guess.[28]

Discussions of disruptive technology in Africa often reflect a framing of technology as progress. However, technology interacts with broader sociocultural contexts in varied ways. For example, new technologies may offer unparalleled opportunities for varied types of destruction. Disruptive technologies may also have distributional consequences that may impact their reception. Further, areas where disruptive technologies emerge may experience magnification of existing societal problems and inequalities. In Silicon Valley, a global center of technology disruption, digital-era technologies have exacerbated existing societal schisms, leading to greater income inequality and a decrease in available affordable housing, among other things. Aspects of the broader societal impact of disruptive technologies in the developed world should be a cautionary lesson to countries in Africa that seek to harness technology to solve Africa's problems. This is particularly true, given the profound social and economic inequality that already exists in Nigeria and other countries in Africa.

THE DIGITAL ECONOMY, CAPACITY, AND SCARCITY OF OPPORTUNITY

The digital economy has heralded a change that some refer to as the fourth industrial revolution, in which digital transformation is a core aspect.[29] At its core, this digital transformation has reshaped how we think about, share, and use knowledge and information. Digital-era technologies highlight the need to consider disruption beyond its effects in the commercial sphere. Disruptive technologies may have broader implications that extend far beyond any intended markets or commercial networks of their origination and may have a significant impact on a broad range of people in diverse places. How technology disruption ultimately plays out in African contexts will depend in part on the actions of external actors and varied internal factors, including new entrants, incumbents, civil society organizations, and policymakers, as well as business, legal, and other institutional frameworks.

Technology disruption in Africa is most evident today with users who interact with technologies largely developed outside of Africa. Such technologies include hardware such as mobile phones, and varied software applications, often deployed to a significant degree over mobile devices in Africa, including Twitter, Facebook, WhatsApp, and Instagram; the latter two of these are both owned by Facebook. Companies based in the United States have a dominant presence in the technology arena in Africa, as well as globally. China now plays a dominant role in Africa in infrastructure projects and an increasingly important role in technology products and services.

Technology disruption in Africa occurs in contexts permeated with shadows of past experience, particularly in relation to various past and continuing internal and external sources of disruption. Precolonial and colonial encounters in Africa have led to institutional structures that reflect ongoing external intervention and indiscriminate adoption of external frameworks and institutions, including legal ones. Internal sources of disruption have, in many countries and regions, been closely related to patterns of external relationships. Technology diffusion in contemporary contexts thus occurs in a broader environment in which certain countries, regions, and languages have become dominant global forces. Technology relationships intertwine with existing patterns present in countries such as Nigeria that significantly shape the diffusion of disruptive and other technologies.

Talent accelerator Andela is an example of external engagement with local connections in Africa. Andela, which has received significant external funding, including from the Chan Zuckerberg Initiative,[30] is based in New York City, and seeks to connect top African software developers with global technology firms.[31] As of mid-2020, Andela had raised $181 million and described itself as a company that builds remote engineering teams.[32] Andela, which had layoffs in May 2020 due to the impact of the COVID-19 pandemic, at that time had offices in four African countries: Nigeria, Kenya, Rwanda, and Uganda.[33] As of mid-2020, Andela had positioned itself as a technology company operating in Africa with core business operations outside of the continent. A future path for technology companies with connections in Africa that replicates Andela's business model may limit benefits that might flow from such companies within Africa. Andela reflects the continuing impact of the external within Africa. As such, Andela sends a message and perhaps may signal a reality that technology companies that could be based in an African country may need to start or at some point move outside of Africa to attain success by global measures. A key digital economy challenge for institutional frameworks within Nigeria and other countries in Africa is to create a better enabling environment for local creativity and innovation, with a goal of having a greater share of benefits from African creativity and innovation flow internally within African countries.

Existing patterns of technology creation and usage have implications for potential future paths of development of technology from Africa. Technologies from Africa would typically emerge in some instances from contexts of creation, use, and adaptation of technologies to specific African contexts. Development of technologies from Africa, at least in the near future, will probably take place in the broader context of a global technological arena that is based on American business and culture and the English language. The English language has become a dominant language in global communication, particularly in the science and technology arena. Furthermore, the United States has played a dominant global role in a number of high technology industries during much of the post–World War II era. Although the dominance of English in the early Internet era is fading, English usage is pervasive in many technical areas, including programming; most programming languages are English-based,[34] and the English language remains at present a widespread global lingua franca for programmers.[35]

Global languages of technology interface in Africa with a complex topography of language use. The pervasive presence of global English as a dominant language of technology may, in fact, reinforce trends in countries in Africa such as Nigeria, where English is a dominant language of communication among elites. English language dominance in the technical arena is present even in countries that have widespread usage of African lingua francas, such as Swahili in Kenya.[36]

People involved in the creation, development, and financing of technologies within Africa are typically enmeshed in global webs of interchange. Future paths of African participation in the broader global digital economy will depend on institutional contexts and capacity within Africa to not only consume and use new technologies, but also to create, harness, and reproduce such technologies. Scientific and technological capacity is a key element of such participation. African countries currently suffer from a tremendous deficit in scientific and technological infrastructure that contributes a significant gap in research capacity between sub-Sahara Africa (SSA) and the rest of the world: "[sub-Saharan Africa] accounts for less than 1 percent of the world's research output while being home to 13.5 percent of the global population … In 2008, [countries in Africa] produced the same number [of research papers] as the Netherlands."[37] The number of scientists engaged in research and development (R&D) per million population is an important measure of development capacity, particularly since such scientists "are key performers of R&D aimed at increasing the stock of knowledge and devising new applications in order to ensure sustainable development."[38] SSA significantly lags most of the world in R&D expenditures as a percentage of gross domestic product (GDP) and the number of R&D scientists per million people.[39]

Research activities within Africa reflect the same externalized patterns that are evident in other arenas with limited internal connectivity. Research output in countries in SSA relies to a significant degree on external networks, including through international collaborations and visiting researchers. In 2012, southern, eastern, and western Africa produced 79 percent, 70 percent, and 45 percent of their research, respectively, "in collaboration with external actors, while only 2-3 percent of the research in Eastern and Southern African involved collaboration with partners in Africa."[40] Current internal research capacity reflects low levels of local R&D investment in SSA, which has led to research being "highly dependent on external funding support, often through intermediary institutions, and thus not optimal for effectively addressing research problems in the region."[41]

Recognition of the R&D investment gap has not led to remediation of the situation by policymakers and internal decision-makers within most African countries. Disrupting existing ways of interfacing with the external and developing robust internal networks of connectivity within Africa will be important in future policies designed to narrow the research capacity gap. This does not mean that this process must be entirely internal. Rather, the process should have involved a careful examination of any external models or networks used with a focus on how those might be used to achieve discernible internal goals, as well as continuing measurement of outcomes of such policies.

Current R&D capacity and other conditions within Africa may significantly limit future paths of technology development within Africa. In addition to limited R&D capacity, a limited number of developers are present in Africa today. A 2020 report by Google and the International Finance Corporation (IFC) notes that African countries have approximately 700,000 professional developers, primarily in Egypt, Kenya, Morocco, Nigeria, and South Africa.[42] Nigeria's 12-percent share of total professional developers in Africa is less than its share of Africa's total population.[43] More developers will be needed throughout Africa to improve digital economic capacity.[44] The number of professional developers in Africa is just a bit more than the 630,000 professional developers in the state of California. Notably, women are 21 percent of the total population of developers in Africa as compared with 15 percent of junior developers in the United States.[45]

The externalized vision that shapes low levels of R&D investment in SSA remains a key colonial legacy. As a result, even long after colonialism, internal activities within countries in Africa related to technology may be based on priorities of external decision-makers, including from states, businesses, and other nongovernmental actors. As a result, although local businesses may be involved as intermediaries in the import of technologies for users in varied spaces, what is made available may not be reflective of local considerations or needs. The gap between what is available and what might be needed locally, makes local contexts of technology use and consumption sites of potential creativity and innovation, often by necessity. Desperation and scarcity of opportunity may drive many things, including a need to innovate for comfort, and at times, survival. A robust, internally oriented and truly postcolonial policy design would try to identify and alleviate suffering and scarcity of opportunity but also create processes to harness the innovation and flexibility that everyday life requires in far too many African contexts.

As Clapperton Chakanetsa Mavhunga notes in his study of technology and innovation related to poaching from an African perspective, technology is created in everyday practices in Zimbabwe where knowledge is made and turned into practical outcomes, even in contexts such as national parks or game reserves that he describes as "a colonial relic struggling to adjust to a postcolonial reality."[46] The poaching practices in Zimbabwe discussed by Mavhunga implicate law because such practices were criminalized during colonialism and then retained by the postcolonial state, as has been the case with many other colonial-era laws and legal processes.

Jenna Burrell notes that sites of activities surrounding technologies used by young people in internet cafés in Ghana may be:

> outside of formal design, manufacturing, and distribution processes . . . [secondhand computers found in Internet cafés of Accra] came to be distributed via gray market processes . . . imported from abroad typically through the efforts of Ghanaian transnational small businesses. A lack of influence on the production end of the process limited the adaptive practices of Ghanaian youth to post hoc efforts to make up for the gaps between technological possibilities and local needs, realties, and interests by leveraging unintentional and serendipitous compatibilities.[47]

Imported secondhand technology products found in internet cafés in Ghana and elsewhere in SSA have also been a source of electronic waste in countries in Africa.[48] The export of e-waste to Africa has implications for potential future paths for digital economy participation by countries in SSA. E-waste also constitutes a significant public health burden. Future paths that reflect Africa as an e-waste dumping ground may continue past patterns of external engagement with costs that may outweigh their benefits. Facilitating the innovation and creativity noted by Mavhunga and Burrell is critical for disrupting colonial legacies, and for treating knowledge and information that comes from within Africa as valuable and potentially transformative. Approaches based on this recognition can also be critical in problem-solving within Africa because they reflect "the means and ways with which ordinary people engage in creative activities directed toward solving their problems and generating values relevant to their needs and aspirations."[49]

PLATFORMS, REGULATORY COMPETENCE, AND COLONIAL POLICY DESIGN

Technology is a major arena in which competing visions of the past, present, and future may play out. Technologies today facilitate widespread dissemination of information and visual images and rapid communication to billions of people across the globe. Many things about such technologies are positive developments that enhance the lives of many. At the same time, uses of such technologies may also be troubling. Technology commentators may emphasize liberating aspects of such technologies in that they enable exchanges and communications that are not mediated by traditional media intermediaries. Although this can be a positive factor in some contexts, Facebook, Twitter, and YouTube, for example, have a serious problem with fake news and hate speech that has led to real-world harm. In 2019, the House of Commons of the United Kingdom issued a report that identified and discussed the "proliferation of online harms" in social media that is made more dangerous by microtargeting messaging through advertisements and use of "deep fake" audios and videos.[50] During the COVID-19 pandemic in 2020 and 2021, significant fake news was disseminated using social media.[51]

Hate speech on Facebook has been evident in a number of different contexts and contributed to genocide in Myanmar in 2018.[52] Hate speech on Facebook, including a "politically-motivated disinformation campaign orchestrated on Facebook through a network of newly created pages and designed to demonize [the singer Hachalu] Hundessa,"[53] preceded the singer's assassination in Ethiopia in June 2020. The violence after Hachalu's murder "was supercharged by the almost-instant and widespread sharing of hate speech and incitement to violence on Facebook, which whipped up people's anger. Mobs destroyed and burned property. They lynched, beheaded, and dismembered their victims."[54] In India, Facebook is alleged to have ignored its own hate speech rules to stay in the good graces of members of the ruling Bharatiya Janata Party (BJP), who were important for the company's business prospects in India.[55]

The 2019 House of Commons report discusses the impact of Facebook and other companies that are part of what many refer to as the platform economy. This report is part of an ongoing global discussion about how to regulate the platform economy. Other terms used to refer to this space include sharing economy, gig economy, and peer economy. Companies with platform business models include Airbnb, Amazon, Etsy, Facebook, Google, Salesforce, TikTok, Twitter, WeChat, and Weibo. Platform companies create "online structures that enable a wide range of human activities ... [which] opens the way for radical changes in how we work, socialize, create value in the economy, and compete for the resulting profits."[56] Platform companies may provide services, products, payments, software development, and other things. Digital platforms are "complicated mixtures of software, hardware, operations, and networks."[57] The business models of platform companies are causing significant economic disruption. A number of platform companies raise issues about the status and role of workers.

Platforms may also be in "winner-take-all" markets, which may enable platform owners to become "virtual monopolists."[58] A 2020 US House of Representatives report based on a sixteen-month investigation found that technology companies exercise significant market power, which the report suggests merits regulatory scrutiny and action to restore greater competition.[59] Google has been sued for anticompetitive practices in both the European Union (EU) and the United States, while Facebook has been under investigation in the EU and has been sued by US federal and state regulators.[60] Amazon has been sued for anticompetitive practices by the EU.[61] Global discussions by regulators and others highlight difficulties in applying existing laws and regulations in new spaces, in part because "the appropriate market rules for competition/antitrust, labor market, and intellectual property among many others are becoming increasingly difficult to specify and legislate."[62] Julie Cohen characterizes the platform as the "core organizational form of the emerging informational economy" in which "the data extracted from individuals plays an increasingly important role as raw material in the political economy of informational capitalism."[63] Facebook, Google, and other digital technology companies that collect significant amounts of data raise concerns related to the privacy and protection of the data they collect and use in their business activities.

Global debates about regulating platform companies are of critical importance for countries in Africa. As is the case elsewhere in the world, platform companies operate throughout Africa, which raises questions about how such companies are regulated in African countries. The treatment of information as a raw material in platform economy contexts also echoes important elements of existing relationships between many African countries and the rest of the world. From the early days of interactions with Europe, African countries have been seen primarily as sources of raw materials, including agricultural products, minerals, and human beings, who during the trans-Atlantic slave trade were accounted for as physical assets.[64] The platform economy thus comes to Africa in the midst of countries that have long been primarily sources of raw material whose value was extracted for the benefit of others, who upon receipt of such benefits often did little to use such benefits for internal improvement. If current patterns are not disrupted, the platform economy and likely future iterations of digital economy-based business models pose the potential for African countries to become further enmeshed in the global economy as exploitable suppliers of raw materials and dumping grounds for digital economy waste.

New technologies unfold in African countries in a legal environment in which colonial overhang is pervasive. Colonial-era laws were often problematic both in their conception and their application. Colonial laws were initially conceived of by colonial powers as mechanism for exerting social control or maintaining what colonialists thought of as existing social relations, which were often assumed to be static. The 1938 *African Survey*, which "played a decisive role in shaping research priorities in both Britain and colonial Africa,"[65] included an essay on law and justice that sought to position legislation as follows:

> means of expressing the changes which a community deems best suited to improve its social and material life; in Africa, the law imposed by the European powers is passing beyond its rudimentary purpose as an instrument for securing order, or

maintaining existing social relations, and is entering a more extended phase, requiring the enactment of a wide range of laws necessitated by new conditions."[66]

Colonial powers' conceptions about law led to inflexible approaches to lawmaking that were out of step with widespread social, cultural, political, economic, and other changes that were taking place during colonialism. This colonial era–derived approach to law, which has not been sufficiently disrupted in postcolonial lawmaking contexts in many countries in Africa, is a poor fit for legal approaches needed in digital economy contexts.

The *African Survey* passage, however, reflects acknowledgment that law must adjust to changing contexts. Colonial views of change in British colonies in Africa were shaped by assumptions of an unquestioned future path toward a state of existence for which British laws, institutions, and frameworks should be a model. This led to widespread cut-and-paste approaches to law and legal process during colonialism that did not end with independence.

Colonial legal overhang has led many countries in Africa to rely on cut-and-paste borrowings from external legal frameworks, laws, and regulations with insufficient attention to adaptation for local contexts. Further, once enacted, laws may not be updated with any speed, even when external source laws are modified. In 2020, Nigeria made a comprehensive revision of its company law for the first time in thirty years, while Kenya's 2015 update took twenty years. Swaziland (landlocked and bordered by South Africa and Mozambique), which changed its name to Eswatini in 2018, is the last absolute monarchy in SSA. Eswatini took almost a century to revise its company law, replacing its Companies Act of 1912 with the Companies Act of 2009.[67] Laws that lag technology constitute a pervasive digital economy problem. In areas with colonial overhang, digital economy legal reforms may have extra lag time reflecting colonial overhang and, as a result, may not be implemented expeditiously. Given changing technologies, existing approaches in countries such as Nigeria may leave many in Africa vulnerable to the activities of platform and other companies with little effective legal protection, even on paper.

Approaches to lawmaking processes in Nigeria have not been conducive to the development of legislative or regulatory competence in contexts of rapidly changing digital technologies that may involve close understanding of highly technical issues. Limited scientific and technological capacity in SSA and insufficient internal investment in developing such capacity may also hinder robust digital economy legal and regulatory responses. Issues of legislative competence about digital economy issues are not just an issue of concern in African countries and have been raised with respect to the US Congress, for example.[68]

Limited legislative and regulatory competence on a range of issues related to business and commerce, including digital economy issues, has been one consequence of the combined colonial and postcolonial legal legacy in Africa. Regulation of fundamental digital economy measures in the electronics sector in Nigeria has reflected what Andrew Ubaka Iwobi has characterized as legislative ineptitude.[69] Early attempts in Nigeria to adopt a data protection regime were troubled. These attempts highlighted troubling approaches to legal borrowing that reflect patterns established during colonialism:

> regulatory authorities have utilized the mechanism of legal transplantation in the fledgling field of data protection in a manner that has been detrimental to the nation's quest for an appropriate statutory framework. Their approach has been desultory and ill-conceived, and their various pieces of draft legislation reveal an alarming lack of in-depth knowledge of the transplanted laws and an absence of the sophisticated mindset needed to render those laws amenable to the Nigerian context. This is unfortunate because it exposes serious failings within the Nigerian legislative process, which will inevitably hinder the nation's progress towards the legal modernization that is vital to compete with other nations in the highly complex and rapidly evolving technological sphere.[70]

Local regulatory frameworks matter, particularly in contexts involving powerful platform companies. In what was at the time the largest known leak in Facebook history, Cambridge Analytica, a British political consulting firm, acquired private Facebook data for more than 50 million Facebook users without their consent. This data was used to build voter profiles that were used in its work on the campaign of President Trump in 2015. Cambridge Analytica was also involved in elections in Africa, including the successful campaigns of Kenyan President Uhuru Kenyatta in the 2013 and 2017 elections, where concern exists about electoral manipulation.[71] Although "[t]he exact details of CA's [Cambridge Analytica's] work in Kenya are the subject of dispute, but it is safe to assume that Kenya in 2013 was the testing ground for at least some of the methodology later used in the Brexit and Trump campaigns."[72]

The activities of Cambridge Analytica may reflect experimentation and a form of regulatory arbitrage that enabled Cambridge Analytica to engage in activities in African countries that might have been more difficult to undertake in countries with more robust data protection, privacy, and other legal regimes regulating the activities of platforms and other digital economy companies. The activities of Cambridge Analytica may reflect use of Africa as a location for digital colonial experimentation that is not likely to be of internal benefit within Africa.

Events surrounding Cambridge Analytica and other data leaks have highlighted widespread concern about data protection that even prior to disclosures about the activities of Cambridge Analytica had led to adoption of data protection legal frameworks throughout the world, including the European Union General Data Protection Regulation,[73] which has become a worldwide model for data protection. In January 2019, the Nigerian National Information Technology Development Agency (NITDA) adopted a data protection regulation.[74] This regulation was adopted by NITDA after the Nigerian National Assembly was not able to adopt legislation after multiple attempts. By October 2019, twenty-five of fifty-four countries in Africa had adopted data protection frameworks.[75] In 2020, the Nigerian National Assembly published a draft data protection law.[76] In doing so, Nigeria came closer to joining a number of African countries in adopting data protection laws.

Laws adopted in digital economy contexts in Nigeria and other former colonies should be scrutinized to evaluate the impact of colonial legal overhang, particularly in relation to governance. Laws intended to address digital economy issues may also be used to pursue authoritarian goals that are consistent with colonial and postcolonial governance in Nigeria, as well as other countries in Africa. For example, the 2015 Nigerian Cybercrime Act, was intended to provide "an effective, unified and comprehensive legal, regulatory and institutional framework for the prohibition, prevention, detection, prosecution and punishment of cybercrimes in Nigeria."[77] The Nigerian government has used the Cybercrime Act to suppress critical speech:

> Cyber stalking ... carries a fine of up to 7 million naira (USD$22,000) and a maximum three-year jail term for anyone convicted of knowingly sending an online message that "he knows to be false, for the purpose of causing annoyance, inconvenience danger, obstruction, insult, injury, criminal intimidation, enmity, hatred, ill will or needless anxiety to another." ... the law was cited in the arrest of Musa Babale Azare who was detained in the capital, Abuja, by police from Bauchi state. He was accused of allegedly criticising the state governor, Muhammad Abdullah Abubakar, on social media, according to news reports. Azare, who uses Facebook and Twitter as platforms to criticize the actions and policies of Abubakar and his administration, said he was denied access to his lawyer, and that police did not have authority to arrest him outside Bauchi state jurisdiction.[78]

Despite Nigerian government efforts to contain the digital economy within approaches that reflect pre-digital-era authoritarian governance tendencies, the Nigerian government has not been able thus far to control or entirely contain digital-era protests, most notably the #EndSARS protests that erupted in Nigeria in October 2020. These protests highlight ways in which Nigeria is at a crossroads of past and present authoritarian paths and future digital economy possibilities. At the time of their emergence, the #EndSARS protests were a spark in the midst of a forest that is ripe for conflagration. The presence of other simultaneous fires from insurgencies and other spaces in Nigeria where the government in Nigeria no longer effectively governs, magnifies prospects for future conflagrations.

The #EndSARS protests also highlight zones of internal contestation, particularly between the young and those who govern, who in Africa tend to be advanced in years. This contestation is evident all over the African continent. The young tend to be more technologically savvy and may seek future paths that disrupt past forms of governance that have contributed to scarcity of opportunity for them evident in scarce jobs and limited educational options. Those who govern may be locked into past paths that may lead them to seek to implement future paths that follow from past and current ones. This confrontation between the old and the young, the past and potential futures is about governance in large part and how diverse countries in Africa full of young people should be governed in the future in light of past and present paths that have led to marginalization, not only of the young but of the vast majority of people.

Despite government attempts to contain critical speech and protests in Nigeria and elsewhere in Africa, digital economy technologies are carving out new spaces, particularly for younger people. Although these spaces disrupt some aspects of past paths, they may reinforce others. #EndSARS, for example, highlights and seeks to disrupt existing patterns of governance in Nigeria that are not inclusive and that could lead to a dire future for many young people. Likely futures for the young may be driven by population growth in coming decades that will far outpace economic growth given current government approaches to managing the economy. At the same time, the technological tools used in protests have emerged from contexts of digital economy private governance that bear similarities to colonial governance. Global technology companies may not be highly regulated in contexts of origin or may reflect norms of governance from contexts of origin that may be questionable in African contexts. Digital economy tools, products, and services have become essential for many. However, access to core digital economy apps and platforms may be subject to arbitrary, nontransparent decisions of technology companies who often do not explain their decisions or offer recourse for consequences of such decisions. From the perspective of users, platform governance may resemble aspects of colonial governance evident in colonial petitions where colonial authorities could and did act in an arbitrary fashion.[79]

Social media companies play a gatekeeping role and might promote or suppress certain types of speech, which highlights their power. The role of platform companies as gatekeepers was evident in the early stages of the #EndSARS protests in Nigeria where Facebook and Instagram (which is owned by Facebook) blocked #EndSARS postings while Twitter did not. Twitter enabled the rapid spread of knowledge about and expressions of support for the #EndSARS protests. #EndSARS thrived on Twitter:

> The campaign to shut down the controversial and brutal Special Anti-Robbery Squad (SARS) thrived on Twitter in particular and a series of significant #EndSARS hashtags trended globally with millions of retweets. Even Twitter's enigmatic founder Jack Dorsey joined young Nigerians in encouraging the global Twitter community to donate to the protest organizers using bitcoin … Twitter gave the EndSARS hashtag an official emoji and verified the Twitter accounts of several users at the forefront of the protest. This act of support contributed to the global credibility of the protest and boosted the movement both online and offline.[80]

In contrast, Facebook and Instagram labeled some of the #EndSARS postings as "fake news":

> Instagram and Facebook platforms, which are both owned by Facebook Inc, both flagged posts containing words such as "#EndSARS" and "Pray for Nigeria" and of photos of a blood-stained Nigerian flag and a burning candle as fake news, and users were directed to an unrelated fact check article for explanations.[81]

Facebook and Instagram responses to #EndSARS highlight problems with the algorithms that make decisions about how to label and exclude or include posts. Decisions by Facebook and Instagram allied them with Nigerian government responses to videos, social media postings, and news reports about the October 2020 shootings of unarmed protestors at Lekki toll gate in Lagos. The Nigerian government initially ignored, and then denied, the killings.[82] Platform companies may play an important role in varied contexts about which they may have limited knowledge. Decisions by such companies may effectively lead to these companies' taking sides in disputes much like colonialists choosing sides in colonial-era disputes.

Uses of Twitter in the #EndSARS protests highlight the impact of social media today. Twitter, which is widely used in Africa and elsewhere in the world, illustrates the potentially varied impact of digital economy companies and applications in Africa. Twitter is a free microblogging service that enables users to send and receive messages or *tweets* that contain video, photos, links, and up to 280 characters of text from mobile devices and computers. Tweets can in turn be *retweeted* by Twitter users, which enables widespread sharing of original tweets. Twitter users may subscribe to streams of tweets by other Twitter users, becoming followers of the streams they select.

Twitter, Instagram, and other social media companies have changed communication in profound ways, at times disrupting incumbent media organizations and significantly affecting varied communicative activities.[83] Twitter has become a dominant platform for sharing breaking news and has been used for coordination and communication by protestors in Belarus, Egypt, Hong Kong, Iran, Ukraine, and the United States, for example. Because its structure permits any user to tweet, Twitter enables communication of information that might not receive attention from traditional media sources.[84] In African countries, Twitter offers possibilities of communication outside of traditional media channels that have often been subject to extensive government control in the past, in part as a result of a "culture of silence … imposed first under colonialism and then by postcolonial military dictatorships and autocratic one-party states."[85] Although government media monopolies began being challenged in the 1980s in some countries in Africa, Twitter has further disrupted government power over media content evident in the past through intimidation and/or control and intermediation in many parts of Africa.

Despite the impact of Twitter and other alternative forms of digital-era communication, government control of the media remains strong across Africa. This was evident during the #EndSARS protests in Nigeria in October 2020. On October 8,

2020, just one week after the sixtieth anniversary of Nigeria's independence, nationwide protests erupted in Nigeria about police brutality. These protests were a response to a video that emerged online on October 3, 2020 showing a young man in Delta state in southern Nigeria allegedly being shot by the Special Anti-Robbery Squad (SARS), "a notoriously corrupt unit that critics contend is exactly the type of criminal syndicate it was created to eradicate."[86] Events surrounding protests about this shooting illustrate how protest and government repression may unfold in specific contexts in Nigeria. The shooting in the October 3 video led to widespread protests on the ground and an eruption on Twitter with the hashtag #EndSARS,[87] which had emerged in earlier protests against SARS in 2017.

On October 10, 2020, a young man, Jimoh Isiaka, was said to have been killed by police in Ogbomosho in Oyo state in southwestern Nigeria, with at least two people said to have been killed the following day. Protests across Nigeria continued. On October 21, 2020, TechCabal Daily noted the Nigerian media silence in response to the shooting of an estimated twelve unarmed protestors by the Nigerian security forces at Lekki toll gate in Lagos, an event referred to as the Lekki Massacre (#LekkiMassacre). Eyewitness accounts and verified mobile phone videos indicated that the Nigerian security forces had shot live ammunition into a crowd of protestors, killing an estimated twelve to fifteen people. TechCabal Daily reported the following media responses:

> Nigeria's traditional media houses have been at the forefront of misinformation since the protests began.
>
> Despite several verified videos of security forces shooting at unarmed protesters, Channels TV ran this headline: *Security Operatives Fire Gunshots To Disperse Protesters in Lekki*.
>
> The *Daily Post of Nigeria* ran this headline: *Lagos: Bullets hit End SARS protesters in Lekki, many feared dead*. The Nigerian newspaper, *Punch*, chose an even stranger headline: *Heavy gunfire as soldiers clear Lekki EndSARs protesters*.
>
> If you're in Nigeria and your TV is turned on, you may very well have no idea that protesters are being killed by the country's security forces.[88]

TechCabal Daily also draws attention to the role of the Nigerian National Broadcasting Commission, a parastatal of the Nigerian government,[89] in shaping media responses to the shootings:

> **Nigeria's broadcast regulator is keeping media houses in line** Nigeria's National Broadcasting Commission (NBC) told broadcasters to "approach the use of materials from user generated content in order not to *embarrass individuals, organisations, government* ... " It also asked broadcasters to perform the role of 'peace agents.' The NBC's stance may explain in part why broadcasters in Nigeria have essentially looked the other way.[90]

As media responses to #EndSARS protests in Nigeria suggest, governments that seek to suppress critical speech and protests in digital economy contexts continue to have varied means to suppress communication, including through traditional media, social media activities countering protestors' activities, violence, detention and imprisonment. The Nigerian government has appointed reform panels while repressing protestors through detention and other acts, including freezing bank accounts of protestors and their supporters and allies: "at least 20 activists and organizations have had their accounts frozen by the [Nigerian] Central Bank."[91] Government attempts to freeze protestors' bank accounts have led protestors to shift to use of Bitcoin,[92] which along with the booming cryptocurrency trade in Nigeria in recent years, may have contributed to the February 2021 decision of the Central Bank of Nigeria to direct financial institutions to close accounts of persons or entities transacting in or operating on cryptocurrency exchanges.

Nigerian government repression in response to the #EndSARS protests follows models of authoritarian governments outside of Africa. In China, for example, people have been detained and interrogated for posting on Twitter.[93] Although Twitter is officially blocked in China, people in China may use VPNs to access Twitter and other blocked websites.[94] Notably, Twitter has in the past run promoted tweets, a form of advertisement for which it is paid, by China Xinhua News, the largest state news agency, that spread disinformation about the violent nature of prodemocracy protests in Hong Kong and repression of Uighurs in western China.[95] In June 2020, Twitter removed more than 20,000 accounts linked to the Chinese government that were promoting the Chinese government response to COVID-19. China uses sophisticated methods of monitoring and surveillance both inside and outside of China.[96] Thus far, governments in Africa that seek to block protests and social media communications have tended to use blunter technological methods to suppress speech, including through use of surveillance, social media blackouts, and internet shutdowns.

The use of Twitter to spread information, communicate alternative messages, and monitor election results highlights how Twitter has become deeply embedded in contemporary communicative activities. The creation of the Nigerian-based Twitter hashtag #BringBackOurGirls in April 2014 vividly demonstrates the potential impact and limitations of disruptive technologies in Africa. The #BringBackOurGirls hashtag became a global phenomenon. This campaign was a direct response to the 2014 kidnappings of over 250 young women from a school by the Nigerian Islamist extremist group Boko Haram. The Boko Haram insurgency has escalated in recent years, from an "internal security problem into a massive political, economic and social disaster."[97] As of October 9, 2020, the Council for Foreign Relations Global Conflict Tracker estimated that since May 2011, more than 37,500 people have been killed by Boko Haram, with more than 2.5 million displaced people in the Lake Chad Basin, where Boko Haram is primarily based, and an estimated 244,000 Nigerian refugees in neighboring countries.[98] Boko Haram and other insurgency movements in Nigeria reflect, and are in part an outcome of, persistent poverty resulting from corruption, poor governance, and broader institutional failures in

Nigeria.[99] Despite the fact that Nigeria is now the largest economy in Africa, many Nigerians are poorer today than at independence, and the northeast region where the Boko Haram insurgency emerged is among the poorest and made even poorer in the aftermath of Boko Haram's activities.

#BringBackOurGirls, which emerged in the context of wider institutional and governance failures in Nigeria, as well a perceived government lack of response to the kidnappings in Chibok, highlights the power of social networking for varied purposes. The kidnapped young women who inspired the #BringBackOurGirls campaign were not immediately rescued and only some fifty had escaped by late 2014. As of April 2020, 112 young women were still missing. #BringBackOurGirls has also drawn greater attention to the human toll of Boko Haram kidnappings: more than 2,000 young women were likely kidnapped in Nigeria by Boko Haram from early 2014 to early 2015, with many being forced into sexual slavery.[100] In 2020, The #BringBackOurGirls movement and 164 women's groups in Nigeria asked the Nigerian government to rescue all girls abducted by Boko Haram and address the continued abductions of women and girls, including an abduction in Borno state in late June of 2020.

#EndSARS and #BringBackOurGirls highlight the interaction of the local and global in digital economy contexts. Digital economy technologies facilitate the establishment of local and transnational networks,[101] which interface in African countries with pre-digital-era networks that reflect a colonial imprint. Colonialism shaped internal and external networks throughout Africa in important ways that continue to reverberate in the digital era. During colonialism, physical and knowledge infrastructures had an external orientation. Physical infrastructures, including roads and railways, reflected a mine-to-port routing to facilitate extraction of natural resources.[102] In contrast to the outward direction of physical infrastructures flows of natural resources, formal flows of knowledge involved borrowings that reflected patterns of borrowings involving external domination to a significant degree. Trade reflected an outward flow of raw materials and inward flow of manufactured goods that Walter Rodney characterized as a core aspect of underdevelopment in Africa.[103] These flows and infrastructures have led to a characteristic network design throughout Africa that has resulted in limited internal networked connectivity within Africa. This limited internal connectivity has reinforced the externalized nature of colonial networks to the present day. This externalized networked interconnectivity, which led to pervasive zones of economic and other types of exclusion of many local people in African colonies during colonialism, has not fundamentally been disrupted, even long after the end of formal colonialism.

Colonial policy design reflects choices about policy tools to achieve particular goals that were largely external in derivation and orientation. In addition, colonial policy design did not reflect an approach that is consistent with good governance or an approach that a robust internally focused policy decision-making process would entail. An internally focused policy design approach would entail "the conscious and deliberate effort to define policy aims and map them instrumentally to policy tools that aim to achieve those goals ... policy design signifies a particular type of policy formulation that involves activities like collecting knowledge about the outcomes of a policy instrument use on policy targets and analyzing its relevance to the creation and implementation of policies meant to attain specific policy goals and aspirations."[104]

Although elites in many African countries may continue to benefit from a colonial legacy of externalized network design, the essentially externalized features of colonial policy design have contributed to the widespread poverty, exclusion, and marginalization of the vast majority of the population in countries such as Nigeria. Jenna Burrell uses the term *invisible users* to characterize experiences of marginality among youths in internet cafés in Ghana.[105] The invisibility ascribed to such youths by Burrell reflects an existence of many marginalized people as imperceptible to those designing policies in many African countries. The limited vision of policymakers goes along with a persistent lack of data about key population statistics in many African countries.

Many local people thus continue to be excluded from access to the benefits of existing externally focused networks developed during colonialism. These networks were never designed to facilitate opportunities for the vast majority of local people in former colonies in Africa. Rather, the design of most colonies in Africa was for the benefit of colonizers and a selected group of local intermediaries and beneficiaries. As a result, a scarcity of opportunity is pervasive in Nigeria and other former colonies in Africa. This scarcity of opportunity limits access for many to education, housing, electricity, clean water, healthcare, employment, economic possibilities, and other things.

Disrupting colonial policy choices would facilitate inclusion and potentially reduce marginalization within Africa and the global marginalization of African countries. Patterns of internal inclusion "tell us something about the complex role of the state in governing and managing poverty and inequality."[106] Although technology may offer potential for giving those without access to wider networks and potential opportunities,[107] technologies spread in environments infused with past design choices that themselves influence the impact of such technologies. Consequently, technologies alone are unlikely to disrupt past networks and policy design choices. These policy design choices, as reflected in varied physical and knowledge infrastructures, including legal frameworks, must be disrupted.

GLOBAL TECHNOLOGY COMPANIES AND DIGITAL COLONIALISM

In late 2015 and early 2016, a controversy erupted that connected Facebook, India, and colonialism. This controversy concerned the Facebook Free Basics program, which at the time offered free stripped down internet access in an estimated thirty countries. In 2016, Facebook Free Basics provided free internet access through a platform that allowed access to thirty-six bookmarked sites and Facebook. Facebook decided which sites were to be included in this platform.[108] Facebook's Internet.org initiative was launched in 2013 to make stripped down internet access available at no cost through an app, and was presented by Facebook as a philanthropic effort, reflected in the Facebook's decision to use the .org top-level domain,[109] which is often associated with nonprofits. Internet.org launched in Zambia in 2014 in partnership with local carrier Airtel, which provided free access with the hope that Zambians would buy prepaid data through the app to explore the Internet.[110] In 2015, Facebook, in "rebranded Internet.org as 'FreeBasics'."[111] By 2016, Facebook Free Basics had reached 25 million people with 500 apps available in thirty-seven countries.[112]

At the time of the controversy in India, Facebook Free Basics explicitly branded itself as targeting people who might otherwise have limited or no internet access.[113] Although attempts to target people with access to fewer opportunities than others in their societies are laudable in theory, this type of *poverty* branding may obscure the actual impact of the Free Basics program. Much like the civilizing mission of past imperialists and colonialists, Facebook Free Basics is an initiative to improve the circumstances of the disadvantaged by offering services that are related to core services from which Facebook and its local partners will benefit. Furthermore, as was often the case during colonialism, the activities of those with civilizing or improving missions often do not take sufficient account of the structural and institutional factors that lead to many lacking access to opportunities in far too many contexts.

Free Basics generated significant opposition in India. Many people in India did not uncritically accept Facebook's positioning of Free Basics' stated improvement mission. One skeptic described Facebook's initiative as follows: "what Zuckerberg means by internet for all, is essentially Facebook for all, along with a few non-profit services thrown in to give it the appearance of philanthropy, and maybe a few co-opted competitors to make it appear as if it isn't about Facebook only . . . Internet.org allows Facebook to increase its dominance and get new users hooked on the service."[114] Of particular concern was the potential for Facebook to hinder competition and dominate the social networking space in India.[115] Facebook's plan led more than 500 people, including technology entrepreneurs, and start-up founders and employees, to sign a letter to Indian Prime Minister Narendra Modi arguing that the Indian government should be "strongly in support of safeguarding of the principle of Net Neutrality".[116]

Under Facebook's plan, Internet.org would permit some commercial services selected by Facebook to be offered for free on its platform, which would mean excluding competitors of selected firms and thus subsidizing firms chosen by Facebook.[117] Opponents of Free Basics in India included a group of activists who, under the banner of Save the Internet, successfully convinced the public of the importance of net neutrality: "[t]he SaveTheInternet.in website pulled off a staggering achievement in the area of online public participation when it managed to garner 1 million email submissions to the Telecom Regulatory Authority of India (TRAI) in 12 days, pleading the case for net neutrality."[118] #SaveTheInternet became a top trending hashtag on Twitter. After temporarily suspending Free Basics in November 2015, in early 2016, TRAI adopted a new set of regulations, Prohibition of Discriminatory Tariffs for Data Services Regulations 2016,[119] which prohibit discriminatory pricing on the basis of content,[120] using principles of net neutrality as a justification for the prohibition. This set of regulations meant that Facebook Basics could not operate as planned in India. The Save the Internet movement represents a successful response to global technology company practices that had potential to have significant internal impact. Many hailed this online social movement as a victory for democratic process.[121]

Mark Zuckerberg responded to the setback in India indicating: "[w]hile we're disappointed with today's decision, I want to personally communicate that we are committed to keep working to break down barriers to connectivity in India and around the world ...[c]onnecting India is an important goal we won't give up on, because more than a billion people in India don't have access to the internet. We know that connecting them can lift people out of poverty, create millions of jobs and spread education opportunities. We care about these people, and that's why we're so committed to connecting them."[122]

Around the same time as Mark Zuckerberg's Facebook post, a member of Facebook's Board of Directors also responded to the situation in India with a tweet that generated yet more controversy. Marc Andreessen, a celebrated venture capitalist who was a founder of the early internet pioneer Netscape, weighed in on Twitter about the Indian regulatory action, tweeting: "[a]nti-colonialism has been economically catastrophic for the Indian people for decades. Why stop now?"[123] Andreessen's tweet, not surprisingly, led to an internet eruption. He soon deleted the tweet and issued statements about his opposition to colonialism. Within a day, Facebook CEO Mark Zuckerberg had issued a statement distancing Facebook from the Andreessen tweet and indicating that he found the Andreessen comments to be deeply upsetting and not representative of Facebook,[124] although not so upsetting that Andreessen was penalized in any visible way. Andreessen, who joined the Facebook board in June 2008, remained a member of the board as of November 2020.

This controversy about modern-day technologies highlights themes of enduring relevance in arenas of the colonized, particularly in relation to civilizing missions, civilizing protagonists, and the local environments within which missionaries and bringers of civilization may act. This is particularly true in cases where external powers, be they colonialists of earlier eras or digital economy purveyors of free things, are narrow in background and orientation and purport to fulfill local needs through a largely external lens. Like their colonial predecessors, Silicon Valley companies are remarkably homogenous, particularly at the highest levels of companies. One critic connected homogeneity in Silicon Valley to events in India: "[Rohit] Sharma saw it as part of a broader issue of homogeneity in Silicon Valley, a region run by a narrow set of oligarchs who famously eschew hiring women or people of color."[125]

Underlying Silicon Valley attitudes toward women and people of color are apparent in employment decisions. At Google, for example, Andy Rubin, the creator of the Android mobile operating system, was permitted to resign from Google in October 2014 with an exit package of $90 million, despite having been accused of sexual misconduct based on claims that Google investigated and found credible.[126] Google praised Rubin and protected him and two other executives accused of sexual misconduct, firing the other two senior executives, but paying them millions of dollars upon their departure, despite having no legal obligation to pay Rubin or the other two employees.[127] In December 2020, Google fired Timnit Gebru, a computer scientist born in Ethiopia whose family is from Eritrea, which gained independence from Ethiopia in 1993 after a thirty-year war. Before her firing, Gebru was technical coleader of the Ethical Artificial Intelligence Team at Google. Gebru attributes her firing to her "criticizing [Google's] approach to minority hiring and the biases built into today's artificial intelligence systems" and in a tweet noted that she was summarily fired due to an email she sent to a listserv that included Google employees.[128] The contrast between the treatment of Rubin and Gebru is striking and reflective of broader patterns related to diversity and inclusion at Google and other prominent digital technology companies.

Varied forms of exclusion shape the technology that is developed by digital economy companies. Digital technologies may facilitate patterns of demeaning representations and exclusion that have long been evident in pre-digital-era contexts. For example, digital blackface has become a pervasive feature of digital worlds. In 2017, FaceApp, a photo editing app that offers a number of filters through which to edit photos, was forced to pull a functionality that permitted digital blackface.[129] This digital blackface option, like the Bob Marley Snapchat filter from 2016 which gave an option for "instant" blackface,[130] is a digital-era manifestation of imagery connected to a long history of demeaning representations of people of African descent.

Simultaneously with pervasive misrepresentations of people of African descent, digital economy companies have engaged in continuing patterns of exclusion in critical contexts in which technologies are conceptualized, created, tested, and deployed. Algorithmic biases, which may be a product of various things, including biases that mirror real-world biases, pervade decision-making within digital economy firms.[131] Facial recognition and voice recognition technologies often fail to recognize women and people with dark skin and African American voices, which reflects continuing patterns of exclusion.[132]

Technologies may also embed cultural assumptions that reflect their sources of origin. The impact of cultural assumptions may not be sufficiently considered when technologies are developed, tested, and deployed. In 2016, Microsoft deployed an AI chatbot named Tay via Twitter. Tay was targeted at millennials and was described as an experiment in "conversational understanding, [that] was designed to engage people in dialogue through tweets or direct messages, while emulating the style and slang of a teenage girl."[133] The creators of Tay expected Tay to learn to sound like the Internet: "[t]he plan was to release Tay online, then let the bot discover patterns of language through its interactions, which she would emulate in subsequent conversations. Eventually, her programmers hoped, Tay would sound just like the Internet."[134] Tay soon came to sound like a racist, sexist, and misogynist: "[w] ithin 16 hours of her release, Tay had tweeted more than 95,000 times, and a troubling percentage of her messages were abusive and offensive. Twitter users started registering their outrage, and Microsoft had little choice but to suspend the account . . . just a few hours after Tay was released, a post on the troll-laden bulletin board, 4chan, shared a link to Tay's Twitter account and encouraged users to inundate the bot with racist, misogynistic, and anti-Semitic language."[135]

The Tay chatbot reflects an astounding inattention to the context in which technologies are developed and released. Given the dominance of companies based in the United States in the technological arena, issues arising from the racial context in the United States are likely to appear in contexts of global technology usage globally. Of particular relevance in African contexts are forms of bias in decision-making by platform companies and other digital economy firms. Past and present racial attitudes about people of African descent are evident in a wide range of digital economy spaces, making algorithmic and other forms of digital economy bias a potentially pressing concern in African contexts.

These concerns extend beyond algorithmic bias. Decisions about acceptable content on Facebook reveal a narrow, US-centered cultural vision that is not surprising, given the lack of diversity within Facebook. Facebook posts have facilitated genocide in Myanmar and violence in Ethiopia. The narrow cultural vision of Facebook is also apparent within the United States, where Facebook discriminates and excludes in determining which posts on Facebook are acceptable and which are unacceptable.[136]

African countries could play a leading role in promoting better inclusion of people of African descent in digital technology contexts through purchasing decisions, and in the development of alternative technologies that correct existing biases in facial recognition and other technologies. Undertaking this role would require development of robust innovation policies that look critically at technology adoption and development, needs within Africa, and opportunities presented by existing gaps. Companies within Africa could also have a goal of identifying and taking advantage of opportunities presented by such gaps that would enhance local innovation ecosystems.

Responses to Facebook Free Basics and existing approaches to innovation in many African countries demonstrate the need for critical perspectives about externally developed technologies and the impact of such technologies. The reception of Facebook Free Basics outside of India has been less critical. In contrast to India, which banned Facebook Free Basics, in Africa, Free Basics has "expanded without much public scrutiny to some thirty-two countries."[137]

Nigeria is Facebook's largest market in Africa. During a visit to Nigeria in August 2016, Facebook CEO Mark Zuckerberg encountered an audience generally receptive to Facebook. The narrative surrounding Mark Zuckerberg's visit to Nigeria largely followed Facebook's script and highlighted Facebook in terms of the development and facilitation of start-up company ecosystems in Nigeria and in Africa more generally.[138] By emphasizing this narrative, discussions of Facebook and other digital economy companies in Nigeria and elsewhere in Africa may obscure important continuities in past, present, and likely future relationships between African countries and external powers, including both states and private actors: "[a]lthough Africa as a market may form an interesting narrative in the digital mobile phone industry, this has not changed its role as a supplier of raw materials for global capitalist innovations."[139] Facebook exemplifies the rise of companies, largely originating in the United States and to a significant degree in California's Silicon Valley, that have forged global digital empires that bear similarities to colonial empires of past years.[140] The activities of companies such as Facebook in India and countries in Africa take place within contexts defined by past relationships and histories of exploitation and colonialism.

The connection made by Indian netizens between Facebook Free Basics and colonial patterns and relationships underscores the fact that colonial hangovers, both in patterns of relationships and legal and other institutions, continue to put entrepreneurs and innovators in former colonies in Africa at significant disadvantage relative to companies such as Facebook that have emerged from the United States and other developed countries. The disadvantaged position of local entrepreneurs and innovators is marked in Africa, where existing institutions make it difficult for local entrepreneurs and innovators to even begin to compete with companies such as Facebook. Digital economy relationships highlight how colonial policies continue to resonate in many countries in Africa.

Notes

1. Steven Levy. "Zuckerberg in Africa." *Wired*, October 5, 2016, accessed October 23, 2020, www.wired.com/2016/10/zuckerberg-in-africa/.
2. Jeremy Horwitz. "Vodacom Launches Africa's First Commercial 5G Service in Lesotho." VentureBeat, August 27, 2018, accessed December 2, 2020, https://venturebeat.com/2018/08/27/vodacom-launches-africas-first-commercial-5g-service-in-lesotho/.
3. Daniel Michaels. "Europe is Falling Behind on 5G Rollout, Top Companies Warn." *Wall Street Journal*, September 18, 2020, accessed December 2, 2020, www.wsj.com/articles/europe-is-falling-behind-on-5g-rollout-top-companies-warn-11600408801.

4. GSM Association. 2020. *The Mobile Economy* 2020, p. 3, accessed December 2, 2020, www.gsma.com/mobileeconomy/wp-content/uploads/2020/03/GSMA_MobileEconomy 2020_Global.pdf.
5. Ibid. at 14.
6. Nigeria Evidence Act, 2011, https://nass.gov.ng/document/download/5945; High Court of Lagos State (Civil Procedure) Rules 2012, http://edojudiciary.gov.ng/wp-content /uploads/2016/10/Lagos-State-Of-Nigeria-High-Court-Civil-ProcedureRule-2012.pdf; Richmond Ekhosuehi Idaeho, Digitalisation of the Supreme Court: Way Forward for the Nigerian Legal Profession, ThisDay, February 27, 2018, accessed October 23, 2020, www.pressreader.com/nigeria/thisday/20180227/282046212589817.
7. Lessig, 2006: 5.
8. Headrick, 1981: 12.
9. Adas, 2015: xiv.
10. Churchill, 1902: 300.
11. Hailey, 1938.
12. Tilley, 2011: 4.
13. Ibid.
14. Ibid. at 12.
15. Cell, 1989: 486.
16. Stocking, 1968: 114; Tylor, 1871.
17. Bauer, 1963: 3.
18. Maine, 1861: 15, 20, 22, 25, 116, 121.
19. TNA CO 583/255/9.
20. Buchan, 2001: 144–145. For a discussion of the naming of Australia, see "How Was Australia Named?" The National Library of Australia, www.nla.gov.au/faq/how-was-australia-named.
21. Buchan, 2005: 2. As the case *Mabo* v. *Queensland*, 175 CLR 1 (1992), which overturned the doctrine of terra nullius in Australia, notes, "[t]o these territories the European colonial nations applied the doctrines relating to acquisition of territory that was terra nullius. They recognized the sovereignty of the respective European nations over the territory of 'backward peoples' and, by State practice, permitted the acquisition of sovereignty of such territory by occupation rather than by conquest." *Mabo* at ¶ 33.
22. Buchan, 2005: 3.
23. Banner, 2005: 101.
24. Pascoe, 2018: 9.
25. Ibid. at 7.
26. Williams, Wright, Crowther, and Denham, 2020.
27. Colonial Office, 1927: 5.
28. Kartik Akileswaran and Georgina Hutchinson. 2019. *Adapting to 4IR: Africa's Development in the Age of Automation*, p. 4. Tony Blair Institute for Global Change, accessed October 23, 2020, https://institute.global/sites/default/files/articles/Adapting-to-the-4IR-Africa-s-development-in-the-age-of-automation.pdf.
29. World Economic Forum. 2016. What is the Fourth Industrial Revolution?, accessed October 23, 2020, www.weforum.org/agenda/2016/01/what-is-the-fourth-industrial-revolution/.

30. Alex Konrad. "Andela Raises $24 Million from Mark Zuckerberg and Priscilla Chan's Fund to Train African Engineers." *Forbes*, June 16, 2016, www.forbes.com/sites/alexkonrad/2016/06/16/andela-raises-24-million-from-zuckerberg-chan-initiative-and-gv/#16ea12c411e0; Steve Lohr. "Start-Up Bets on Tech Talent Pipeline from Africa." *New York Times*, October 10, 2017, accessed October 23, 2020, www.nytimes.com/2017/10/10/business/andela-start-up-coding-africa.html.
31. At one point news articles described Andela as Africa-focused. Jake Bright. "Africa-Focused Andela cuts 400 Staff as it Confirms $50M in Revenue." TechCrunch, September 17, 2019, accessed October 23, 2020, https://techcrunch.com/2019/09/17/africa-focused-andela-cuts-400-staff-as-it-confirms-50m-in-revenue/.
32. www.crunchbase.com/organization/andela#section-overview and www.andela.com.
33. Jake Bright. "Andela CEO Confirms Staff Cuts as Layoffs Hit African Tech." TechCrunch, May 6, 2020, accessed October 23, 2020, https://techcrunch.com/2020/05/06/andela-ceo-confirms-staff-cuts-as-layoffs-hit-african-tech/.
34. Gretchen McCulloch. "Coding Is for Everyone—as Long as You Speak English." *Wired Magazine*, April 8, 2019, accessed October 24, 2020, www.wired.com/story/coding-is-for-everyoneas-long-as-you-speak-english/.
35. Christina Murillo, Why are most major programming languages only in English? Medium.com, March 9, 2019, https://medium.com/@cristina_9416/why-are-most-major-programming-languages-only-in-english-7ae2f6d256b1.
36. Ipala and Mbori, 2009.
37. Sharon Ronn. "How to Build Research-Focused Universities in Africa." QuartzAfrica, September 7, 2018, accessed October 23, 2020, https://qz.com/africa/1382151/africa-needs-research-universities-like-cape-town-makerere/.
38. United Nations Department of Economic and Social Affairs, Division for Sustainable Development, Chapter 35: Science for Sustainable Development, Section 3(b), Scientists and engineers are the key performers of R&D aimed at increasing the stock of knowledge and devising new applications in order to ensure sustainable development, accessed October 23, 2020, www.un.org/esa/sustdev/natlinfo/indicators/indisd/english/chapt35e.htm.
39. Drahos, 2002; UNESCO. R&D Data Release, June 28, 2018, accessed October 23, 2020, http://uis.unesco.org/en/news/rd-data-release.
40. Ezeh and Lu, 2019: 2.
41. Ibid.
42. Google and the IFC. 2020. e-Conomy Africa 2020, accessed November 16, 2020, p. 28, www.ifc.org/wps/wcm/connect/e358c23f-afe3-49c5-a509-034257688580/e-Conomy-Africa-2020.pdf?MOD=AJPERES&CVID=nmuGYF2.
43. According to World Bank figures, the total estimated SSA population in SSA in 2019 was 1,106,957,900, with an estimated population in Nigeria of 200,963,599. United States Census International Database gives an estimated 2020 population in Africa of 1,339,492,000, which would make Nigeria's population some 15 percent of the total population of Africa. The World Bank, Population, Total – Sub-Saharan Africa, https://data.worldbank.org/indicator/SP.POP.TOTL?locations=ZG; United States Census, International Database, Demographic Overview – UN – Africa, www.census.gov/data-tools/demo/idb/region.php?T=13&RT=0&A=aggregate&Y=2020&C=&R=110.

44. Yinka Adegoke. "Africa's internet economy is booming but it needs more homegrown software developers." QuartzAfrica, November 16, 2020, accessed November 16, 2020, https://qz.com/africa/1933529/africas-booming-internet-economy-needs-more-software-developers/.
45. Google and the IFC, *supra* note 42, at 39.
46. Mavhunga, 2014: 5.
47. Burrell, 2012: 7–8.
48. Adam Minter. "The Burning Truth Behind an E-Waste Dump in Africa." *Smithsonian Magazine*, January 13, 2016, accessed October 23, 2020, www.smithsonianmag.com/science-nature/burning-truth-behind-e-waste-dump-africa-180957597/; Amy Yee. "Electronic Marvels Turn Into Dangerous Trash in East Africa." *New York Times*, May 12, 2019, accessed October 23, 2020, www.nytimes.com/2019/05/12/climate/electronic-marvels-turn-into-dangerous-trash-in-east-africa.html; Orisakwe et al., 2019.
49. Mavhunga, 2014: 7.
50. House of Commons, Digital, Culture, Media and Sports Committee. *Disinformation and 'Fake News': Final Report*. Eighth Report of Session, 2017-19, February 14, 2019, https://publications.parliament.uk/pa/cm201719/cmselect/cmcumeds/1791/1791.pdf.
51. Chrysalis L. Wright. "COVID-19 Fake News and Its Impact on Consumers. *Psychology Today*, April 30, 2020, accessed October 23, 2020, www.psychologytoday.com/us/blog/everyday-media/202004/covid-19-fake-news-and-its-impact-consumers.
52. Paul Mozur. "A Genocide Incited on Facebook, with Posts from Myanmar's Military." *New York Times*, October 15, 2018, accessed October 23, 2020, www.nytimes.com/2018/10/15/technology/myanmar-facebook-genocide.html?action=click&module=Top%20Stories&pgtype=Homepage.
53. David Gilbert. "Hate Speech on Facebook Is Pushing Ethiopia Dangerously Close to a Genocide." Vice.com, September 14, 2020, accessed October 23, 2020, www.vice.com/en/article/xg897a/hate-speech-on-facebook-is-pushing-ethiopia-dangerously-close-to-a-genocide.
54. Ibid.
55. Newley Purnell and Jeff Horwitz. "Facebook's Hate-Speech Rules Collide with Indian Politics." *Wall Street Journal*, August 14, 2020, accessed October 23, 2020, www.wsj.com/articles/facebook-hate-speech-india-politics-muslim-hindu-modi-zuckerberg-11597423346.
56. Kenney and Zysman, 2016.
57. Ibid.
58. Ibid.
59. Investigation of Competition in the Digital Marketplace: Majority Staff Report and Recommendations, Subcommittee on Antitrust, Commercial and Administrative Law of the Committee on the Judiciary, US House of Representatives, October 2020, accessed October 24, 2020, https://judiciary.house.gov/uploadedfiles/competition_in_digital_markets.pdf.
60. Complaint, *United States* v. *Google LLC*, Case 1:20-cv-03010, filed October 20, 2020, www.justice.gov/opa/press-release/file/1328941/download; Summary of Commission decision of 27 June 2017 relating to a proceeding under Article 102 of the Treaty on the Functioning of the European Union and Article 54 of the EEA Agreement (Case

AT.39740 – Google Search (Shopping)), accessed October 24, 2020, https://eur-lex.europa.eu/legal-content/EN/TXT/PDF/?uri=CELEX:52018XC0112(01)&from=EN; FTC ; Complaint, *Federal Trade Commission* v. *Facebook, Inc.*, Case No.: 1:20-cv-03590, filed January 21, 2021, www.ftc.gov/system/files/documents/cases/051_2021.01.21_revised_partially_redacted_complaint.pdf.

61. European Commission, Press Release – Antitrust: Commission sends Statement of Objections to Amazon for the use of nonpublic independent seller data and opens second investigation into its e-commerce business practices, November 10, 2020, accessed November 10, 2020, https://ec.europa.eu/commission/presscorner/detail/en/ip_20_2077.
62. Kenney and Zysman, 2016.
63. Cohen, 2017: 135, 157.
64. Rosenthal, 2018.
65. Tilley, 2011: 5.
66. Hailey, 1938: 263–264.
67. Kabir, 2011: 37.
68. Mike Miesen, Maeve Campbell, Chris Klang, Laura Manley and Emily Roseman. *Building a 21st Century Congress: Improving Congress's Science and Technology Expertise*. Harvard Kennedy School Belfer Center for Science and International Affairs, September, 2019, accessed October 23, 2020, www.belfercenter.org/sites/default/files/2019-09/ST/Building21stCenturyCongress.pdf.
69. Iwobi, 2019.
70. Iwobi, 2017: 15.
71. Martin Plaut. "Cambridge Analytica and the Digital War in Africa." NewStatesman, March 20, 2018, accessed October 23, 2020, www.newstatesman.com/world/2018/03/cambridge-analytica-facebook-elections-africa-kenya.
72. Nyabola, 2018: 160.
73. Regulation (EU) 2016/679 of the European Parliament and of the Council of 27 April 2016. Official Journal of the European Union. May 5, 2016, https://eur-lex.europa.eu/legal-content/EN/TXT/PDF/?uri=CELEX:32016R0679.
74. Nigeria Data Protection Regulation. National Information Technology Development Agency. January 2019, https://nitda.gov.ng/wp-content/uploads/2019/01/Nigeria%20Data%20Protection%20Regulation.pdf.
75. Aissatou Sylla and Alex Ford-Cox. "Overview of Data Protection Laws in Africa." Hogan Lovells, October 14, 2019, accessed October 23, 2020, www.lexology.com/library/detail.aspx?g=82196d1c-2faa-43c2-983b-be3b0f1747f2.
76. Nigerian Data Protection Bill, 2020, www.nimc.gov.ng/docs/Draft_Data_Protection_Bill_2020.pdf.
77. Cybercrimes (Prohibition, Prevention, Etc) Act, 2015, Explanatory Memorandum, www.cert.gov.ng/ngcert/resources/CyberCrime__Prohibition_Prevention_etc_Act_2015.pdf.
78. Peter Nkanga. "How Nigeria's Cybercrime Law Is Being Used to Try to Muzzle the Press." Committee to Protect Journalists, September 21, 2016, accessed October 23, 2020, https://cpj.org/2016/09/how-nigerias-cybercrime-law-is-being-used-to-try-t/.
79. Issues related to platform governance have been discussed by many, including Robert Gorwa and Frank Pasquale. Gorwa, 2019; Pasquale, 2018.

80. Uwagbale Edward-Ekpu. "Facebook and Instagram made missteps on Nigeria's EndSARS protest while Twitter boosted it." QuartzAfrica, October 24, 2020, accessed October 24, 2020, https://qz.com/africa/1922372/facebook-hurt-nigerias-endsars-protest-while-twitter-boosted-it/.
81. Ibid.
82. Ajeck Mangut, Angela Dewan and Nada Bashir. "Nigeria threatens CNN with sanctions but provides no evidence Lekki toll gate investigation is inaccurate." CNN.com, November 19, 2020, accessed November 19, 2020, www.cnn.com/2020/11/19/africa/nigeria-shooting-lekki-toll-gate-investigation-response-intl/index.html.
83. Weller, Bruns, Burgess, and Mahrt, 2013; Murthy, 2013.
84. Zhao, 2011: 12.
85. Karikari, Kwame. "African Media Breaks 'Culture of Silence'." *Africa Renewal*, May 2010, accessed October 23, 2020, www.un.org/africarenewal/magazine/august-2010/african-media-breaks-%E2%80%98culture-silence%E2%80%99-0.
86. Rick Gladstone and Megan Specia. "Nigeria's Police Brutality Crisis: What's Happening Now." *New York Times*, November 14, 2020, accessed November 14, 2020, www.nytimes.com/article/sars-nigeria-police.html.
87. Human Rights Watch. Nigeria: Crackdown on Police Brutality Protests. October 16, 2020, accessed October 23, 2020, www.hrw.org/news/2020/10/16/nigeria-crackdown-police-brutality-protests#.
88. Fighting Police Brutality and Media Silence, TechCabal Daily, October 21, 2020, accessed October 23, 2020, https://techcabal.com/2020/10/21/techcabal-daily-media-silence/.
89. National Broadcasting Commission, www.nbc.gov.ng/.
90. TechCabal Daily, *supra note* 88.
91. Ruth Maclean. "Nigeria Goes on Offensive Against Youth Protesting Police Brutality." *New York Times*, November 13, 2020, accessed November 13, 2020, www.nytimes.com/2020/11/13/world/africa/Nigeria-EndSARS-protests.html.
92. Yomi Kazeem. "How bitcoin powered the largest Nigerian protests in a generation." QuartzAfrica, October, 26, 2020, accessed October 26, 2020, https://qz.com/africa/1922466/how-bitcoin-powered-nigerias-endsars-protests/.
93. Paul Mozur. "Twitter Users in China Face Detention and Threats in New Beijing Crackdown." *New York Times*, January 10, 2019, accessed October 23, 2020, www.nytimes.com/2019/01/10/business/china-twitter-censorship-online.html.
94. VPNs or virtual private networks are encrypted connections over the Internet from a device to a network that prevent unauthorized people from eavesdropping on the traffic. Cisco, What is a VPN? – Virtual Private Network, accessed October 23, 2020, www.cisco.com/c/en/us/products/security/vpn-endpoint-security-clients/what-is-vpn.html.
95. Ryan Gallagher. "Twitter Helped Chinese Government Promote Disinformation on Repression of Uighurs." *Intercept*, August 19, 2019, accessed October 23, 2020, https://theintercept.com/2019/08/19/twitter-ads-china-uighurs/; Matthew Ingram. "Facebook and Twitter Profit from Chinese Propaganda." *Columbia Journalism Review*, August 29, 2019, accessed October 23, 2020, www.cjr.org/the_media_today/facebook-twitter-china.php.
96. Danny O'Brien. "China's Global Reach: Surveillance and Censorship Beyond the Great Firewall." Electronic Frontier Foundation, October 10, 2019, accessed October 23, 2020,

www.eff.org/deeplinks/2019/10/chinas-global-reach-surveillance-and-censorship-beyond-great-firewall.

97. Amnesty International. *'Our Job is to Shoot, Slaughter and Kill': Boko Haram's Reign of Terror in North-East Nigeria*. London: Amnesty International Ltd. April 15, 2015, accessed October 24, 2020, www.amnesty.org/download/Documents/AFR4413602015ENGLISH.PDF.
98. www.cfr.org/global-conflict-tracker/conflict/boko-haram-nigeria.
99. International Crisis Group, 2014: 2–6.
100. Anna Leach. "Six months after Chibok Mass Abduction, 'The World Has Moved On'." *Guardian*, October 13, 2014, accessed October 24, 2020, www.theguardian.com/global-development-professionals-network/2014/oct/13/nigeria-chibok-schoolgirl-abduction-kidnap-bringbackourgirls.
101. Benkler, 2006.
102. French, 2014: 4.
103. Rodney, 1972.
104. Howlett, 2019: 3.
105. Burrell, 2012: 7.
106. Roy, 2018: 19.
107. Jenna Burrell's study of urban youth in internet cafés in Accra, Ghana notes the "general shared view among these youths of the Internet as a mechanism for expanding one's social network, specifically in order to acquire foreign contacts." Burrell, 2012: 3.
108. Rahyul Bhatia. "The Inside Story of Facebook's Biggest Setback. *Guardian*, May 12, 2016, accessed October 24, 2020, www.theguardian.com/technology/2016/may/12/facebook-free-basics-india-zuckerberg.
109. Jessi Hempel. "What Happened to Facebook's Grand Plan to Wire the World? *Wired*, May 17, 2018, accessed October 24, 2020, www.wired.com/story/what-happened-to-facebooks-grand-plan-to-wire-the-world/.
110. Josh Constine. "Internet.Org's App with Free Access to Facebook, Google, Wikipedia, Local Info Launches in Zambia. techcrunch.com, July 31, 2014, accessed October 24, 2020, https://techcrunch.com/2014/07/31/internet-org-app/.
111. Mukerjee, 2016: 359.
112. Nellie Bowles. "Facebook's 'Colonial' Free Basics Reaches 25 Million People – Despite Hiccups. *Guardian*, April 12, 2016, accessed October 24, 2020, www.theguardian.com/technology/2016/apr/12/facebook-free-basics-program-reach-f8-developer-conference.
113. Facebook Free Basics, accessed October 24, 2020, https://web.archive.org/web/20160413072449/https://info.internet.org/en/story/free-basics-from-internet-org/; Andrew Hutchinson. "The internet.org Debate and the Important Role it Plays in Facebook's Future." Socialmediatoday.com, January 15, 2016, accessed October 24, 2020, www.socialmediatoday.com/social-networks/internetorg-debate-and-important-role-it-plays-facebooks-future; Our Impact, accessed October 24, 2020, https://web.archive.org/web/20160312143434/https://info.internet.org/en/impact/.
114. Nikhil Pahwa. "What Mark Zuckerberg Didn't Say about Internet.org." Medianama, October 10, 2014, accessed October 24, 2020, www.medianama.com/2014/10/223-zuckerberg-india-internet-org/.

115. Ibid.
116. Save the Internet, January 26, 2016, accessed October 24, 2020, https://pixr8.com/news/an-open-letter-to-prime-minister-of-india-from-tech-startups-to-save-the-internet/. The term *network* or *net neutrality* was coined by law professor Tim Wu, who used it to describe a set of principles under which internet services providers and governments should treat all data on the Internet in the same manner and not discriminate against or charge different fees for varied modalities of use, including from differences among users, platforms, applications, and other factors.
117. Rahyul Bhatia. "The Inside Story of Facebook's Biggest Setback." *Guardian*, May 12, 2016, accessed October 24, 2020, www.theguardian.com/technology/2016/may/12/facebook-free-basics-india-zuckerberg.
118. Mukerjee, 2016: 359.
119. Telecom Regulatory Authority of India, No. 2 of 2016, February 8, 2016 (Prohibition of Discriminatory Tariffs for Data Services), accessed October 24, 2020, https://trai.gov.in/sites/default/files/Regulation_Data_Service.pdf.
120. Ibid. at Chapter 2, Section 3(1) ("No service provider shall offer or charge discriminatory tariffs for data services on the basis of content.").
121. Mukerjee, 2016: 359–360.
122. Mark Zuckerberg Facebook Post, February 8, 2016 at 7:15 pm, accessed October 24, 2020, https://m.facebook.com/story.php?story_fbid=10102641883915251&id=4&_ft_=top_level_post_id.1693808464230721%3Atl_objid.1693808464230721%3Athid.1651122061832695%3A306061129499414%3A3%3A0%3A1483257599%3A8613020229387056159&__tn__=C.
123. Nellie Bowles. "Why is Silicon Valley so 'tone deaf' to India?" *The Guardian*, February 12, 2016, accessed October 24, 2020, www.theguardian.com/technology/2016/feb/11/marc-andreessens-colonialism-tweet-silicon-valley-facebook-india.
124. Mark Zuckerberg Facebook Post, February 10, 2016, accessed October 24, 2020, www.facebook.com/zuck/posts/10102645335962321.
125. Bowles, *supra* note 123.
126. Daisuke Wakabayashi and Katie Benner. "How Google Protected Andy Rubin, the 'Father of Android'." *New York Times*, October 25, 2018, accessed December 2, 2020, www.nytimes.com/2018/10/25/technology/google-sexual-harassment-andy-rubin.html.
127. Ibid.
128. Cade Metz and Daisuke Wakabayashi. "Google Researcher Says She Was Fired Over Paper Highlighting Bias in A.I." *New York Times*, December 3, 2020, accessed December 3, 2020, www.nytimes.com/2020/12/03/technology/google-researcher-timnit-gebru.html. In her tweet, Gebru noted "I was fired by @JeffDean for my email to Brain women and Allies. My corp account has been cutoff. So I've been immediately fired :-)", https://twitter.com/timnitGebru/status/1334352694664957952, 11:24 pm, December 2, 2020.
129. Alex Hern. "FaceApp Forced to Pull 'Racist' Filters That Allow 'Digital Blackface'." *Guardian*, August 10, 2017, accessed October 24, 2020, www.theguardian.com/technology/2017/aug/10/faceapp-forced-to-pull-racist-filters-digital-blackface.
130. Sophie Kleeman. "Snapchat's Offensive 'Bob Marley' Filter Gives You Instant Blackface." Gizmodo.com, April 20, 2016, accessed October 24, 2020, https://gizmodo.com/snapchat-s-offensive-bob-marley-filter-gives-you-inst-1772008981.
131. Baer, 2019; Noble, 2018; Buolamwini and Gebru, 2018.

132. Patrick Grother, Mei Ngan & Kayee Hanaoka. *Face Recognition Vendor Test (FRVT) Part 3: Demographic Effects*, NISTIR 8280, National Institute of Standards, December 2019, accessed October 24, 2020, https://nvlpubs.nist.gov/nistpubs/ir/2019/NIST.IR.8280.pdf; Allison Koenecke, Andrew Nam, Emily Lake, Joe Nudell, Minnie Quartey, Zion Mengesha, Connor Toups, John R. Rickford, Dan Jurafsky and Sharad Goel. "Racial Disparities in Automated Speech Recognition Systems." Proceedings of the National Academy of Sciences, March 23, 2020, accessed October 24, 2020, www.pnas.org/content/early/2020/03/17/1915768117.
133. Oscar Schwartz. "In 2016, Microsoft's Racist Chatbot Revealed the Dangers of Online Conversation." *IEEE Spectrum*, November 25, 2019, accessed October 24, 2020, https://spectrum.ieee.org/tech-talk/artificial-intelligence/machine-learning/in-2016-microsofts-racist-chatbot-revealed-the-dangers-of-online-conversation.
134. Ibid.
135. Ibid.; Sophie Kleeman. "Here Are the Microsoft Twitter Bot's Craziest Racist Rants." Gizmodo.com, March 24, 2016, accessed October 24, 2020, https://gizmodo.com/here-are-the-microsoft-twitter-bot-s-craziest-racist-ra-1766820160.
136. Julia Angwin and Hannes Grassegger. "Facebook's Secret Censorship Rules Protect White Men from Hate Speech But Not Black Children." ProPublica, June 28, 2017, accessed October 23, 2020, www.propublica.org/article/facebook-hate-speech-censorship-internal-documents-algorithms.
137. Notais, 2020.
138. Yomi Kazeem. "Mark Zuckerberg is on a Surprise Visit to Nigeria, Facebook's largest African Market." QuartzAfrica, August 30, 2016, accessed October 24, 2020, https://qz.com/africa/770002/mark-zuckerberg-is-in-nigeria-facebooks-largest-african-market/.
139. Oyedemi, 2019: 2046.
140. LaFrance, 2016.

7

Nigerian Princes, Start-Up Companies, and Potential Future Paths

"[A]fter you register your own company, you must find a white man ... doors will open for you because you have an oyinbo General Manager."

Chiamamanda Ngozi Adichie, *Americanah* (2013)

Oyinbo. Definition: white people. Example: see that oyinbo for there.

Naijalingo.com – A Nigerian Pidgin English Dictionary

DISRUPTION, NIGERIAN PRINCES, AND START-UP COMPANIES

Start-up companies have become emblematic of the digital economy. Significant investments have been made in start-up companies all over the world, leading some commentators to suggest that an *app* boom valuation bubble had developed by 2019. This boom was thought to be evident in valuations for start-ups and other companies that were too high relative to the actual value of such companies.[1]

In March 2019, Jumia, an online retailer with significant presence in Africa,[2] went public on the New York Stock Exchange. By going public, Jumia changed from a private company, which would typically receive investments from a legally limited set of sophisticated and wealthy investors, including investment funds and corporate investors, to a public company whose stock could be purchased by anyone with the funds to do so. This event was heralded as an important moment for African countries' digital economy ecosystems. Jumia is a leading e-commerce company in Africa. Because it provides e-commerce services in Africa, Jumia is thought by many to be African. The identification of Jumia as an African or Nigerian company is strong, despite the fact that Jumia was formed in Germany and has end users and subsidiaries, but notably not core business operations, within Africa.

Jumia, which reached a $1 billion valuation in 2016, has been described as the first African technology unicorn.[3] Unicorns, which exist, at least in the technology arena, refer to private start-up companies with a valuation of more than $1 billion. Start-up companies, which are also referred to as emerging growth companies, are fledgling enterprises that have become a hallmark of the digital economy in many places, particularly Silicon Valley, which has become an epicenter of a digital economy that has spread to all regions of the world.[4] Start-up companies typically rely on private capital in their earliest days and have failure rates estimated to be as high as 90 percent.[5] Venture capitalists have traditionally been the primary investors in the start-up universe.[6]

On the surface, Jumia represents the IPO of an African e-commerce website and a watershed moment for African start-ups. Beneath the surface, however, the story of Jumia is more complex. Jumia reflects the interaction of the internal and external, as well as the likely impact of institutional limitations in business contexts in Nigeria and other countries in Africa.

As is the case with many start-up companies in Africa and elsewhere, Jumia, which was founded in 2012, started out by copying an existing model, notably the eBay auction marketplace. By 2017, with inspiration from Instagram, Jumia had changed its business model to an online social shopping site.[7] By the time of its IPO,[8] Jumia had become the largest e-commerce company operating in Africa, which is notable. At the time of its IPO, Jumia operated in fourteen countries, including Nigeria, Egypt, Cameroon, Ghana, Ivory Coast, Senegal, Algeria, Morocco, Tunisia, Kenya, Rwanda, Tanzania, Uganda, and South Africa.[9] Jumia later exited its operations in Cameroon, Rwanda, and Tanzania.

Jumia Technologies AG, which went public in March 2019, was at the time of its IPO, actually headquartered in Berlin, Germany, with technology operations in Porto, Portugal, and administrative function teams based in Dubai, UAE.[10] Jumia Technologies AG is a holding company and appears to operate in Africa through subsidiaries.[11] At the time of its IPO, Jumia's financial statements listed some seventy subsidiaries, including seven subsidiaries in Nigeria, Jumia's largest market.[12] At the time of its IPO, Jumia's German parent company owned 99 to 100 percent of its Africa-based consolidated subsidiaries, other than one or more subsidiary in each of Algeria, Angola, Egypt, and Zimbabwe, which suggests a minimal level of direct local ownership of Jumia's Nigerian subsidiaries.[13]

Tension between the internal and the external in Africa are apparent in Jumia's choice to establish itself as a German company and locate its technological, administrative, and holding company management operations outside of Africa. Nigeria and a number of other countries in Africa can be difficult places to do business. This is partially due to legal frameworks and legal processes that may not be clear and transparent. African legal systems also reflect considerable colonial overhang and persistent postcolonial inattention to the needs of small and medium enterprises (SMEs). The Jumia IPO Prospectus describes legal uncertainties doing business in Africa:

> Governments in Africa frequently intervene in the economies of their respective countries and occasionally make significant changes in policy and regulations [with] actions [that have involved] nationalizations and expropriations, price controls, currency devaluations, mandatory increases on wages and employee benefits,

capital controls and limits on imports . . . . In the future, the level of intervention by African governments may continue to increase . . . . Many countries in Africa have not yet developed a fully integrated legal system, and recently-enacted laws and regulations may not sufficiently cover all aspects of economic activities in such markets. In particular, the interpretation and enforcement of these laws and regulations involve uncertainties . . . . Many African legal systems are based in part on government policies and internal rules, some of which are not published on a timely basis, or at all, and may have retroactive effect. There are other circumstances where key regulatory definitions are unclear, imprecise or missing, or where interpretations that are adopted by regulators are inconsistent with interpretations adopted by a court in analogous cases. As a result, we may not be aware of our violation of certain policies and rules until after the violation. In addition, any administrative and court proceedings in Africa may be protracted, resulting in substantial costs and the diversion of resources and management attention.[14]

The uncertain legal and regulatory environment in Nigeria makes it more difficult than it should be for start-up companies to establish themselves as legal entities in Africa, obtain financing, operate, and grow on a large scale. In addition, this legal environment imposes significant costs on SMEs generally. As a result, far too much innovation and activities and practices of everyday people are consigned to the informal sector, not by choice but by necessity and institutional design. Financing gaps are also a pervasive problem. Conditions in many African countries, however, may lead to greater reliance on external sources of financing, which may import patterns of racial and other biases into African contexts.

A July 2020 posting at TechCabal, a digital media company based in Nigeria that describes itself as a "future-focused publication that speaks to African innovation and technology in depth,"[15] notes that the bias for the "white" pitch (i.e., a pitch seeking investor funding by companies where the founders are white) is evident in African contexts. For example, of seventeen companies that raised $1 million or more from venture capital in Kenya in 2019, only one was founded by locals, four by a mix of expatriates and locals, and eleven by expats only.[16] Some describe this funding situation as "another form of neo-colonialism."[17] The tendency to fund people other than Africans was highlighted in a July 2020 article in *The Guardian*, with the title "Silicon Valley has Deep Pockets for African Startups – If You're Not African."[18] This pattern replicates racial patterns and funding biases evident in Silicon Valley and other contexts.[19]

The establishment and growth of companies such as Jumia could provide impetus for needed changes in business and commercial law and other legal frameworks in Nigeria and other countries in Africa. Such changes might ease the path for local companies with regional, pan-African, or global prospects and facilitate the establishment of varied types of legal entities within Africa. This legal reform process, if implemented with care and attention to detail, could potentially benefit a broad range of people in Nigeria and elsewhere in Africa. Such reforms require strategies within African countries that blend the internal and the external in a flexible and hybrid way and that take account of past experience, present needs, and likely futures. Although start-up companies and entrepreneurship are increasingly celebrated in Nigeria, Kenya, and other countries in Africa,[20] the legal frameworks and reforms that might put start-ups and other small businesses in Africa on an even footing with externally based enterprises remain surprisingly elusive.[21]

Jumia's operations also raise significant questions about what it means to be an African company.[22] Short seller Citron Research made allegations in 2019 that Jumia is a fraud, describing Jumia as a Nigerian e-commerce company. Citron Research also referred to Nigerian Princes in a discussion of Jumia.[23] The reference to Nigerian Princes in the Citron Research report refers to a type of scam that has become associated with Nigeria.[24] The Nigerian Prince scam, which is used by people inside and outside of Nigeria, is likely the most famous digital economy "innovation" credited to Nigeria. Also referred to as advance fee or 419 scams (in reference to the section of the Nigerian criminal code that outlaws fraud), the Nigerian Prince scam involves a communication that solicits funds from the target of the communication as follows:

> They originate with e-mails to all sorts of people, usually from business and academic lists, claiming that millions of dollars reside in an overlooked account for shipment of some goods into or out of an African country. The sender asks for a person's help in transferring the money to a legitimate bank account outside Africa and will share a percentage of the frozen funds with the recipient of the message. The owner of the account is invariably dead.[25]

Many people all over the world have received these advance fee scam communications or may know people who have become enmeshed in an advance fee scam. The advance fee scam has contributed to global perceptions of Nigerians as scammers. In 1995, for example, former US Secretary of State Colin Powell referred to Nigerians as a group of *scammers*.[26] In late 2018, roughly around the same time as Jumia was preparing for its IPO, the US Department of Justice impaneled a grand jury in a fraud case that led to a 252-count indictment of 80, mostly Nigerian, nationals on charges related to international fraud and money laundering.[27] The Nigerian nationals in this case were alleged to be involved in schemes involving the "fraudulent transfer of at least $6 million in fraudulently-obtained funds . . . and the overall conspiracy was responsible for the attempted theft of at least an additional $40 million."[28]

The activities of advance fee scammers in Nigeria and elsewhere reflect a type of digital economy innovation that exists in certain spaces of unauthorized and in this instance illegal activities. These activities highlight types of negative disruption and negative consequences from disruption that may be ignored in discussions of innovation and disruption. Scammers in Nigeria, also referred to as Yahoo Boys, are one symptom of the scarcity of opportunity for many, including young people, in Nigeria: "Okechukwu Nnadi would not say that to be a scammer is the best career choice for a young Nigerian, but, he adds, it will do in a situation where young graduates like himself have little to no other career opportunities."[29]

In a digital economy in which hype and brand have become paramount, the association of the advance fee scam with Nigeria, justifiable or not, has fundamentally shaped perceptions of Nigeria in a negative way. This brand association of Nigeria with internet princes and fraud may also have implications for innovative Nigerian companies that seek to operate in seemingly more positive spaces of innovation. As the Jumia IPO prospectus notes, doing business in Nigeria through formal avenues can be difficult, which facilitates informal, and even illicit or illegal, activities.

In August 2019, some months after its IPO, Jumia disclosed that it had experienced internal fraud and legal threats, which would tend to fulfill expectations of those who associate Nigeria with scams.[30] Ironically, however, Jumia is best described as a company with operations in Africa, rather than as an African company. Jumia's status as an African company is more than just a question of naming and touches directly on longstanding problems in Africa about relationships with external models, external networks, and external powers. Jumia's structure also raises critical questions about where the benefits of Jumia's establishment and growth will flow and what types of tangible and other benefits from Jumia's activities will actually flow within Africa.

Although Jumia is described as an African company, and at times, a Nigerian company, media reports specify the founders of Jumia as French.[31] Jumia appears to have local staff within at least some of the countries where it operates, including CEOs of Jumia's Nigerian operations. A key question in assessing the overall impact of start-up companies in Africa requires attention to the flows of wealth that such companies generate. Although having successful digital economy companies with business operations on the ground in African countries is an important and positive step, wealth generation in start-up company ecosystems comes to a significant degree from the benefits that come with ownership of such entities. Start-up companies generally grant stock to founders at formation and, as they hire people, grant stock or options to employees as an incentive to retain high-quality and hard-working employees. The equity received by employees is often referred to as *sweat* equity because it essentially rewards the employees' labor, a form of nonmonetary investment.[32] In contrast, much of the funding for the growth and development of start-up companies is provided by venture capitalists and other investors who receive a share of equity in exchange for the provision of needed funds.

Start-up companies typically have one of three potential future paths. The vast majority fail. Start-ups that do not fail generally lead to two exit paths for their investors and employee stockholders: the company can either go public with an IPO or get acquired by another company or new investors. Patterns of start-up company share ownership have implications for the direction of wealth flows generated by acquisitions and IPOs of start-up companies. To the extent that local employees and local founders have an ownership stake in start-up companies operating in Africa, more particularly in the entity that actually goes public or is acquired, such local employees and founders based within Africa will likely benefit when such companies go public or are purchased. These benefits may flow into broader communities where such employees and founders are based. For many African start-ups, going public on a stock market in Africa may not be feasible. Nigeria-based financial technology (fintech) unicorn Interswitch, which is a leading company in the African digital payments space, reportedly delayed plans to go public until at least 2021.[33] The market for exits for start-ups in Africa is not well developed, which makes significant deals noteworthy. In October 2020, the global fintech company Stripe announced its acquisition of fintech company Paystack, a Nigerian payments start-up company, for over $200 million, which is slightly more than Visa paid in November 2019 to acquire 20 percent of Interswitch.[34] Paystack was the first Nigerian start-up company admitted to Y combinator,[35] the leading global start-up accelerator based in Silicon Valley.[36] The success of these two companies could help to redefine perceptions of technology spaces in Nigeria and Nigerian start-up companies.

The typical amount of equity ownership reserved for employees varies by company and region. One estimate suggests that some 50 percent of start-up companies in the United States reserve between 10 and 15 percent of their total capitalization for option pools.[37] Employee ownerships in start-up companies is typically higher in parts of the United States, particularly the San Francisco Bay Area and New York City, than elsewhere in the United States and the world.[38] At the time a start-up company goes public, its share ownership would typically reflect ownership of stock by outside investors, stock owned by founders, who typically receive their stock when the start-up company is formed, often at a low price, and stock options and/or stock granted to employees, directors, and others.[39] This structure of stock ownership in many start-up companies means that employees, who typically receive some type of equity ownership stake in the start-up company, may become quite wealthy when a company goes public or is purchased. The 2012 Facebook IPO created 10 billionaires and over 900 millionaires, at least on paper.[40] In 2013, Google purchased Waze, an Israeli social mapping start-up company with little or no revenue, for more than $1 billion. Each of Waze's 100 employees received an estimated $1.2 million as a result of the Google acquisition, which was at the time the most lucrative payout ever in the Israeli start-up ecosystem.[41]

The Jumia pre-IPO ownership structure may not leave much room for ownership by local staff, at least at the Jumia German holding company level. The Jumia IPO Prospectus indicates that just over 1 million shares were awarded as equity compensation to directors and employees in 2017 and 2018, which constituted just over 1 percent of Jumia's pre-IPO capitalization, while option and virtual restricted stock unit plans appear to constitute approximately 10 percent of Jumia's pre-IPO capitalization.[42] However, at the time of the Jumia IPO, some 41 percent of these option and virtual restricted stock plan units were granted to Jumia's founders,[43] which might leave just over 6 percent for others, who might include Jumia employees. More than 60 percent of the outstanding shares of Jumia prior to its IPO were owned by shareholders based in Europe, with only one shareholder with a greater than 5 percent ownership stake being based in Africa. That shareholder, Mobile Telephone Networks Holdings Limited, the owner of 29.7 percent of Jumia's pre-IPO share capitalization, is a wholly-owned subsidiary of MTN Group Limited, a South African multinational mobile telecommunications company (MTN).[44] MTN exited its Jumia investment in late October 2020, selling its 18.9 percent stake for $142 million in net proceeds.[45]

The identity of founders and shareholders matters in Africa, where external extraction of value has been a longstanding pattern. If the digital era is to be take root in Nigeria and other countries in Africa by companies, founders or shareholders largely based outside of Africa, the benefits of the digital economy will flow into countries within Africa in far more limited ways than might otherwise be the case. Jumia highlights that the digital economy can be an opportunity for transformation and disruption of existing patterns of external relations of Nigeria and other countries in Africa, which will be facilitated by legal reform of governance practices and laws affecting the landscape of available opportunities.[46] Alternatively, the digital economy can represent a continuation of past patterns and practices of uses of external models, external networks, and external relationships that result in benefits largely flowing outside of Africa, which would likely not enhance stability within countries in Africa.

Where start-up companies are based can also have implications for the development of capacity to enable others to establish, scale, and operate large-scale digital economy and other enterprises based in Africa. If Jumia and other companies that operate in Africa but are based elsewhere, including Andela, a software development company based in New York, and Zola Electric, a solar power company based in Silicon Valley, become characteristic digital economy models in Africa, the future of the digital economy within Africa will be fundamentally different from what it would be if such companies were developed to a greater extent within Africa. Externally based "African" companies may send a message that success, at least in some African contexts, requires being external to Africa.

As aspects of Jumia's operations suggest, the introduction of new technologies may mirror patterns of relationships established during colonialism when colonies that were externally defined and subject to unequal power relationships that facilitated significant extraction of wealth and resources. Although the externalized nature of colonial relationships has been widely discussed, such relationships continue to have an impact on patterns of relationships in the digital era. Rather than dividing geographic territory on a map, digital-era companies divide spheres of technological and commercial significance such as varied hardware configurations, software applications, and a variety of internet and social media business models that may be based on internet search algorithms and varied spaces of networked communication. Instead of establishing rights and spheres of influence over physical property as was the norm in earlier eras, digital-era companies establish rights of ownership in intangibles such as intellectual property. Not surprisingly, owners of rights in the digital era tend to be based in countries that were owners with established property rights over actual physical terrain in their roles as imperial and colonial powers in earlier times.

Many dominant digital-era companies were at one time themselves start-ups. However, despite their origins as small enterprises that grow and become large companies, such companies may play a role in exacerbating established relationships of dominance and inequality. In the United States, the impact of disruptive technologies is evident in the San Francisco Bay area, including Silicon Valley, which has been a key region in the world for the development, dissemination, and commercialization of disruptive and innovative technologies in recent decades. The success of Silicon Valley reflects the current global dominance of American technology companies and immense wealth that this dominance has generated. However, current debates in the city of San Francisco offer a warning sign for potential consequences of disruptive technologies in the broader social contexts within which such technologies may be deployed.

Disruptive technologies do not necessarily disrupt existing institutions. Patterns of disruption and nondisruption can illuminate key limitations of disruptive technologies and their impact. In the San Francisco Bay area, technological innovations have created immense wealth for some but have also contributed to greater socioeconomic inequality. Debates surrounding the cost of housing, the placement of bus stops that carry workers from San Francisco to Silicon Valley, dealing with human waste from the large number of homeless people on the streets of San Francisco, and other social concerns highlight points of tension that have emerged in the midst of immense wealth and prosperity, at least for some. With this has come notable new categories of employment, including the San Francisco Poop Patrol,[47] people employed by the City of San Francisco to clean up human waste from the large numbers of homeless people living on the streets of San Francisco.[48] The *Poop Patrol* approach, notably, does not provide homeless people with access to public toilets or affordable housing, both of which are likely necessary to truly address the problem of human feces in the streets.

NETWORKS, INFRASTRUCTURE, AND BIOMETRICS

Terminal 3 at Kotoka International Airport in Accra, Ghana, which opened in September 2018, is an impressive facility that some have called the "pride of Ghana." Traveling by air in much of sub-Saharan Africa (SSA) gives testament to infrastructural and other limitations that are commonplace in far too many African countries. Although Africa has 12 percent of the world's population, African countries in recent years have held less than 2 percent of world passenger aviation market and less than 1 percent of the cargo market.[49] It is often expensive and logistically difficult to fly within Africa due to protectionist legal and regulatory hurdles, inadequate infrastructure, high taxes, and nationalism that has exacerbated a lack of competition in some markets; further "[a]irlines trying to launch a new route between African nations need to first secure permission from both countries, which can be a lengthy and expensive prospect that may or may not involve significant bribes."[50] Difficulties in air transportation in Africa reflect broader patterns of networked relationships and decision-making that continue to play a role in impeding economic prosperity for many.

The modern infrastructure evident in the new terminal in Accra is not yet typical in Africa outside of a few markets such as South Africa. Notably, the Kotoka Airport terminal received support from airport Companies in both Ghana and South Africa. This collaborative effort resulted in a distinctively African world-class airport. The Kotoka Airport thus highlights what is possible within Africa.

The Kotoka Airport terminal highlights the extent to which past and present relationships have also fostered networks that continue to be defined to a significant degree by patterns of external relationships. This means that essential networks developed during colonialism have become a pattern upon which networks of relationships and infrastructures are based and developed anew. These networks are not uniformly formed.

As is the case with other networks in Africa, air transportation networks today reflect historic patterns of relationships between and among African countries and the rest of the world. Air transport networked connectivity within Africa is limited, while external air networks reflect a continuing colonial imprint. These networks reflect patterns that had become predominant during colonialism, when European powers became the center of networks formed with colonial possessions that fell under their sphere of influence with limited internal connectivity within Africa.

The patterns evident in air transportation networks are evident in a broad range of infrastructures. Land transportation and other infrastructure networks within Africa, including in relation to rail, port, electricity, and telecommunications, are also quite limited.[51] This makes trade within Africa expensive and often logistically difficult. These limited internal networks have led to limited economic relationships within African countries: much of African countries' trade today is with Europe, the United States, China, and emerging economies. Moreover, Africa's intraregional trade is well below that of most other regions; in 2017, intra-African exports were less than 17 percent of total formal trade, which was comparable to numbers for Latin America and the Caribbean, more than Oceania, but well below the 59 percent for intra-Asian, 68 percent for intra-European, and 31 percent for intra-Northern American trade.[52] These trade flows persist despite the presence of fourteen separate trading blocs within Africa with overlapping members.[53] The paucity of internal infrastructural and other networks of connectivity and actions within Africa make prospects for the 2019 African Continental Free Trade Agreement (AfCTA) less than optimal, unless significant attention is also paid to improving internal networks and infrastructures.[54]

These network patterns also reflect levels of capacity in many African countries. As was the case during colonialism, Africa still exports raw materials and imports manufactured goods. Much of the equipment for the Kotoka Airport was purchased outside of Africa. The airport has also put in place state-of-the-art biometric scanning and data collection instruments and procedures, largely developed by companies outside of Africa. In a promotional document, thyssenkrupp, the German multinational conglomerate, states that it played a "key role in equipping the new Terminal 3" and notes that it provided three new escalators, sixteen new high-tech elevators, and seven state-of-the-art passenger boarding bridges.[55] The e-immigration systems at Kotoka Airport were developed by Gemalto, an international digital security company with headquarters in Amsterdam, that was acquired in April 2019 by Thales Group, a French multinational company.[56] It is not yet clear whether Kotoka Airport will follow a pattern common during and after colonialism in which external parties have built infrastructure in Africa that is not, and likely cannot be, sustained locally. This pattern of externally sourced infrastructure development has contributed to persistent infrastructure deficits in many African countries.[57]

Entering into infrastructure arrangements with external parties that do not include the development of internal capacity to maintain and renew the infrastructure often results in infrastructure that cannot be properly maintained. This was evident in 2017 in Nigeria, when the Nnamdi Azikiwe International Airport in Abuja, Nigeria's capital city, was closed for some six weeks to repair the airport's sole runway, which had not been properly maintained.[58] As the acting general manager of corporate affairs for the Department for the Federal Airports Authority of Nigeria noted in 2017: "[p]roper maintenance should have been done, but it wasn't done."[59] This state of affairs is "a reflection of the poor performance of successive governments, none of which took up the task of resurfacing the runway after its lifespan ended in 2002."[60]

The closing of the Nnamdi Azikiwe International Airport in Abuja, Nigeria caused significant hardship and economic damage. However, Nigeria's infrastructure is generally not well maintained, which leads to inflexibility in dealing with circumstances such as closed airports. Attempts to find other potential paths for passengers flying to Abuja were hindered by poor facilities at the closest international airport at Kaduna, which typically has far fewer daily flights than the Nnamdi Azikiwe International Airport in Abuja. The Nigerian government had sought to direct planes and passengers to Kaduna Airport. Ethiopian Airlines was the only major airline to agree to fly to Kaduna instead of Abuja. Road transportation in Nigeria is often difficult and perilous. High levels of security were needed for redirected passengers on roads and trains to transit from another airport to Abuja by land. The poor state of the roads between Abuja and Kaduna and between Abuja and Lagos, which has a major international airport, made travel to other airports by land from Abuja during the airport closure challenging. The Abuja-Kaduna-Kano road is "famous for kidnappings and banditry in a region where nomadic herdsmen and farmers engage in frequent deadly clashes."[61]

A new terminal opened at Nnamdi Azikiwe International Airport in Abuja, Nigeria, in January 2019 – one of four new terminals being constructed by the China Civil Engineering and Construction Corporation (CCECC), a Chinese state construction company. The construction process, degree of local collaboration, extent to which the new airport reflects approaches focused on sustainability, and incorporation of processes to facilitate maintenance of the new infrastructure within Nigeria are not clear. These factors are likely to be important if experiences such as the Abuja airport runway closure are to be averted in the future.

The activities of the CCECC in Nigeria reflect a rising influence of China in infrastructure and other types of projects in Africa.[62] Airport development is surging across Africa,[63] and China has played a role in a number of airport projects. China's role in the aviation sector reflects the rise of what is likely the most important cluster of external networked relationships between African countries since the colonial era. In 2009, China became Africa's dominant trading partner.[64] The extent to which these new networks with China yield different results from those from earlier eras remains to be seen. Activities in Africa may be undertaken by varied actors based in China, including central state-owned enterprises and policy banks, provincial state-owned enterprises, private companies, and entrepreneurial or family firms.[65]

Relationships between China and Africa are transforming networks of external relationships of many African countries. The growing relationship between China and African countries is evident in air transportation networks: flights between China and Africa increased by 630 percent in the decade leading up to 2019, with average daily flights increasing from less than one per day in 2010 to an average of eight flights per day between China and Africa by 2019.[66] Much of this growth has been driven by Ethiopian Airlines, which had become the largest airline in Africa by 2020.[67] The growth of Ethiopian Airlines highlights the growing economic power of Ethiopia itself, which has been one of the fastest-growing countries in the world in recent years.

Kotoka Airport makes extensive use of biometrics. Uses of biometrics evident at Kotoka Airport are increasingly evident across Africa. Biometric recognition refers to the automatic identification of a person based on a person's physical (e.g., fingerprint, face, voice, iris) or behavioral (e.g., signature) characteristics or traits.[68] African countries are increasingly using biometrics for varied purposes.[69] Biometrics are being used in political processes, in the financial sector, in the telecommunications sector, and/or in identity management. A 2018 joint Strathmore University and Privacy International report has noted that the use of biometrics in political processes has swept across Africa as biometrics have been adopted in electoral processes by many African countries.[70] Part of the rationale for the use of biometrics is the low trust of majority of citizens with electoral bodies. Consequently, those adopting biometrics typically assume that the use of biometrics will increase confidence, effectiveness, and efficiency in elections. This assumption has, however, not yet been substantially validated, at least in the 2017 Kenyan elections.[71]

In Nigeria, biometrics have been or are being implemented for a number of purposes, including the registration of mobile telephone subscriber identity module (SIM) cards, opening bank accounts, the issuance of drivers' licenses, and international passports. Biometrics are used in the electoral process – for the national identity management scheme and for other purposes.[72] The use of biometrics has helped to create identity databases, and therefore provided data for planning and crime prevention and resolution. Nigeria currently has multiple points of collection of biometric data, which has underscored the need for greater attention to data privacy and protection.

THE CFA FRANC, CURRENCY CONTROLS, AND CRYPTOCURRENCIES

Currency policies in African countries demonstrate the continuing impact of external networks based on relationships established during colonialism. French networks with former African colonies remain among the strongest. For example, twelve francophone countries, one former Portuguese colony, and one former Spanish colony – in West and Central Africa – use a colonial monetary system involving two currencies, the West African CFA franc and the Central African CFA franc. This system, developed in 1945 during colonialism, was originally pegged at a fixed rate to the French franc and is now pegged to the euro.[73]

The CFA franc system is controversial and has been criticized. In 2017, a group of ten African musicians from seven countries released a rap song opposing the CFA franc (7 Minutes Contre le CFA Franc),[74] with the message: "The CFA franc will die and we will dance at its funeral."[75] Until 2020, the CFA franc system required participating countries to deposit 50 percent of their foreign exchange reserves in France. The French central bank then guaranteed the value of both currencies. The anti-CFA franc rap song reflects continuing controversy about this overhang from the colonial era. Although participation in the CFA franc system is, in theory voluntary, Mali, which tried to exit the system, experienced economic instability that led to its return to the CFA franc system.[76] As is the case with other colonial legacies, the CFA franc system gives France significant power over the economies of countries within the system. The CFA franc tends to benefit external interests, including the French government and French commercial interests, and internal elites within CFA franc countries, but hinders the ability of countries within the system to export competitive products:

> The CFA franc is a good currency for those who benefit from it: the major French and overseas corporations, the executives of the zone's central banks, the elites wishing to repatriate wealth acquired legally or otherwise, heads of state unwilling to upset France etc. But for those hoping to export competitive products, obtain affordable credit, find work, work for the integration of continental trade, or fight for an Africa free from colonial relics, the CFA franc is an anachronism demanding orderly and methodical elimination.[77]

In late 2020, West African CFA franc countries, which include former French West African colonies and Guinea Bissau, a former Portuguese colony, announced an agreement with France to rename the West African CFA franc as the *Eco*. The Eco will still be pegged to the euro, but countries using the Eco will not be required to maintain 50 percent of their foreign reserves in the French treasury.[78]

Currency policy in Nigeria demonstrates the impact of foreign exchange rate management that facilitates jurisdictional arbitrage by enabling selected internal actors to profit from their access to currency exchange rates not available to most people in Nigeria. Nigeria has a currency regime that has included as many as eight different exchange rates, some of which are much more favorable than the official exchange rate. Exchange rate policies for the Nigerian naira offer a lesson in how to create a black market for a country's currency, as well as how to foster jurisdictional arbitrage by those with access to preferential exchange rates. Under the Abacha regime, Nigeria maintained a fixed official exchange rate of twenty-two naira to one dollar from the day Abacha took power until the day he died. The black market foreign exchange rate for the Naira was as high as eighty-eight naira to one dollar during that time period. This exchange rate policy affected incentives for banks and facilitated arbitrage by banks:

> This rigid exchange rate gave birth to a phenomenon that is now a permanent fixture today – the mainstreaming of the forex black market. Bankers came up with what they used to call the 'blended' rate. Say a client requested $1 million from their bank, the bank would inflate it to say $10 million and then take the request to the AFEM [Autonomous Foreign Exchange Market] knowing that the CBN [Central Bank of Nigeria] would never approve the full request anyway. Whatever was obtained from CBN was then 'blended' with the rest obtained from the black market. It does not take a genius to know that if the black market rate was four times the official rate, people made an absolute fortune from the arbitrage. A lot of banking fortunes that remain to this day in Nigeria were made in this period. It was sweet business.[79]

This exchange rate regime has shaped incentives for banks. The regime builds in opportunities for jurisdictional arbitrage as a matter of policy, in much the same way in which colonial legal systems offered arbitrage opportunities for favored intermediaries. This exchange rate regime has resulted in confusion and the continuation of practices that are harmful to the integrity of institutions. In 2017, with differences between exchange rates as high as 200 naira to the dollar, so-called forex billionaires made "huge fortunes on the back of this difference."[80]

Although the Nigerian government has tried to impose penalties on currency resellers, the currency black market is pervasive in Nigeria. Rather than punishing those who take advantage of opportunities for this type of arbitrage, a better policy would be to implement a currency management regime that eliminates opportunities for arbitrage through foreign exchange rates and other mechanisms. At this point in time in Nigeria and other countries in Africa, policies that enable jurisdictional and other forms of internal arbitrage based on preferential access should also be scrutinized and eliminated to the greatest extent possible. This would likely lead to devaluation of the Naira, which would be painful, particularly for those who profit from arbitrage of internal currency rates. Nigeria has attempted to float its currency freely. The Naira weakened immediately when the Central Bank of Nigeria (CBN) attempted to float the Naira, sinking by 31 percent in one day in June 2016 after the first day of trading of a floating currency,[81] which led the CBN to move quickly to restore fixed exchange rates.

Current currency controls in Nigeria were introduced in 2015 when crude oil prices were falling. Currency controls have led to restricted access to US dollars and have actually choked off investment.[82] Nigeria's foreign exchange policy also requires significant investment from the Nigerian government to defend and maintain the value of the Naira. In 2018, the CBN spent some $36.6 billion ($17.87 billion net) defending the Naira fixed exchange rate, a 130 percent increase over the $15.8 billion spent ($9.73 billion net) in 2017.[83] The government's defense of the Naira has been described as "disastrous" in "creating shortages of products such as milk and fuel, and bringing factories to a standstill for want to imported inputs."[84] The current Nigerian foreign exchange regime, which the government is unlikely to change,[85] reflects historical practices – also evident during colonialism – of laws, regulations, and policies that enable certain intermediaries to profit from jurisdictional arbitrage that extracts rent internally. The availability of such "opportunities" distorts behaviors and diminishes incentives for productive behaviors that might create opportunities for greater and more broad-based growth and prosperity.

In the face of currency controls, people across Africa are increasingly turning to cryptocurrencies. The growth of cryptocurrency trade across Africa underscores the regulatory challenges posed by emerging technologies in the digital era. Cryptocurrencies are a form of virtual currency that are largely unregulated, usually issued and controlled by their developers and used and accepted within a specific virtual community. Cryptocurrencies, which include Bitcoin, Ethereum, and Ripple, are secured with cryptographic techniques that use public and private digital keys.[86] AmbaCoin is one indication of a growing cryptocurrency trade across Africa. In 2018, an Ecobank report noted that twenty-one African countries had made no public stance on cryptocurrency regulation and African governments and central banks were "mostly adopting a 'wait and see' approach when it comes to regulating cryptocurrencies."[87]

By 2020, however, both South Africa and Nigeria had begun to move toward establishing concrete frameworks for regulation of cryptocurrencies. In South Africa, financial regulators issued a position paper on cryptoassets in April 2020 that included thirty recommendations for cryptocurrency regulation.[88] Regulation of cryptocurrencies in Nigeria has not been a model of clarity in the regulation of new technologies. The Nigerian Securities and Exchange Commission issued a statement in September 2020 declaring the commission's position that "virtual crypto assets are securities, unless proven otherwise,"[89] while in February 2021, the CBN directed financial institutions to close accounts transacting in or operating cryptocurrency exchanges. The CBN decision to ban cryptocurrencies then led the Nigerian SEC to suspend its planned regulation of cryptocurrencies. This CBN decision is also said to have led people in Nigeria transacting in cryptocurrencies to move to peer-to-peer exchange platforms to continue trading.

The Nigerian attempt to ban cryptocurrencies is a delayed regulatory reaction to the fact that people using cryptocurrencies in Nigeria have moved far ahead of regulatory frameworks. Luno, a leading cryptocurrency exchange,[90] was founded in South Africa in 2013, but is now headquartered in London with regional hubs in Singapore and Cape Town and local offices in Australia, Indonesia, Nigeria, South Africa, Uganda, the United Kingdom, and Zambia. Although bitcoin activity in Nigeria may include speculative trading, the currency crisis and dollar shortage there have led to cryptocurrencies becoming prominent. Companies in Nigeria are using bitcoin to settle payments for international transactions. In August 2020, Nigeria overtook the United States as the country with the most downloads in one week of the Bitcoin.com wallet.[91] Luna reports that bitcoin monthly trading volume in Nigeria and South Africa exceeded $549 million in August 2020, a 49 percent increase since the beginning of 2020. New customers across Africa increased 122 percent between the fourth quarter of 2019 and the second quarter of 2020, likely in response to the challenges of fluctuating exchange rates and the COVID-19 pandemic.[92]

Although regulatory frameworks for cryptocurrency are nascent across Africa, people in Nigeria use bitcoin in an attempt to move money out of the country and circumvent government restrictions on foreign exchange transactions.[93] The appeal of cryptocurrencies draws attention to pervasive economic insecurity and regulatory uncertainty that is policy-driven to a significant degree. Insecurity is exacerbated by the lack of certainty of the legal and regulatory environment for bitcoin:

> [C]ryptocurrency startups welcome regulation . . . . The theme of regulation as a building block for fostering consumer confidence is a recurring one among cryptocurrency startup founders and insiders. By setting out requirements for

cryptocurrency start-ups to operate, the belief is regulation will ultimately make it easier for interested customers to identify credible and licensed exchanges .... Crucially, it will also offer a differentiation from unlicensed operators and outright scams. It's a key factor given the relative anonymity of how cryptocurrencies operate also provides room for bad faith actors to thrive: fraudulent cryptocurrency platforms received just over $8 million from users in Africa in June alone.[94]

Notes

1. John Loeber. 2018. What Happens to Startup Companies in the Next Recession?. *Crunchbase News*, https://news.crunchbase.com/news/what-happens-to-startups-in-the-next-recession/.
2. John Bowker and Yueqi Yang. 2019. "Jumia Files for New York IPO as African Unicorn Seeks Funds." *Bloomberg*, March 12, www.bloomberg.com/news/articles/2019-03-12/jumia-files-for-new-york-ipo-as-african-unicorn-seeks-funding.
3. Ibid.
4. Center for American Entrepreneurship, The Rise of the Global Startup City, http://startupsusa.org/global-startup-cities/.
5. Max Marmer, Bjoern Lasse Herrmann, Ertan Dogrultan, and Ron Berman, Startup Genome. 2011. Startup Genome Report Extra on Premature Scaling, http://innovationfootprints.com/wp-content/uploads/2015/07/startup-genome-report-extra-on-premature-scaling.pdf?source=post_page.
6. These patterns may, however, be changing in the current start-up company investment boom. Investors in high growth entrepreneurial firms now include those other than the venture capital funds that had traditionally invested in this space, including mutual funds and private equity buyout funds. Sergey Chernenko, Josh Lerner and Yao Zeng. 2017. Mutual Funds as Venture Capitalists? Evidence from Unicorns, p. 3. National Bureau of Economic Research, Working Paper No. 23981, www.nber.org/papers/w23981 [https://perma.cc/3MYK-L6NR].
7. Baraka Jefwa. "Jumia Market launches new business model with inspiration from Instagram." CIO East AfricaMay 31, 2017, accessed October 23, 2020, www.cio.co.ke/jumia-market-launches-new-business-model-with-inspiration-from-instagram-2/.
8. Jumia went public by registering its shares on the New York Stock Exchange. Jumia actually registered American Depositary Shares (ADSs), which are frequently used by foreign companies based outside of the United States to register their shares for sale in US stock markets. Each ADS listed on the New York Stock Exchange represents two Ordinary Shares of Jumia Technologies AG, the Germany company. In December 2018, in preparation for its IPO, Jumia changed both its legal name and its legal form of entity in Germany from Africa Internet Holding GmbH to Jumia Technologies AG. Jumia, Initial Public Offering Prospectus. Filed with the United States Securities and Exchange Commission on April 15, 2019 ("Jumia IPO Prospectus"), accessed December 2, 2020, www.sec.gov/Archives/edgar/data/1756708/000119312519105752/d650749d424b4.htm.
9. Ibid. at 2, 83, 110,
10. Ibid. at 10, 46, 60, 126, 151.

11. Jumia's 2018 financial statements include five major subsidiaries: ECART Internet Services Nigeria, formed in Nigeria, Jumia Egypt LLC, formed in Egypt, ECART Services Morocco Sarl, formed in Morocco, ECART Services Kenya Limited, formed in Kenya, ECART services Ivory Coast SRL, formed in the Ivory Coast, and Jade E-Services South AfricaPTY Ltd, formed in South Africa. Jumia subsidiaries include Jumia UG & Co. KG, AIH General Merchandise Nigeria UG & Co. KG, and entities based in Tanzania that were sold to Jumia's co-CEO in 2016 and repurchased in 2018 Ibid. at 141, 150.
12. Jumia Technologies AG (vormals: Africa Internet Holding GmbH), Konzernabschluss zum Geschäftsjahr vom 01.01.2018 bis zum 31.12.2018 [Jumia Technologies AG (formerly Africa Internet Holding GmbH), Consolidated Financial Statements for the financial year from 1/1/2018 to 12/31/2018], pp. 21–24.
13. Ibid.
14. Jumia IPO Prospectus, *supra* note 8, at 23, 24.
15. About TechCabal, https://techcabal.com/about/.
16. Alexander O. Onukwue. Nudges and Shoves: Tackling Venture Capital Bias in Africa. TechCabal, July 29, 2020, accessed October 23, 2020, https://techcabal.com/2020/07/29/funding-bias-venture-capital/.
17. Ibid. (citing Swaady Martin, an Ivorian entrepreneur).
18. Larry Madowo. "Silicon Valley has Deep Pockets for African Startups – If you're not African." *Guardian*, July 17, 2020, accessed October 23, 2020, www.theguardian.com/business/2020/jul/17/african-businesses-black-entrepreneurs-us-investors; David Pilling. "Are Tech Companies Africa's New Colonialists?" *Financial Times*, July 5, 2019, accessed October 23, 2020, www.ft.com/content/4625d9b8-9c16-11e9-b8ce-8b459ed04726/.
19. Lyons-Padilla et al., 2019; Morgan Stanley, *The Growing Market Investors are Missing: The Trillion Dollar Case for Investment in Female and Multicultural Entrepreneurs*, December 11, 2018, www.morganstanley.com/pub/content/dam/msdotcom/mcil/growing-market-investors-are-missing.pdf [https://perma.cc/6VMX-N6HL]; Andria Thomas et al., Intel & Dalberg, Decoding Diversity: The Financial and Economic Returns to Diversity in Tech, 2016, accessed October 23, 2020, https://dalberg.com/our-ideas/decoding-diversity-financial-and-economic-returns-diversity-tech/ [https://perma.cc/5TCA-JD28].
20. Ndemo and Weiss, 2017.
21. Gathii, 2020.
22. Yomi Kazeem. "What makes Africa's largest e-commerce platform African?" Quartz Africa, March 19, 2019, accessed October 24, 2020, https://qz.com/africa/1572318/what-makes-jumia-an-african-startup/, Jumia IPO Prospectus, *supra* note 8, at 2, 6, 46, 60, 88, 102, 108, 120.
23. Citron Research. 2019. Not all IPOs are Created Equal. Jumia is a Fraud, https://citronresearch.com/wp-content/uploads/2019/05/Not-All_IPOs-Are-Created-Equal-Jumia-is-a-Fraud-.pdf.
24. Daniel Engber. "Who Made that Nigerian Scam," *New York Times*, January 3, 2014, accessed October 24, 2020, www.nytimes.com/2014/01/05/magazine/who-made-that-nigerian-scam.html.
25. Glickman, 2005: 460.

26. The reference to Nigerians as scammers was part of a statement concerning Nigeria's use of its resources: "Nigeria is a nation of ninety million people. With enormous wealth. And what they could have done with that wealth over the last twenty years – they just pissed it away. They just tend not to be honest. Nigerians as a group, frankly, are marvellous scammers." Henry Louis Gates, Jr., "Powell and the Black Elite," *New Yorker*, September 25, 1995; see also Howard W. French. "The Leader of the Nation is Elusive," *New York Times*, October 20, 1995, accessed October 24, 2020, Section A, p. 5, www.nytimes.com/1995/10/20/world/the-leader-of-nigeria-is-elusive.html.
27. *United States* v. *Iro et al.*, Indictment. June 19, 2019, CV No. 190R00308, United States District Court for the Central District California, October 2018 Grand Jury, www.justice.gov/usao-cdca/press-release/file/1197341/download.
28. US Attorney's Office, Central District California. August 22, 2019, Massive International Fraud and Money Laundering Conspiracy Detailed in Federal Grand Jury Indictment that Charges 80 Defendants, www.justice.gov/usao-cdca/pr/massive-international-fraud-and-money-laundering-conspiracy-detailed-federal-grand-jury.
29. Olivia Ndubuisi, "Nigeria Internet Scamming. The Yahoo Boys Universe Chronicle #37, ZAM Magazine, accessed October 24, 2020, www.zammagazine.com/chronicle/chronicle-37/695-nigeria-internet-scamming-the-yahoo-boys-universe.
30. Jumia Q2 2019 Earnings Call, August 21, 2019, https://services.choruscall.com/links/jmia190821.html.
31. Jeremy Hodara worked as an engagement manager at McKinsey and Company from 2006 to 2012, where he specialized in retail and e-commerce consulting and earned a master's degree in business management from the HEC School of Management in Paris, France. Sacha Poignonnec also worked at McKinsey and Company from 2007 to 2012, first as an associate, then as an engagement manager, and finally as an associate partner, was a manager at Aon Accuracy and from 2002 to 2004, an associate at Ernst & Young and holds a master's degree in finance from the EDHEC Business School. Jumia IPO Prospectus, *supra* note 8, at 138.
32. Zenichi Shishido. 2009. "Sweat Equity as a Gift: Venture Capital Investments and Tax Law in Japan." In *Proceedings from the 2009 Sho Sato Conference on Tax Law*, www.law.berkeley.edu/files/sho_sato_tax_conf_web_paper–shishido(2).pdf.
33. Jake Bright. "Why COVID-19 Could Delay Interswitch, Africa's Next Big IPO." TechCrunch, May 4, 2020, accessed December 2, 2020, https://techcrunch.com/2020/05/04/why-covid-19-could-delay-interswitch-africas-next-big-ipo/.
34. Olumuyiwa Olowogboyega. "Stripe acquires Nigerian fintech startup, Paystack for over $200 million." Techcabal.com, October 15, 2020, accessed October 23, 2020, https://techcabal.com/2020/10/15/stripe-acquires-paystack/.
35. Paystack's Y-Combinator Application, September 11, 2017, accessed October 23, 2020, https://paystack.com/blog/company-news/paystacks-y-combinator-application.
36. Yomi Kazeem. "Payments giant Stripe has bought Nigerian payments startup Paystack for Africa Expansion." QuartzAfrica, October 15, 2020, accessed October 23, 2020, https://qz.com/africa/1917940/stripes-buys-nigerias-paystack-for-africa-expansion/.
37. This total capitalization would include stock actually issued and stock that could be issued upon exercise of stock options and other convertible securities. One study from 2017 notes that over 50 percent of startups reserve between 10 and 20 percent of their

capitalization table for the option pool. Marcus Gosling. "Option Pool Sizing – By the Numbers." LTSE Tools, July 19, 2017, accessed October 23, 2020, https://tools.ltse.com/sizing-the-option-pool-whats-normal-95e0f2bc0b88

38. Notably, as venture capitalist and prolific blogger Fred Wilson notes, ownership percentages for employees are highest in the United States, with lower rates in Europe and even lower rates outside of Europe. Fred Wilson. Employee Equity: How Much? avc blog, August 1, 2019, accessed October 23, 2020, https://avc.com/2019/08/employee-equity-how-much-2/. and Fred Wilson. Employee Equity: How Much? avc blog, November 22, 2010, accessed October 23, 2020, https://avc.com/2010/11/employee-equity-how-much/.
39. Stock options would typically have been granted must be exercised and an exercise price paid to actually obtain the company's stock. Stock options are exercisable for a price established at the time the stock option was granted. Upon exercise of the stock option and payment of the exercise price, the stock option holder would receive stock in the start-up company.
40. Barry Evangelista. "Facebook IPO will create billionaires." *SF Gate*, January 8, 2013, accessed October 23, 2020, www.sfgate.com/business/article/Facebook-IPO-will-create-billionaires-3036102.php.
41. Amir Teig. "Waze Employees Clinch Most Lucrative Exit in Israeli History." *Haaretz*, June 13, 20113, accessed October 23, 2020, www.haaretz.com/israel-news/business/.premium-waze-workers-sharing-in-google-buyout-1.5278721; Ingrid Lunden. "Google Bought Waze for $1.1 Billion, Giving a Social Data Boost to its Mapping." Techcrunch.com, June 11, 2013, accessed October 23, 2020, https://techcrunch.com/2013/06/11/its-official-google-buys-waze-giving-a-social-data-boost-to-its-location-and-mapping-business/.
42. Jumia IPO Prospectus, *supra* note 8, at 18, 100, 141–143.
43. Ibid. at 140–141.
44. At the time of the Jumia IPO, shareholders based in Europe included AEH New Africa eCommerce I GmbH, based in Germany (8.4 percent), Atlas Countries Support S.A., based in Belgium (5.8 percent), AXA Africa Holding S.A.S., based in France (5.8 percent), Chelsea Wharf Holdings S.à r.l., based in Luxembourg (5.2 percent), Millicom International Cellular S.A., based in Luxembourg (5.8 percent), Pernod Ricard Deutschland GmbH, based in Germany (5.1 percent), and Rocket Internet SE, an incubator based in Germany (20.6 percent). Ibid. at 147–148.
45. Emma Rumney. "S. Africa's MTN raises $142 million from sale of Jumia stake." Nasdaq.com, October 30, 2020, accessed October 30, 2020, www.nasdaq.com/articles/s.africas-mtn-raises-%24142-million-from-sale-of-jumia-stake-2020-10-30.
46. China has undertaken significant legal reforms in the business and commercial law and intellectual property law areas. In the securities law arena, China, which evolved from a one-bank system under Mao to a four-bank system under Deng, has undertaken legal reforms to establish securities markets that grew five-fold in the decade leading up to 2017. Carpenter and Whitelaw, 2017; Wei, 2008.
47. Nathan Robinson. "Why is San Francisco … Covered in Human Feces?" *Guardian*, August 18, 2018, accessed March 10, 2020, www.theguardian.com/commentisfree/2018/aug/18/san-francisco-poop-problem-inequality-homelessness.
48. Ibid.

49. Julian Hattem, Why Is African Air Travel So Terrible, CityLab.com, November 21, 2017, accessed October 23, 2020, www.citylab.com/transportation/2017/11/why-is-african-air-travel-so-terrible/546422/; Button, Brugnoli, Martini and Scotti, 2015: 85.
50. Ibid.
51. Arewa, 2016.
52. UNCTAD. 2018. *e-Handbook of Statistics*, https://stats.unctad.org/handbook/MerchandiseTrade/ByPartner.html.
53. Masimba Tafirenyika. "Intra-Africa Trade: Going Beyond Political Commitments." *AfricaRenewal*, August, 2014, p. 5, www.un.org/africarenewal/magazine/august-2014/intra-africa-trade-going-beyond-political-commitments.
54. This free trade zone creates the largest free trade zone since the creation of the World Trade Organization. Agreement Establishing the African Continental Free Trade Area, Date of Adoption: March 21, 2018, Date of Entry into Force: May 30, 2019, accessed October 23, 2020, https://au.int/entreaties/agreement-establishing-african-continental-free-trade-area.
55. Marcel Bender. 2018. "Accra – the Modern Heart of West Africa#engineered blog, engineered.thyssenkrupp.com/en/accra-the-modern-heart-of-west-africa/.
56. *Gemalto Case Study: Ghana's e-Immigration Solution: Controlling Borders to Shape a Bright Future*, www.gemalto.com/brochures-site/download-site/Documents/gov-ghana.pdf.
57. Arewa, 2016.
58. The Nigerian aviation minister noted that the runway had an expected life of twenty years, had been in service for thirty-five years, fifteen years beyond its expected life, and that no major maintenance had been carried out on the runway resulting in runway failure. Nigerian govt mulls second runway at Abuja Airport. Logistics Update Africa, March 22, 2017, accessed October 24, 2020, www.logupdateafrica.com/index.php/nigerian-govt-mulls-second-runway-at-abuja-airport-aviation.
59. Dionne Searcey. 2017. "Airport Will Temporarily Shut, Disrupting a Nigerian Lifeline." *New York Times*, March 5, 2017, accessed October 24, 2020, www.nytimes.com/2017/03/05/world/africa/airport-will-temporarily-shut-disrupting-a-nigerian-lifeline.html.
60. Maggie Fick. 2017. "Nigeria's woes worsened by Abuja airport runway potholes." *Financial Times*, January 19, 2017, accessed October 24, 2020, www.ft.com/content/10dad8be-d8da-11e6-944b-e7eb37a6aa8e.
61. Dionne Searcey. "Airport Will Temporarily Shut, Disrupting a Nigerian Lifeline." *New York Times*, March 5, 2017, accessed October 24, 2020, www.nytimes.com/2017/03/05/world/africa/airport-will-temporarily-shut-disrupting-a-nigerian-lifeline.html.
62. Arewa, 2016.
63. Mapping Africa's biggest airport projects. Airport Technology Blog, July 23, 2018, accessed October 24, 2020, www.airport-technology.com/features/africas-airport-projects/.
64. Irene Yuan Sun, Kartik Jayaram and Omid Kassir. *Dance of the Lions and Dragons*. McKinsey & Company, June 2017, www.mckinsey.com/~/media/McKinsey/Featured%20Insights/Middle%20East%20and%20Africa/The%20closest%20look%20yet%20at%20Chinese%20economic%20engagement%20in%20Africa/Dance-of-the-lions-and-dragons.ashx.
65. Lee, 2017: 4.

66. Youyou Zhou. "Air traffic between China and Africa has jumped 630% in the last decade." QuartzAfrica, July 28, 2019, accessed October 23, 2020, https://qz.com/africa/1675287/china-to-africa-flights-jumped-630-in-the-past-nine-years/.
67. Matina Stevis-Gridneff. "Crash Puts Spotlight on Ethiopian Airlines, Pride of a Nation." *Wall Street Journal*, March 17, 2019, accessed October 23, 2020, www.wsj.com/articles/crash-puts-spotlight-on-ethiopian-airlines-pride-of-a-nation-11552737600.
68. What is Biometrics?, Biometrics Research Group, Department of Computer Science and Engineering, Michigan State University, http://biometrics.cse.msu.edu/info/index.html.
69. Muthuri, Monyango & Karanja, 2018; Biometrics, Surveillance Technologies and the Rise of the 'Security State' in South Africa, LSE Centre for Africa Blog, March 22, 2017, accessed October 24, 2020, http://blogs.lse.ac.uk/africaatlse/2017/03/22/biometrics-surveillance-technologies-and-the-rise-of-the-security-state-in-south-africa/.
70. Muthuri, Monyango & Karanja, 2018: 1.
71. "Despite such costs, the adoption of biometrics has not restored the public's trust in the electoral process, as illustrated by post-election violence and legal challenges to the results of the 2017 Kenyan elections." Ibid.
72. Biometrics Bank Project, Dermalog.com, www.dermalog.com/success-stories/nigeria/; Nigerian Officials Registering Foreigners' Biometrics, Findbiometrics.com, June 26, 2018, https://findbiometrics.com/nigerian-officials-registering-foreigners-biometrics-506261/; Overview of Biometric Identification System in Nigeria, CommunicationsWeek.com, March 27, 2017, http://nigeriacommunicationsweek.com.ng/overview-of-biometric-identification-system-in-nigeria/; 20 Million Records for Nigerian Biometric Voter Registration Project, m2sys.com, www.m2sys.com/biometric-fingerprint-software-case-studies-nigerian-voter-registration/.
73. Central Bank of West African States (BCEAO), History of the CFA Franc, accessed October 23, 2020, www.bceao.int/en/content/history-cfa-franc.
74. 7 Minutes Contre le CFA Franc, https://youtu.be/OO-s94Rf36k.
75. "The CFA franc in West Africa: Time for a Change?" DeutscheWelle, June 22, 2018, accessed October 23, 2020, www.dw.com/en/the-cfa-franc-in-west-africa-time-for-a-change/a-44348656.
76. Christopher Giles and Jack Goodman. 2019. African migration: Is the CFA franc forcing people to leave? BBC, January 25, 2019, accessed October 23, 2020, www.bbc.com/news/world-africa-46960532.
77. Ndongo Samba Sylla. The CFA Franc: French Monetary Imperialism in Africa. LSE Blog, July 12, 2017, accessed October 24, 2020, https://blogs.lse.ac.uk/africaatlse/2017/07/12/the-cfa-franc-french-monetary-imperialism-in-africa/.
78. David Pilling. "Death to the CFA franc. Long live the CFA franc." *Financial Times*, June 24, 2020, accessed October 24, 2020, www.ft.com/content/0a6c8f91-cfc0-4352-b8b3-2fbe4a52bdd5.
79. Feyi Fawenhimi. "A (not so) Brief History of the Fall and Fall of the Nigerian Naira." QuartzAfrica, December 6, 2015, accessed October 24, 2020, https://qz.com/africa/564513/a-not-so-brief-history-of-the-fall-and-fall-of-the-nigerian-naira/.
80. David Ajikobi, FACTSHEET: Nigeria's numerous dollar exchange rates, March 13, 2017, accessed October 24, 2020, https://africacheck.org/factsheets/factsheet-nigerias-numerous-dollar-exchange-rates/.

81. Yomi Kazeem. "Nigeria's Naira is Tumbling after a Currency Float, but That's a Good Thing." QuartzAfrica, June 21, 2016, accessed October 23, 2020, https://qz.com/africa/712371/nigerias-naira-is-tumbling-after-a-currency-float-but-thats-a-good-thing/.
82. Libby George. "Nigeria Unlikely to Change Forex Policy, Information Minister Says." Reuters, April 18, 2019, accessed October 24, 2020, www.reuters.com/article/nigeria-politics-idUSL5N220272.
83. The 2018 CBN Annual Activity report notes that the CBN "maintained its direct intervention in the inter-bank foreign exchange market to fusion demand pressure and ensure exchange rate stability," selling $25.67 billion in spot sales and $11.05 billion in forward sales, as compared with $15.81 billion in 2017, with $4.62 billion in spot transactions and $11.20 billion in forward transactions. Central Bank of Nigeria, Annual Activity Report 2018, accessed October 23, 2020, p. 17, www.proshareng.com/admin/upload/report/12340-AnnualActivityReport2018-proshare.pdf.
84. Olumide Adesina. "Defending the Naira at a Cost." Nairametrics, March 17, 2020, accessed on October 23, 2020, https://nairametrics.com/2020/03/17/defending-the-naira-at-a-cost/.
85. Ibid.
86. Robby Houben and Alexander Snyers. *Cryptocurrencies and Blockchain*, p 20. Policy Department for Economic, Scientific and Quality of Life Policies, European Parliament, June 2018, accessed October 23, 2020, www.europarl.europa.eu/cmsdata/150761/TAX3%20Study%20on%20cryptocurrencies%20and%20blockchain.pdf.
87. Ecobank. Middle Africa Briefing Note-Digital-African crypto Regulation, August 1, 2018, accessed October 23, 2020, www.ecobank.com/upload/publication/20180801125146120TM6YM8S7HG/20180801124738625 3.pdf.
88. The 2020 position paper followed an initial public statement on crypto assets in 2014. Crypto Assets Regulatory Working Group, Position Paper on Crypto Assets, www.treasury.gov.za/comm_media/press/2020/20200414%20IFWG%20Position%20Paper%20on%20Crypto%20Assets.pdf.
89. Securities and Exchange Commission, Nigeria. Statement on Digital Assets and Their Classification and Treatment, September 14, 2020, accessed October 23, 2020, https://sec.gov.ng/statement-on-digital-assets-and-their-classification-and-treatment/.
90. Luno was acquired by New York-based Digital Currency Group in September 2020. BusinessWire, Digital Currency Group Acquires Luno, a Leading Bitcoin and Digital Asset Exchange, September 9, 2020, accessed October 23, 2020, www.businesswire.com/news/home/20200909005262/en/Digital-Currency-Group-Acquires-Luno-a-Leading-Bitcoin-and-Digital-Asset-Exchange.
91. Terence Zimwara. "Nigeria' Foreign Currency Crisis Boon for Bitcoin: Country Tops Wallet Downloads Ahead of the US." Bitcoin.com, August 21, 2020, accessed October 23, 2020, https://news.bitcoin.com/nigerias-foreign-currency-crisis-boon-for-bitcoin-country-tops-wallet-downloads-ahead-of-the-us/.
92. Yomi Kazeem. "Regulators in Africa's Big Economies are Scrambling to Get on Top of a Spike in Cryptocurrency Trade." QuartzAfrica, September 22, 2020, accessed October 23, 2020, https://qz.com/africa/1904921/are-cryptocurrencies-regulated-in-africa/.
93. Ibid.
94. Ibid.

8

Technology, Precarity, and Protest

The Republic is in labour
Screaming
pacing the political ward
cursing the colonial midwife
for telling her to push.

Her head is spinning
vision blurred
mind inside out.

She drinks a cup of counterfeit morality
and blubbers a prayer of hope
for the stillborn baby.

The Republic is a headless chicken
with a body that can only flip
and flap in labour.

She curses the future
for coming too soon
clings to a grandfather clock
that's out of tune
hoping it'll correct a future
that's gone askew.

Harriet Anena, "A Nation in Labour"[1]

PROTEST, FUTURE VISIONS, AND INTERNET SHUTDOWNS

Economies in sub-Saharan Africa (SSA) grew markedly in the early years of the twenty-first century and continued to grow,[2] albeit more slowly, in the second decade of the century.[3] Prior to 2000, economic growth in many SSA countries was at best sluggish and was roughly half of more recent growth levels.[4] Political circumstances in many African countries have been tenuous. In the postcolonial era, many African countries have experienced persistent civil war and violence.[5] In 1999, for example, armed conflicts occurred in sixteen of the fifty-four countries in Africa.[6] Recent armed conflict has occurred in South Sudan, Sudan, the Democratic Republic of the Congo (DRC), Central African Republic, and Mali. In the DRC alone, more than 5 million people are estimated to have died in conflicts between 1998 and 2010.[7] South Sudan, which became independent from the Sudan in 2011 in an agreement ending the longest running civil war in Africa, began its own civil war in 2013. A cease fire was reached in the South Sudan civil war in 2018, followed by the swearing in of a new unity government in February 2020.[8]

Digital-era technologies in Africa must be considered in light of existing conditions in many African contexts. New technologies may offer opportunities for the enhancement of human potentiality but may have other consequences, some of which may be difficult to ascertain in advance. New technologies may intensify existing sources of disruption and conflict. The facial recognition technology and digital fingerprinting used at Kotoka Airport reflect important trends today in use of biometrics. Collection of biometric data in many African countries has run far ahead of laws and regulations intended to address potential negative consequences that might flow from collection and storage of vast amounts of critical private and personal information. Of particular concern are questions relating to privacy and data security. Views of technology and technology companies are changing in the aftermath of repeated scandals relating to inadequate attention to users' privacy, what some view as the threat of social media companies to democracy, and a perception that many technology companies, who have in recent years pursued business strategies of moving and breaking things, have been less willing to deal with or even acknowledge the consequences of their breakage.[9]

A 2019 *Harvard Business Review* article notes that the "public will continue to grow weary of perceived abuses by tech companies, and will favor businesses that address economic, social, and environmental problems."[10] Understanding the potential opportunities and limitations of digital-era technologies in African countries requires recognition of the tremendous diversity within and among countries in Africa in terms of historical experiences, capacity, and other measures. Truly engaging with technology's potential and limits also requires a clear vision of potential future paths at the local level and deep interrogation of historical and contemporary contexts and relationships between technology and political and economic power, among other things. This means taking into account the future possibilities in light of potential negative consequences of digital-era technologies that have been noted in recent criticisms of technology companies, including on account of their activities in African countries.

Technology disruption in many African contexts reflects not only the potential promise of technology but also significant limitations of digital technologies. The impact of seemingly disruptive social media has, however, been uneven. Despite the advent of social media in African countries, governments in many countries continue to exert significant control over access to information. Twitter and other social media technologies may have had less of an impact in giving citizens access to verified and credible information. A pervasive lack of access to information contributes to a viral culture of rumors in Nigeria, which has likely been made worse with the advent of social media in Nigeria.

In many countries in Africa (and elsewhere), limited information is made available to the public concerning the health of leaders. In Nigeria, President Mohammadu Buhari was the focus of death rumors in 2018 and 2019, perhaps instigated by political opponents, with frequent reports of his having died. The spread of these rumors was fostered by lack of information about the president's health and the five months President Buhari spent in London in 2017 for medical treatment for an ailment that was not identified. In 2018 and 2019 when Buhari's appearance improved following apparently successful treatment for his undisclosed condition, rumors abounded that he had been replaced by a body double, leading to a public denial by President Buhari of his replacement and remarkable global headlines such as "Nigerian President Denies Rumour He Died and Was Replaced by Clone" in the *Independent* and "Nigeria's President Denies Death Rumor and replacement by Sudanese look-alike 'Jubril'" in *Deutsche Welle*, both in December 2018.[11]

Reactions to and commentary about President Buhari's health within Nigeria are likely driven by politics and past experiences with Nigerian leaders in poor health. A pervasive culture of rumors in Nigeria and elsewhere in Africa flourishes in an environment with little transparency where citizens are given limited access to accurate and verified information. Rather than widening access to information, politicians in Nigeria in 2015 introduced an anti–social media bill ("Act to Prohibit Frivolous Petitions and Other Matters Connected Therewith") that criminalized false statements made in newspapers and social media. The proposed 2015 bill was withdrawn after vehement and vocal public opposition.

A new anti–social media bill was introduced in Nigeria in late 2019.[12] This bill, which passed second reading on the floor of the Nigerian Senate, led to significant opposition, including a Change.org online petition campaign,[13] which received over 90,000 signatures within 24 hours. The Twitter hashtags #SayNoToSocialMediaBill and #ResistTheSocialMediaBill have been used by opponents of the bill, which Human Rights Watch noted would criminalize criticism of the government.[14]

Sources of the 2019 anti–social media bill law may reveal something about desired future governance paths, at least from the Nigerian government perspective. If these desired models become a template for Nigeria, future digital economy paths are likely to entail significant authoritarianism and repression that are also enshrined in new laws that are more than colonial hangovers. The private bill proposed in the Senate is also likely not compatible with the Nigerian Constitution. The text of the Nigerian legislation was copied from a bill entitled *Protection from Online Falsehoods and Manipulation Bill*, adopted in 2019 in Singapore,[15] just a few months before introduction in the Nigerian Senate of the Nigerian bill "Protection from Internet Falsehoods and Manipulation and Other Related Matters Bill."

The Singapore and Nigerian bills are substantially similar. The Nigerian bill copies Parts 1 to 5 of Singapore Law but does not copy Parts 6 to 9. This is consistent with the significantly lower word count of the Nigerian bill (just under 11,000 words as compared with the Singapore law, which is just over 23,000 words). Comparison of the two bills suggests that the Nigerian bill has approximately 69 percent similarity with the text of the Singapore law. Understanding what these differences mean requires a closer visual analysis of the text and structure of each bill.

Part 1 of the Nigerian bill is taken in part from the preamble to the Singapore bill with the addition of language that is not relevant to the substance of the Nigerian bill (e.g., "The Aims and objectives of this Act is."). The first aim and objective in Part 1 Section 1(a) is identical to the Singapore bill except "electronic communication" in the Singapore bill is replaced by the word "transmission" in the Nigerian bill. This is potentially problematic because the Nigerian bill has removed the defined terms section present in the Singapore law. The meaning of the term transmission of false statements/declarations of facts is not entirely clear in the Nigerian bill. Part 1 of the Nigerian bill is substantially similar to Part 1 (Preliminary) Section 5 of the Singapore bill. Although the Nigerian bill is substantially similar to the Singapore bill, the changes generally make the potential operation of the law less clear. Despite some clear differences, much of the substance of the Nigerian bill is directly copied from the Singapore legislation.

Although Singapore is at the top of many indexes that rank countries in terms of economic performance and development, it is not as highly ranked in terms of press freedom, political rights, and civil liberties. Singapore might be a good model for aspects of governance, particularly as they relate to government integrity, honesty, and lack of corruption. Singapore would, however, be a questionable model for Nigeria to follow as a model for freedom of expression. The combination of current modes of economic and political governance in Nigeria with restrictions on government criticism modeled after Singapore, would be problematic, given Nigerian economic performance, demographics, and the marginalization of so much of the population.

Aisha Buhari, the First Lady of Nigeria, was criticized for using China as a desired model for Nigeria for regulation of social media: "On this issue of social media, you cannot just sit in the comfort of your house and tweet that the Vice President has resigned. It is a serious issue," Aisha said. If China can control over 1.3 billion people on social media, I see no reason why Nigeria cannot attempt controlling only 180 million people," she said.[16]

The choice of the Nigerian government to emulate parts of other models of authoritarian countries with strong economic performance is telling, particularly because the Nigerian government does not appear to seek to emulate the economic management models of China and Singapore that are thought to have contributed to their economic successes. Whether Nigerians would be willing to accept a trade-off of better economic management for restrictions on political freedom is an open question. Further, it is not clear whether such a trade-off is even necessary. In Nigeria, past authoritarianism and restrictions on economic and political freedom have tended to benefit a select and small portion of the Nigerian population. As Omoyele Sowore of Sahara Reporters has noted, the anti–social media bill was enacted for the benefit of politicians, not the Nigerian people.[17]

The #EndSARS protests underscore fundamental differences between visions of governance evident in the desire of both the legislative and executive branches in Nigeria to substantially restrict freedom, including freedom of expression, seemingly without any other major reforms of government practices that led many to protest. This view of governance appears contrary to the desire of many Nigerians to have a government that actually invests in Nigeria and Nigerian people, rather than serving as a platform for performance of the prebendal politics noted by political scientist Richard Joseph of use of public resources by those in government for personal benefit. Government responses to #EndSARS protests may play a significant role in setting future paths for Nigeria. Initial government responses to the protests seemed likely to result in attempts to regulate social media communications and suppress criticism of government, rather than initiatives that reform the aspects of government that have led so many people, particularly young people, to protest.

One apparent goal of Nigerian government attempts to limit social media criticism is greater government control of the flow of information, which is why China is an example that appears to inform approaches of the executive. Controlling information, however, is unlikely to ameliorate the myriad problems that Nigeria faces, and could actually exacerbate instability. Events in Gabon in 2019 point to potential consequences of an authoritarian government's limiting information and not being transparent in digital-era contexts in relation to health information about the president. This is a particular issue throughout Africa because rulers in Africa tend to be old, with many in power for decades.

Gabon has been ruled by a single dynasty, the Bongo family, since 1967. Governance in Gabon reflects a familiar pattern of internal governance that is extractive,[18] with pernicious consequences for most people in Gabon, combined with external relationships reflecting colonial-era patterns that facilitate internal extraction. In 2015, an inheritance battle involving the ruling Bongo family revealed a "shady system of informal political and commercial networks of patronage, graft and corruption privileging French multi-national companies and politicians, a system known as *Francafrique* has been exposed."[19] Gabon also illustrates a familiar pattern in resource rich countries in Africa with mass poverty in the midst of significant wealth, at least for a few:

> After formal independence in 1960, many white expatriates remained in the country and continued to staff important economic firms and the national administration. President Léon Mba's influence, like the compositional tactics of most local politicians, relied on opportunistic deference to French interests . . . his successor, Omar Bongo, refined the system in unprecedented ways. Hailed abroad for its political stability and relative wealth, the country suffocated in the regime's regional compromises and haphazard alliances to preserve itself, while failing to lift the bulk of the population out of poverty. At the time of Bongo's death in 2009, Gabon was a rich nation with a poor citizenry, and a country ridden with grave social and political tensions.[20]

In 2009, Omar Bongo was replaced as president by his son Ali Bongo. Between October 2018 and March 2019, President Ali Bongo was out of the country receiving medical treatment in Saudi Arabia and London. Little was disclosed about the president's health, leading to rumors and suspicious about his health,[21] including speculation that Bongo was dead or had been replaced by a body double. President Bongo was not seen in public in 2018 following his departure from the public eye, and he appeared only in a silent video and in a few still pictures of him released.

In December 2018, the government of Gabon released a video of President Bongo giving New Year's greetings.[22] The president's appearance in the video was thought to be strange, which caused a furor, leading to the circulation of various theories, including that the video was a deepfake.[23] *Deepfakes* are fake audio or video recordings that look and sound real: "once the bailiwick of Hollywood special effects studios and intelligence agencies producing propaganda . . . today anyone can download deepfake software and create convincing fake videos in their spare time."[24] One analysis suggests that President Bongo's strange appearance in the video was perhaps a result of a combination of Botox and weakness on one side of his body.[25] The lack of transparency about the health of rulers that can itself be a source of significant instability. In Gabon, allegations about the deepfake video led to an attempted but ultimately unsuccessful coup.[26] Events in Gabon illustrate the uncertain topography between repressive forms of postcolonial governance in Africa and digital-era technologies, suggesting that future paths may exist that may be even more unstable and unpredictable than present ones.

In Zimbabwe, citizens tracked the late President Robert Mugabe's heath by tracking the location of his plane.[27] The impact of Twitter in Zimbabwe was evident in early 2015 when a fall by President Mugabe became a trending topic on Twitter. Traditional media and others captured the fall on camera. State security officials denied that Mugabe fell and attempted to control dissemination of the images of Mugabe falling by forcing journalists to erase the images on their cameras, which would have likely been successful in suppressing the images in earlier eras with no smart phones or social media. Despite attempts to block the images, photos of the fall spread rapidly on Twitter under the hashtag #MugabeFalls, leading to the fall becoming a trending topic on Twitter.[28] The image of President Mugabe falling was widely retweeted with pictures of President Mugabe's fall positioned by Twitter users in varied imagined contexts, including photos that showed President Mugabe dancing with Beyonce in her "All the Single Ladies" video, running from Zimbabwe security forces, and surfing.

The Mugabe falling episode reflects something of what users can do in digital spaces that was not as possible in past times and spaces. However, assessing the impact of Twitter in Zimbabwe and elsewhere forces attention on how change involving technology may actually occur in real-world contexts in ways that may at times reflect significant continuity with the past. President Mugabe was replaced in 2018 by his onetime ally, Emmerson Mnangagwa. Politics in the era of Twitter in Zimbabwe reflects significant continuity with the past, and social media applications such as Twitter have not fundamentally changed the political system in Zimbabwe. Human Rights Watch notes a pattern of continuity in human rights abuses in Zimbabwe in 2018 despite the country having had the first democratic elections in some thirty years in which Robert Mugabe was not on the ballot.[29]

On the ground, however, things may be changing, and not just in Zimbabwe. The changes in communication possibilities in Zimbabwe and elsewhere are causing governments to react, in part, due to the prospect of changes that might flow from changing modes of communication and community building in ways that are particularly notable among young urban elites. As Jacquelin Kataneksza notes:

> Over the last two years, the country has seen the evolution of a digitally-driven, and increasingly vocal and politically active local and diaspora population. Much of this socio-political transformation has taken place online, outside a formalized, State-sanctioned political forum. Yes, this transformation has largely fallen under the purview of a 'young urban elite' and critics have correctly noted the absence of a distinctly rural voice. Nevertheless, Zimbabwean Twitter feeds, WhatsApp threads and Facebook walls have become digital town halls for expressing dissent and debating the goals, merits and methods of political and social transformation, and more recently even as spaces for engagement between citizens and the State.[30]

In Kenya, Nanjala Nyabola notes that virtual spaces, including Twitter, WhatsApp, Facebook, and other platforms have become a "collective powerful force that institutions have been forced to reckon with."[31] Although Twitter has changed communication possibilities in Nigeria, Zimbabwe, Kenya, and other countries in Africa, its ultimate impact may be less immediately clear. The #EndSARS movement in Nigeria shows the potential for violent government responses to protests that use digital-era modes of communication and community building. Internet shutdowns, social media blackouts, and repression and violence by African governments during times of protest attest to the potential disruptive power of social media and other digital-era technologies in Africa. The specific naming of technologies such as WhatsApp in the 2015 Nigerian social media bill reflects political concern about the potential impact of such technologies. The growing political reaction to social media applications such as Twitter and WhatsApp is as important as the increasing reach of such technologies. Government reactions to uses of social media applications in Zimbabwe, even during the Mugabe era, reflected a shutdown approach that has become prominent in a number of African countries that may lead to counter-responses by social media users that seek to avoid government restrictions:

> When Mugabe's government reacted in typically repressive form against an atypical digitally-mediated adversary (by squeezing bandwidth, temporarily blocking WhatsApp, raising the rates of data bundles and introducing a cyber security bill), Zimbabweans creatively circumvented those actions (for example, by installing VPNs).[32]

Rather than focus their attention to how to best participate in the digital economy, including through necessary business, legal, and other reforms, a number of African countries have developed digital economy policies that center around blocking internet and mobile access for political purposes. Political scientist Chipo Dendere tracked 19 total shutdowns, 43 social media blackouts and 237 days of delayed internet in 2016 and 2017, with shutdowns ranging from a few hours to as long as 40 weeks in Cameroon from June 2017 to January 2018.[33] In the first half of 2019, internet shutdowns occurred in at least six countries in Africa, including Chad, the DRC, Ethiopia, Zimbabwe, Sudan, and Gabon.[34] In Africa in 2019, internet shutdowns were more frequent, increasing by 47 percent over 2018, and longer in duration, at an estimated cost of over $2 billion.[35] Of the fourteen countries that shut down the Internet in 2019, "at least seven have either never shut down the internet or did not do so in 2018 and 2017. This includes Benin, Gabon, Eritrea, Liberia, Malawi, Mauritania, and Zimbabwe."[36]

Authoritarian governments account for some 77 percent of internet shutdowns in Africa in the five years leading up to 2019.[37] Chad cut access to social media platforms, including WhatsApp, Twitter, Facebook, Instagram, and YouTube, for sixteen months ending in 2019. Internet shutdowns in Africa are often justified on account of security: "[i]n most cases, under the guise of security, governments simply want to hamper opposition leaders from organizing protests or riling up citizens about their policy decisions. A fair number of internet shutdowns or social media blocks also happen around elections."[38] In late October 2020, Guinea shut down its internet shortly before announcement of the results of a presidential election.[39]

Internet shutdowns in Ethiopia have led to a manifest tension between stated government goals of providing an environment to facilitate the technology sector, including by promoting technology start-up companies,[40] and its seeking to maintain control reflective of authoritarian approaches of the past. In 2017, the government shut down internet access in English-speaking regions of Cameroon in an attempt to stifle protests by English speakers about their marginalization in the majority French-speaking country.[41] A number of countries have attempted to tax internet transactions. In 2018, Uganda attempted to tax uses of social media and messaging platforms such WhatsApp, Facebook, and Twitter. Uganda ended up raising far less than it had anticipated from these new taxes, in part, because many in Uganda started to use virtual private networks (VPNs), which enabled them to shield their actual location and avoid paying the taxes.

Although the availability and use of telecommunication services are linked to economic growth and living standards,[42] new technologies may also intensify existing sources of disruption. Not surprisingly, access to digital technologies often track existing societal gaps. Although digital technologies are increasingly present in Africa, available data suggests that significant differences exist by varied measures, including rural and urban contexts, as well as by gender. Furthermore, |participation in the digital economy is significantly limited throughout Africa by a lack of electricity.[43] SSA is experiencing a power crisis. Electrical power is unreliable and power generation in the region is the lowest in the world:

> Electricity consumption per person in large African countries such as Ethiopia, Kenya, and Nigeria is less than one-tenth that of Brazil or China. In poorer countries such as Mali, a typical household uses less electricity in a year than a Londoner uses to boil a kettle each day. And nearly 600 million people in sub-Saharan Africa lack access to electricity altogether – with the result that whole communities literally live half their lives in the dark.[44]

Africa continues to lag the world in a number of key digital economy measures. In 2017, African countries had an estimated internet penetration of 27 percent. and mobile broadband penetration estimated to be just under 23 percent,[45]with a growing internet user gender gap.[46] In 2013, the contribution of the Internet to GDP in Africa was half the level of other emerging regions.[47] Internet penetration is projected to reach over 50 percent by 2025.[48] Due to the relative predominance of mobile devices in the SSA region, internet access in Africa will likely reflect a greater proportion of mobile devices than is typically the case outside of SSA.

The limited networked connectivity of countries in Africa with air traffic and other physical networks is also evident in the digital economy where similar patterns of infrastructural gaps are present. Notably, new infrastructure projects that seek to increase bandwidth have been funded to a significant degree externally, including by Facebook, which is building an undersea cable around Africa that will increase internet access for twenty-three countries in Africa, the Middle East, and Europe.[49]

The advent of the digital economy in recent decades has underscored the fact that many countries in SSA have not effectively integrated into the industrial economy,[50] to say nothing of the digital economy that followed it. Current conditions in SSA suggest that "Africa's development crisis is in indeed largely a policy crisis."[51] This policy crisis is rooted in the historical experience of African countries during the eras of the slave trade and colonialism and the continuing dominance of institutional frameworks created during such time periods in the postcolonial era.

Policy crises and legal overhangs highlight the importance of innovations in law that have not always received sufficient attention in discussions of conditions in countries in Africa. The adoption of laws and regulations, and even lawmaking processes themselves, have reflected problematic patterns of borrowing in African countries that use models not sufficiently adapted for local contexts. The needed development of robust and new hybrid models will require disrupting these established patterns and innovative approaches to law and policymaking processes.

FOOD SECURITY AND RURAL AND URBAN SPACES

Technology and continuing urbanization are important forces in Africa in the digital era. In Nigeria and other countries in Africa, urbanization was a key characteristic of colonialism, even in areas such as southwestern Nigeria and Botswana, where large human agglomerations existed prior to colonialism: the city of Ilé-Ifẹ̀ in southwestern Nigeria is thought to date back to at least the tenth century.[52] Estimates suggest that the percentage of Africans living in cities increased from 4.8 percent in 1920 to 14.2 percent in 1960.[53] Population increases in urban areas in Africa have continued after independence. Between 1950 and 2015, the share of population living in rural areas decreased from 85 percent in 1950 to 57 percent by 2018; United Nations estimates suggest that the urban population in Africa is likely to triple between 2018 and 2050.[54]

Categories such as urban and rural may vary significantly among countries in Africa, with complex and multifaceted networks of relationships and back and forth movements that may complicate categorization of what is urban or rural. Despite these potential complexities, urbanization is an important colonial legacy.[55] The footprint of the British colonial empire is readily apparent in urban spaces. Cities in Africa also reflect a legacy of racial residential segregation that was characteristic of colonialism in many African contexts.[56] In Madagascar, residential racial segregation was "achieved through subtle measures such as building and subdivision codes that severely disadvantaged the non-White population."[57]

Africa is the least urbanized but most rapidly urbanizing continent.[58] The topography of cities in Africa is complex and includes cities that might be categorized as indigenous, Islamic, European, colonial, dual, and hybrid.[59] Although diverse in many respects, African cities share features that underscore consequences of external orientation and external determination during and after colonialism. African cities are often poor today, and marginalized masses form a majority of the population.[60] African cities are often crowded, disconnected, and costly.[61] Political, economic, and ethnic group cleavages can be striking in cities where elites and the masses have come together. In Nigeria, the:

> very nature of urban development contributed to the gulf between the ordinary citizens and the officials of the state . . . [s]imilarly, government institutions failed to keep up with the forces of urbanization . . . hampered by a lack of funds, trained personnel, and organizational elasticity, leaving them unable to respond to most residents' needs for basic services and protection.[62]

Circumstances in cities throughout Africa underscore profound sources of insecurity for many in Africa. Land insecurity, food insecurity, and personal insecurity are pronounced but certainly not limited to urban areas. In urban areas, some may not have clear rights to land, leading to land tenure insecurity. According to World Bank data, tenure insecurity in Africa measured in terms of the share of the population without formally recognized land tenure rights increased from 55 percent in 2009 to about 66 percent in 2012.[63] Overlapping and sometimes contradictory property rights systems, including formal, customary, and informal ones,[64] reflect how a lack of reconciliation among different legal regimes remains a source of uncertainty and insecurity.

Urbanization in most parts of Africa has been driven by complex and varied forces, including migration from rural areas and transformation of rural areas into urban ones. Many internal migrants are driven by economic factors. Education has also been a driver for migration. Migration may also take on different patterns in different subregions within Africa. For example, the southern African region has long had significant migration, including particular forms of labor migration that had become institutionalized in the region by the time of apartheid in South Africa.[65] Migration from rural areas may relieve pressures in some rural areas where significant population pressure on land exists.[66] Migration within Africa is complex in terms of its duration, the composition of migrants, and other factors.

The footprint of the British colonial empire is also readily apparent in rural areas, reflecting ways in which the "control of people and of agricultural production was central to the missionary and colonial project" as well as to that of local rulers.[67] In Nigeria, colonial ordinances played an important role in continuing infrastructure deficits in rural areas by prioritizing the provision of infrastructure to areas with significant European presence.[68] Colonial agricultural marketing boards, established in varied colonies during the 1940s, "were more at the service of the colonial interest of local resource exploitation, which ended up impoverishing the rural sources of economic capital through commodity price distortion and excessive taxation."[69]

Colonial policies, including agricultural policies that channeled resources toward production of cash crops intended for export and tax policies,[70] had an impact on gender and female agricultural producers,[71] shaped available resources for people in urban and rural areas, and influenced patterns of internal and external migration.[72] Postcolonial agricultural development policies may reflect a continuation of colonial-era policies that focused to a significant degree on production for export.

African economies tend to depend on a small number of export commodities,[73] many of which were established during colonialism. This has led to significant reliance on commodity world market prices for government operating budgets and fiscal security, which creates forces within African countries that are inherently unstable given volatility in commodity prices, particularly without robust risk management practices.[74]

During colonialism, despite the lack of a consistent plan or blueprint, clear-cut policies concerning the role of agriculture led agriculture in Nigeria to "serve as the major arm for the satisfaction of the economic needs of the mother country, providing raw materials and offering a training ground for British experts experimenting on tropical agriculture ... [and] a division of functions between the participants, namely British administrators and commercial interests, on the one hand, and African peasants on the other."[75] As a result of colonial policies, export crops became dominant, and the food crops sector neglected.[76] Agricultural policies that developed during colonialism, including in relation to cash crops, export crops, and government purchasing boards, may not reflect the full complexity of African cultivation. In colonial Kenya, for example, African cultivators produced for the black market, which gave them higher returns than terms of trade offered by government purchasing boards.[77] Patterns established during colonialism continued to have an impact after formal independence and have contributed to continuing food deficits throughout Africa today.[78]

Although migration to urban areas has been significant in many African countries in recent decades and the proportion of population living in rural areas has decreased since 1950, the absolute number of rural dwellers is increasing and has doubled since 1980.[79] As is the case with urban areas in Africa, although the agricultural sector may be a dominant source of employment and contribute significantly to GDP, rural areas in Nigeria and other countries in Africa are often poor with significant cultivation by small-scale farmers:

> Agriculture is the mainstay of the [Nigerian] economy, contributing about 45 per cent of GDP. The agriculture sector employs about two-thirds of the country's total labour force and provides a livelihood for about 90 per cent of the rural population. Nigeria is the world's largest producer of cassava, ... yam and cowpea – all staple foods in sub-Saharan Africa. It is also a major producer of fish. Yet it is a food-deficit nation and imports large amounts of grain, livestock products and fish ... rural areas are involved in a whole lot of primary economic activities that are important in sustaining the entire Nigerian economic system ... Poverty is especially severe in rural areas, where up to 80 per cent of the population lives below the poverty line and social services and infrastructure are limited. The country's poor rural women and men depend on agriculture for food and income. About 90 per cent of Nigeria's food is produced by small-scale farmers who cultivate small plots of land and depend on rainfall rather than irrigation systems.[80]

Colonialism also led to regionalization of the Nigerian economy, with three semi-autonomous regions (north, east, and west), each associated with a primary export commodity and in the postwar period with "a Marketing Board that extracted peasant surpluses to finance party loyalists, administrators and a nascent bourgeoisie."[81] Agricultural production in Nigeria reflects familiar patterns of lack of internal infrastructure, low productivity, and external facing policies. The Nigerian oil boom in the 1970s also influenced the agricultural policy, leading agricultural to be relegated to the background.[82] The granting of import licenses for food became a source of state patronage and rent-seeking in Nigeria in the 1970s:

> Food imports were in themselves an important source of speculative profits and private accumulation, and hence became a political arm of state coalition building. The existence of cheap imports in any case exerted a depressing effect on domestic production, especially in light of the prevailing cost squeeze in agriculture.[83]

Food deficits in Africa reflect widespread and continuing food insecurity throughout Africa. This is not a new phenomenon. In Congo-Brazzaville during colonialism:

> The most serious problem facing African workers on a daily basis was hunger. Although those employed by the administration had rations as part of their pay, many had to spend a great deal of time finding food. Reports of undernourished and starving people are common in early accounts, and they continued as late as the 1920s. It was a problem created by colonialism. Having disrupted the pre-colonial exchange system which delivered food to the Pool markets, the administration was unable to ensure a supply itself.[84]

Between 2016 and 2018, United Nations Conference on Trade and Development (UNCTAD) estimates suggest Africa "imported about 85% of its food from outside the continent, leading to an annual food import bill of $35 billion, which is forecast to reach $100 billion by 2025."[85] Food and Agriculture Organization of the United Nations (FAO) estimates suggest that to feed the world population of 9.1 billion people in 2050, global food production will need to grow by 70 percent.[86] In Africa, productivity will need to increase at an even faster rate to avoid continued mass hunger.[87] In addition to governance and policy reforms, technology that is truly targeted towards local needs may be a key element facilitating sufficient agricultural production in Africa to meet population growth. Varied technologies have potential to have a sustained positive impact on agricultural production in Africa, including automated systems, advice, and payment systems, evident in use of aerial images from satellites and drones, weather forecasts, and soil sensors.[88] Notably, weaknesses in agricultural statistics persist in SSA, which hinders the development of sound agricultural policies.[89]

Even prior to the impact of the COVID-19 pandemic, which likely diminished food security in Africa, hunger was rising in almost all subregions of Africa, with a prevalence of undernourishment in SSA of 22.8 percent, according to 2018 FAO estimates.[90] Total food insecurity is significantly higher in Africa than elsewhere in the world.[91] Notably, climate change, which is already having an impact in Africa, is likely to have a continuing impact, and may worsen food security.[92]

(IN)SECURITY, CONTESTATION, AND EXTERNAL POWERS

What people say about security in Africa can reveal much about legal and policy priorities. Discussions about security in African contexts highlight two important postcolonial conditions. The first is the extent to which those in power may ignore critical sources of insecurity for the many. In addition, circumstances of insecurity interrelate in important ways to conceptions of security, particularly as elucidated by those who govern. Shifting conceptions of security were evident in Nigeria in the #EndSARS protests in October 2020.

How governments construe security also reflects continuing colonial legacies. For example, in the Congo-Brazzaville, which was colonized by France, colonial authorities used public security as a "pretext for instituting draconian policies that strictly limited the movement of Africans," including through institution of a law in December 1926 that imposed a 9:00 p.m. curfew on Africans.[93] A 1904 colonial decree had imposed restrictions on playing drums and dancing during certain hours in Brazzaville.[94] Contravention of this decree was punishable by a fine, one to five days in prison, or both.[95] Bans on drumming in Congo-Brazzaville are one example of widespread efforts by colonial authorities to censor musical expression.[96]

Digital worlds increasingly shape varied types of relationships throughout the world, including in Africa. In addition to face-to-face interactions, various forms of online interaction within African countries, and with external diasporic and other populations, have become pervasive. Further, how governments construe security is particularly important in the digital era. In the digital era, considerations of the personal security and privacy of individuals increasingly collide with conceptions about national security.[97]

The controversy surrounding the American whistleblower Edward Snowden underscores tension between competing conceptions of security and whose security should take precedence in different digital-era contexts. This tension is particularly evident in a number of African contexts where national security may essentially mean the security and maintenance of power of authoritarian rulers, rather than the personal and economic security of those over whom they govern. This is of particular concern as digital technologies become increasingly widespread in Africa, including those that enable surveillance and the collection of biometrics and other personal information. Digital technologies have significant potential uses for suppression and surveillance.[98] As such, the digital era, rather than serving the forces of freedom in Africa, could lead to future paths of greater repression.

Responses in contemporary contexts of continuing authoritarianism and oppression in Africa may compel particular survival strategies and responses, from exit through migration to nonviolent protest to insurgency and the taking up of arms.

Migration, protest, and insurgency may reveal, blur, and even shift boundaries between the internal and external. For much of the postcolonial era, many outside of Africa have effectively ignored the suffering of the many within African countries and histories of exploitation, linkages with external powers, and internal governance failures that enabled this suffering. For much of the postcolonial era, consequences of such suffering were seemingly contained and seemingly did not have much external impact outside of Africa.

Through alliances with internal elites who benefit from external networks, external powers, including former European colonial powers and countries such as the United States, mentioned human rights, but still undertook actions in Africa that were consistent with human rights as being important in theory rather than in practice. These actions of external powers, which have often advanced their self-interest, at times involved supporting or turning a blind eye to various forms of oppression in contexts of governments with authoritarian tendencies or worse, who have used internal governance structures that are a legacy of colonialism. External enablers have long been a factor in authoritarianism and oppression in postcolonial Africa. In Uganda, for example, President Museveni, who, by 2020, had been in power for more than three decades, used facial recognition surveillance technology purchased from Huawei to suppress dissent following protests in November 2020.[99] External enablers have facilitated the creation of an oppressive security state in Uganda.[100]

Even during later time periods when *democracy* became a buzzword, in many contexts, democracy in Africa meant elections, and could reflect forms of performative behaviors connected to elections and other things associated with democracy in Western countries, followed by continuing authoritarian forms of governance. All of this seemingly occurred with little impact on external powers whose support of internal authoritarians and various forms of extraction have often facilitated authoritarian rule. What many refer to as the migration crisis in Europe and externally networked insurgent movements throughout Africa are examples of internal conditions of oppression and scarcity that drive movements of ideas and people into and outside of Africa. The nexus of the internal and external and external impact of migration, in particular, are making external powers pay more attention to the external consequences of seemingly internal decisions. The external reverberations of internal circumstances are likely to be increasingly important factors in the interface of the internal and external in African countries.

Contestation and Violence

Colonialist and missionaries imposed governance and other models from Europe as a key part of their civilizing mission. Access to benefits made available through external powers during colonialism became a point of differentiation among ethnic groups. Colonial policies also played a key role in shaping ethnic affiliation and conflict throughout much of Africa:

> Whereas the European ethno-political power constellation emerged from an extensive period of state formation and nation building, this was not the case for most post-colonial states. Here, particular groups' chances of gaining access to state power in the postindependence period depended heavily on colonial policy, which typically treated its subjects very differently conditional on ethnic affiliation.[101]

Colonial power and the nexus of access to state power and ethnic, linguistic, religious, and other affiliations has contributed to pervasive contestation in postcolonial Africa. This contestation and competition over state control have contributed to policy instability and pervasive insecurity. In 1966, the ethnic-political power constellation within Nigeria exploded into violence and led to a civil war in Biafra with an estimated loss of 1 to 3 million lives, many from starvation after Biafra was blockaded by the Nigerian government.[102] Many who died in Biafra were civilians, including women and children. The cycle of death in the early days of an independent Nigeria continues to be an open wound that is a living force that continues to shape events and actions.

The Biafran War highlights the complexities and devastating consequences of ethnic contestation within Nigeria, which includes hegemonic ethnic groups that define core regions of Nigeria, as well as minority groups within such regions. In the former Eastern Region of Nigeria, the Niger Delta contains many minority ethnic groups, including the Ijaw, Ibibio, Itsekiri, and Ogoni. Ken Saro-Wiwa's war memoir, *On a Darkling Plain*, describes his experiences during the Biafran War. Although Ogoniland is located within the territory of Biafra, Saro-Wiwa opposed the war. His narrative attests to the experience of minority ethnic groups, who may also suffer at the hands of hegemonic ethnic groups. As Onookome Okome notes: "Ken Saro-Wiwa's political life questions this [tableaux of the three major privileged ethnic discourses], calling attention to all other (un)manned sites of antagonism in Nigeria's nation-building."[103]

Sites of antagonism form a potential basis for instability, even in times of apparent calm. In recent years Cameroon has faced increased instability and conflict. Cameroon was unusual in Africa in having two concurrent colonial powers in different regions of the country. After Germany was stripped of its colonies in 1919 in the Treaty of Versailles,[104] Cameroon was partitioned in unequal divisions in an arbitrary manner between the United Kingdom and France under a League of Nations mandate that was later superseded by a United Nations trusteeship agreement. Britain and France administered their respective parts of Cameroon separately. After independence, this led to a hybrid legal system with English common law, French civil law, and customary law. This system of bijuralism, imposed by historical circumstances, has led to difficulties in practice.[105] The failure to effectively unify and implement a dual legal system in Cameroon reflects a broader cleavage between anglophone and francophone Cameroon that became more acute in 2016 after twenty years of relative quiescence.

In 2016, the frustration and marginalization of Cameroonians living in anglophone regions, who constitute 20 percent of Cameroon's population, grew into a movement that led to increased repression.[106] Separatists in Cameroon have renamed the former British Southern Cameroons as the Federal Republic of Ambazonia and have even created a cryptocurrency known as AmbaCoin.[107] The creation of AmbaCoin reflects ways in which Cameroonian separatists have mobilized online through social media and other virtual means.[108] Notably, the Cameroonian government shut down the Internet in response to unrest in anglophone Cameroon, at considerable cost.

Various forms of violent conflict and civil strife present in countries in Africa, continue to reflect configurations of the internal and external.[109] Insurgents reflect one notable type of response to precarity that may be a harbinger for potential future paths of widespread chaos and violence if current governance failures are not reformed to alleviate sources of unfreedom and temper scarcity of opportunity.

In addition to being a destabilizing force in Mali, which experienced coups in 2012 and 2020 in the face of Islamist insurgents in northern Mali. Islamist insurgencies are present in various regions in Africa today, including Boko Haram, which has carried out attacks across Nigeria. Al-Shabaab, based in Somalia, has carried out attacks across the east Africa region, including the 2013 attack at the Westgate Shopping Centre in Nairobi, Kenya where some seventy people, mostly civilians, were killed.[110] In August 2020, the ISIS affiliated militant group, Islamic State Central Africa captured the northern port town of Mocímboa da Praia in Mozambique's oil rich Cabo Delgado.[111] This area of Mozambique has seen an Islamic insurgency unfold that has led to an a quarter of a million people being displaced and 1,500 civilians killed since 2017.

Insurgents such as Boko Haram, which has operated since 2002–2003, undertaking a campaign of terror based in Nigeria,[112] reflect new patterns of engagement with external forces and new internal networks within Africa that reflect pervasive usage of social media and other digital-era technologies. Furthermore, the "spread of social media in Africa has brought many economic and political benefits, while also equipping terrorist groups with a tool for recruitment and propaganda."[113] These insurgencies illustrate the rise of jihadist groups with both global and local reach in local contexts where many are marginalized and where repression is common:[114]

> [i]ssues concerning poor governance, state corruption, unemployment and instability can all increase the appeal of extremist groups, and are often the subject of extensive discussion on social media. In a number of cases, terrorist groups are said to present tailored narratives on social media to position themselves as an alternative to corrupt and oppressive governments.[115]

The activities of jihadist and other extremist groups illustrate ways in which online interactions increasingly shape daily activities and social movements throughout Africa. Online networks are transforming both the internal and external by providing a direct reach into diaspora populations, as well as a more generalized global audience, as potential sources for recruitment and financing. This is increasingly evident throughout Africa where diasporic populations may play a key role in mobilization online.[116]

Insecurity, Protest, and Response

The 2020 cryptocurrency surge across Africa highlights the interface between new digital-era technological possibilities amid struggle and contested spaces. Contestation of the kind that is evident in Cameroon has also contributed to widespread insecurity throughout Africa where human insecurity "has attained high levels," with significant poverty, conflict, and instability.[117] This leads to a sense of insecurity that "leads people to struggle for resources."[118] Nigeria illustrates this struggle. In Nigeria, insecurity and scarcity of opportunity are pervasive features of life for many, with limited access to clean water and electricity, widespread economic insecurity, pervasive food insecurity, personal insecurity from violence by bandits and kidnappings,[119] various forms of civil strife, commonplace abuses by government security forces and the military, threat of attack from Islamist and other insurgents, and conflicts and violence between herders and farmers.[120] The growth of the kidnapping industry in Nigeria highlights forms of innovation in "negative" spaces that may exacerbate insecurity: "between June 2011 and the end of March 2020, at least $18.34 million was paid to kidnappers as ransom. Even more frightening is that the larger proportion of that figure (just below $11 million), was paid out between January 2016 and March 2020, indicating that kidnapping is becoming more lucrative."[121]

In early 2021, Wole Soyinka expressed concerns about the widespread insecurity across Nigeria: "it is a common problem (insecurity); it is a national, collective issue . . . the most impotent individual has become a prime target . . . . The sovereignty of this nation is in the hands of murdering herdsmen. The sovereignty of this nation has already been taken over by Boko Haram, it's been taken over by ISWAP [Islamic State West Africa Province], it's been taken over by those with absolutely no respect for what is called national integrity."[122]

Nigerian government responses in the name of restoring security have instead exacerbated insecurity because human rights violations by government security forces and the Nigerian military have themselves become a source of insecurity for many. Government responses to the #EndSARS protests reflect the inability and inflexibility of the Nigerian government in addressing profound fissures in Nigeria that could be the source of significant ongoing disruption if not adequately addressed. On October 11, 2020, in response to ongoing protests, the Nigerian government announced the disbanding of SARS, which had had a longstanding practice of abuse and violence:

> SARS was formed in 1992 to combat armed robbery and other serious crimes. Yet since its inception, the unit has allegedly been implicated in widespread human rights abuses, including extrajudicial killings, torture, arbitrary arrests, unlawful detention, and extortion. Many Nigerians feel that the unit has deliberately profiled and targeted young people, especially those with tattoos, dreadlocks, and visible possessions such as phones and laptops. Over the years, Nigerian authorities have repeatedly promised to reform SARS and ensure accountability for abuses by its officers, but with few results.[123]

As is the case with so many other manifestations of the government in Nigeria, SARS operated with impunity, largely without accountability or effective legal or other constraints. The replacement of SARS with the Special Weapons and Tactical Team did not immediately stop the protests, instead leading to the rise of the #EndSWAT Twitter hashtag. The SARS protests, which have been led by the young, highlight potential generational conflict in Nigeria that may be defined by various uses of digital-era technologies. The Nigerian Army made a statement on October 15 threatening "to deal decisively with 'subversive elements' and 'trouble makers,' and indicating that it stands 'ready to fully support the civil authority in whatever capacity to maintain law and order and deal with any situation decisively'."[124] If effectuated, the army's threat is unlikely to lead to the grievances underlying the SARS protests being addressed, because even if these current protests are suppressed, "[t]he Nigerian army has also been implicated in human rights abuses, including the use of lethal force against peaceful protesters."[125]

The Nigerian federal government also had an unsatisfactory response. In a twelve-minute speech on October 22, 2020, President Buhari:

> began with a warning 'to those who have hijacked and misdirected the . . . protest of some of our youths,' and ended by declaring that his government 'will not allow anybody or groups to disrupt the peace.' On social media, the response was mostly shock. Was that all he had to say?
>
> Nigerians had demanded a statement from the government after people all over the world watched via Instagram Live on October 20 as the army opened fire on a crowd of young people demonstrating against police violence at the Lekki tollgate in Lagos. Eyewitnesses reported up to fifteen dead. Who ordered the shooting of peaceful protesters in a democracy? Nigerians wanted to know. But the president ignored the subject.[126]

Initial government responses to the Lekki killings reflected the typical lack of government accountability that is characteristic of governance in Nigeria. Whether recent events will change past patterns remains to be seen. Some suggest the #EndSARS protests will disrupt past patterns:

> The initial denials and changing stories reflect a leadership unaccustomed to being held accountable by the citizenry. But that is changing as young Nigerians are refusing to accept the status quo. To them, a generation of out-of-touch

> gerontocratic leaders that cannot see the folly in claiming that live video footage has been photoshopped are unsurprisingly aligned with a police unit that cannot understand how young people, notably those in the tech industry, might be able to buy a car without dabbling in crime. Older Nigerians were surprised at the ease with which the Feminist Coalition switched to bitcoin after its bank account suffered restrictions.[127]

Without comprehensive restructuring of governance in Nigeria, including through legal and institutional reform, Nigeria is likely to experience instability that might, at some point, burn out of control or be contained only through even greater government repression than exists at present. Even this might not block criticism and protests against the government in an era of widespread mobile phones and varied means of digital communication. Past approaches to contestation that have led to significant periods of military rule in postcolonial Nigeria may not be sustainable in a digital-era world of rapid population growth and an increasing youth population without significant strife and violence by the government and its military and police forces.

Notes

1. Anena, 2015.
2. International Monetary Fund, World Economic Outlook April 2013: Hope, Realities, Risks 67–69 (2013), www.imf.org/external/pubs/ft/weo/2013/01; McKinsey & Company, The Lions on the Move: The Progress and Potential of African Economies (2010), www.mckinsey.com/~/media/McKinsey/Featured%20Insights/Middle%20East%20and%20Africa/Lions%20on%20the%20move/MGI_Lions_on_the_move_african_economies_full_report.pdf.
3. African Development Bank. 2020. African Development Outlook 2020: Developing Africa's Workforce for the Future, p. 15.
4. Ibid.
5. Addison, Le Billion and Murshed, 2002; Richards, 1996: xiii; Taylor, 2002.
6. Tony Addison, *Reconstruction from War in Africa: Communities, Entrepreneurs and States* (2001), United Nations University/World Institute for Development Economic Research/WIDER Discussion Paper #2001/18, at www.wider.unu.edu/publications/dps/dp2001-18.pdf.
7. Jeffrey Gettleman, "Africa's Forever Wars," *Foreign Policy*, March/April 2010, accessed October 23, 2020, www.foreignpolicy.com/articles/2010/02/22/africas_forever_wars.
8. International Crisis Group. "A Major Step Toward Ending South Sudan's Civil War," February 25, 2020, www.crisisgroup.org/africa/horn-africa/south-sudan/major-step-toward-ending-south-sudans-civil-war.
9. Taplin, 2017.
10. Taneja, 2019.
11. Adam Forrest. "Nigerian president denies rumour he died and was replaced by clone." *Independent*, December 3, 2018, accessed October 23, 2020, www.independent.co.uk/news/world/africa/nigerian-president-buhari-denies-rumour-dead-replaced-lookalike-

clone-jubril-a8664571.html; "Nigeria's president denies death rumor and replacement by Sudanese lookalike 'Jubril.'" Deutsche Welle, December 3, 2018, accessed October 23, 2020, www.dw.com/en/nigerias-president-denies-death-rumor-and-replacement-by-sudanese-lookalike-jubril/a-46545666

12. Protection from Internet Falsehoods and Manipulation and Other Related Matters Bill 2019, www.nassnig.org/documents/billdownload/10965.pdf.
13. Stop the Social Media Bill! You can no longer take our rights from us, www.change.org/p/the-national-assembly-of-the-federal-republic-of-nigeria-stop-the-social-media-bill-you-can-no-longer-take-our-rights-from-us.
14. Anietie Ewang. "Nigerians Should Say No to Social Media Bill." Human Rights Watch, November 26, 2019, accessed October 23, 2020, www.hrw.org/news/2019/11/26/nigerians-should-say-no-social-media-bill#.
15. "From title to content, Nigeria's 'social media bill' is a 'replica' of Singapore's act." TheCable.ng, November 26, 2019, accessed October 23, 2020, www.thecable.ng/fact-check-is-nigerias-social-media-bill-truly-a-replica-of-singapores-act.
16. Bayo Wahab. "Aisha Buhari wants FG to regulate social media like China." Pulse.ng, November 30, 2019, accessed October 23, 2020, www.pulse.ng/news/local/aisha-buhari-wants-fg-to-regulate-social-media-like-china/kf2g2py
17. Alexander O. Onukwue. "Nigeria's Social Media Bill suffers its biggest defeat yet." TechCabal, March 9, 2020, accessed October 23, 2020, https://techcabal.com/2020/03/09/social-media-bill-public-hearing/.
18. Adam Nossiter. "Underneath Palatial Skin, Corruption Rules Gabon." *New York Times*, September 14, 2009, accessed October 23, 2020, www.nytimes.com/2009/09/15/world/africa/15libreville.html.
19. Emma-Kate Symons. "A Fight Inside Gabon's Kleptocratic Dynasty Exposes the Complicity of French Business." QuartzAfrica, May 1, 2015, accessed October 23, 2020, https://qz.com/395572/a-fight-inside-gabons-kleptocratic-dynasty-reveals-the-complicity-of-french-business/.
20. Bernault, 2019: 19–20.
21. Ali Breland. "The Bizarre and Terrifying Case of the 'Deepfake' Video that Helped Bring an African Nation to the Brink." *Mother Jones*, March 15, 2019, accessed October 23, 2020, www.motherjones.com/politics/2019/03/deepfake-gabon-ali-bongo/.
22. www.facebook.com/tvgabon24/videos/discours-à-la-nation-du-président-ali-bongo-ondimba/324528215059254/.
23. Breland, *supra* note 21.
24. J. M. Porup. "How and Why Deepfake Videos Work – And What Is At Risk." CSOonline.com, April 10, 2019, accessed October 23, 2020, www.csoonline.com/article/3293002/deepfake-videos-how-and-why-they-work.html.
25. "The Suspicious Video that Helped Spark an Attempted Coup in Gabon." The Fact Checker, *Washington Post*, February 13, 2020, accessed October 23, 2020, www.youtube.com/watch?v=F5vzKs4z1dc&vl=en-US.
26. Sarah Cahlan. "How Misinformation Helped Spark an Attempted Coup in Gabon." *Washington Post*, February 13, 2020, accessed October 23, 2020, www.washingtonpost.com/politics/2020/02/13/how-sick-president-suspect-video-helped-sparked-an-attempted-coup-gabon/.

27. Hopewell Chin'ono and Norimitsu Onishi. "Zimbabwe Follows Robert Mugabe's Health by Following His Plane," *New York Times*, September 6, 2016, accessed October 23, 2020, www.nytimes.com/2016/09/07/world/africa/zimbabwe-follows-robert-mugabes-health-by-following-his-plane.html.
28. Maeve Shearlaw. "Mugabe Falls: Comedy Memes of Zimbabwe's President Go Viral." *Guardian*, February 5, 2015, accessed October 23, 2020, www.theguardian.com/world/2015/feb/05/mugabe-falls-comedy-memes-of-zimbabwes-president-viral.
29. Human Rights Watch Report 2019, accessed October 23, 2020, www.hrw.org/world-report/2019/country-chapters/zimbabwe.
30. Jacquelin Kataneksza. "Zimbabwean Twitter is Shifting Politics." Africa Is a Country Blog, October 2018, accessed October 23, 2020, https://africasacountry.com/2018/10/social-media-and-politics-in-zimbabwe.
31. Nyabola, 2018: 4.
32. Kataneksza, *supra* note 30.
33. Chipo Dendere, "Why Are So Many African Leaders Shutting off the Internet in 2019?" *Washington Post*, January 30, 2019, accessed October 23, 2020, www.washingtonpost.com/news/monkey-cage/wp/2019/01/30/why-are-so-many-african-leaders-shutting-off-the-internet-in-2019/?utm_term=.9e774d9661b0.
34. Ibid. Abdi Latif Dahir. "The Numbing Experience of Living through Africa's Growing Internet Shutdowns." Quartz.com, June 24, 2019, accessed October 23, 2020, https://qz.com/africa/1650545/what-does-it-feel-like-to-experience-an-internet-shutdown/.
35. Yomi Kazeem. "Internet shutdowns in Africa were more frequent and lasted longer in 2019." QuartzAfrica, February 27, 2020, accessed October 23, 2020, https://qz.com/africa/1808728/african-internet-shutdowns-were-more-frequent-in-2019/.
36. #KeepitOn. Targeted, Cut off and Left in the Dark: The #KeepItOn Report on Internet shutdowns in 2019, p. 3, www.accessnow.org/cms/assets/uploads/2020/02/KeepItOn-2019-report-1.pdf.
37. Samuel Woodhams. "Chad social media ban reaches one-year mark." African Arguments, March 28, 2019, accessed October 23, 2020, https://africanarguments.org/2019/03/28/chad-social-media-shutdown-has-now-lasted-a-whole-year/.
38. Kazeem, *supra* note 35.
39. "Internet disrupted in Guinea ahead of presidential election result announcement." Netblocks.org, October 23, 2020, accessed October 23, 2020, https://netblocks.org/reports/internet-disrupted-in-guinea-ahead-of-presidential-election-result-announcement-DA3lQ3BW.
40. Abdi Latif Dahir. "Ethiopia's tech startups are ready to run the world, but the internet keeps getting blocked." June 18, 2019, accessed October 23, 2020, https://qz.com/africa/1646789/ethiopia-tech-startups-hurt-by-social-media-block-internet-shutdown/
41. Julie Owono. 2017. "New Internet Shutdown Ordered in Cameroon." Internet sans frontières, accessed October 23, 2020, https://internetwithoutborders.org/fr/new-internet-shutdown-ordered-in-cameroon/.
42. Garbacza and Thompson, 2007.
43. Onkokame Mothobi. Empowering African Economies in the Digital Era, Africa E-Commerce Week Presentation, December 2018, accessed October 23, 2020, https://

researchictafrica.net/wp/wp-content/uploads/2018/12/2018_Measurement-of-the-digital-economy_Africa-E-Week.pdf.

44. Leke, Chironga, and Desvaux, 2019.
45. Babatunde Okunoye. "Building an Internet of Opportunity for Africa." Council on Foreign Relations Blog, March 21, 2019, accessed October 23, 2020, www.cfr.org/blog/building-internet-opportunity-africa.
46. ITU. Measuring Digital Development: Facts and Figures 2019, p. 3, www.itu.int/en/ITU-D/Statistics/Documents/facts/FactsFigures2019_r1.pdf.
47. McKinsey & Company. 2013 *Lions Go Digital: The Internet's Transformative Potential in Africa*, p. 1, accessed October 23, 2020, www.mckinsey.com/Insights/High_Tech_Telecoms_Internet/Lions_go_digital_The_Internets_transformative_potential_in_Africa?cid=other-eml-alt-mgi-mck-oth-1311.
48. GSMA. 2018. The Mobile Economy: Sub-Saharan Africa Mobile Economy, accessed October 23, 2020, www.gsmaintelligence.com/research/?file=809c442550e5487f3b1d025fdc70e23b&download.
49. Ray Browne. "Facebook is building a huge undersea cable around Africa to boost internet access in the continent." *CNBC.com*, May 14, 2020, accessed October 23, 2020, www.cnbc.com/2020/05/14/facebook-building-undersea-cable-in-africa-to-boost-internet-access.html.
50. Nwokeabia, 2001: 12; Langdon, 1986: 181; Commission on Intellectual Property Rights. *Integrating Intellectual Property Rights and Development Policy*, Sept. 2002, accessed October 23, 2020, www.iprcommission.org/papers/pdfs/final_report/CIPRfullfinal.pdf.
51. Englebert, 2000: 1822.
52. O'Connor, 1983: 27.
53. Freund, 2007: 2–5.
54. United Nations. *World Urbanization Prospects: The 2018 Revision*, p. 24, https://population.un.org/wup/Publications/Files/WUP2018-Report.pdf.
55. Hunt, 2014: 9.
56. Njoh, 2008: 581–582.
57. Ibid. at 584.
58. Otiso and Falola, 2017.
59. O'Connor, 1983: 27–41.
60. Otiso and Falola, 2017.
61. Lall, Henderson, and Venables, 2017: 10.
62. Barnes, 1986:16.
63. Lall, Henderson, and Venables, 2017: 123.
64. Ibid. at 123.
65. Schierup, 2016.
66. O'Connor, 1983: 84
67. Moore and Vaughan, 1994: 3.
68. Akpan, 2012: 99.
69. Ibid. at 100.
70. Taxes mandated by colonial authorities led African agricultural producers to grow cash crops for export. These crops displaced food for local consumption. Darkoh and Ould-May, 1992: 40.

71. Korieh, 2001.
72. Mbakwe, 2015: 139; Sutton, 1989.
73. Watts and Bassett, 1986: 122.
74. Ibid.
75. Ijere, 1974: 303.
76. Ibid. at 303–304.
77. Anderson and Throup, 1985: 338.
78. Darkoh and Ould-Mey, 1992: 37.
79. Gastineau and Golaz, 2016.
80. Akpan, 2012: 98.
81. Watts and Bassett, 1986: 107.
82. Akpan, 2012: 101.
83. Watts and Bassett, 1986: 111.
84. Martin, 1995: 37.
85. Paul Akiwumi. "COVID-19: A Threat to Food Security Africa." OECD Development Matters Blog, August 11, 2020, accessed October 23, 2020, https://oecd-development-matters.org/2020/08/11/covid-19-a-threat-to-food-security-in-africa/.
86. FAO. 2009. "How to Feed the World in 2015. High Level Expert Forum – The Special Challenge for Sub-Saharan Africa," p. 8, accessed October 23, 2020, www.fao.org/fileadmin/templates/wsfs/docs/expert_paper/How_to_Feed_the_World_in_2050.pdf.
87. Ekekwe, 2017.
88. Ibid.
89. Carletto, 2010.
90. FAO, 2019: 8.
91. Ibid. at 20; 2019 Global Hunger Index by Severity, accessed October 23, 2020, www.globalhungerindex.org/results.html.
92. UNECA, Subregional Office for Southern Africa. *Climate Change and the Rural Economy in Southern Africa: Issues, Challenges and Opportunities*. Issues Paper, accessed October 23, 2020, www.uneca.org/sites/default/files/PublicationFiles/climate-change-and-the-ruraleconomy-in-southern-africa.pdf.
93. This law copied a law in effect across the Congo River in Leopoldville (now Kinshasha) in the Belgian Congo. Njoh, 2008: 586.
94. Martin, 1995: 37.
95. Ibid.
96. Cloonan, 2006.
97. Donohue, 2015.
98. Zuboff, 2019.
99. Stephen Kafeero. "Uganda is using Huawei's facial recognition tech to crack down on dissent after anti-government protests." QuartzAfrica, November 27, 2020, accessed December 2, 2020, https://qz.com/africa/1938976/uganda-uses-chinas-huawei-facial-recognition-to-snare-protesters/.
100. Helen Epstein. "In Uganda, Another Museveni Crackdown." *New York Review of Books*, November 25, 2020, accessed December 2, 2020, www.nybooks.com/daily/2020/11/25/in-uganda-another-museveni-crackdown/.
101. Wucherpfennig, Hunziker and Cederman, 2016: 885.

102. Emmanuel Iduma. "'Gone Like a Meteor': Epitaph for the Lost Youth of the Biafra War." *New York Review of Books*, May 30, 2019, accessed October 23, 2020, www.nybooks.com/daily/2019/05/30/gone-like-a-meteor-epitaph-for-the-lost-youth-of-the-biafran-war/.
103. Okome, 1999: xxiii.
104. Treaty of Versailles. 1919, Article 119.
105. Fombad, 1999.
106. International Crisis Group. 2017. *Cameroon's Anglophone Crisis at the Crossroads*. Africa Report No. 250,), accessed October 23, 2020, https://d2071andvipowj.cloudfront.net/250-cameroons-anglophone-crisis-at-the-crossroads_0.pdf.
107. https://ambacoin.io/; Amindeh Blaise Atabong. "Cameroon's Anglophone Separatists Have Created Their Own Cryptocurrency." QuartzAfrica, December 12, 2018, accessed October 23, 2020, https://qz.com/africa/1492745/cameroon-anglophone-separtists-create-cryptocurrency-ambacoin/.
108. Jules Roger, Sombaye Eyango, 2018.
109. Annan, 2014; Malu, 2019.
110. Tristan McConnell. "Close Your Eyes and Pretend to Be Dead." *Foreign Policy*, September 20, 2015, accessed October 23, 2020, https://foreignpolicy.com/2015/09/20/nairobi-kenya-westgate-mall-attack-al-shabab/.
111. Costas Paris, Sarah McFarlane and Benoit Faucon. "Islamist Attacks in Mozambique Threaten to Disrupt Total-Led Natural-Gas Project." *Wall Street Journal*, August 20, 2020, accessed October 23, 2020, www.wsj.com/articles/islamist-attacks-in-mozambique-threaten-to-disrupt-total-led-natural-gas-project-11597944723; Leighton G. Luke. "Countering Islamist Insurgency in Northern Mozambique Requires New Approach." Future Directions International, August 19, 2020, accessed October 23, 2020, www.futuredirections.org.au/publication/countering-islamist-insurgency-in-northern-mozambique-requires-new-approach/.
112. Boko Haram "is the popular title for a group that calls itself Jama'at ahl al-sunna li-da'wa wa-l-qital, and it has operated in Nigeria since 2002–2003." David Cook. "The Rise of Boko Haram in Nigeria." *CTC Sentinel* 4, 9 (September 2011), accessed October 23, 2020, https://ctc.usma.edu/the-rise-of-boko-haram-in-nigeria/.
113. RAND Europe. *Social Media in Africa presents double-edged sword for security and development*, November 2018, accessed October 23, 2020, www.rand.org/randeurope/research/projects/social-media-in-africa.html.
114. Morier-Genoud, 2018.
115. Cox et al., 2018: 10.
116. Bernal, 2014.
117. Akokpari, 2007.
118. Mochizuki, n.d.
119. SB Morgen, 2020.
120. Chukwuma, 2020.
121. SB Morgen, 2020: 4; Malu, 2019.
122. Adejumo Kabir. "Soyinka laments insecurity, says Nigeria's sovereignty taken over by armed groups." *Premium Times*, January 10, 2021, accessed January 10, 2021, www.premiumtimesng.com/news/headlines/435863-soyinka-laments-insecurity-says-nigerias-sovereignty-taken-over-by-armed-groups.html.

123. Human Rights Watch. Nigeria: Crackdown on Police Brutality Protests. October 16, 2020, accessed October 23, 2020, www.hrw.org/news/2020/10/16/nigeria-crackdown-police-brutality-protests#.
124. Adejumo Kabir. "Nigerian Army Threatens Decisive Action Against 'Subversive Elements, Trouble Makers'." *Premium Times*, October 15, 2020, accessed October 23, 2020, www.premiumtimesng.com/news/top-news/420898-nigerian-army-threatens-decisive-action-against-subversive-elements-trouble-makers.html.
125. Human Rights Watch, *supra* note 123.
126. Oris Aigbokhaevbolo. "Nigeria's Protests Against Police Violence." *New York Review of Books*, November 1, 2020, accessed November 1, 2020, www.nybooks.com/daily/2020/11/01/nigeria-protest-against-police-violence/.
127. Ibid.

9

Elites, Ornamentation, and Future Visions

Perhaps I am just a disembodied self usurping my body, strapped into a business-class seat in the plane, being borne to my designated burial ground . . . .

Wole Soyinka, *You Must Set Forth at Dawn: A Memoir* (2006)

Would You Give Up Your Airline Seat for Wole Soyinka?

Instagram Page of Tonye Patrick Cole (June 23, 2019) @professorwolesoyinka #celebrategreatness #relationshipsmatter

Is it too much to ask that an elderly man be allowed to remain in a seat allotted to you in the same business class cabin . . . ?[1]

STATUS AND HIERARCHY IN NIGERIA

An Instagram post by Tonye Patrick Cole described what happened on his flight when a man insisted on sitting in his assigned business class seat and asked globally renowned author Wole Soyinka to move because Wole Soyinka was in his seat. Wole Soyinka moved without issue but others aboard the plane were unhappy that Wole Soyinka had been asked to change his seat. This post began a revealing series of exchanges in social media and reports in traditional media about seats in business class on an airplane. This 2019 exchange involving Wole Soyinka's plane seat underscores critical fissures in Nigeria surrounding age, status, and other characteristics that reached a boiling point just over a year later during the #EndSARS protests. The public reaction to the events described in the Instagram post led Wole Soyinka to respond: "[t]hose who permit themselves to be persuaded, even for one second that I, Wole Soyinka, having wrongly identified a seat number like millions of travellers all the time, and all over the world, would then attempt to consolidate the error in any form, through act, word, or gesture, qualify to be the first beneficiaries of this vastly improved humanitarian policy."[2]

Notably, Wole Soyinka has long been a strong critic of the Nigerian government, which led to his imprisonment and exile. The debate that arose concerning his business class seat reflected his status as a leading luminary and Nobel Prize in

Literature laureate in 1986, but not the sentiments and criticisms that he has long expressed about governance failures in Nigeria.

The Instagram post touches on an issue of tension and increased contestation in Nigeria, particularly for many young people. Even prior to any digital revolution, if one were to occur, Nigeria is a country with staggering levels of inequality. Status hierarchies in Nigeria reflect a hybrid weave of precolonial, colonial, and postcolonial practices as interpreted and interpolated in present-day contexts. Patterns of hierarchy and elite privilege were a prominent characteristic of colonialism, when colonial administrators played a significant role in picking winners and losers by virtue of varied colonial policies. Colonial administrators also created hybrid rituals surrounding indigenous rulers that both intensified and reinscribed power hierarchies.

Patterns of elite formation in Ghana and Nigeria reflect types of elite categories that arose in British colonies in Africa during and after colonialism. Missionaries contributed to elite formation in Nigeria, playing an important role in providing educational opportunities.[3] In early colonial Ghana and Nigeria, local rulers who participated in colonial administrations formed a key early element of the elite category.[4] These local rulers included existing rulers, as well as those selected by colonial administrators. In Ghana, this group, which might be referred to as "traditional" elites, was joined by a "national bourgeoisie" group of elites who supported the colonial administration, including "lawyers, judges top civil servants, senior army and police officers" who helped "the imperial powers rule more effectively."[5]

Other beneficiaries of colonialism became part of this national bourgeoisie, including wealthy peasants and others involved in successful commercial activities. The bourgeois nationalist elites were the core of the independence movement in Ghana and took power at independence. In Ghana and elsewhere, African elites were molded through education to accept hierarchies of value that saw the European as superior to the African. As a result, elites tended to not only benefit from but also accept colonial hierarchies of status, which is an impediment to disruption of colonial overhang. In a "Letter from Ghana" published in *The New York Review of Books* in October 1967, an anonymous author notes the following:

> The British were most skeptical of the ability of Africans to rise on the ladder, and made no serious attempts to assimilate their colonized. In Ghana, however, the coolness of the British was offset by the ardent faith with which the educated Ghanaians embraced the doctrine. A number seriously desired to become black Englishmen. The not-so-ambitious assumed as a matter of course that if they could acquire British habits they would eventually be invited to share the ruling of their less fortunate brothers with the white master, thus constituting a modern colonial ruling elite... the education of the Ghanaian was nothing less than an organized, systematic flight from all things African – culture, values, roots – to things European. As a result, the educated Ghanaian had two very marked traits in his

psychology: first, an uncritical adoration of everything British; second, a profound contempt for his own people.[6]

Things falling within the elite category thus came to be positioned in opposition to things African:

> This profound dislike of Africans and African institutions manifested itself in a disapproval of the masses, who formed the large base of the dual society, and in a marked separation between the masses and the elite.[7]

Conceptions of eliteness and elites' marking of elite boundaries thus naturally continued one-way patterns of borrowing and acceptance of the external, rather than disrupting externally derived colonial institutions to replace them with locally based hybrid ones. Elites may also play an important role in ethnic politics,[8] which may reflect a legacy of colonial divide-and-rule policies. Attitudes toward the external and the internal continue to play an important role in many African contexts today, shaping conceptions of entitlements to public resources that underlie jurisdictional arbitrage and other extractive behaviors.

The reaction to the business class seating arrangements on a plane highlights important issues about place and status in Nigeria and other countries in Africa today. During colonialism, education, relative wealth, and high status in state institutions became "basic determinants of elite status" in Nigeria.[9] Positions held by Europeans were at independence filled by "a highly educated Western-oriented African ruling elite."[10] These elites were separated from the masses within former colonies by their Western orientation and access to opportunities provided by state institutions. In Sudan, educational policies favoring those with high status were a pragmatic attempt to quell potential anticolonial resistance by "giving potential opponents – precolonial elites and their offspring – a stake in the system."[11] British reinforced existing status hierarchies in colonial Sudan through education policies that channeled Black Sudanese into technical education rather than academic education.[12]

The elite imprint in state institutions was marked in Nigeria, where 87 percent of college educated people were employed by government following independence, primarily in senior service positions.[13] This concentration of colonial government economic power carried over to governments in the postcolonial era. Postcolonial elites have thus held concentrated economic and political power in an institutional environment with few effective constraints on that power, which has facilitated extractive behaviors.

Elites mark status in myriad ways that are fueled by the large share of Nigerian oil wealth that is funneled to those at the top. Although Nigeria generates significant proceeds from oil resources, the vast majority of the population in Nigeria lives in abject poverty. In contrast, Nigerian elites often live large. Nigerian government officials may travel in caravans of multiple, and at times, luxury cars. In

September 2019, a coalition of civil society groups attempted to block importation of over $15 million worth of luxury cars for use by the Nigerian Senate.[14] In response to protests about the automobile purchases, the Nigerian Senate spokesman stated: "[d]irectors of agencies, even minor officials in agencies use official cars. So why will the National Assembly be different? Why should it be a problem that the National Assembly is entitled to cars, to use official cars?"[15]

Nigerian legislators are among the most highly compensated in the world. The compensation and perquisites of Nigerian legislators are increasingly a source of contestation and significant negative publicity for Nigeria. A controversy arises whenever legislative compensation figures are disclosed.[16] The BBC has a Nigerian senator salary calculator that enables people to compare their compensation with those of Nigerian senators.[17] According to this calculator, a person earning 500,000 Naira (₦) per month, which was the approximate equivalent of just over $1,200 in early 2021, would earn in thirty days what a Nigerian senator earns in two hours and twenty minutes. In 2018, compensation and expense allowances for Nigerian senators were reported to be close to $40,000 per month.[18] These levels of compensation are largely unregulated and reflect a general lack of transparency and accountability at the highest levels of the Nigerian legislative branch. The amounts received by senators contrast with the less than $2 per day on which the average Nigerian is estimated to live, and is notably higher than the less than the $200,000 in compensation per year that is granted members of the US Congress.[19] These levels of compensation are striking, given the increasing number of poor people in Nigeria.

In addition to poverty, the digital divide remains a concern in African countries. The digital divide, which concerns unequal access to and usage of new technologies,[20] has also grown in certain respects as digital-era technologies have become more widespread in Africa. As mobile technologies have been deployed in Africa, the urban–rural and gender digital divides are increasing,[21] which has significant implications for future inequality. Trends in Africa are consistent with those elsewhere in the world. Disruptive technologies in Silicon Valley and elsewhere have had significant distributional effects and have exacerbated inequality, sometimes in ways that were likely predictable.

COLONIALISM, INTERMEDIARIES, AND JURISDICTIONAL ARBITRAGE

Colonialism created opportunities for rent-seeking by intermediaries in ways that were largely not checked at the time. In Sierra Leone, for example, "[i]ndirect rule created new opportunities for chiefs to seek rents and distort local economic activity," including through opportunities provided by legal frameworks that placed "ultimate ownership of all land in the hands of the paramount chief" and made paramount chiefs "eligible for direct payments of 'surface rent' from miners."[22] Laws in Sierra Leone thus "created opportunities for chiefs to capture rents from both private citizens and the central government," enabled them to pervert justice through corrupt judicial decisions, and allowed them to exploit their power by compelling their "subjects to undertake 'communal labor'."[23]

Economic rent is a measure of market power and reflects excess or monopoly profits. Rent-seeking refers to the expenditure of resources to create, maintain, or transfer rent or that seek to acquire access to or control over opportunities for earning rent.[24] This might involve, for example, activities in which "the governmental apparatus is employed to create and extract rents."[25] The desire to capture the "rent-creating governmental control of markets for the purpose of creating and extracting rents" drives competition for control of government in African contexts.[26] Rent-seeking activities in these contexts are unproductive, produce private profits to those who undertake such activities, and impose social costs. These costs include political instability from battles over government control, diversion of resources from productive uses to rent-seeking and political contests, and increased costs of doing business.[27]

Treatment of local intermediaries during colonialism has played an important role in determining the perquisites of elite status and structures that facilitate exploitation and rent-seeking. The latitude given such intermediaries during colonialism continues to shape entitlements and elite behavior. Intermediaries during colonialism came to rely on varied methods of extraction. Intermediaries could also wield power in ways that were abusive. Wielding of power and extractive behaviors by intermediaries have contributed to the creation of legal and other institutions that are distorted. Even if not intentional, the benefits to intermediaries that might accrue from such institutions may minimize incentives to reform such structures.

The distinct legal systems evident during colonialism continue to operate side-by-side in Nigeria. These distinct systems reflect fundamentally different conceptions about, and approaches to, law that remain unreconciled and incompatible to a significant degree. The lack of reconciliation between English and customary law has also created ongoing opportunities for jurisdictional arbitrage, which had become evident by the time of colonialism. The term *arbitrage* comes from trading in financial markets where traders take advantage of different prices in different markets or derivative forms to receive a profit. Jurisdictional arbitrage occurs when people exploit laws in different jurisdictions to obtain a benefit. Jurisdictional arbitrage is commonly used by multinational corporations and wealthy individuals to minimize taxes.[28] The manner of implementation of English law and customary law in Nigeria effectively created multiple legal systems in the same jurisdiction without sufficient attention to the full implications of having these different systems. Indirect rule reinforced the importance of social networks and relationships as determining factors for access to resources. Further, in "seeking to maintain social and administrative stability by building on tradition, officials wove instability – in the form of changing relations of authority and conflicting interpretations of rules – into the fabric of colonial administration."[29]

Customary law consists of hundreds of different sets of law that may vary by ethnic group and even by village.[30] Conflicts between customary law and English law–derived frameworks have created opportunities for jurisdictional arbitrage and blocking behaviors. The initial implementation and continued operation of legal systems in Nigeria and elsewhere have largely not addressed opportunities for arbitrage that remain. In the postcolonial era, this type of arbitrage has been detrimental to the operation of law in Nigeria and elsewhere in Africa. Jurisdictional arbitrage creates opportunities for people to garner a private profit from their public or quasi-public position or status. The failure to constrain jurisdictional arbitrage during colonialism is a negative colonial legacy.

Jurisdictional arbitrage was used by varied intermediaries. Interpreters were often well positioned to take advantage of their understanding of differences between external and internal systems of governance in ways that enabled them to extract rent:

> the interpreter soon assumed a central position as a broker between the French and the Banjal. In addition to advising on land questions and settling disputes throughout the Lower Casamance, he exercised considerable influence in the selection of cantonal chiefs in the Banjal zone. Initially the French sought chiefs from clans whom they believed to hold 'traditional' authority . . . . Beginning in this pre-war period the interpreter maintained close relations with the priestly patronymic groups, over the years becoming known as such an authority on their rites that in the 1960s he sometimes advised those responsible on the correct ritual procedures! Subsequently colonial criteria for chiefs included a minimal ability to speak French or overt signs of political compliance.[31]

Colonial authorities in Nigeria were often tolerant of jurisdictional arbitrage, other abuses of power, and corruption:

> At an interview with Mr E. R. Chadwick, a former D. O. in Warri Province, in London on 20 Dec., 1962, I was told that Dogho's relations with the Residents were extremely cordial. The more junior officers were aware of his abuse of office and other failings, though as Mr Chadwick pointed out, Dogho was clever to choose his time and place. In the circumstances, it was always difficult to bring his faults home to him.[32]

In Nigerian contexts, British tolerance of abuse of power was colored by colonial administrators' conceptions of sovereignty that were not consistent with democracy or institutional limitations on the power of their designated local rulers. In a discussion in relation to a local chief, a colonial officer made a comparison between the power of African rulers and medieval European rulers by invoking conceptions of the ruler as suzerain. The recourse to feudal law was noted by William Geary, the lawyer who represented Oba Olofin of Isheri in the case under discussion.[33] The failure of British colonial authorities to adequately address abuse of power, jurisdictional arbitrage, blocking behaviors, and other forms of exploitation contributed to an institutional structure in which those with power could often act with impunity. This also meant that the power of British colonial authorities was largely unchecked. At independence, the legal and institutional legacy in Nigeria and other former British colonies was fundamentally skewed in ways that have in many instances still not been addressed.

Use of the term *suzerain* in the case involving Oba Olofin of Isheri reflects the use of underlying European political, economic, cultural, and other conceptions that were critical aspects of the imposition of colonialism. These underlying conceptions were not always explicitly stated, and likely, not always well understood by those seemingly using such concepts. Not surprisingly, the legal systems that came with colonialism had an impact on the legibility of local institutions for many local people. Local people in colonies in Africa became subject to new legal systems, significant portion of which was unfamiliar to them. Many in local communities likely had some familiarity with customary law. English law was alien in multiple ways. It required a language that few local people read or even understood and was based on cultural values and histories that were unknown to local people and misunderstood even by colonial officers who were tasked with implementing English law.

The British needed local intermediaries to bridge these differences. These local intermediaries developed an understanding of the new systems, institutions, and policies being introduced by the British. Some undoubtedly used this knowledge to benefit local people. Some took advantage of this knowledge by using jurisdictional arbitrage for personal benefit. These types of extractive approaches could have been recognized and limited by colonial powers, but were largely not constrained. As conflicts among legal systems within the same jurisdiction arose, opportunities for jurisdictional arbitrage continued to emerge.

In their study of rural paramount chiefs in Sierra Leone, Acemoglu, Reed and Robinson found that for "those born in places where there are fewer ruling families, a variety of development outcomes are significantly worse."[34] The availability of jurisdictional and other forms of arbitrage led to a focus by some elites on activities that were not necessarily beneficial to the society as a whole but that could be highly beneficial to them. These types of opportunities have skewed incentives and behaviors. The initial implementation and continued operation of legal systems in Nigeria and elsewhere in Africa have largely not addressed opportunities for jurisdictional and other forms of arbitrage and blocking behaviors that remain present and that continue to be created. In the postcolonial era, this type of arbitrage and other opportunities for extraction continue to be detrimental to the operation of law.

Law in colonial and postcolonial contexts has unfolded within zones of contestation and changing local and global circumstances that highlight conflicts between the internal and external, as well as competing visions of both the external and the internal. The actions of colonial administrators were not neutral. Part of understanding the impact of the external in colonial and postcolonial African countries is clarifying how the external has impacted competing internal conceptions and empowered those whose views were accepted by colonial and other externally based authorities. Moreover, the internal and external are interrelated, and interact with and impact one another in myriad ways. Elizabeth Colson has noted how internal contestation played out in the development of customary land law, particularly in contexts where scarcity became a factor and people "became aware of the conflict between the old political obligation to maintain general access to adequate resources for all citizens, and the possibility of extracting an individual profit from areas preempted under the rule that a man might enjoy the fruits of his labor."[35]

Rulers selected by the British were kept in check by threat of force. The penalty for opposing British interests could be quite high. Benin City was once the seat of the great African medieval Kingdom of Benin, which today is located within Nigeria. Prior to its destruction, Benin City was situated on a plain with massive walls. The earthworks around Benin City were constructed between 800 and 1500 AD and:

> extend for some 16 000 kilometres in all, in a mosaic of more than 500 interconnected settlement boundaries. They cover 6500 square kilometres and were all dug by the Edo people. In all, they are four times longer than the Great Wall of China, and consumed a hundred times more material than the Great Pyramid of Cheops. They took an estimated 150 million hours of digging to construct, and are perhaps the largest single archaeological phenomenon on the planet.[36]

Benin City was one of the first cities to have lighting and was planned using fractal design.[37] Patterns of fractal geometry, which is "one of the most exciting frontiers in the fusion between mathematics and information technology," are "surprisingly common in traditional African designs and some of its basic concepts are fundamental to African knowledge systems."[38] When the Portuguese first encountered Benin City in 1485, "they were stunned to find this vast kingdom made of hundreds of interlocked cities and villages in the middle of the African jungle. They called it the 'Great City of Benin', at a time when there were hardly any other places in Africa the Europeans acknowledged as a city. Indeed, they classified Benin City as one of the most beautiful and best planned cities in the world."[39]

In 1897, following the ambush and killing in Benin of members of a British delegation, British military forces conducted a punitive military expedition against the Kingdom of Benin. British military forces invaded, looted, and ransacked Benin City, setting buildings on fire and killing many people. They seized thousands of works of art in the process, including the now world-famous plaques, sculptures, and other objects, including elephant tusks, known as the Benin Bronzes. The British then deposed, shackled, and exiled Oba Ovonramwen, the ruler of Benin, to Calabar, where he died in 1914. The British attack led to the end of Benin's existence as an independent kingdom.[40] Benin's cultural heritage was seized by British authorities and by individual soldiers in some instances, and kept by the British government or the families of soldiers or sold in European art markets. Few artifacts have been returned to Nigeria.[41] Ironically, during a later time period in the mid-1930s, after the imposition of indirect rule and during the reign of Oba Akenzua II, the grandson of Oba Ovonramwen, British colonial officials attempted to locate and purchase on behalf of Oba Akenzua II stools that had been taken in 1897.[42]

ELITE ORNAMENTATION AND POVERTY IN NIGERIA

As Muna Ndulo has noted, "the dreams of post-independence prosperity and self-rule [in Africa] have become the nightmare of insecurity and poverty."[43] Elites and elite visions in African countries have played an important role in these outcomes. Pervasive conditions of insecurity and poverty in Africa reflect policy environments inherited after colonialism that have been recreated and sustained by internal elites, often with various forms of external support. Continuities between the colonial and postcolonial era are, in part, a consequence of how postcolonial elites have conceptualized and applied postcolonial legal frameworks, which have been largely based on colonial-era laws and lawmaking approaches that have still not been sufficiently disrupted.

Most importantly, postcolonial elites in Africa have in more than a few instances adopted the mindset of European colonialists in their conceptualizations of their place within their societies. As David Cannandine has noted, British colonialism as adopted in India, and later in colonies in Africa, included pervasive hierarchies and ornamentalism:

> Nigerian emirs and African kings rarely ruled over societies that were as venerable, as settled, as ornamental or as rich as the grandest princely states seemed to be. But traditional India remained the model, which meant that the new empire of indirect rule depended on the cooperation and support of kings who were presumed to be at the apex of 'a clearly defined hierarchical society' . . . . As a result, chiefs and emirs and sultans were treated with great shows of public respect by British officials, especially on such ceremonial occasions as installations, coronations, investitures, birthdays and jubilees . . . at Budo in Uganda, the British built a public school, just after the First World War, for the education of local rulers and notables . . . coronation services took place in the college chapel, combining British and African ceremonial elements.[44]

Indirect rule was grafted onto existing hierarchies in places such as northern Nigeria and Buganda. In societies that had less extensive or visible hierarchies, chiefs were identified and given extensive authority, which had a significant impact on such chiefs' communities. Although the British made great shows of public respect to rulers whom they anointed, the actual status of such rulers was precarious and noncooperative rulers could be displaced by British authorities.[45] British choices of local rulers also tended to prioritize rulers who did not oppose British interests or priorities. This tended to make such rulers ineffective agents for those over whom they ostensibly ruled, which has continuing implications today.

Ornamentalism reflects what Georg Simmel characterized as adornment, which he notes is the "egoistic element as such: it singles out its wearer, whose self-feeling it embodies and increases at the cost of others (for the same adornment of all would no longer adorn the individual)."[46] Simmel also notes that "by virtue of adornment, a representative of one's group, with whose whole significance one is 'adorned.' It is as if the significance of his status, symbolized by jewels, returned to the individual on the very beams which originate in him and enlarge his sphere of impact. Adornment, thus, appears as the means by which his social power or dignity is transformed into visible, personal excellence."[47]

The impact of ornamentalism is pervasive throughout Africa today. The vast spending on mansions, cars, yachts, and other amenities and the documentation of his life on Instagram by Teodoro Nguema Obiang Mangue of Equatorial Guinea, reflects adornment. In Nigeria, oil wealth has facilitated grand acts of adornment. Stories, some of which are not true or wildly exaggerated, abound about the activities of Nigerian elites.

In 2019, during a formal hearing for which a YouTube clip was posted, the Nigerian Agriculture Minister lamented the loss of foreign exchange from the activities of wealthy Nigerians who order pizza in London and have it delivered to Nigeria on British Airways.[48] The minister's remarks were widely reported. The story is a remarkable example of elite ornamentalism that, taken collectively, has a profound impact on all Nigerians. Even if the story is not true, it reflects beliefs about things that Nigerian elites could do and the implications of such decisions. Comedian Trevor Noah highlighted the clip and questioned the decision to bypass Italy and order pizza from London.[49] Bringing pizza to Nigeria from London reflects the external orientation of those who would undertake such activities. Other paths for obtaining pizza might have a greater benefit within Nigeria, including, for example, investing in a local pizzeria, which could provide local opportunities and employment, but perhaps would not fulfill same function in terms of adornment. A story about ordering pizza illuminates patterns of decision-making that reflect a continuing postcolonial external orientation and valorization that must be disrupted.

Externally derived policy decisions and internal decision-making that does not adequately consider the needs of the many contribute to the profound poverty that exists in Nigeria. The number of people in poverty in Nigeria, combined with the activities of at least some elites, is not a positive harbinger for the future. It also reflects choices within Nigeria that demonstrate questionable uses of proceeds from Nigeria's oil resources.

Elite ornamentation is present even in countries that lack the oil resources of Nigeria. Burundi – a tiny landlocked country in East Africa bordered by Rwanda, Tanzania, and the DRC – is one of the poorest countries in the world. In early 2019, travel blogs and media reports indicated that the government of Burundi had rejected a proposed new flight route from Nairobi, Kenya. The proposed route was to be flown by JamboJet, which is affiliated with Kenyan Airways. JamboJet was planning to use a small jet for the proposed Nairobi flight. The government of Burundi rejected the flight because it had no business class, which according to the letter said to have been sent from the Ministry of Transport, Public Works, Equipment and Land Use to the airline: "I would like to kindly inform you, as I informed your partner Kenya Airways before, that our high State officials travel to the world mainly via Nairobi and need to be treated in business class conditions that are acceptable considering their rank."[50]

MIGRANTS, INSURGENTS, AND POSTINDEPENDENCE REALITIES

Conditions on the grounds in many African countries are driving many to attempt to escape, even at the cost of losing their lives or liberty. What some refer to as the migrant crisis in Europe is at least in part a reaction to lack of opportunities within migrants' countries of origin. This pervasive scarcity of opportunity in many areas is a consequence of colonial and postcolonial internal and external policies. Migrants from Africa have died while crossing the Mediterranean.[51] Some people have been auctioned off in slave markets in Libya.[52]

Recent migration statistics across the Mediterranean underscore the continuing impact of colonial governance in Africa. In the past, although some left Africa, the vast majority of people within African countries had few options but to remain, often experiencing significant adversity and scarcity of opportunity. The conditions within African countries thus typically benefitted external powers both by permitting continued patterns of resource extraction and enabling migration of talented people from such countries, contributing to an ongoing brain drain from many countries in Africa.[53]

Although ongoing aid to Africa has been a focus of many external powers and donors, insufficient attention has been paid to structures of extraction and exploitation that benefit external powers and internal elites within Africa, typically to the detriment of many. In recent years, a persistent scarcity of opportunity has led increasing numbers of people to seek opportunities in Europe, through official and unofficial paths. Unofficial migration from Africa and elsewhere, which is having a decided impact in Europe, may be drawing attention to structures that perpetuate inequality and lack of opportunity within countries in Africa. External powers, including former colonial powers, are deeply implicated in such structures. The inflow of migrants into Europe has also highlighted tensions within Europe. In January 2019, Italy's then deputy prime minister, a member of the anti-immigration Five Star Movement, accused France of forcing poor Africans to flee their countries because it runs those countries as de facto colonies: "France has never stopped colonizing tens of African states . . . . The EU should sanction France, and all countries like France, that impoverish Africa and make these people leave, because Africans should be in Africa, not at the bottom of the Mediterranean."[54]

The same technologies that have facilitated digital economy commercial networks have fostered the development of global networks connecting insurgents in different parts of the world. Boko Haram and other forms of organized violence in Nigeria – including robbers, bandits, and kidnappers – reflect, and are in part, an outcome of persistent poverty resulting from corruption, poor governance, and broader institutional failures in Nigeria.[55]

The impact of the migration "crisis" and networks of insurgents may focus attention on internal policies within countries that drive people to migrate or become insurgents and on the impact of external powers on such policies. Today, the vast majority of citizens in far too many African countries face a policy-induced environment of scarcity. Many people must scramble to find work, food, shelter, water, electricity, education and, before the advent of mobile phones, the ability to communicate in other than in face-to-face contexts. Scarcity of opportunity tends to limit future possibilities, which may be subsumed under everyday conditions in which the focus is survival. Unemployment and underemployment are pervasive throughout Africa, particularly among the young: "[c]urrently, Africa is the world's youngest continent, with an estimated 10 to 12 million young Africans joining the labour force each year. Yet the continent is able to create only about 3 million jobs annually. With limited economic opportunities, many young Africans are migrating to Europe and America for economic opportunities."[56]

Employment in many parts of Africa is informal to a great degree. Rather than serving as a basis for innovation and small business growth, the informal sector in many African countries remains largely marginalized. Furthermore, opportunities for all but the most connected are constricted by widespread failure to facilitate local small business and entrepreneurship, high levels of corruption, insufficient infrastructure investment, high costs, and other factors.[57]

Scarcity of opportunity restricts future possibilities in myriad ways. It prevents people from realizing their full potential. The implications of scarcity of opportunity extend far beyond tangible resources. The scarcity of opportunity can severely limit hopes and dreams of the future because of the necessities of survival that may cause many people to function in survival mode, which has serious consequences for the human body and psyche.

Present-day realities in many African countries are far removed from the visions of Africa's potential futures at the time of independence. The disconnect between future visions at independence and postindependence realities is, in part, a consequence of changing conceptualizations of Africa's future among elites and ruling classes. On a more concrete level, the disconnection between past visions of the future and actual outcomes also reflects inattention to the gap between rhetoric and reality, a failure to fully appreciate the limitations within which African countries were to operate in the postindependence era with respect to external powers, lack of a strategic vision, and, perhaps most importantly, widespread failures of rulers to govern with integrity and accountability in various times and places.

Independence leaders at the cusp of African independence had a vision of freedom from colonialism that was compelling. They also creatively borrowed from Western conceptions about freedom, independence, and human rights, in effect recasting colonialism through a lens that made its continuation less tenable. Colonial-era nationalist leaders were particularly effective in using Western discourse about rights and freedoms to make their case for the necessity for colonialism to end. Anticolonial movements were both nationalist movements and human rights movements; the connection between anticolonial movements and contemporary human rights frameworks is increasingly recognized.[58] This creative vision, paired with events in the developed world after World War II, particularly in Europe, led to a cascading fall in formal colonial rule in the roughly two decades following the end of World War II. However, as Phyllis Taoua has noted, national liberation in African contexts "did not deliver meaningful freedom to the majority of people in Africa."[59]

Meaningful freedom for the majority of people in Africa will require freedom from the institutional and legal legacies of colonialism. This would require disruption of laws, regulations, legal processes, and patterns of borrowing that has yet to be undertaken in much of the African continent. Without such disruption, future paths at independence largely followed the path that already existed prior to independence, with little fundamental transformation of available paths. The acceptance of European institutional models with little scrutiny of the implications of such models in Africa and little ongoing readjustment of paths in light of actual outcomes is a critical background factor that has led to current conditions throughout Africa:

> It was to be these emerging elites who were to lead the African nationalist movement. They harnessed the popular resistance of the multitudes to minimum wages, extremely low crop prices and the frequent employment of forced labour. Their own interests, however, were rather different, namely the gaining of power and the use to which it could be put for the accumulation of wealth. These few were trained in the European universities or military academies and in the colonial administrations. The elites accepted the European models as being the only ones for Africa. They accepted the ruling ideology and institutions whether or not they were applicable and, sadly, all too often they were found wanting in practice.[60]

The failure to disrupt key aspects of colonial institutions reflects contradictions within African liberation movements whose leaders sought to overthrow European colonizers, but ended up essentially replacing them.

Notes

1. From the Instagram Page of Tonye Patrick Cole as quoted in Adams Odunayo, "Nigerians react as aircraft passenger asks Wole Soyinka to get off his seat." Legit.ng., accessed October 23, 2020, www.legit.ng/1245150-outrage-aircraft-passenger-asks-wole-soyinka-seat.html.

2. I can't wrongly pick airline seat and justify action – Soyinka, Punchng.com, June 29, 2019, accessed October 23, 2020, https://punchng.com/i-cant-wrongly-pick-airline-seat-and-justify-action-soyinka/.
3. Ajayi, 1969.
4. Kofi, 1972: 97.
5. Ibid.
6. Name Withheld. "A Letter from Ghana." *The New York Review of Books*, October 12, 1967, www.nybooks.com/articles/1967/10/12/letter-from-ghana/.
7. Kofi, 1972: 99.
8. Adebanwi, 2014.
9. Barnes, 1986: 14.
10. Ibid.
11. Sharkey, 2003: 24.
12. Ibid. at 23.
13. Barnes, 1986: 14.
14. Bukola Adebayo, "Nigerian Lawmakers Face Public Anger over Planned Purchase of Luxury Cars." CNN.com, September 2, 2019, accessed October 23, 2020, www.cnn.com/2019/09/02/africa/nigeria-senate-luxury-car-controversy-intl/.
15. Ibid.
16. Muhammed Adedeji Akinyemi. "Nigerian Lawmakers Are Eating the Country with Insane Allowances." African Liberty, May 17, 2019, accessed October 23, 2020, www.africanliberty.org/2019/05/17/nigerian-lawmakers-are-eating-the-countrys-wealth-with-insane-allowances/.
17. Nigerian senator salary calculator: How do you compare? *BBC News*, April 1, 2018, accessed October 23, 2020, www.bbc.com/news/world-africa-43516825.
18. John Campbell. "Uproar over Parliamentary Salaries in Nigeria, Again." Council on Foreign Relations Blog, March 20, 2019, accessed October 23, 2020, www.cfr.org/blog/uproar-over-parliamentary-salaries-nigeria-again.
19. Ibid.
20. Fuchs and Horvath, 2008.
21. Nour, 2017.
22. Acemoglu, Reed and Robinson, 2014: 327.
23. Ibid. at 327, 329.
24. Coolidge and Rose-Ackerman, 1997: 2–3; Khan, 2000.
25. Mbaku and Paul, 1989: 64.
26. Ibid.
27. Ibid. at 63.
28. Palan and Mangraviti, 2016: 422.
29. Berry, 1993: 32.
30. Rahmatian, 1996: 283.
31. Snyder, 1981: 59.
32. Ikime, 1965: 320–321.
33. TNA CO 583/235/14.
34. Acemoglu, Reed and Robinson, 2014: 362.
35. Colson, 1971: 195–196.

36. Fred Pearce. "The African Queen." *New Scientist*, September 11, 1999, accessed October 23, 2020, www.newscientist.com/article/mg16322035-100-the-african-queen/.
37. Mawuna Koutonin. "Story of Cities #5: Benin City, the Mighty Medieval Capital Now Lost Without Trace." *Guardian*, March 8, 2016, accessed October 23, 2020, www.theguardian.com/cities/2016/mar/18/story-of-cities-5-benin-city-edo-nigeria-mighty-medieval-capital-lost-without-trace.
38. Eglash, 1999: 3.
39. Koutonin, *supra* note 37.
40. Igbafe, 1970.
41. Akenzua, 2000; Plankensteiner, 2016.
42. TNA CO 583/211/10.
43. Ndulo, 2003: 334.
44. Cannandine, 2001: 102–103.
45. British colonial records include a number of disputes involving local rulers' entitlements, including who is authorized to rule and who is authorized to receive payments made by the British to local rulers.
46. Simmel, 1950: 339.
47. Ibid. at 343.
48. www.youtube.com/watch?v=iyLlii1WDjA, at 2:35.
49. www.youtube.com/watch?v=hmn_I_4rpo8.
50. John Njiru. "Burundi Rejects JamboJet as It Lacks Business Class." The Kenyan Wall Street, November 14, 2018, accessed October 23, 2020, https://kenyanwallstreet.com/burundi-rejects-jambojet-as-it-lacks-business-class/.
51. UN News. "Thousands Suffer Extreme Rights Abuses Journeying to Africa's Mediterranean Coast, Say Humanitarians." July 29, 2020, accessed October 23, 2020, https://news.un.org/en/story/2020/07/1069231.
52. Nour Youssef. "Sale of Migrants as Slaves in Libya Causes Outrage in Africa and Paris." *New York Times*, November 19, 2017, accessed October 23, 2020, www.nytimes.com/2017/11/19/world/africa/libya-migrants-slavery.html.
53. Mo Ibrahim Foundation. Brain Drain: A Bane for Africa, August 9, 2018, accessed October 23, 2020, https://mo.ibrahim.foundation/news/2018/brain-drain-bane-africas-potential.
54. Kim Willsher. "Italy and France's Refugee Dispute Awakens a Dark Colonial Legacy." *Guardian*, January 27, 2019, accessed October 23, 2020, www.theguardian.com/world/2019/jan/27/italy-france-refugee-dispute-awakens-dark-colonial-legacy-migration.
55. International Crisis Group, 2014: 2–6.
56. Mo Ibrahim Foundation, supra note 53.
57. Jallow, 2014.
58. Ibahwoh, 2007: 5.
59. Taoua, 2018: 8.
60. Munslow, 1983: 223.

10

Colonial Portfolios, Monopolies, and Competition

In much of Africa formal economies are dominated by large firms that rip off consumers . . . firm markups are about 11% larger . . .[and] prices . . . 20% higher.

The Economist, October 3, 2020[1]

POLICY DESIGN AND THE RACIAL IMAGINATION

As Achille Mbembe notes in *On the Postcolony*, understanding African "historicities" requires and understanding of history, the history of ideas, and theories that shaped interactions with Africa and Africans, particularly in Europe, but increasingly today in other areas of the world, including China. In early 2018 and again in 2021, the *CCTV New Year's Gala* (Spring Festival Gala), an annual variety show broadcast for the Lunar New Year that receives as many as 800 million viewers, featured a skit, intended to celebrate China's relationship with African countries that included performers in blackface.[2] As part of the 2018 celebration, a well-known Chinese actress appeared in blackface as an African woman with exaggerated buttocks and a large chest. She was accompanied by an African man dressed as a monkey.[3] Images of the 2018 and 2021 galas were widely shared throughout the world. The sharing of racist imagery out of China was also evident in 2016, when a black man smeared with paint was washed and came out of the laundry as a Chinese man in an advertisement for the Chinese laundry detergent Qiaobi.[4] The laundry detergent ad was a curious inversion of an Italian advertisement in which an Italian man is washed and then becomes a black man.[5]

In a 2016 Daily Comment in *The New Yorker*, Jiayang Fan notes:

> In many respects, China's historical insuloarity means that it has largely lived homogeneously – or thought of itself as doing so, writing off minorities like the Uighurs – quarantined from the outside world. In the past few decades, through market reform and the embrace of globalization, that has changed dramatically. There are growing pains, chief among them provincialism and ignorance. These characteristics do not absolve the Chinese of racism or take away from the pain of the injury, but comprehension of the country's historical and

cultural passage may help pave a path forward. Everyone who has written or spoken about racial awareness in China has emphasized the importance of education and diversity training, but the concrete details of what that might look like have been harder to define.[6]

Blackface eruptions and racism in advertisements are not only present in China. Since coming of age in the nineteenth century as one of first major cultural exports from the United States, blackface eruptions are still commonplace globally. The 2018 blackface incident in China, however, involved the predominant state-owned television network in China. Perhaps more telling have been responses by the Chinese government to criticisms and accusations of racism. In responding to criticism and accusations of racism, a spokesman for the Foreign Ministry reiterated China's opposition to any form of racism.[7] Despite the assertions of the Foreign Ministry spokesman, the attitudes toward Africans and people of African descent in the 2018 Spring Festival Gala do not appear to be isolated ones.[8] They reflect longstanding attitudes about skin color in China filtered through colonial experiences that have led to "whiteness" becoming "an important element in contemporary postcolonial Asian understandings of beauty" and "a commodity in the marketplace."[9] These racial attitudes have also been shaped by historical experiences of external domination in China, including during a series of wars with Western imperial powers, beginning with the nineteenth-century opium wars.[10]

Antiblack racism in China is not a new phenomenon.[11] However, racial eruptions now occur in a broader context in which China is broadening its footprint as a global power, particularly in Africa. The racial attitudes expressed in the laundry advertisement and television program have broader real-world implications. China is now a chief trading partner with Africa and has extensive trading and other relationships with African countries. The racist attitudes expressed in the advertisement have, not surprisingly carried over in interactions between Chinese and local people in Africa, as well as in the experiences of Africans and other black people in China, particularly during the COVID-19 pandemic.

In the 1970s, before China became the global power of today, China funded the TAZARA railway between Zambia and Tanzania. Chinese funding of the railway represented an attempt to counter Soviet and American influences in Africa, and the Chinese government offered generous credit terms for the railway. Significant segregation existed at railway work camps, and Chinese workers were said to be reluctant to interact with Africans.[12] In 2015 an incident in Kenya involving racial exclusion of Kenyan locals drew widespread attention, leading to the arrest of the owner of a Chinese restaurant in Nairobi that had a "no Africans" policy following a social media furor and the emergence of the Twitter hashtag #noblacksallowed.[13]

Treatment of Africans and other black people in China during the COVID-19 pandemic highlights continuing racial attitudes that are contrary to China's policy initiatives. In May 2020, Human Rights Watch called for the Chinese government to end discriminatory treatment of Africans in the COVID-19 pandemic, asking for authorities to protect Africans and people of African descent from discrimination in employment, housing, and other areas throughout China.[14] Early in the COVID-19 response in China, the local government in Guangzhou implemented surveillance, conducted compulsory testing, and enforced a fourteen-day quarantine for all African nationals, even those with prior negative COVID-19 tests who had not recently travelled outside of China:

> In Yuexiu district, the largest African migrant community in China, many Africans were evicted by landlords – despite having paid their rents – and left to sleep rough on the street. In an echo of apartheid South Africa or segregation-era United States, a color bar was imposed across the city: Africans were refused entry by hospitals, hotels, supermarkets, shops and food outlets. At one hospital, even a pregnant woman was denied access. In a department store, an African woman was stopped at the entrance while her white friend was allowed in. In a McDonald's restaurant, a notice was put up saying 'black people cannot come in'. The widespread racism has caused a huge public outcry across Africa, shared on social media under the hashtag #ChinaMustExplain.[15]

Treatment of Africans in China in relation to COVID-19 also reflects a contradiction noted by Chi-Yu Shi: "[l]ofty policy concessions and aid, as well as normative support for autonomy, are not sufficient to reconcile Africans to Chinese racism toward black people … Ironically, the longer African students stay in China, the more negative are their feelings toward the country."[16]

Discrimination against people perceived as "others" became visible globally during the COVID-19 pandemic. In the United States, government officials during the administration of former President Trump, referred to COVID-19 as the "Chinese Virus."[17] Asian people have increasingly faced public attacks and racist violence in the United States, including being spat upon, yelled at, and physically attacked,[18] with an increasing number of hate crimes directed at Asians, and in Atlanta in March 2021, a shooting rampage at three spas that led to eight murders, including of six Asian women Racists attacks have also taken place in Europe, where the European Union Agency for Fundamental Rights noted in April 2020 that the "[c]oronavirus pandemic triggered an increase in racist and xenophobic incidents against people of (perceived) Chinese or Asian origin, including verbal insults, harassment, physical aggression and online hate speech."[19]

Treatment of Africans in China, as well as Asian people in the United States and Europe, are tied together by conceptions of an external other who must be blamed or constrained in the context of the devastating COVID-19 pandemic. Treatment in both contexts reveals deep underlying strains of racism.

China, however, is not alone in having significant contradictions between what it says about Africa and what it actually does in its treatment of African people. Treatment of Africans in China under COVID-19 may lead to increased tension in relationships between China and African countries. Racist attacks unfolding before our eyes during the COVID-19 epidemic show how underlying attitudes can translate into actions. Ideas about black people that were evident in the Spring Festival Gala reflect attitudes toward people of African descent that have long been evident in Europe and United States.

Chinese racial attitudes and treatment of ethnic minority groups in China may have implications for future paths in Africa if countries in Africa were to adopt technological surveillance and other methods of control used against protestors and ethnic minority groups in China.[20] This is one potential path African governments might attempt to follow in light of issues of contestation embodied in protests such as #EndSARS and in likely future contestation. The demographics and historical experiences of countries in Africa would likely lead to tremendous devastation and human suffering should governments in Africa choose that path.

We may have a tendency to look back from the present and assume that the path that led to the present was somehow inevitable. However, paths may not appear to be necessarily predestined particularly when one looks forward from past events at various future paths that might have existed in the past as opposed to backward from the present along only a single path. Looking backward may also lead to incomplete understandings of the past because visions of the past may be distorted by later events and various types of manipulation. The path that led to Africans' becoming subjugated and enslaved through the transatlantic slave trade and plantation slavery were supported by conceptions about the racial inferiority of people of African descent that was used as a justification of slavery. Notably, this path does not appear to reflect attitudes toward Africans in Renaissance and Stuart England. Historian Miranda Kaufmann has found records of hundreds of black Tudors in Renaissance England who were not slaves, and who "played an active part in some of the best-known stories of the age."[21] The status of Black Tudors gives testament to other potential paths of relationships between Africans and external powers and actors:

> experiences of Africans in Tudor and early Stuart England described here show that slavery was not an inevitable result of the Anglo-African encounter. Coupled with evidence of free Africans in early Virginia, this book adds weight to the conclusion that American slavery was instead something that emerged in the very specific economic and social circumstances of the early colonies.[22]

Dr. Kaufmann's research suggests that the path toward a racialized chattel slavery that developed in colonial America and other parts of the New World might relate to the nature of crops harvested in the colonies, particularly sugar, that created a demand for imported slave labor that shaped future paths.[23]

EASE OF DOING BUSINESS AND COMPANY LAW REFORM

Law and policymaking in the shadow of European domination were shaped by underlying conceptions and attitudes about Africans and assumed racial and societal hierarchies that typically placed Africans at or near the bottom. This placement led to things considered African being devalued and contributed to the unquestioned one-way directionality of borrowings from external models. From the earliest days of engagement with British interests, lawmaking in British colonies in Africa typically reflected a continuing pattern of largely one-way imposition of external legal and other frameworks to a significant degree with little or no negotiation, customization, or adaptation to specific local contexts. This was particularly true in the realm of business and commercial relations. Law in British colonies was not implemented in the same way in all colonial possessions. Some colonies, particularly those with European settlers, were subject to soft imperial law, which left room for local legal activities. In contrast, most colonial possessions in Africa were on the hard imperial law side of the imperial law spectrum, which left African colonies with less legislative autonomy and little room for truly local legal initiatives.[24]

The discrepancy between sources of legal borrowings and local contexts of adoption was particularly evident in the business and commercial realms. In these realms, statutes enacted by colonial authorities were often at least implicitly perceived as being applicable primarily to Europeans. Such statutes were often verbatim copies of laws adopted in England or other British colonial possessions. To the extent that the sources of law were modified (such modifications are evident in the many markups of laws present in colonial records and correspondence), such modifications rarely took serious account of local contexts or local needs.

Colonial legal relics have significant implications for digital-era participation, particularly because digital economy policies and laws relating to business, entrepreneurship, and innovation in Africa continue to lag behind those of other areas of the world. The legal environment for local business plays an important role in current outcomes. During colonialism, institutions and legal frameworks were imposed throughout Africa that were defined to a significant degree by outside interests, particularly in the context of colonial power, political, and commercial interests. This tendency to external determination did not end with the end of formal colonialism, in large part, because this external orientation, albeit from different sources from the colonizing power, has become deeply imbedded in legal frameworks and institutions, and in conceptions about appropriate ways to borrow policies, laws, and institutional frameworks. As a result, in far too many discussions about business and law in Africa, when people talk about the legal environment for business, they actually mean foreign businesses with insufficient attention to the implications of such environments for local businesses, particularly smaller ones. This is one of many hangovers from the colonial era.

Future paths in which African economies are competitive and structured to benefit the vast majority of their citizens must be based around legal and business environments that, in addition to being responsive to external circumstances, must be for the benefit of local people and local companies. Lawmaking processes and institutions developed during colonialism have not been sufficiently disrupted to date, and insufficient attention has been given to the importance and need for new types of flexible and hybrid laws and institutions. Laws and institutions that reflect questionable forms of borrowing still shape law, legal processes, and policy, and contribute to poor economic outcomes for far too many today.

The evolution of entity forms that typified twentieth-century business practices in much of the developed world has been much slower to develop in much of sub-Saharan African (SSA). Countries with a common law tradition, including Nigeria, typically have statutes in force that reflect outdated versions of laws copied from statutes in the United Kingdom or other British colonies. For example, an estimated 90 percent of the provisions of the Nigerian Companies Act 1968, the act that immediately preceded the Companies and Allied Matters Act 1990, were identical or substantially similar to the UK Companies Act 1948; Nigerian courts also rely to a "substantial degree on English case law."[25] Close copies of British business entity legal frameworks were initially introduced during the colonial period. For example, commercial codes and conduct consistent with British practice were introduced following the cession of Lagos to the British Crown in 1861.[26] From 1861 until 1876, no local laws governed companies operating in Nigeria, and all companies operating in Nigerian were foreign; English corporations operating in Nigeria had limited liability only if they were registered in England. From 1876 to 1912, the lack of local laws continued and English common law and doctrines of equity were "deemed applicable to Nigeria" and continue to form part of Nigerian company law today.[27] The first local company law in Nigeria was adopted in 1912.

Entrepreneurs seeking to incorporate do so today pursuant to the Nigerian Companies and Allied Matters Act 2020 (CAMA 2020), which repealed and replaced the Companies and Allied Matters Act, 1990 (CAMA 1990).[28] CAMA 2020 is intended to promote the ease of doing business in Nigeria and make it easier and cheaper for Small and Medium Enterprises (SMEs), which was a significant shortcoming under CAMA 1990. CAMA 2020 reduces formalities in ways that are likely to aid the ease of doing business for small companies.[29]

During the summer of 2020, official copies of the draft bill and enacted law were not widely available, although unofficial copies were in circulation. The lack of transparency in the adoption of CAMA 2020 and lack of ready availability of an official version of the law draw attention to shortcomings in legislative processes in Nigeria. It is also significant that it took Nigeria thirty years to modify its company law. In a digital economy environment where things may change very quickly, modification and amendment of laws should be an ongoing process. More incremental modification of key statutes and regulations would likely be beneficial. CAMA also does little to rectify other laws in Nigeria that have, in some instances, gone even longer than thirty years without significant modification – including copyright, patent, and trademark laws – all of which have become of critical importance in digital economy contexts.

The topography of business organizations in Nigeria today plays a potentially important role in economic outcomes. Prior to reforms in 2006, companies legislation in the United Kingdom was not favorable to small companies: "[p]revious UK companies legislation was notoriously and indefensibly complex, hitting most brutally on small businesses."[30] The fact that laws governing business entities in former British colonies such as Nigeria tend to be based on earlier, largely unmodified versions of laws in the United Kingdom has contributed to a legal environment in former colonies that is often not favorable to SMEs. Mirroring a colonial-era inattention to small and emergent local businesses, African governments during the postcolonial period have, until recently, typically made policy choices that focus on supporting big businesses, with less support given to SMEs. Although initiatives to address SMEs have been undertaken in a number of countries,[31] SMEs may still experience gaps in critical areas, including access to financing.[32] This tendency to support big businesses is evident, for example, in the 2013 Ghana Investment Centre Promotion Act (GICPA), which includes minimum capital requirements for investors of foreign capital.[33] These requirements make it difficult for international technology investors to invest in start-up companies in Ghana.[34]

Policy choices that favor larger enterprises are reflected in the types of menu options for business entities available to entrepreneurs. Although the 2020 Nigerian company law reforms are moving in a direction of taking better account of SMEs, current legal frameworks in Nigeria and elsewhere could do more to promote the development of business laws and business forms more suited to SMEs. Business law frameworks, together with the financing environment for businesses, have implications for the development of digital economy businesses, which often start as small start-up entities, the most successful of which may then scale and grow astronomically, as well as other types of SMEs.

Legal reform processes may not yet reflect flexible and responsive approaches needed in digital-era contexts. In 2015, Kenya enacted the Companies Act 2015, which significantly reformed its company law. Kenya's 2015 law directly copied from the United Kingdom Companies Act 2006.[35] James Thuo Gathii notes that the legal reforms in Kenya were driven by a desire to increase Kenya's ranking in the World Bank's Ease of Doing Business (EDB) reports. Gathii notes that the reform process of the Companies Act in Kenya is contrary to the view evident in the 2010 Kenyan Constitution, which "is premised on creating autochthonous laws, jurisprudence, policies and regulations that serve the interest of the Kenyan people."[36] The Kenyan reforms, which reflected a two-decade reform process that had failed prior to the 2015 reforms being finalized, underscores the role of indexes and rankings in various contexts. Reforms that respond to the desire to increase rankings based on external measures of ease of doing business may not be responsive to the circumstances of local people and local businesses in Kenya. Gathii suggests that the Companies Act 2015 represents "a failure of the imagination on the part of elite business interests in Kenya."[37] In Gathii's view, contestation over the legal reforms reflect fundamentally different visions that are based on different networks that shape views of the law:

> these elite interests or the transnational capitalist class ... promote a kind of dependent development because their primary interlocutors are foreign not local business interests. For these elites who are embedded in transnational business networks, transplanting foreign business laws is a precondition for development... By contrast, the elites whose efforts to reform company law started in 1993 but ultimately failed are primarily embedded in local business networks. Without high-level political access to have their vision of corporate law reform prevail, the agenda of supporting the indigenization of the economy and of autonomous national development with the aid of foreign capital only as a backup or as a second-best option has taken a distant second place.[38]

The view that shaped the final enacted version of the Kenyan Companies Act 2015 reflects the type of externalized vision of law and policy that has been prominent during and after colonialism. Kenya's reforms led Kenya to be cited as the third most improved country in the 2015 EDB rankings, which is consistent with the externally oriented nature of the reform process. Policies and laws based on externalized visions should not continue to be the primary vision shaping law and policy in former colonies. Rather, the externalized vision underlying the Kenyan Companies Act 2015 and many other laws in Kenya and elsewhere in SSA should rest on a vision of law and policy as a tool for internal development.

The long revision process in Kenya offered an opportunity to disrupt past patterns of lawmaking but ultimately did not do so. External measures and rankings play a role in decisions about legal and policy reform, and not just in Kenya. However, the fundamental question that should be asked is for whom reforms are intended. Discussions about ease of doing business in Africa often implicitly mean ease of doing business for foreign businesses, without proper attention to the needs of local people who may engage in varied types of formal and informal business activities.

Given past approaches to law and colonial overhang, African countries are, not surprisingly, clustered at the bottom of the World Bank Ease of Doing Business (EDB) index. These rankings measure a broad range of factors that contribute to the overall environment for doing business, including the ease of starting a business, getting electricity, access to credit, registering property, and enforcing contracts. As the Kenyan company law reform process illustrates, the EDB index has had a global impact and has enabled the World Bank to shape the global regulatory environment because states often respond to a low ranking and make reforms to enhance their rankings.[39] EDB rankings magnify the influence of the World Bank on states and encourage regulatory changes in line with the bank's largely deregulatory policy objectives.[40]

The EDB rankings often raise reputational and status concerns within countries with low rankings, leading such countries to make reforms with the goal of improving EDB rankings. Reforms that respond to the external impetus of EDB rankings may continue past patterns of incorporating the external in African countries. The EDB rankings do, however, provide potentially useful information about the business environment within a country. If countries in Africa were actually responsive to local business conditions, they should not need the EDB rankings to incentivize them to make reforms, because at least some of the things measured by the EDB rankings should be obvious targets for reform. The EDB rankings, however, implicitly assume a similar path for improving business environments across all countries. This path, like many others in the past for African countries, comes from external authorities and reflects external approaches to issues of significant internal concern. Without new approaches that robustly incorporate the internal, responses to EDB ranking concerns in Africa may be yet another example of the external driving the internal.

At times, EDB rankings have been contested and even problematic. The rankings are based on formal laws, which may not reflect law in practice or actual business practice.[41] The simplification inherent in EDB rankings may lead countries to seek solutions that game the numbers but might not have a real internal impact. As is the case with other indexes and rankings, the underlying methodology used to develop the EDB index may not be transparent or consistent. In 2018, the World Bank's chief economist, Paul Romer, stated that the World Bank had repeatedly changed the methodology over several years in ways that "were unfair and misleading."[42] The World Bank then indicated that it would correct and recalculate rankings going back for at least four years. In August 2020, the World Bank announced in a data irregularities statement that it was suspending the EDB rankings after discovering that a "number of irregularities have been reported regarding changes to the data in the Doing Business 2018 and Doing Business 2020 reports."[43] The Bank indicated that it was conducting a systematic review and would "act based on the findings" and "retrospectively correct the data of the countries that were most affected by the irregularities."[44]

Although the EDB rankings have given countries incentives to compete to improve rankings, fundamental reforms that benefit local people and businesses may remain elusive. The policy choices of many current governments in Africa must not, however, be taken in isolation, but must be seen as a continuation of essential policy choices made during colonialism when colonizing powers such as Britain established policies that favored British commercial interests over the interests of local ones. Modern colonialism recoded conquest as commerce.[45] This process by which conquest became recoded as commerce is particularly evident in the experiences of local entrepreneurs in the Niger Delta region of what later became Nigeria and other areas of Africa.

Prior to the advent of legitimate trade in palm oil and colonialism in the nineteenth century, the primary basis of commercial relations between Niger Delta traders and European commercial interests centered around the slave trade.

In the precolonial era, powerful local trading intermediaries were present in the Niger Delta.[46] These intermediaries had a significant degree of control over the slave trade and restricted European access to the sources of slaves.

With the imposition of colonialism, local merchants were increasingly constrained. This limiting of opportunities for local merchants was not unique to the Niger Delta region and was evident in other colonial contexts, including colonial Zambia. In Zambia prior to independence, the colonial administration protected rich white storekeepers by suppressing competition from poor white hawkers and Africans, including by preventing Africans from engaging in trade, except in certain areas such as African shanty towns.[47]

The widespread use of indigenization measures (which legally restrict the activities of multinational corporations) in a number of postcolonial contexts is a direct response to limitations on local business activities imposed during colonialism.[48] Although indigenization measures have sought to address the consequences of African exclusion from the commercial sphere in former colonies, they do not truly address the largely externally derived institutional configurations that perpetuate such exclusion. In the Nigerian case, the indigenization statute did not fundamentally change previous patterns:

> With respect to the promotion of indigenous enterprises the policy achieved very little; no new opportunities or challenges were offered ... the expected even or equitable redistribution of income accruing from stock sales is nothing more than a fanciful farce. Only an infinitesimal fraction of the population has benefited .... In fact, the policy has aggravated the urban-rural income inequality since the bulk of the beneficiaries have been urban dwellers.[49]

The continuing presence of rigid laws and limited opportunities for the development of commercial enterprises from within Africa has significant implications for socioeconomic development in general, for the emergence of new technologies from within Africa, and for efforts by local innovators and entrepreneurs within such countries to engage in digital economy undertakings. Rigid legal frameworks, institutional failures, and difficulties in establishing formal businesses also contribute to pervasive informality in Africa. Nigeria has a large informal economy that is thought to account for as much as 70 percent of Nigeria's gross domestic product.[50]

INTELLECTUAL PROPERTY LAW, LOCAL KNOWLEDGE, AND MARGINALIZATION

Policies that continue essential colonial-era approaches have contributed to the global marginalization of African countries and to the internal marginalization of many within African countries. Valentin Mudimbe has noted the marginality that "designates the intermediate space between the so-called African tradition and the projected modernity of colonialism."[51] Intellectual property laws, which have become increasingly important during the digital era, give evidence of the marginalization of forms of local knowledge present in Africa and other developing countries and ways in which externally derived legal frameworks have enabled exploitation of such knowledge, typically by people outside of Africa.

Rigid business frameworks are compounded by limitations in intellectual property frameworks in many African countries, which has particular importance for digital-era disruption within Africa and the emergence of technologies from Africa. As is the case with business laws, intellectual property laws in much of SSA reflect a legacy of external determination.[52] Intellectual property frameworks in Africa are highly fragmented, "comprising an array of partially overlapping and sometimes conflicting agreements, laws, policies and sub-regional organisations."[53] Nigeria and many other countries in Africa have entered into international agreements that obligate them to provide minimum levels of intellectual property protection. For example, the 1994 Agreement on Trade-Related Aspects of Intellectual Property Rights (TRIPs Agreement) sets global minimum standards for intellectual property. Many African countries implement these minimum standards without customizing them for local contexts, including by taking advantage of exceptions and limitations that might be advisable for developing countries.[54]

Without robust intellectual property frameworks within Africa to facilitate local innovations, knowledge and information from Africa may not be protected from appropriation, which might lead to patterns that mirror past appropriations of local knowledge and art.[55] Companies today throughout the world operate in a postindustrial, digital economy that is based to a significant degree on the use and exploitation of intangible assets such as information technology, research and development, brand equity, and intellectual property rights. Full participation in the knowledge economy by African entrepreneurs and countries requires intellectual property frameworks and strategies that are targeted to the needs of local environments and take account of anticipated future paths given local circumstances.

The globalization of intellectual property that is evident in the TRIPs Agreement means that countries in Africa today often face intellectual property frameworks that are to a significant degree externally determined and derived. Within such constraints, countries such as Nigeria have not developed intellectual property frameworks that seek to maximize domestic opportunities and socioeconomic development potential. Customization of intellectual property laws to meet local needs and local requirements would require, for example, that countries find a balance between external constraints and local considerations with respect to proprietary intellectual property interests and open innovation, and also take advantage of exceptions and limitations that are critical for developing countries. Insufficiently scrutinized acceptance of, and failure to modify, externally derived legal frameworks has thus been problematic in business, intellectual property, and other contexts.

In Nigeria, for example, the consequences of inattention to local needs in legal design has resulted in intellectual property frameworks with, at times, significant shortcomings. The cultural industries in Nigeria have tremendous potential and capacity. Some cultural industry participants are, however, unable to capitalize fully on Nigeria's creative potential due to Nigeria's inadequate and antiquated copyright law frameworks.[56] Inadequacies in copyright legal frameworks have contributed to low levels of awareness among key stakeholders about the importance of copyright protection.[57]

These shortcomings extend to multiple areas of intellectual property in Nigeria. Trademarks and branding play a critical role in business today. Nigeria's trademark law,[58] is modeled after the 1938 United Kingdom Trade Mark Act,[59] which was repealed in the United Kingdom in 1994. Trademark law in Nigeria would benefit from modernization and reform, similar to the reforms undertaken in Ghana in 2004 and South Africa in 1993. Nigerian trademark law does not provide for service marks, which are critical in the digital economy era.[60] Trade secret, which is often used to protect valuable and secret commercial information such as the Kentucky Fried Chicken (KFC) recipe and the Coca-Cola formula, is an important body of intellectual property law in many areas of the world. As of 2021, Nigeria lacked a comprehensive legislative framework for trade secret protection.[61] Implementation of appropriate trade secret laws would be an additional avenue to enable protection of local companies and local innovation within Nigeria.[62]

Similar inadequacies are apparent in patent frameworks. The patent landscape in Nigeria can be traced back to colonial-era policies. Patent laws were first enacted in Nigeria in 1900 in Lagos Colony and Southern Nigeria, and in 1902 in Northern Nigeria. These first patent laws were robust ones that provided for the filing and granting of patents within what later became Nigeria, and were comparable to institutional structures in the United Kingdom at the time.[63] These laws were, however, repealed just after amalgamation of Northern and Southern Nigeria in 1914. The 1916 patent ordinance, which remained valid until 1970, no longer permitted patent applications to be filed in Nigeria. The new legal framework, which was altered in 1925 to a "Registration of United Kingdom Patents Ordinance," permitted holders of patents in the United Kingdom to obtain patents in Nigeria based on such prior patents.[64]

The current Nigerian patent system in Nigeria is a registration system that came into force in 1971.[65] Patent registration systems are the norm throughout SSA. In a patent registration system, the examination or review of the patent only scrutinizes whether the patent fulfills requirements of form, with no substantive examination of the quality of the patent itself. Patent registration systems tend to lead to patent grants to a relatively high ratio of patent applicants. Patent registration systems enable patent holders to receive broader patent rights than they might otherwise receive in a system based on patent examination. As such, patent frameworks replicate past patterns of the external and internal in laws that do not operate for the benefit of most people in Africa. Countries with substantive patent examination, which include developed countries, scrutinize the substance of a patent and grant patents to only a proportion of applicants.[66] South Africa's 2018 intellectual property policy has proposed implementation of substantive patent search and examination as a key reform.[67] Not surprisingly, the South African reforms have encountered significant external opposition echoing the same types of external influences that were pervasive during colonialism.[68]As a result of past and present policies, patents have not been levers for growth and development in Nigeria.[69] The current Nigerian legal topography in business and innovation spaces is disadvantageous to people in Nigeria generally and may make Nigerian creators and innovators less able to protect their creations and inventions in relation to external actors. The lack of a comprehensive Nigerian intellectual property and innovation policy also means that doctrines that may be used to constrain assertions of intellectual property rights that are important for developing countries and that facilitate development and human wellbeing, including those related to access to knowledge and access to medicines, may not be formally incorporated into policy approaches or legal frameworks.

The importance of access to medicines became apparent with the HIV/AIDS pandemic. HIV/AIDS has had its greatest impact in Africa, which has experienced significant regional variation in HIV prevalence: "[t]he burden of the global HIV epidemic is disproportionately concentrated in sub-Saharan Africa, where – in 2017 – 75% of deaths and 65% of new infections occurred and where 71% of people living with HIV resided . . . Country-level estimates of HIV prevalence . . . highlight extensive differences in HIV prevalence between countries within sub-Saharan Africa . . . studies consistently find extensive within-country geographical variation in HIV prevalence."[70] Patents for anti-retroviral therapies (ART),[71] have been a point of contestation between pharmaceutical companies, trade representatives of countries where such companies are based, and health activists.[72] Debates surrounding access to medicines, including ART, highlight a key arena of the interaction of law, policy, and issues related to human well-being that are of critical importance in many African countries today.[73] In July 2020, for example, South Africa had an estimated HIV prevalence rate for adults aged 15–49 of 18.7 percent.[74] The COVID-19 pandemic, which also raises patent-related issues for African countries, may intersect with and worsen HIV/AIDS outcomes due to COVID-19 related disruptions in HIV/AIDS services and treatment.[75]

Although the extent to which patents specifically stimulate growth is contested,[76] intellectual property rights are important aspects of innovation policy. Existing copyright, trademark, and patent frameworks in Nigeria were inherited from Britain to a significant degree, and have not been sufficiently modified to take account of, and meet, Nigeria's domestic needs, including balancing incentives for innovation with critical societal needs such as access to medicines.[77]

Two African regional patent systems exist under the rubric of ARIPO (African Regional Intellectual Property Organization) and OAPI (Organisation Africaine de la Propriété Intellectuelle or African Intellectual Property Organization). The presence of two regional patent systems creates a challenging environment for patent applicants; the patenting process at both ARIPO and OAPI is also quite expensive, as much as six to seven times the cost of obtaining a national patent in South Africa, which has the most robust patent infrastructure in SSA.[78] Most African countries lack robust national patent infrastructures.

Patent registration systems such as those in Nigeria that do not require substantive patent examination are likely to lead to patent grants that may result in patent monopolies that are too broad, stifle competition, and keep prices high, while disadvantaging local inventors by restricting their ability to enter relevant markets.[79] As a result of the current patent landscape and innovation policies, inventors in African countries are a negligible presence on the global patent scene.

COLONIAL PORTFOLIOS, CULTURE, AND COPYRIGHT

Colonial records highlight the extent to which various legal frameworks were externally determined and driven by the needs of British colonial and commercial interests. They also illustrate what might be characterized as a portfolio approach to colonial policies and lawmaking. This portfolio approach meant that British colonial office officials often paid close attention to cultivating the overall British colonial portfolio of various countries in diverse locations, often at the expense of local priorities and needs. Legal and policy decisions undertaken with a portfolio mindset are likely to diverge, sometimes significantly, from those undertaken on a country-by-country basis. These decisions could also radically shift policy in a short period of time. For example, in February 1943, the Cotton Control of the United Kingdom decided that quotas would be calculated separately for each colony in West Africa, fixing the Gold Coast quota at 22 percent and the Nigerian quota at 70 percent, leaving the balance available for Sierra Leone and Gambia.[80] This revision of quotas was retroactive and reflected an increase in the share for Nigeria and a "substantial" reduction in the share for the Gold Coast. The new quotas were driven by British needs:

> The reason for this drastic measure was said to be the desperate need for oilseeds from Nigeria. It was hoped to improve the production by increasing the supply of textiles to act as an inducement to producers of oilseeds. Yet the same oilseeds were at the time bought on a strict quota basis with rigid exclusion of new buyers.[81]

As a result of externalized portfolio approaches to lawmaking, insufficient attention was given to the implications of such legal and policy frameworks within local contexts. Further, legal frameworks in each colonial possession might diverge from other similarly positioned colonial possessions merely because of differences in the dates on which English law was received and the dates of independence. Uniformity is also a helpful attribute in the creation of basic laws in colonial portfolio holdings, which has likely led to greater uniformity of laws in former British colonial possessions than might otherwise be the case.

Colonial approaches to copyright reflect the significant impact of colonial portfolio approaches. The impact of marginality in law and culture is also evident in the realm of copyright and cultural products. Laws and regulations may shape varied types of activities, including creative endeavors. The impact of colonialism on culture in Africa has been significant. Censorship and the policing of culture, including of music, was characteristic of colonial control. This was certainly true in the case of film during the colonial era, when filmmaking in Nigeria and elsewhere in Africa was largely reserved for European directors and producers, because films were thought to be too complex for Africans to produce or understand.[82] The governance of economic activities and exclusionary policies in the cultural arena during colonialism reflected a topography of lawmaking that extended beyond what would typically fall within the realm of copyright today. Colonial-era exclusion of Africans from various economic activities was accomplished through varied laws and regulations, including those that required registration to undertake certain types of activities.

Patterns of regulation of internal activities, which have not been disrupted to a sufficient degree since independence in many countries, also effectively suppressed African competition with colonial commercial interests in a broad range of economic and creative activities. As was the case with colonialism generally, funneling activities through specified regulatory paths, gave colonial administrators significant discretionary power to censor, enable, or block a particular activity – often with little or no transparency, explanation, or recourse. The discretion that was characteristic of colonial administrators has contributed to poor postcolonial outcomes: "empires, through their lack of foresight and the wide discretion they give administrators, lead to instability and the development of chronic problems."[83] Colonial administrations were also highly bureaucratic, a tendency that was not significantly disrupted at independence. Colonial era approaches to regulation gave colonial authorities wide-ranging ability to suppress activities that might criticize the colonial administration or oppose colonial government policies or objectives.

In the case of films, for example, Pierre Laval, the French Colonial Minister, issued a decree in 1934 that regulated the production of films in French colonies in French West Africa.[84] This decree required that films could not be shown or shot and phono records could not be imported or distributed without the approval of the governor general. In order to receive this approval, certain other requirements also applied, including a substantive review of the creative work's content. This decree thus regulated creative activity and limited the creative contributions of Africans.[85] Anticolonial films, even when made by Europeans, were also banned.[86] Consistent with colonialism's "civilizing" mission, the French creative regulations sought to impose French cultural norms and discourage the development of indigenous filmmaking activity that might compete with colonial endeavors or any filmmaking that criticized or expressed opposition to colonialism.[87]

British colonial policy in the cultural realm was similarly intertwined with its "civilizing" mission. British film policy centered around economic self-interest, concern for "susceptible natives" who were thought not to be able to discern what was true or false, and a desire that the white race, particularly the British, be depicted in something other than an unsavory fashion.[88] British film policy was closely intertwined with censorship, and colonial governments:

> were told that in the exercise of their censorship powers they should take into account 'the special character and susceptibilities of the native people' and to beware of anything 'which is calculated to rouse undesirable racial feeling . . . . More specifically the Colonial Secretary drew the attention of colonial governors to the request of the War Office that 'films of a nature calculated to bring into disrepute the Forces of the Crown and His Majesty's uniform are prevented from being shown in the territory under your administration'.[89]

As is the case with other legal institutions, censorship policies initiated by the British carried over after the end of colonialism. In Nigeria, censorship boards remain an essential part of the regulation of films. The National Film and Video Censors Board (NFVCB), formed by a 1993 decree, is an institutional force in the Nigerian film industry.[90] Legal frameworks adopted just following independence established the Film Censors Board, which specifically applied to film production, but which did not encompass video.[91] In contrast, the 1993 decree establishing the NFVCB, which repealed the Cinematograph Act of 1963,[92] specifically applies to both film and video.[93] The Nollywood industry arose in large part by taking advantage of regulatory gaps and a characteristic inattention to the need to update regulations in Nigeria in light of changing technological and other circumstances. At the time of emergence of the now globally recognized Nollywood industry, the Cinematograph Act did not cover the video genre,[94] which likely facilitated the development of the Nollywood industry.

During the colonial period, most British colonies in Africa did not enact laws and regulations in contexts of English law borrowings that were truly adapted to local contexts. Colonial-era laws and correspondence reflect a continuing concern with the local impact of colonial legislation on the Dominions and relative lack of concern with local impacts within most colonial possessions in Africa. The differences between approaches in the Dominions and elsewhere are evident in the implementation of the Copyright Act 1911, which was also known as the Imperial Copyright Act. The Imperial Copyright Act was extended to British colonial possessions by a Privy Council Order in Council, which effectively created a dual system of application of copyright law that distinguished the Dominions from other territories.[95]

The Imperial Copyright Act governed copyright matters in African colonies for a significant portion of the twentieth century. The implementation of the Imperial Copyright Act demonstrates the external impetus in colonial lawmaking in Africa. The British Cabinet expresses intent as early as 1906 to amend copyright laws.[96] The Imperial Copyright Act repealed local laws, which was acknowledged in colonial correspondence.[97]

In internal correspondence concerning the Imperial Copyright Act, colonial officials noted that by effectively repealing local copyright laws, the Imperial Act could lead to problems. Colonial administrators were concerned about the impact of the Imperial Copyright Act in the Dominions, which included South Africa.[98] The Imperial Copyright Act did not provide for a system of registration in African colonies, which created problems for African colonies that remain evident today in a number of postcolonial contexts. Because most African colonies had far more circumscribed space for modifying colonial laws, at independence, significant gaps existed, including the lack of effective copyright registration systems. Copyright registration systems can be an important element in copyright administration because they facilitate information disclosure of those claiming copyright ownership rights. During the colonial era, known legal shortcomings may not have been addressed unless they negatively affected British interests.

To a significant degree, the British colonial approach to lawmaking was closely connected to patterns of English lawmaking and the needs of British commercial interests. Further, decades old laws from England or other reaches of the empire might be used to create laws in African contexts. The adoption of the Copyright Act 1956 in British colonies reflects this dynamic. Between 1956 and 1963, just as countries in Africa were becoming independent, colonial records reflect a heightened urgency that remaining British colonial possessions adopt the Copyright Act 1956.[99] This urgency was driven after 1961, at least in part, by the adoption of laws in Ghana that British copyright interests characterized as "confiscatory."

As was the case with other British colonial possessions, Ghana inherited a copyright system based on the Copyright Act 1911.[100] Ghana became independent on March 6, 1957.[101] The Ghana Independence Act 1957 contained specific provisions relating to copyright.[102] A few years after independence, Ghana replaced colonial copyright laws with its first postindependence copyright laws.[103] In addition to adding new copyright subject matter, the Ghanaian Copyright Act of 1961 "contained relatively shorter terms of protection .... In the case of published literary works, copyright protection lasted only until the end of the year in which the author died or 25 years (instead of 50 years under the earlier Ordinance) after the end of the year in which the work was first published, whichever was later in time."[104]

These Ghanaian laws alarmed British copyright interests, particularly publishers and performing rights societies who did not want former colonies to pass local laws that might give fewer rights to them than those available under the Copyright Act

1956, which provided for a copyright term of life plus fifty years for literary, dramatic, and musical works.[105] The Performing Rights Society noted:

> We are naturally pleased to see that by the Copyright (Kenya) Order 1967 (SI 1963 No. 1147) the 1956 Act has been extended appropriately to Kenya before that territory becomes independent. We feel that this will prevent or at least materially delay the enactment of a Kenya Copyright Act on the confiscatory lines of the present Ghana Copyright Act .... With this in mind, may I venture to urge upon Her Majesty's Government that every step open to them should be taken to ensure that the Copyright Act, 1956 is appropriately extended to every one of the British Overseas territories that are present still operating under the 1911 Act, so that an up-to-date copyright law will be operating in each of those territories when, as seems inevitable in every case sooner or later, it becomes independent and, more likely than not, a near dictatorship.[106]

The British Joint Copyright Council similarly noted that "[i]t is certainly very much to be hoped that the Colonial Administration will opt for extension of the Act to their territories rather than for local legislation."[107] The Publisher's Association noted "hopes that the various Colonial Territories will accept your suggestion that our Act should be extended to cover them, rather than new local legislation should be introduced."[108]

This lobbying by copyright interests laid the groundwork for the Colonial Office to move quickly to ensure that all remaining colonies enacted the Copyright Act 1956. Little attention was paid to local concerns. In a communication from the Colonial Office to the Board of Trade, Industrial Property Department, Sierra Leone is described as having specifically asked for a shorter term of protection (apparently something less than life plus 50):

> A reply from Sierra Leone states that, whilst there is no objection to the making of an Order-in-Council applying the Act to that territory, it is "considered that 50 years is too long a period for a Copyright to last in regard to a country as yet without any professional, musical or literary activity". No alternative period is suggested, however, and, subject to your views as to whether there is objection in principle to a variation of the period laid down in the Act, we shall have to ask the Sierra Leone authorities what shorter period they would propose.[109]

The Industrial Property Department refuses to accommodate the request from Sierra Leone and responds to the Colonial Office correspondence by stating: "[w]e feel that we cannot agree, in principle, to extending the Act to Sierra Leone in such a way as to reduce the period of copyright protection. The term of protection, we consider, is a basic feature of the Act of 1956 which we cannot modify when extending the Act to any other territory. Moreover, Sierra Leone, could not, if such a change were made, become part to the Brussels text of the Berne Convention."[110] In denying the request from Sierra Leone, the Industrial Property Office focuses on external concerns related to international treaties and British commercial interests and does not take account of the perceived local needs in Sierra Leone that motivated the request for a more customized approach to intellectual property lawmaking.

This historical note in intellectual property lawmaking is not surprising. However, it lends credence to the need today to scrutinize more carefully continuing patterns of externally-derived lawmaking that do not take account of local considerations and needs. Further, at the time of independence, existing colonial legal frameworks and patterns of commercial relationship were not significantly disrupted, which continues to influence legal frameworks and institutions in Africa today.

COLONIALISM, MONOPOLY GAMES, AND COMPETITION

In late 2012, the world famous game Monopoly added Lagos to its roster of cities. The Lagos version of Monopoly is similar to other versions of the game with some changes that reflect the local environment. For example, recognized locations in Lagos are used in the game, including Banana Island, which serves as an upscale property replacing Boardwalk and Mayfair in the United States and British versions. The arrival of Monopoly in Lagos is both notable and ironic. The casual trading of properties characteristic of the game of Monopoly today echoes the actual division of Africa geographically into formal colonies of varied European powers.[111] The division of African countries into zones of European ownership has had continuing consequences for Africa today, because as Thomas Piketty notes, the "only continent not in equilibrium is Africa, where a substantial share of capital is owned by foreigners ... Despite the fact that there are many imperfections in the balance of payments data, foreign ownership is clearly an important reality in Africa today."[112]

The creation of an African version of Monopoly also reflects increasing visibility of Nigeria and other countries in Africa as consumer markets that are targets of opportunity for multinational corporations. The development of the Lagos version of Monopoly was sponsored by Lagos State for marketing purposes and to encourage adherence to traffic laws as is apparently evident in the game cards in Lagos Monopoly. The price of Monopoly in Lagos was significantly more than the price in the United States and United Kingdom.[113] The price differential was substantial, particularly given that per capita gross domestic product in Nigeria has in recent years been a fraction of that in the United States and United Kingdom. The game Monopoly serves as a powerful symbol for engagement of countries in Africa with the broader global economy and cultural flows. Continuities between the past and present are evident in countries in Africa and other areas that have experienced colonialism. As Amy Wilentz has highlighted in her discussions of Haiti, early experiences of globalization evident in Haiti were a template for later experiences:

> The colonial economy that followed the destruction of the indigenous islanders [in Haiti] was one of the first entirely globalized economies in human history, at every

level a model for the modern global economy. . . . Like the heads of multinational employers today, plantation owners sometimes lived a world away, in their French chateaux. The product the slave workers made was, as is so often the case today, almost exclusively for export.[114]

The externalized approach that was characteristic of colonialism in much of Africa is evident in approaches to monopolies and competition. Monopolies and anticompetitive conceptions shaped policies and laws during colonialism both within African countries and between African countries and external powers. Imperialism and colonialism were effectuated through use of state sponsored companies. Chartered companies that were given monopolies over geographic areas and areas of trade played a critical role in early contacts between Africa and Europe, for example. Notably, Adam Smith, was critical of the anticompetitive abuses of companies such as the British East India Company,[115] which was formed in 1600 and given a Crown Charter that granted it "monopoly privileges to all overseas trade with the extensive area then called the East Indies, indicating the entire area east of the Cape of Good Hope and west of Cape Horn."[116] The British East India Company and other state sponsored enterprises were far more than commercial entities. They at times engaged in military activities, including the acquisition of territories and in the case of the British East India Company, the Dutch East India Company, and early versions of the French East India Company "were formed with the specific intent to further state interests by aggressively colonizing and settling areas of Asia."[117]

The creation of monopolistic zones of European interest and ownership underscore the tremendously anticompetitive nature of the colonial endeavor itself in ways that have continuing resonance today in countries such as Nigeria. In his study of competition and trade in West Africa just as formal colonialism was ending, development economist P.T. Bauer identified a number of factors underlying what he characterized as monopolistic tendencies in West African external trade. These policies and practices did not end with colonialism.

Bauer's report indicates that colonial West African import and export trade had a high degree of concentration, with "a large share of the trade being handled by a small number of firms," reflecting the oligopolistic and occasionally monopolistic nature of West African trade.[118] Markets with a high concentration of firms were more likely to have formal or informal market-sharing agreements, particularly prior to the end of World War II.[119] Concentration and exclusionary practices made it difficult for new firms to enter import trading markets.

Concentration in colonial West African import and export trading was in part a result of colonial government policies that favored expediency and administrative convenience: "administrators prefer to deal with a few large firms rather than with a small number of enterprises."[120] Colonial administrators were not as responsive to SMEs as they were to larger firms. The focus on large firms underscores the role of external competition with non-African competitors in shaping internal colonial policies. Restrictive colonial immigration policies, including towards Lebanese and Indian business people, also reduced competition. As P.T. Bauer notes, "[c]ommercial life in West African has been much affected by dislike and distrust of the Levantine communities, which is marked in official circles."[121] Immigration policy reduced competition, increased firm profits, strengthened the position of existing firms and had important economic effects on capital formation, employment opportunities, and development.[122]

In the agricultural sector, colonial structures and policies put in place varied, depending on the interests involved. In East Africa and southern Africa, settler farmers secured favorable arrangements. Agricultural marketing boards, which were established in British West Africa in the 1940s, had a sustained impact. The cocoa marketing board in Gold Coast (later Ghana) was made permanent after World War II and represented an attempt by the Colonial Office and Gold Coast colonial government to "preempt charges that continued 'underpayment' of African farmers amounted to colonial exploitation."[123] During the late 1930s, global economic conditions had triggered colonial protests, including cocoa holdups in West Africa and riots in the West Indies. Marketing boards resulted in seasonally required statutory minimum prices and were structured as permanent export monopolies.

Although wartime control schemes and later marketing boards were attempts to deal with social conflict arising from global crop price volatility, P.T. Bauer suggests that statutory marketing boards more likely weakened rather than strengthened the position of farmers with respect to intermediaries.[124] Although the Gold Coast cocoa marketing board was initially "devised to protect farmers, from 1943 at the latest the control board's policies were redirected to the opposing goal of depressing farmers' income."[125] British attention to primary producing areas in Africa reflected external pressures on Britain, which, beginning in the 1870s, had a declining share of manufacturing in comparison to the United States and Germany.[126]

Marketing boards expanded state involvement in the economy. Farmers were required to sell to a statutory board that had authority to set prices.[127] The activities of colonial administrators underscore the high degree of government intervention in the economic sphere in colonies in Africa. This dominance of the public sphere has continued long after the end of colonialism. This has led to a private sector in many African countries in which the state role in the economy continues to be dominant. Private sectors in many African countries remain weak, which poses challenges to goals of many countries to increase levels of entrepreneurship. The small size of enterprises, which is a colonial legacy in many African countries, is one of several challenges to the private sector in African countries.[128] Although SMEs are important elements of future paths throughout Africa, the growth of SMEs is limited in many African countries, and SMEs in Africa have in many cases not grown to become larger in size: "there is very little upward mobility of enterprises in

Africa."[129] High and rising levels of informality, weak interfirm linkages, low levels of competitiveness, and a lack of innovation capabilities are other factors identified by UNCTAD in 2013 as needing to be addressed to promote entrepreneurship, private sector development, and intra-African trade.[130]

Low levels of competitiveness are a hangover of colonial policies. Anticompetitive structures in West Africa led to trading relationships that favored external interests over internal ones. Citing statistics from customs records in Nigeria, P.T. Bauer notes that in 1949, 85 percent of import trade was handled by European firms, 10 percent by Levantine (Syrian and Lebanese) firms and Indian firms, and 5 percent by African firms.[131] These numbers are striking, given population numbers. The 1931 census, which was the most recent census at the time Bauer undertook his analysis of West African trade, indicated that Nigeria had 5,442 non-Africans, including 419 Syrians (which included Lebanese) and 97 Indians, out of a total population of well over 20 million.[132] This suggests that non-Africans controlled 95 percent of the import trade while constituting approximately 0.027 percent of the population.

Colonial policies contributed to noncompetitive spaces within colonies in Africa, with marginalization of Africans in key colonial economic zones. Colonialism established colonies in SSA as spaces that were intentionally structured to not be competitive with colonial power commercial interests. Countries in SSA were also locked into exclusive relationships with the European colonial power claiming ownership rights to the colonial possession. These relationships and the authoritarian nature of colonial rule were used to suppress activities within colonies that might pose a competitive challenge to colonial commercial interests, or colonial authority, or both. A British colonial administrator in the early 1940s described key anticompetitive features of colonial policy design:

> It is probably true that the natives have not been encouraged to develop large handicraft industries for export because such export would compete with similar industries in the United Kingdom. You always have to remember that there is a reason for owning a colony. I will say this much, that the hard-boiled principle of running a colony is to develop it only in the sense that you develop its production and export of raw materials. Don't allow any outside capital to be put into developing colonial industries, because in many cases they will compete too successfully with mother-country industries. Every finished article most [sic] be imported into the colony from their mother country, with the exception of certain things which it is not advantageous to ship to the colony – such as wicker furniture, ginger ale, and such things, which would take up cargo space which can be better occupied by more expensive things.[133]

As a result of colonial policies that sought to suppress competition, countries in Africa had limited ability to seek competitive terms of economic and other forms of engagement from alternative sources. The intensification in recent years of various forms of South-South engagement in Africa today, including from China and India, may be modifying these historical patterns of relationships.[134] The exclusive vertical relationships between colonial powers and colonial possessions were often beneficial to the colonial power. In addition to being exclusionary, the terms of such relationships were extractive ones in which colonized countries provided raw materials and in turn purchased British manufactured products.[135] As a British official noted in 1928: "[t]he cannibal dancing on the beach in Nigeria buys more from Great Britain than Henry Ford."[136]

The terms of engagement between colonial powers and their colonies were often exploitative. In a 1941 letter concerning the exploitative terms of engagement with local cocoa growers in West Africa, the Anti-Slavery and Aborigines' Protection Society noted:

> Africans grow their own food and spend the proceeds of their export crops on manufactured goods. The first cost of those goods has greatly advanced since the outbreak of war and Import Duties on many of them have been increased. The African's consumption of manufactured goods is always minimal and a reduction of £2 to £3, a ton in the price of one of his principal export crops at the same time that the prices of manufactured goods which he uses have greatly advanced, cannot but cause him great hardship .... The Committee feels that the great disparity between the price at which raw cocoa is bought from the growers and the price at which processed cocoa is sold to the consumer has been one of the major injustices of the trade in cocoa by private enterprise, and it had hoped that when Government took control of the buying and selling of cocoa, it would have been more generous and more just towards cocoa growers than private industry had been, but the reverse has been the case. At the present time, the price at which raw cocoa is bought from growers is 1.4d (one decimal pound four pence) per pound, and the price at which it is sold to consumers is 19d per pound, or more than thirteen and a half times the price of the raw product.[137]

In addition to limiting competition by constraining colonial possessions' relationships with those other than the colonial power, colonialism also limited competition within colonial possessions. Promotion of British commerce and suppression of competition was a core aspect of British colonialism.[138] This also had implications within the legal sphere. The suppression of competition meant that British colonial authorities had little interest in laws that would promote domestic competition. This posture toward competition was reflected in law and led to weak or absent competition law frameworks in many former colonies. Until relatively recently, most countries in Africa did not have competition law regimes. Although a number of countries have adopted competition law regimes in recent years, with the number of countries in Africa with competition law frameworks tripling in a fifteen-year period,[139] such regimes remain weak with insufficient resources in many countries. Nigeria, now the largest economy in Africa, did not have a competition law regime until adoption of the Federal Competition and Consumer Protection Act (FCCP),[140] which was signed into law in January 2019.

Fear and suppression of competition was the key ethos underlying colonial governance in Africa. For example, during the early years of formal colonialism, the Royal Niger Company (RNC) sought to establish a monopoly, which was contrary to its charter.[141] Sir George Goldie, a founder of the RNC, sought for and achieved "a complete dislodgment of both African and non-British European competitors in the Niger trade both before and after he obtained the Royal Charter in 1886."[142] These preferred policies reflected a particular vision of colonialism and its civilizing mission that led to conflict with Bishop Samuel Ajayi Crowther and his supporters. Bishop Ajayi Crowther "envisaged for the Lower Niger a prosperous, peaceful and peace-loving, literate and Christian population, with modern roads and navigable waterways that would put the territory's inhabitants in mutually beneficial contact with the industrial countries of the world. He also hoped to see the territory under the guidance and protection of the British Crown."[143] Bishop Ajayi Crowther was pleased to see a large number of *Saro* who were "active participants of the Niger trade in an individual capacity."[144] The Bishop's conviction was that "Christian teaching could not have any meaning for peoples of the country unless, and until, their material needs were first looked after ... [sharing] the notion of his missionary colleagues ... that Christianity could not be expected to flourish in Africa until a social and economic transformation similar to that of contemporary Europe and America had been achieved."[145]

In RNC territories and elsewhere, including during later time periods, African competition was typically suppressed, at times with significant military force. As historian Kenneth Dike has outlined in his classic history of trade in the Nigeria Delta, in the precolonial era, powerful indigenous trading intermediaries emerged in the Niger Delta.[146] In the precolonial period, forms of traditional unincorporated trading associations appear to have existed.[147] African merchant princes, including Nana of Warri and JaJa of Opobo, developed commercial organizations that encompassed significant amounts of territory, employing several thousand people in varied capacities.[148] These and other Niger Delta intermediaries had a significant degree of control over the slave trade and controlled European access to sources of slaves. As trading activities transitioned to products such as palm oil, and Europeans began traveling further inland, these trading relationships changed, particularly as European traders were placed in direct competition with African traders.

Europeans accepted the role of African middlemen for a time, but eventually sought to depose them, in part because they became competitors. Ja Ja, for example, sought to compete against European traders who monopolized the export trade to Europe, seeking to establish himself as an exporter independent of European firms.[149] In doing so, he could obtain a higher price for his products than he was able to obtain in Opobo. English officials did not react well to Ja Ja's attempts to compete in the export trade:

> Ja Ja has identified himself with that curse of western Africa, the middlemen, and is resolved to prevent any intercommunication between the white traders on the coast and the industrious thrifty tribes of the interior. . . . I venture, with all due deference,

> to suggest to your Lordship that the most effectual aid to peace and commerce in the British Protectorate of the Oil Rivers would be administered by the humiliation or banishment of Ja Ja. It would be a fatal blow dealt at the assumptions of the middlemen, and it would necessitate no other display of force than the action of a gun-boat .... The traders here are of opinion that with the fall of Ja Ja all serious opposition on the part of the middlemen would cease, and direct communication with the markets of the interior become feasible. Not only would the increase in trade be enormous and unchecked, but in many minor points the condition of the coast traders would be benefited.[150]

The threat of Ja Ja's competition led to his being deposed in 1887, detained and exiled to St. Vincent. His treading on a space reserved for white men was the justification for his being deposed:

> Now they are about to reap the long-waited-for and sadly-needed profits of their praiseworthy enterprise, their trade stopped by the machinations of one of the most grasping, unscrupulous, and overbearing of mushroom Kings who ever attempted to throttle the growing commerce of white men with the rich interior .... Should Ja Ja agree to my conditions, the difficulty will be at an end. But if he continues to resist them, I must respectfully ask your Lordship for means of properly and effectually supporting British authority.[151]

While in St. Vincent, Ja Ja petitioned many times to be returned to Nigeria.[152] Ja Ja was not granted permission to return until 1891.[153] In poor health, he died during his return to Nigeria, with rumors of his having died on account of being poisoned. The removal of Ja Ja significantly reduced potential export trade competition because "[b]y removing Ja Ja and Nana, the administration was removing the only Delta Africans who had the resources even to attempt to establish an African export trade, as had a few of the Sierra Leonean merchants in Lagos."[154] In Ja Ja's absence, the power and wealth of Opobo declined.

The exclusion of African competition from portions of trade reserved for Europeans facilitated exploitation and contributed to the development of countries at independence that were not globally competitive. The British reaction to Ja Ja's attempt to go around their emerging control over external access of Africans reflects ways in which colonial states were "gatekeeper states" that sat at the nexus of the internal and external.

Institutions and legal structures put in place during colonialism supported the anticompetitive aspects of colonialism that sought to prevent African competition. More procompetitive policies have been slow to be implemented in many African countries in the postindependence era. However, competitiveness will be important in shaping Africa's digital economy participation, as well as in disrupting internal institutional structures that are not competitive. The 2016–2017 World Economic Forum Africa Competitiveness Report suggests a number of reforms to improve competitiveness, including: strengthening of institutions, adopting sector-specific policies to increase labor demand, improving competitiveness of cities, reducing the housing backlog to improve lives of city dwellers, creating jobs, enhancing productivity, and developing effective technical vocational education and training programs to reduce a growing skills mismatch.[155]

Although the level of competitiveness varies among countries in Africa, African countries are generally among the most uncompetitive countries in the world by many measures: in the World Economic Forum 2016–2017 Global Competitiveness Index, no African country was ranked in the top quartile, while African countries comprised twenty-four of the bottom thirty-eight countries.[156] The rankings also reflect significant regional variation, with the West African region stagnating in the rankings and being the least competitive region, and the highest country (Ivory Coast) ranking at ninety-nine with Sierra Leone and Nigeria in the bottom fifteen.[157] Future prospects for improved competitiveness do not look good: "if past performance is relied on as an indicator of future results, Africa's competitiveness outlook appears grim, as performance has been relatively stagnant for over a decade."[158] Legal frameworks to promote internal competition within African countries did not exist at the time of independence. African countries have, however, increasingly adopted competition law frameworks that have potential to draw greater attention to issues related to competition and competitiveness.[159]

The competing visions of Goldie, which was premised on economic and political subjugation under the weight of force, and Crowther's vision of social and economic empowerment were not compatible. Implementation of Goldie's vision required suppression of African competition. Some came to believe that Samuel Ajayi Crowther "was training Africans to compete for wealth and power in this world, something that had to be stopped."[160] Suppression of African competition was a key aspect of colonialism in various contexts. In Kenya, for example, settlers and Africans "competed for control over the economy in the political arena."[161] In the end, the future path of Goldie, rather than Crowther, came to pass in colonial Nigeria. This reflects ways that the "goal and result of imperialism – one which was in fact achieved in most territories before decolonization – was the creation of colonies politically submissive and economically profitable to their European metropoles."[162] As a result, the fundamental social and economic transformation envisaged by Bishop Ajayi Crowther remains a path not taken, or as yet, even fully conceptualized.

Notes

1. "How Big Firms Rip Off African Consumers." *Economist*, October 3, 2020, accessed October 23, 2020, www.economist.com/middle-east-and-africa/2020/10/03/how-big-firms-rip-off-african-consumers.
2. James Wilkinson. "'Racist' Chinese Spring Festival Gala TV Show Causes Uproar over 'Blackface and Big Bottoms'." *South China Morning Post*, February 16, 2018, accessed October 24, 2020, www.scmp.com/news/china/society/article/2133558/racist-chinese-spring-

festival-gala-tv-show-causes-consternation; Adam Taylor. "Chinese State Media's New Year Gala Once Again Features Blackface in Segment Depicting Africa." *Washington Post*, February 12, 2021, accessed March 12, 2021, www.washingtonpost.com/world/2021/02/11/cctv-gala-blackface-chunwan/.

3. Jane Perlez. "With Blackface and Monkey Suit, Chinese Gala on Africa Causes Uproar." *New York Times*, February 16, 2018, accessed October 24, 2020, www.nytimes.com/2018/02/16/world/asia/china-africa-blackface-lunar-new-year.html.
4. Racism in a Chinese Laundry Detergent Advertisement, May 7, 2016, accessed October 24, 2020, www.youtube.com/watch?v=Few8kJozfnY.
5. Coloria, www.youtube.com/watch?v=4douYfyzFhI&feature=youtu.be.
6. Jiayang Fan. "Lessons About China and Race from a Detergent Ad." *New Yorker*, June 9, 2016, accessed October 24, 2020, www.newyorker.com/news/daily-comment/lessons-about-china-and-race-from-a-detergent-ad.
7. "China Denies Racism, Says Hyping up TV Blackface Skit 'Futile'." Reuters, February 22, 2018, accessed October 24, 2020, www.reuters.com/article/us-lunar-newyear-china-blackface/china-denies-racism-says-hyping-up-tv-blackface-skit-futile-idUSKCN1G60ZE.
8. Sautman, 1994.
9. Goon and Craven, 2003.
10. Hung, 2015: 32–33.
11. Sautman, 1994.
12. Monson, 2009.
13. Murithi Mutiga. "'No Africans' Chinese Restaurant Owner Arrested in Nairobi." *Guardian*, March 24, 2015, accessed October 23, 2020, www.theguardian.com/world/2015/mar/24/no-africans-restaurant-owner-arrested-nairobi-kenya/.
14. Human Rights Watch. "China: Covid-19 Discrimination Against Africans." May 5, 2020, accessed October 23, 2020, www.hrw.org/news/2020/05/05/china-covid-19-discrimination-against-africans.
15. Hsaio-Hung Pai. "The Coronavirus Crisis Has Exposed China's Long History of Racism." *Guardian*, April 25, 2020, accessed October 23, 2020, www.theguardian.com/commentisfree/2020/apr/25/coronavirus-exposed-china-history-racism-africans-guangzhou.
16. Shih, 2013: 38.
17. Allyson Chiu. "Trump Has No Qualms About Calling Coronavirus the 'Chinese Virus.' That's a Dangerous Attitude, Experts Say." *Washington Post*, March 20, 2020, accessed October 23, 2020, www.washingtonpost.com/nation/2020/03/20/coronavirus-trump-chinese-virus/.
18. Sabrina Tavernise and Richard A. Oppel, Jr. "Spit On, Yelled At, Attached: Chinese Americans Fear for Their Safety." *New York Times*, March 23, 2020 (updated April 10, 2020), accessed October 23, 2020, www.nytimes.com/2020/03/23/us/chinese-coronavirus-racist-attacks.html.
19. European Union Agency for Fundamental Rights. Coronavirus pandemic in the EU – Fundamental Rights Implications – Bulletin 1, p. 11, April 8, 2020, https://fra.europa.eu/en/publication/2020/covid19-rights-impact-april-1.
20. Leibold, 2020.
21. Kaufman, 2018: 277.
22. Ibid. at 279.

23. Ibid.
24. Birnhack, 2012: 30.
25. Mwalimu, 2009: 430, 432.
26. Asomugha, 1994: 2; Mwalumu, 2009: 419.
27. Mwalimu, 2009: 419.
28. Banwho & Ighodalo. Companies and Allied Matters Act 2020: Reforming Provisions that Impact the Nigerian Business Community, August 10, 2020, accessed October 23, 2020, www.banwo-ighodalo.com/assets/grey-matter/e6fb6e556c4a854b62179365eea3ec36.pdf.
29. CAMA 2020 makes corporate seals not mandatory, provides for virtual annual general meetings, exempts SMEs from appointing auditors, makes appointments of the Company Secretary optional for SMEs and provides for single-member/shareholder companies. Abiola Odutola, How New CAMA 2020 Will Enhance SMEs' Ease of Doing Business. Nairametrics, August 9, 2020, accessed October 23, 2020, https://nairametrics.com/2020/08/09/how-new-cama-2020-will-enhance-smes-ease-of-doing-business/.
30. Reisberg, 2010: 317.
31. José Filomeno de Sousa dos Santos. 2015. "Why SMEs Are Key to Growth in Africa." World Economic Forum Agenda, October 5, accessed October 23, 2020, www.weforum.org/agenda/2015/08/why-smes-are-key-to-growth-in-africa/.
32. The World Bank. Small and Medium Enterprises (SMES) Finance, accessed October 23, 2020, www.worldbank.org/en/topic/smefinance.
33. Ghana Investment Promotion Centre Act, 2013 (Act 865), §28, www.gis.gov.gh/PDFs/GIPC%20Act%202013.pdf.
34. Auria Styles. "Why Africa's Startup Scenes Need Better Investment Promotion Legislation – Learnings from Ghana." Venture Capital for Africa Blog, October 10, 2014, accessed March 14, 2020, https://perma.cc/D7WH-3JCW?type=image.
35. Gathii, 2020: 1.
36. Ibid. at 1
37. Ibid. at 3.
38. Ibid. at 3–4.
39. Doshi, Kelley and Simmons, 2019.
40. Ibid. at 613.
41. Ibid. at 619.
42. Josh Zumbrun and Iain Talley. "World Bank Unfairly Influenced Its Own Competitiveness Rankings." *Wall Street Journal*, January 12, 2018, accessed October 24, 2020, www.wsj.com/articles/world-bank-unfairly-influenced-its-own-competitiveness-rankings-1515797620.
43. World Bank. Doing Business – Data Irregularities Statement, August 27, 2020, accessed October 24, 2020, www.worldbank.org/en/news/statement/2020/08/27/doing-business–data-irregularities-statement.
44. Ibid.
45. Birla, 2011: 1018.
46. Asomugha, 1994: 1–2.
47. Seleti, 1992: 155; Beveridge, 1974: 478.
48. Beveridge, 1974; Nigerian Enterprises Promotion Decree, 1972; Nigerian Enterprises Promotion Decree, 1977.

49. Adejugbe, 1984: 587–588.
50. Neuwirth, 2012: 34.
51. Mudimbe, 1988: 4.
52. Mgbeoji, 2014.
53. Adebola, 2020: 234.
54. Okediji, 2006.
55. Arewa, 2006: 173–175.
56. The Nigerian Copyright Commission launched a copyright reform process in 2012 and published a draft copyright reform bill in November 2015.
57. Adelowo et al., 2010.
58. Trade Marks Act, Cap T 13, Laws of the Federation of Nigeria 2004 ("TMA") and the Trademark Regulations 1990.
59. Mordi, 2011: 193.
60. As Mordi notes: "The non-inclusion of services as covered in the definition of trademark is clearly one of the shortcomings of the Nigerian Act" (2011: 196). See also § 4 ("A trade mark must be registered in respect of particular goods or classes of goods, and any question arising as to the class within which any goods fall shall be determined by the Registrar, whose decision shall be final."). Trade Marks Act, Laws of the Federation of Nigeria 2004.
61. LeLaw Barristers & Solicitors, 2021.
62. Pam and Mantu, 2019.
63. Ezejiofor, 1973: 40.
64. Ibid.
65. Ibid. at 45.
66. Dhar, Biswajit and C. Niranjan Rao. 2002. "International Patent System: An Empirical Analysis." Research and Information System for the Non-Aligned and Other Developing Countries. New Delhi: India, pp. 12, 33, Habitat Centre, accessed October 23, 2020, www.wipo.int/about-ip/en/studies/pdf/study_b_dhar.pdf.
67. Department Trade and Industry. 2018. Intellectual Property Policy of the Republic of South Africa, Phase I, www.gov.za/sites/default/files/gcis_document/201808/ippolicy2018-phasei.pdf; Zulu et al., 2018.
68. International Centre for Trade and Sustainable Development. 2014. South Africa, Pharmaceutical Industry Face Off on Patent Reform, www.ictsd.org/bridges-news/bridges-africa/news/south-africa-pharmaceutical-industry-face-off-on-patent-reform-0.
69. Oyedepo, 2012.
70. Laura Dwyer-Lindgren, Michael A. Cork, Amber Sligar, et al. "Mapping HIV Prevalence in Sub-Saharan Africa Between 2000 and 2017." *Nature* 570 (2019): 189–193, at 189.
71. Steven S. Forsythe, William McGreeve, Alan Whiteside et al., "Twenty Years of Antiretroviral Therapy for People Living with HIV: Global Costs, Health Achievements, Economic Benefits." *Health Affairs* 38, 6 (2019): 1163–1172.
72. Arachu Castro and Michael Westerhaus. "Access to Generic Antiretrovirals: Inequality, Intellectual Property Law, and International Trade Agreements." *Cadernos de Saúde Pública* 23, 1 (2007): S85–S96.
73. Heinz Klug. "Access to Medicines and the Transformation of the South African State: Exploring the Interactions of Legal and Policy Changes in Health, Intellectual Property,

Trade, and Competition Law in the Context of South Africa's HIV/AIDS Pandemic." *Law & Social Inquiry* 37, 2 (2012): 297–329.

74. Statistics South Africa. *Mid-year population estimates 2020*, at viii, July 9, 2020, accessed December 2, 2020, www.statssa.gov.za/publications/P0302/P03022020.pdf.
75. Editorial. "Maintaining the HIV response in a world shaped by COVID-19." *Lancet* 396 (November 28, 2020): 1703, www.thelancet.com/action/showPdf?pii=S0140-6736%2820%2932526-5.
76. Bessen and Meurer, 2008.
77. Umahi, 2011.
78. Andrade, Anthony de and Venkatesh Viswanath. "The Costs of Patenting in Africa: A Tale of Three Intellectual Property Systems." IPWatchdog.com, August 4, 2017, accessed October 24, 2020, www.ipwatchdog.com/2017/08/04/costs-patenting-in-africa/id=86500/.
79. Editorial. "Reforming South Africa's Procedures for Granting Patents to Improve Access to Medicine." *South African Medical Journal*, September 2015, accessed October 24, 2020, www.scielo.org.za/scielo.php?script=sci_arttext&pid=S0256-95742015000900018.
80. Bauer, 1963: 85.
81. Ibid.
82. Bischoff, 2009; Sauer, 1992: 29; Smyth, 1979.
83. Kwarteng, 2011: 2.
84. Organisation du contrôle des films cinématographiques, des disques phonographique, des prises de vues cinématographiques et des enregistrements sonores en Afrique occidentale française [Decree regulating the organization and control of cinema films and phonographic records, of film shooting and audio recordings in French West Africa], *Journal Officiel de la République française*, March 11, 1934, 2541.
85. Bischoff, 2009: 443.
86. Barlet, 2012: 205.
87. Bischoff, 2009: 443.
88. Smyth, 1979: 437–440.
89. Ibid. at 439.
90. Established pursuant to the National Film and Video Censors Board Decree (Decree 85 of 1993), National Film and Video Censors Board Act, Cap n. 40 ("NFVCB Decree").
91. Cinematograph (Film Censorship) Regulations, 1964, Annual Volume of the Laws of the Federal Republic of Nigeria B63-B70 (1964).
92. Cinematograph Act of 1963 (no. 7), Annual Volume of the Laws of the Federal Republic of Nigeria A35-A38 (1963).
93. NFVCB Decree, at §§ 54-65, 67. Decrees in Nigeria have typically been issued by military governments, which have ruled Nigeria for close to 30 years since Nigerian independence in 1960 (1966 to 1979 and 1983 to 1999).
94. Ugor, 2007: 6.
95. Privy Council Order, May 14, 1912. TNA PC 2/413.
96. Preliminary Notes on Certain Legis. TNA BT 209/1072.
97. Memo to Imperial Secretary from R. Feetham in Johannesburg (July 6, 1912). TNA DO 119/881.

98. Proclamations extending Copyright Act 1911 to Bechuanaland, Swaziland, Basutoland, Southern and Northern Rhodesia. TNA DO 119/881.
99. Extension of the Copyright Acts to the Colonies. TNA BT 209/1072.
100. Ghana adopted the Copyright Ordinance of 1914 (Cap. 126) and enabling Copyright Regulation of 1918, which applied the British Copyright Act of 1911 within the colony of the Gold Coast Colony (which later became Ghana). Adusei, Anyimadu-Antwi and Halm, 2009, p. 10.
101. Ghana Independence Act 1957. 5 & 6 Eliz. 2 ch. 6.
102. Article 12. Ghana Independence Act 1957. 5 & 6 Eliz. 2 ch. 6.
103. Copyright Act 85 of 1961 and the Copyright (Fee) Regulation of 1969 (Legislative Instrument 174).
104. Adusei, Anyimadu-Antwi and Halm, 2009: 10.
105. Copyright Act 1956 § 2(3).
106. Letter to the Board of Trade, Industrial Property Department from Performing Rights Society (8/16/1963) and signed by the General Manager. TNA BT 209/1072.
107. Letter to Board of Trade, Industrial Property Department from The British Joint Copyright Council (9/2/1958). TNA BT 209/1072.
108. Letter to Industrial Property Department from The Publisher's Association (9/2/1958). TNA BT 209/1072.
109. Letter from the Colonial Office to the Industrial Property Department (12/22/1958). TNA BT 209/1072.
110. Letter to the Colonial Office from the Industrial Property Office (2/17/1959). TNA BT 209/1072.
111. Ferguson, 2003: 233.
112. Piketty, 2017: 86–87.
113. Vladimir Duthiers and Teo Kermeliotis. "Monopoly Moves to Africa with Lagos Edition." Cnn.com, December 20, 2012, accessed October 23, 2020, www.cnn.com/2012/12/14/world/africa/lagos-monopoly/index.html.
114. Wilentz, 2013: 93.
115. Smith, 1904: 58–140.
116. Erikson, 2014: vii.
117. Ibid. at v–viii.
118. Bauer, 1963: 65.
119. Ibid. at 77–79.
120. Ibid. at 145.
121. Ibid. at 148.
122. Ibid. at 156–157.
123. Alence, 2001: 398–399.
124. Bauer, 1963: 266.
125. Alence, 2001: 408.
126. Trivedi, 1971: 617.
127. Alence, 2001: 397.
128. UNCTAD, 2013: 66–67.
129. Ibid. at 82.
130. Ibid. at 65.

131. Bauer, 1963: 65.
132. Ibid. at 157.
133. TNA CO 583/262/5.
134. Arewa, 2016.
135. Rodney, 1972: 22.
136. Nigeria, Address by Major Walter E. Elliot, March 28, 1928, p, 7, TPA CPA/1/6/9.
137. Letter dated November 17, 1941 from The Anti-Slavery and Aborigines Protection Society to the Under-Secretary of State for the Colonies; Letter dated July 3, 1941 from The Anti-Slavery and Aborigines Protection Society to the Under-Secretary of State for the Colonies. TNA CO852/446/6.
138. Bannerman, 2013.
139. World Bank. "Breaking down Barriers: Unlocking Africa's Potential Through Vigorous Competition Policy," June 2016, p. 10, accessed October 23, 2020, http://documents.worldbank.org/curated/en/243171467232051787/pdf/106717-REVISED-PUBLIC-WBG-ACF-Report-Printers-Version-21092016.pdf .
140. https://placng.org/i/wp-content/uploads/2019/12/Federal-Competition-and-Consumer-Protection-Act-2018.pdf.
141. Hansard HC Deb 26 July 1899 vol 75 cc370-426. Statement of Mr. Labouchere.
142. Ayandele, 1967: 46.
143. Ibid. at 47.
144. Ibid. at 48.
145. Ibid. at 49.
146. Dike, 1956.
147. Asomugha, 1994: 1–2.
148. Gertzel, 1962: 362-366.
149. Ibid. at 365.
150. No. 7. Vice-Consul Johnston to the Marquis of Salisbury (January 15, 1886). TNA FO 403/534.
151. No. 27. Vice-Consul Johnston to the Marquis of Salisbury (July 28, 1887). TNA FO 403/534.
152. TNA CO 96/831.
153. TNA CO 28/229/47.
154. Gertzel, 1962: 366.
155. World Economic Forum, 2017: xiv–xv.
156. Adeleye et al., 2018: 2.
157. Ibid.
158. Ibid. at 4.
159. Fox and Bakhoum, 2019.
160. Barnes, 2018: 8.
161. Anderson and Throup, 1985: 344.
162. Headrick, 1981: 11.

11

Conclusion

Ghosts, Dreams, and Future Paths

It's difficult to turn a large number of people into radical Islamists or drug gangs if they have jobs and security.[1]

Lamido Sanusi
Governor of the Central Bank of Nigeria (2009–2014)
Emir of Kano (2015–2020)

Government of the people, say by the people and for the people . . . You all are liars just sharing the Nation's proceeds amidst the few you.

Bembe Aladisa "Ewa Fun Mi Ni Visa" (Give me a visa!)[2]

I really wish the international community could make . . . rule of law and respect for human rights . . . a precondition for cooperation with Uganda . . . [and] not . . . appear like a partner in crime.

Bobi Wine (Robert Kyagulanyi Ssentamu)
Ugandan Opposition Presidential Candidate (2021)[3]

BALLET IN LAGOS, SOCIAL MEDIA, AND GLOBAL AUDIENCES

In the summer of 2020, in the midst of the global COVID-19 pandemic, an 11-year-old Nigerian ballet dancer caught the attention of the world.[4] In a video that had been viewed more than 20 million times on social media platforms by August 2020, Anthony Mmesoma Madu danced barefoot in the rain:

> In June, a minute-long video featuring a young ballet student dancing in the rain began circulating on the internet. As the rain falls, forming puddles between the uneven slabs of concrete on which he dances, Anthony Mmesoma Madu, 11, turns pirouette after pirouette . . . . Though the conditions for such dancing are all wrong – dangerous, even – he twirls on, flying barefoot into an arabesque and landing it. He indulges the camera with a smile, but only for a moment, before assuming a look of fierce determination, lifting his eyes toward the sky, his lithe arms and graceful fingers following closely along.[5]

Anthony's video was intended to help him practice his form.[6] Anthony's dance is a testament to the hard work, talent and enduring sense of hope of so many throughout Africa who live their lives dealing with significant adversity. Anthony's story is also about the Leap of Dance Academy in Lagos, Nigeria where he learned to dance; the academy was founded in 2017 by Daniel Owoseni Ajala, who teaches students to dance for free, and has "transformed the lives of its students, affording them a place to dance and to dream … in the last few months, it has inspired influential people in ballet to lend a hand."[7]

The response to Anthony's video has, for Anthony, Daniel and other students at the academy, enabled realization of hopes and dreams. The academy has received donations from around the world. Anthony received a full scholarship to an online summer program at the School of American Ballet theater after the school's director saw Anthony's video. In January 2021, Anthony was to begin a scholarship program in New York. Anthony also gained a sponsor in Nigeria for his and another student's academic education. Other students from the academy have received similar offers. Olamide Olawale, the academy's first and oldest dancer, wants to become the next Misty Copeland and enrolled in an online 2020 summer program with the Elmhurst Ballet School of the Birmingham Royal Ballet in England.[8]

The viral video has had an impact in Nigeria as well, leading to community validation and changing perceptions about ballet, particularly for male dancers. The short video has enabled culmination of dreams and creation of previously unimagined opportunities for those involved with the academy in a fashion that seems like a fairy tale rather than real life. This is particularly the case in Nigeria, where dreams may remain unfulfilled for many, and where the surrounding environment is often not structured to facilitate creation of opportunities or paths by which to fulfill their hopes and dreams. Anthony, Daniel, Olamide, and the other students in the academy and by extension, other people in Nigeria, should not need to rely on viral videos or an "external" lottery to provide them with opportunities:

> Madu's story offers a dangerously easy narrative of change – a young prodigy finally given the opportunity his talent deserves. But this narrative only includes the story of one student; the story would be exponentially more powerful if we sought to include the empowerment of Madu's classmates as well as other underserved communities across the globe.[9]

Nigeria and other countries in Africa need to provide opportunities for local communities to address local needs and facilitate hopes and dreams for the many. This requires eliminating the ghosts of colonialism and disrupting the legal and other institutional structures that sustain these ghosts. Disrupting colonial overhang would entail changing colonial-era legal frameworks but requires far more. It also requires disrupting law and policymaking processes skewed by external determination, disrupting patterns of accumulation enabled by jurisdictional arbitrage, blocking behaviors, and other forms of corruption, and reorienting government for the benefit of the majority of people. A need also exists for long-term sustainable strategies that are flexible and able to respond to changing local and global circumstances.

The digital economy may offer opportunities for such disruption. However, this will require new terms and conditions of engagement that are based to a greater extent on local considerations and local needs than has been the case in the past. Unfortunately, and not surprisingly, Nigeria and other countries in Africa may be in the process of being incorporated in digital economy contexts on terms and conditions that bear important similarities to the past. For example, rather than the digital economy's being a source of innovation that could facilitate development in local, national, and regional contexts within Africa, African countries are increasingly becoming sites for dumping of digital economy electronic waste, which poses significant environmental and health hazards.[10]

Digital-era disruption will also require learning from the young, which may be difficult in Nigeria and other countries in Africa, where elders are treated with respect, even when the respect accorded them may be questionable in light of prior acts.[11] As Atane Ofiaja asks in a blog posting, "[o]ne of the things our cultures have in common is their reverence for elders. But is merely being around for a long time enough? Shouldn't respect be earned? Not all elders are wise. Should we also defer to an elder known to be ignorant, misogynistic and cruel?"[12] Globalization and neoliberal reforms and practices may already be shifting attitudes surrounding the "social values attached to old age."[13]

Africa is a continent full of young people, who because of scarcity of opportunity, often have limited future paths for education, employment, and other fundamental things. Africa is presently the youngest continent in the world, with a median age of 19.5 in 2020,[14] with the oldest leaders in the world.[15] By 2100, "Africa's youth will be equivalent to twice Europe's entire population and almost one half of the world's youth will be from Africa."[16] Africa's position of having the oldest rulers in the world reflects the many African rulers who have held positions of power, at times for for decades in the time since independence:[17] Since 1960, fifteen rulers in Africa have been in power more than two decades and ten held office for more than three decades.[18] The age mismatch between those who govern and the governed is likely to get worse as populations in many countries in Africa explode in the twenty-first century. Future population increases in Africa can be either an opportunity to realize postindependence hopes and dreams for African freedom, or a ticking time bomb for greater instability and chaos.[19] The #EndSARS protests in Nigeria and widespread unrest in Ethiopia and Uganda in late 2020 may be a harbinger of things to come.

As demographics shift in the coming decades, contestation between generations may become increasingly sharp, particularly in light of widespread leadership failures in Africa in the postindependence era. Younger generations in Africa are often enmeshed in the digital economy in ways that their elders are not, which may create problems in digital economy policy and decision-making where those making policies, in addition to following processes that reflect colonial overhang, may not be as well versed as those who are younger in issues related to digital-era technologies and their uses. This is not a problem that is only evident in sub-Saharan Africa (SSA) but may be magnified there because the age gap between leaders and the population is so wide. Listening to and learning from the young should bring greater prominence to places such as TechCabal, where conveners, speakers, and the audience are a testament to the energy and thoughtfulness of entrepreneurs all over Africa. Many similar locations for such discussions are happening throughout the African continent. These discussions need to be given a voice and input into policies that shape digital economy responses in Africa.

Adequate and ongoing assessment of the full impact of new technologies remains a pervasive problem in the digital era, again, not only in Africa. One impediment to assessing outcomes arises from typical assumptions about the impact of technology as a progressive force. This is by no means necessarily the case. Legal trends emerging from, and connected to, colonial era laws and institutions, which were reinforced in important respects after colonialism, are also relevant. These laws and regulations have contributed to profound inequalities on multiple levels that have marginalized significant segments of the population and have contributed to unstable institutional configurations. Technology can facilitate inclusion, but cannot overcome deeply rooted institutional structures and the ghosts of colonialism by itself.

Additional factors also highlight the need for caution in making determinations of successes and failures in digital contexts in Africa. Both poverty levels and aspects of the digital divide have grown at the same time as transformative digital-era technologies have gained a foothold in Africa. The digital divide has also grown as digital-era technologies have become more widespread in Africa,[20, 21] which has significant implications for future inequality, as well as future paths. Demographic and digital divide trends suggest that greater attention should be paid to policy frameworks for implementation of new technologies that take account of the broader impact of such technologies. Trends in Africa are consistent with those in other parts of the world. Disruptive technology in Silicon Valley and elsewhere have had significant distributional effects and have exacerbated inequality. The determination of what constitutes success in the context of new technologies that likely improve overall welfare, but with respect to which the benefits accrue to only a few, is among the most important issues in considering the broader global impact of new technologies, particularly in Africa.

FLEXIBLE REGULATORY APPROACHES AND INTEGRATED INNOVATION ECOSYSTEMS

Present circumstances in Nigeria draw attention to the need for integrated and flexible approaches to innovation that take account of past and present successes and failures in planning future paths. Such approaches should also anticipate, and attempt to ameliorate, adverse consequences of new technologies, as well as the impact of structures reflecting a continuing influence of colonial and neocolonial forces. This would require broader policy approaches to a wide range of technologies and infrastructures that would take account of laws and regulations targeting SMEs and other companies enmeshed in digital-era technologies and reconsideration of intellectual property laws, as has been evident in intellectual property reforms in South Africa in its move to a system of patent examination.[22]

Integrated innovation ecosystem approaches would address a broad range of issues, including internet access and infrastructure, firm formation, firm financing, and laws and regulations, including business law and intellectual property law, competition policy and competition law, regulation of privacy and data security, tax policies, and capital markets policies. These laws and regulations must be customized for African contexts and should incorporate learning from past and present experiences in Africa and elsewhere. Such laws should not be enacted in isolation, and from their inception, should take account of the human impact of economic and business laws and regulations, including questions of human rights, equality, and other relevant factors.

Countries in Africa now recognize the importance of business laws that facilitate development of SMEs, as reflected in the Nigerian CAMA 2020 and the proposed 2020 Kenya Startup Bill, which establishes a framework for development of innovation and entrepreneurship. Kenya follows Tunisia and Senegal in considering start-up–specific legislation, while Rwanda and Ethiopia have also considered such a law.[23] Facilitating entrepreneurship in Africa will, however, require more than just passing new legislation. It will require disruption of existing approaches and processes that reflect the ghosts of colonialism. It will require legal processes that are hybrid, flexible, and responsive, and that continually assess the effectiveness of legal frameworks in light of actual outcomes for people in Africa. Disrupting past approaches will also require assessment of the impact of laws, regulations, and other frameworks on the many, rather than just on the privileged few.

The impact of new technologies and new business models will likely be more sustained and robust in Africa if approaches to these technologies are integrated with innovation and competition policies more generally. Approaches centered around innovation ecosystems can also incorporate ongoing monitoring of the impact and outcomes of new technologies within Africa in light of current and historical experiences within and outside of Africa. This type of integrated innovation ecosystem approach could have a number of advantages. An integrated approach that focuses on the development of innovation ecosystems could incorporate policies that are related to the development of innovative technologies. Such policies could address questions of access to the Internet and other digital economy infrastructures; support for enterprises that develop new technologies; financing considerations; legal considerations related to business formation and intellectual property laws;

regulations that target use of new technologies; regulation of privacy and data security; competition policies and competition law; tax policies; and capital markets policies that enable the purchase, sale, financing, and public offering processes of such enterprises. Such integrated approaches should also assess the social and human impact of new technologies.

An integrated approach requires innovation in how we think about and organize the development and deployment of new technologies and new business models, and not only for companies that are closely enmeshed in the digital economy. An integrated approach also requires innovative approaches to law and institutions that have thus far proven to be unstable, unsustainable, or both in far too many postcolonial African contexts. By undertaking such integrated approaches, African countries could be on the leading edge of addressing issues related to new technologies, many of which might be relevant in other places. Such approaches could address questions related to technology gaps, socioeconomic inequality, the impact of technology on labor and agriculture, technology, e-waste, and environmental issues, among others. Forward-looking technology, legal, and innovation policies within Africa could also enhance the competitive position of African firms within an increasingly digital world in which access to knowledge and information is becoming of paramount importance. Such integrated approaches could enhance our understanding of how success and failure should be defined and assessed in the digital era within potentially shifting contexts of implementation and use. Innovation ecosystem approaches could also cut across existing bureaucratic and other silos and take account of lessons of past and present experiences with digital-era technologies.

An integrated innovation ecosystem would also involve considering positions in external settings, including in international negotiations, in light of their implications for domestic and regional innovation ecosystems. Such ecosystems would tie existing initiatives in Africa relating to biometrics, drones, automation, digital finance and more to broader policy concerns. An integrated innovation ecosystem would assess laws and regulations and new technologies in terms of their impact on the well-being of people within Africa. This type of integrated innovation ecosystem poses a challenge that, if met, has the potential to transform future paths within Africa. One clear lesson of the digital era is that even if disruptive and other new technologies increase social welfare generally, they may also have significant detrimental distributional and other effects. Anticipating and planning for the consequences of such potentially detrimental effects should be one focus of integrated innovation policies.

Models for future paths should take account of local contexts. This would include solutions to local problems within Africa, as well as opportunistic facilitation of unexpected initiatives and industries as they arise. Nigeria's Nollywood film industry and digital money in Kenya represent potential models for how local innovation may arise. Digital money in Kenya also offers an example of flexible regulatory approaches that can incentivize the development of innovative sectors. Legal reform in innovative sectors should be a starting point for comprehensive bottom-up legal reform with goals of creating legal frameworks that enable, rather than block, facilitating creation of local opportunities for local people, and more generally, disrupting and exorcising the ghosts of colonialism.

NOLLYWOOD AS MODEL

The shape of Nigeria's Nollywood film industry has changed significantly its origins. The early institutional structure of Nollywood reflected the leap to digital technology with informal industry structures that lacked centralized and hierarchical industry structures organized around the creation, financing, and distribution of physical video films. This early structure was in part due to the absence of large-scale cinemas at that time in cities such as Lagos, and to the dominance of home viewing.[24] The initial dominance of home viewing has had significant implications for business and legal structures that have arisen surrounding the Nigerian video film industry.

Nollywood's development underscores the physical infrastructure and other institutional challenges that existed in Nigeria at the time of Nollywood's emergence.[25] Lack of reliable electricity is yet another challenge confronting the Nollywood industry: Nigeria is one of the most inefficient producers of electricity in the world with frequent blackouts and brownouts, as well as widespread reliance on self-generated electricity.[26] Unreliable electricity is thought by many to be the biggest constraint in the Nigerian business sector.[27]

These challenges and technological discontinuities underscore why Nigeria was an unlikely locale for the development of a video film industry and illustrate fundamental paradoxes of contemporary Nigeria. Nollywood also highlights the potentially unpredictable nature of innovation, which underscores the need for enabling environments that permit the development of new things that might not always be expected or predictable.

Nollywood has changed as it has matured. Once divided along ethnic lines, the Nigerian film industry is becoming increasingly professionalized and unifying under the term *Nollywood*.[28] New Nigerian cinema has also involved an aesthetic transformation of the industry with films with higher technical quality. Nollywood is becoming increasingly formal and:

> is slowly detaching itself from the industry's informal political economy. Filmmakers in this sector produce and distribute their films via the theaters located in shopping malls that attract the middle- and upper-class elites. Such films are sparsely available within the larger popular audience market as they take several months and sometimes years to become available on DVDs."[29]

The more recent development of Nollywood may raise questions about whether Nollywood is being gentrified.[30] Nollywood films are now also distributed through formal and authorized global distribution chains, including Netflix, which, in 2020, announced its first original Nollywood production, a series from *Vaya* director Akin Omotoso. The six-part series will be set in contemporary Nigeria and filmed in Lagos. It will tell the story of the goddess Kemi, who is reincarnated as a human to avenge her sister's death.[31]

Changing Nollywood business models draw attention to the indifference if not resistance to fundamental legal reform in Nigeria. The successes of Nollywood have not led to fundamental legal reform, which reflects the durability of institutional frameworks and legal processes imbued with the ghosts of colonialism. Nigeria's copyright law is over thirty years old and has not been comprehensively updated to reflect digital economy realities for Nigeria or the need to use copyright as a tool of innovation. As a result, the current copyright law in Nigeria does not take sufficient account of domestic industries such as Nollywood that are important economically or public interest goals of copyright, particularly in relation to access to knowledge.[32] Although a copyright reform process was undertaken and a draft bill was made public in 2015,[33] actual reform legislation has not been enacted.

Nollywood has, however, played a role in changing Nigerian approaches to copyright enforcement. Prior to the advent of Nollywood, copyright enforcement had traditionally been weak.[34] Lack of copyright enforcement in Nigeria was due to a variety of factors, including a traditional lack of domestic copyright constituencies.[35]

As Chidi Oguamanam has noted, Nollywood offers a potential model of entrepreneurship that could be adapted in Nigeria and elsewhere in Africa.[36] This model is based on local innovation, but has connectivity with the global. Nollywood shows the potential for the growth of industries with little or no initial government involvement. At the same time, Nollywood shows limitations and the potential resistance of legal infrastructures in African contexts to internally driven transformations and reform, as well as the long time periods that such reform processes may at present require.

DIGITAL FINANCE IN KENYA

Digital finance in Kenya demonstrates potential transformations driven by a more flexible and innovative approach to regulation. Digital-era disruption has had an impact on a number of sectors, including the financial industry, which has adapted to new technologies.[37] Fintech has facilitated the development of vast networks of varied participants. Such networks may exist on multiple levels and may include knowledge networks that embed technology infrastructures, as well as interconnections among individuals within firms and firms themselves. These interconnections link market participants during both financial market expansions and contractions. As is the case in other areas of economic activity, financial systems are permeated with multiple levels of interrelationships. Through their influence on financial variables such as interest rates and currency prices, financial market networks reach deep into homes and pocketbooks of a significant portion of world's population.[38]

The pervasiveness of global and local financial and other networks today makes questions of financial inclusion all the more urgent. The impact of technologies in the digital finance and other arenas must be assessed continually to better understand the full impact of such technologies. In Africa, mobile telephones have been heralded as a significant positive disruptive force.[39] Although mobile phones and mobile money and payments have transformed the lives of many,[40] including poor rural households in Africa, the positive impact of new technologies should not be assumed, and potential future negative impacts should be anticipated and addressed to the greatest extent possible. New technologies must also be considered in light of existing sources of disruption in Africa that may not be as present in other areas of the world in which disruptive technologies have been deployed.

In much of the postcolonial period, many in Africa have been excluded from financial networks and financial tools that are essential for the development of small businesses, management of household expenses, and ability to make investments in school and health and plan for emergencies.[41] In 2012 only one quarter of adults in Africa experienced financial inclusion. By 2018, that number had increased to some 43 percent, with countries such as Kenya, Tanzania and, the Democratic Republic of the Congo (DRC) doubling the rate of financial inclusion during this time period.[42] This means that many who were unbanked now have access to important tools to manage businesses, family and household expenses, and investments for the future.

Stories about digital finance, fintech, and disruptive technologies today draw needed attention to technologies that may enhance the well-being of many. The development and diffusion of such technologies should not, however, be considered in isolation, either in time or space. Digital money and other types of fintech offer the prospect of alleviation of a range of acknowledged problems, including those connected to access and participation in financial networks that have become so pervasive and prominent today. The promise of digital finance and other disruptive technologies in Africa must, however, be considered within broader local and global contexts. The impact of such technologies will likely be more sustained and robust in Africa if approaches to these technologies are integrated with innovation policies more generally. Approaches centered around innovation ecosystems can also incorporate ongoing monitoring of the impact and outcomes of digital finance and other new technologies within Africa in light of current and historical experiences within and outside of Africa.

Digital finance is often thought of as a digital economy success story in Africa. Digital finance alone cannot fully address problems of poverty and inequality. Rather, digital finance must be aligned with broader innovation policies that link legal and regulatory environments and technology, economic, business, and other policies, with attention to the impact of such policies on human beings. Finally, the impact of digital finance and other new technologies is an empirical question that must be continually evaluated to assess the impact of such technologies on inclusion and inequality and other important indicators of human conditions.

Kenya is among the countries in Africa that could stand at the forefront of an important shift to greater use of technology developed or customized for African contexts that focus on solving local problems. In five years, 19 million Kenyans, close to 70 percent of the adult population, signed up for mobile money services.[43] Over 80 percent of these 19 million Kenyans were customers of M-Pesa (M for mobile and pesa meaning money in Swahili). M-Pesa is a mobile money service developed by the Kenyan telecommunications company Safaricom, which was formerly owned by the Government of Kenya.[44] Kenyan regulators approved a regulatory framework for mobile money that enabled people to use their mobile phones in transactions that had previously involved physical currency. M-Pesa, was deployed by Kenyan telecom Safaricom, based on an idea and technology that was germinated in London at the multinational telecom company Vodafone.[45] M-Pesa was a pilot project of the Vodafone Group with support from a UK Department of International Development (DFID) grant, and Kenya was chosen as a country to pilot M-Pesa.[46]

M-Pesa has put Kenya on a leading edge of digital finance innovation. By 2012, M-Pesa transactions outnumbered Western Union transactions globally and 60 percent of all electronic financial transactions in Kenya were conducted through M-Pesa, which constituted more than 20 percent of Kenyan GDP.[47] M-Pesa has also had a meaningful impact on financial inclusion in Kenya. A 2016 study suggests that M-Pesa increased per capital consumption levels and lifted some 2 percent of Kenyan households out of poverty. Notably, the impact of M-Pesa was more pronounced for female-headed households.[48]

The development of M-Pesa in Kenya is a story of regulators enabling, rather than blocking, new technology. The Central Bank of Kenya (CBK) is thus an important part of the development of M-Pesa. The rapid adoption of mobile money in Kenya contrasts with a number of other countries in Africa, where incumbent banks have been able to block independent innovative mobile money services. Regulators had a flexible approach to the rollout of M-Pesa, which was telecom led, in contrast to approaches in Nigeria that were bank led and were ultimately not nearly as successful as M-Pesa.[49] As Stephen Mwaura Nduati, former Head of National Payments System at the CBK notes, the CBK recognized that access to financial services is a "key to unlocking economic opportunity."[50] The CBK balanced concerns about safety and soundness that are critical to regulation of banks, with the need to put in place complex legal and institutional frameworks in light of technological innovations that are an important source of innovation.[51]

When M-Pesa was launched in Kenya in 2007, Kenya did not have a clear legal framework for regulation of the M-Pesa system. The CBK approved the launch of M-Pesa and permitted its rapid growth after an extensive due diligence and consultation process. Kenyan regulators took a flexible approach to managing the introduction of an innovative new payments system. The launch of M-Pesa took months of engagement with the CBK.[52] M-Pesa grew rapidly, reaching 5 million users in less than two years. The growth of M-Pesa led to concerns by the Kenyan banking community, among others. Although Kenyan law gave the CBK general authority with respect to payment, clearing, and settlement systems, it did not have clear authority over nonbank funds transfer and did not interfere with the launch of M-Pesa.[53]

The story of M-Pesa is a compelling one, a story of uplift that helps poor and marginalized people in Africa. However, continuing evaluation of the impact of technologies in local contexts is a critical aspect of understanding the human impact of innovative things. In *Reimagining Money*, Sibel Kusimba draws attention to the need to interrogate the consequences of digital finance innovations for people on the margins that such innovations are intended to benefit. She notes that stories of positive outcomes and greater inclusion that have been thought to be consequences of digital finance innovations may be countered by stories that question "any direct relationship between digital finance and desirable outcomes like poverty reduction and financial inclusion."[54] Her ethnographic study considers digital finance and financial inclusion from a user perspective, seeking to ask "what money is, what it does, and what it means ... [trying] to get at local understandings of wealth, relationships, and well-being.[55] This perspective is an important one that must be taken account of when considering future paths and shaping how laws, legal process, and policy should interact with technological innovation.

POTENTIAL FUTURE PATHS

The successful launch of M-Pesa in Kenya was facilitated by the support of the Central Bank of Kenya (CBK), whose governor turned down requests from commercial banks that M-Pesa be stopped. These banks had apparently complained that M-Pesa could cause a financial crisis in Kenya.[56] M-Pesa's successful launch also relied on a flexible approach by the regulators, who recognized the importance of financial inclusion. It likely also helped that Safaricom was a former state-owned company. Interconnections among the parties at the table in discussions, including the CBK and Safaricom, likely enhanced relationships of trust that can be of critical importance in contexts of new technology, as well as other arenas. As Ade Atobatele, an investor and founder who was familiar with the nascent start-up scene in Lagos, notes, trust is an essential issue in emerging company spaces in Nigeria: "We have a trust issue .... There's no legacy system. People don't believe they can succeed."[57]

M-Pesa can provide another opportunity for considering the nexus between the internal and external in Africa. M-Pesa highlights the importance of internal relationships of trust in the development of new technologies that may have uncertain paths and futures that further require flexible regulatory approaches and structures of relationships. Some level of trust is important in entrepreneurial activity.[58] Factors that facilitate the development of internal trust within Africa are important for realizing the full potential of the digital economy in African countries. Patterns of government concentration that were established during, and continued after, colonialism may impact structures of trust within countries in Africa. Social trust within countries in SSA is low and "citizens express very low levels of vertical, generalized interpersonal trust."[59] Colonialism and types of contestation that became prominent during colonialism likely influenced levels of interpersonal trust, particularly beyond kinship and ethnic networks. Empirical work by Nathan Nunn and Leonard Wantchekon hypothesizes that cultures of mistrust in Africa may be one channel by which the slave trade may continue to affect economic development in Africa today.[60]

Reputation is another important factor in entrepreneurial and other relationships. Perceptions about Africa continue to function as a negative reputational factor in external facing interactions. This was likely a factor in the reception of M-Pesa when Vodafone attempted to launch the mobile money transfer service in Europe in Romania and Albania.[61] Institutional factors and competitive environments have contributed to M-Pesa's failure to gain traction in some markets, including South Africa.[62] New technologies emerging in Africa confront a world in which external perceptions of Africa as a source of innovation may be quite negative.

Nollywood and M-Pesa show different potential paths that reflect approaches that have been beneficial to at least some in both Nigeria and Kenya. Many potential future paths may exist that should be explored, at times even in an experimental fashion, to discover most promising paths. Nollywood and M-Pesa both reflect the influences of the internal and external, but are rooted in internal needs and experiences as a starting point for their development.

Creating future paths for Africa must disrupt past patterns of unfiltered use of external models. These paths will also require extensive legal and regulatory reform over time, undertaken with sufficient flexibility to enable careful navigation around potential impediments arising from both internal and external sources. These paths will also mandate innovative thinking about the role and operation of law itself, particularly in countries that may continue to experience the imposition of external legal frameworks, laws, and ideas that was so characteristic of colonialism. New paths will require disruption of colonialism's institutional legacy, as well as mental attitudes that continue to valorize this legacy, at times unconsciously. Future paths can play an important role in changing both internal and external perceptions and relationships within and outside of Africa.

Notes

1. Nicholas Norbrook and Patrick Smith. "Sanusi: 'These People Feel There Is No Future.'" *TheAfricaReport*, December 4, 2017, updated March 9, 2020, accessed, October 23, 2020, www.theafricareport.com/769/sanusi-these-people-feel-there-is-no-future/.

2. Bembe Aladisa (Ewafun mi ni visa) Part 1, www.youtube.com/watch?v=rvJm7qGgoaQ Bembe Aladisa (Ewafun mi ni visa) Part 2, www.youtube.com/watch?v=3wgDvU2WbLw. </int_u>
3. Associated Press, Ugandan Police Harass Opposition Candidate, *New York Times Video*, January 8, 2021, accessed January 10, 2021, www.nytimes.com/video/players/offsite/index .html?videoId=100000007541823.
4. www.youtube.com/watch?v=Jhc8fE9-AsU; twitter.com/violadavis/status/127589331314 5434114; www.instagram.com/leapofdanceacademy/?utm_source=ig_embed.
5. Noor Brara. "In Lagos, A Homegrown Ballet Academy Leaps into the Spotlight." *New York Times*, August 19, 2020, accessed, October 23, 2020, www.nytimes.com/2020/08/19/arts/ dance/lagos-ballet-school-viral-video.html.
6. Emmanuel Akinwotu. "Poise and Prestige: Viral Clip Propels Lagos Ballet Class to Global Stage." *Guardian*, September 4, 2020, accessed, October 23, 2020, www.theguardian.com /stage/2020/sep/04/poise-and-prestige-the-lagos-ballet-class-propelled-onto-global-stage.
7. Noor Brara. "In Lagos, A Homegrown Ballet Academy Leaps into the Spotlight." *New York Times*, August 19, 2020, accessed, October 23, 2020, www.nytimes.com/2020/08/19/arts/ dance/lagos-ballet-school-viral-video.html.
8. Ibid.
9. Zoe Phillips. "We May Have Missed the Point About the Boy in the Rain." *Michigan Daily*, August 31, 2020, accessed, October 23, 2020, www.michigandaily.com/section/arts/ we-may-have-missed-point-about-boy-rain.
10. Orisakwe et al., 2019.
11. Natasha Booty. "Respect Your Elders: Why Cultural Norms Benefit Mugabe." BBC News.com, November 19, 2017, accessed, October 23, 2020, .
12. Atane Ofiaja. Why Elders Deserve Only Earned Respect. thisisafrica.me blog, March 6, 2014, accessed, October 23, 2020, https://thisisafrica.me/arts-and-culture/why-elders-deserve-only-earned-respect/.
13. Ojo Melvin Agunbiade. Neoliberalism and Resilience Among Older Yoruba People in a Semiurban Community, South West Nigeria, International Network for Critical Gerontology Blog, March 23, 2017, accessed, October 23, 2020, https://criticalgerontology .com/neoliberalism-resilience/.
14. Camille Rocca and Ines Schultes. "Africa's Youth: Action." Mo Ibrahim Foundation, August 2020, p. 1, accessed October 23, 2020, https://mo.ibrahim.foundation/sites/default/ files/2020-08/international-youth-day-research-brief.pdf.
15. Yinka Adegoke. "The World's Youngest Continent Will Keep Being Run by Its Oldest Leaders." QuartzAfrica.com, December 28. 2017, https://qz.com/africa/1162490/the-youngest-continent-keeps-on-being-run-by-the-oldest-leaders/.
16. Rocca and Schultes, *supra* note 14.
17. Abdullahi Alim. "No Continent for Old Men." *Foreign Policy*, September 12, 2019, accessed, October 23, 2020, https://foreignpolicy.com/2019/09/12/africa-no-continent-for-old-men-social-entrepreneurship-politics-youth/.
18. Claire Felter. "African 'Rulers for Life'." Council for Foreign Relations Blog, Updated June 2020, accessed, October 23, 2020, www.cfr.org/backgrounder/africas-leaders-life.
19. Kingbsley Ighobor. "Africa's Youth: A "ticking time bomb" or an Opportunity." *Africa Renewal*, May 2013, accessed, October 23, 2020, www.un.org/africarenewal/magazine/

may-2013/africa%E2%80%99s-youth-%E2%80%9Cticking-time-bomb%E2%80%9D-or-opportunity.
20. Fuchs and Horvath, 2008.
21. Nour, 2017: 3, 4, 7.
22. Zulu et al., 2018.
23. Tom Jackson. Kenya Looks set to get its own "Startup Act." What exactly does the proposed bill entail? Disrupt-africa.com, September 28, 2020, accessed on October 23, 2020, https://disrupt-africa.com/2020/09/kenya-looks-set-to-get-its-own-startup-act-what-exactly-does-the-proposed-bill-entail/.
24. Marston, Woodward and Jones, 2007: 54.
25. UNCTAD, 2008: 9; Ismail Radwan, *Nollywood Has Talent!*, Nazikiliza World Bank Blog, Aug. 5, 2011, accessed on October 23, 2020, http://blogs.worldbank.org/nasikiliza/fr/node/521
26. Will Connors. "Nigeria Moves to Address Chronic Power Outages." *Wall Street Journal*, April 25, 2009, accessed October 23, 2020, http://online.wsj.com/article/SB124062314911155519.html.
27. Iwayemi, 2008: 18.
28. Ezepue, 2020: 2.
29. Ibid.
30. Ibid.
31. Peter White. "Netflix Orders First Nigerian Original from 'Vaya' Director Akin Omotoso." *Deadline*, February 27, 2020, accessed, October 23, 2020, https://deadline.com/2020/02/netflix-first-nigerian-original-netflix-orders-first-nigerian-original-akin-omotoso-1202869614/.
32. Chuma-Okoro, 2018.
33. Draft Copyright Bill 2015, http://graduatedresponse.org/new/wp-content/uploads/2016/02/DRAFT_COPYRIGHT_BILL_NOVEMBER-_2015.pdf.
34. Will Connors. "Nollywood Babylon." *Wall Street Journal*, May 22, 2009, www.wsj.com/articles/SB10001424052970203771904574177472683696390.
35. Ibid.
36. Oguamanam, 2020.
37. Gomber, Koch, and Siering, 2017.
38. LiPuma and Lee, 2004.
39. Sanya, 2013: 14–16.
40. Lee H. Babcock. 2014. "Mobile Payments: How Digital Finance Is Transforming Agriculture," devex.com, August 20, www.devex.com/news/mobile-payments-how-digital-finance-is-transforming-agriculture-84191; Mastercard Foundation and International Finance Corporation, 2018.
41. Mastercard Foundation and International Finance Corporation, 2018: 5.
42. Ibid.
43. Omwansa and Sullivan, 2012: 8.
44. In 2020, the Government of Kenya owned 35 percent of Safaricom. Safaricom started as a department of Kenya Posts & Telecommunications Corporation, the former monopoly operator and was incorporated as a private liability company in 1997, and then converted into a public company with limited liability in May 2002. The Government of Kenya

divested its ownership of public enterprises, including Safaricom, initially selling 25 percent of issued share capital in 2008. Institute of Developing Economies, Japan External Trade Organization, Safaricom Limited, accessed October 25, 2020, www.ide.go.jp/English/Data/Africa_file/Company/kenya03.html.

45. Omwansa and Sullivan, 2012: 13.
46. Alliance for Financial Inclusion, 2010: 4.
47. Omwansa and Sullivan, 2012: 24.
48. Suri and Jack, 2016.
49. Laura Llewellyn Jones. "Why Mobile Money Transformed Kenya but Failed to Take Off in Nigeria." iea Blog, February 11, 2016, accessed October 24, 2020, https://iea.org.uk/blog/why-mobile-money-transformed-kenya-failed-to-take-in-nigeria.
50. Mwaura, 2011: 37.
51. Ibid. at 40.
52. Alliance for Financial Inclusion, 2010: 3.
53. Ibid. at 4–5.
54. Kusimba, 2021: 4.
55. Ibid. at 6.
56. Msangi S. Kimenyi. Mobile Wars and Political Barriers to Entry: Safaricom vs. Equity Bank. Brookings Africa in Focus Blog, October 29, 2014, www.brookings.edu/blog/africa-in-focus/2014/10/29/mobile-wars-and-political-barriers-to-entry-safaricom-vs-equity-bank/.
57. Steven Levy. "Zuckerberg in Africa." *Wired*, October 5, 2016, accessed October 24, 2020, www.wired.com/2016/10/zuckerberg-in-africa/.
58. Amoako, 2018: 105.
59. Mattes and Moreno, 2018: 357.
60. Nunn and Wantchekon, 2011: 3221.
61. Vodafone Shuts M-Pesa After It Fails to Click in Europe. Businesstoday Kenya, July 5, 2017, accessed October 24, 2020, https://businesstoday.co.ke/m-pesa-fails-click-europe/.
62. Bregu, Anamali, and Shosha, 2019.

Select Bibliography

Acemoglu, Daron, Isaías N. Chaves, Philip Osafo-Kwaako, and James Robinson. 2014. "Indirect Rule and State Weakness in Africa: Sierra Leone in Comparative Perspective." NBER Africa Project Working Paper, accessed on October 23, 2020, https://scholar.harvard.edu/files/jrobinson/files/indirect_rule_nber_4_0.pdf.

Acemoglu, Daron, Simon Johnson, and James Robinson. 2002. "Reversal of Fortune: Geography and Institutions in the Making of the Modern World Income Distribution." *Quarterly Journal of Economics* 117, 1231–1294.

2001. "The Colonial Origins of Comparative Development." *American Economic Review* 91, 1369–1401.

Acemoglu, Daron, Tristan Reed, and James A. Robinson. 2014. "Chiefs: Elite Control of Civil Society and Development in Sierra Leone." *Journal of Political Economy* 122, 2, 319–368.

Acemoglu, Daron, and James A. Robinson. 2012. *Why Nations Fail: The Origins of Power, Prosperity, and Poverty*. New York: Crown.

2010. "Why Is Africa Poor?" *Economic History of Developing Regions* 25, 21–50.

Acemoglu Daron, Thierry Verdier, and James A. Robinson. 2004. "Kleptocracy and Divide - and-Rule: A Model of Personal Rule." *Journal of the European Economic Association* 2, 2–3, 162–192.

Achebe, Chinua. 2012. *There Was a Country: A Memoir*. New York: Penguin.

1994. "The Art of Fiction #139." *Paris Review* 133 (Winter), Interviewed by Jerome Brooks.

1958. *Things Fall Apart*. London: Heinemann.

Adas, Michael. 2015. *Machines as the Measure of Men: Science, Technology and Ideologies of Western Dominance*. Ithaca and London: Cornell University Press.

Addison, Tony, Philippe Le Billion, and S. Mansoob Murshed. 2002. "Conflict in Africa: The Cost of Peaceful Behavior." *Journal of African Economics* 11, 365–386.

Adebanwi, Wale. 2014. *Yorùbá Elites and Ethnic Politics in Nigeria: Ọbáfemi Awólowo and Corporate Agency*. New York: Cambridge University Press.

Adebola, Titilayo. 2020. "Mapping Africa's Complex Regimes: Towards an African Centred AfCFTA Intellectual Property Protocol." *African Journal of International Economic Law* 1, 232–290.

Adegbija, Efurosibina. 2007. "Language Policy and Planning in Nigeria." In Robert B. Kaplan and Richard B. Baldauf, Jr., eds., *Language Planning and Policy in Africa*, vol. 2. Cleveden, UK: Multilingual Matters, pp.190–255.

Adegbulu, Femi. 2011. "From Warrant Chiefs to Ezeship: A Distortion of Traditional Institutions in Igboland? *Afro Asian Journal of Sciences* 2, 2.2, 1-25.

Adejugbe, Michael. 1984. "The Myths and Realities of Nigeria's Business Indigenization." *Development and Change*, 15, 4, 577–592.

Adeleye, Ifedapo, Joseph Amankwah-Amoah, Nathaniel Boso, and Mark Esposito. 2018. "Africa's Competitiveness in the Global Economy: Past, Present and Future." In Ifedapo Adeleye and Mark Esposito, eds., *Africa's Competitiveness in the Global Economy*. New York: Palgrave Macmillan, pp. 1–22.

Adelowo, C.M., A.A. Egbetokun, I. Olunyi, D.A. Abolaji, and W.O. Siyanbola. 2010. "The Management of Copyright in the Creative Country Industry in Nigeria: Nollywood Experience." Working Paper, https://docplayer.net/54409021-The-management-of-copyright-in-the-creative-country-industry-in-nigeria-nollywood-experience.html.

Adjaye, Joseph K. 1990. "Asantehene Agyeman Prempe I, Asante History, and the Historian." *History in Africa* 17, 1–29.

Adichie, Chimamanda Ngozi. 2020. "Opinion – Chimamanda Ngozi Adichie: Nigeria Is Murdering Its Citizens." *The New York Times*, October 21, 2020, accessed on October 23, 2020, www.nytimes.com/2020/10/21/opinion/chimamanda-adichie-nigeria-protests.html.

2014. *Americanah*. New York: Anchor.

Adewoye, Omoniyi. 1987. "Proverbs as a Vehicle of Juristic Thought Among the Yorubá." *Obafemi Awolowo University Law Journal* 3, 4, 1–17.

1977. *The Judicial System in Southern Nigeria 1854–1954*. Atlantic Highlands, NJ: Humanities Press.

1973. "Review: *Law and Social Change in Nigeria* by T.O. Elias." *Journal of the Historical Society of Nigeria* 7, 1, 149–159.

Adusei, Poku, Kwame Anyimadu-Antwi, and Naana Halm. 2009. *ACA2K Country Report: Ghana*, African Copyright and Access to Knowledge (ACA2 K) Project, May, https://idl-bnc-idrc.dspacedirect.org/bitstream/handle/10625/39701/128550.pdf.

Afigbo, A.E. 1972. *The Warrant Chiefs: Indirect Rule in Southeastern Nigeria, 1891–1929*. London: Longman.

Aiyede, E. Remi. 2005."Executive-Legislature Relations in Nigeria's Emerging Presidential Democracy." *Unilag Journal of Politics* 2,1, 64–87.

Ajayi, J.F. Ade. 1969. *Christian Missions in Nigeria, 1841–1891: The Making of a New Elite*, 2nd ed. Chicago: Northwestern University Press.

Akenzua, Edun. 2000. "The Case of Benin." Appendices to the Minutes of Evidence, Appendix 21, House of Commons, The United Kingdom Parliament, March, accessed on October 23, 2020, https://publications.parliament.uk/pa/cm199900/cmselect/cmcumeds/371/371ap27.htm.

Akinwumi, Olayemi. 2002. *The Colonial Contest for the Nigerian Region, 1884–1900: A History of the German Participation*. Hamburg: LIT Verlag. Google Books edition.

Akokpari, John. 2007. The Political Economy of Human Insecurity in Sub-Saharan Africa. V. R.F. Series, Institute of Developing Economies, Japan External Trade Organization, October 2007, accessed on October 23, 2020, http://210.148.106.167/library/English/Publish/Download/Vrf/pdf/431.pdf.

Akpan, Nseabasi S. 2012. "From Agriculture to Petroleum Oil Production: What Has Changed About Nigeria's Rural Development." *International Journal of Developing Societies* 1, 3, 97–106.

Alao, Akin. 2003. "Colonial Rule and Judicial Reforms 1900–1960." In Adebayo Oyebade, ed., *The Foundation of Nigeria: Essays in Honor of Toyin Falola*. Trenton, NJ: Africa World Press, pp. 201–216.

Albert, Isaac Olawale, 2008. "From 'Owo Crisis' to 'Dagbon Dispute': Lessons in the Politicization of Chieftaincy Disputes in Modern Nigeria and Ghana. *The Round Table* 97, 394, 47–60.

Alence, Rod. 2001 "Colonial Government, Social Conflict and State Involvement in Africa's Open Economies: The Origins of the Ghana Cocoa Marketing Board, 1939–46." *Journal of African History* 42, 397–416.

Allen, Judith van. 1972. "'Sitting on a Man': Colonialism and the Lost Political Institutions of Igbo Women." *Canadian Journal of African Studies / Revue Canadienne des Études Africaines* 6,2, 165–181.

Alliance for Financial Inclusion. 2010. "Enabling Mobile Money Transfer: The Central Bank of Kenya's Treatment of M-Pesa," accessed on October 23, 2020, www.gsma.com/mobilefordevelopment/wp-content/uploads/2013/09/enablingmobilemoneytransfer92.pdf.

Amankwah, Harrison A. 1970. "Ghanaian Law: Its Evolution and Interaction with English Law." *Cornell International Law Journal* 4,1, 37–57.

Amoako, Isaac Oduro. 2018. *Trust, Institutions and Managing Entrepreneurial Relationships in Africa*. New York: Palgrave.

Anderson, David and David Throup. 1985. "Africans and Agricultural Production in Colonial Kenya: The Myth of the War as a Watershed." *The Journal of African History* 26, 4, 327–345.

Anena, Harriet. 2015. "A Nation in Labour." In *A Nation in Labour: A Poetry Collection*, Scotts Valley, CA: CreateSpace Independent Publishing Platform, p. 37.

Anghie, Anthony. 2005. *Imperialism, Sovereignty and the Making of International Law*. Cambridge: Cambridge University Press.

Animashaun, Bashir Olalekan. 2018. Amaro (Brazilian Returnees) and Cultural Diffusion in Lagos: A Study of Lagos-Pacific Cultural Relations. The European Conference on Arts & Humanities 2018, Official Conference Proceedings, accessed on October 23, 2020, http://25qt511nswfi49iayd31ch80-wpengine.netdna-ssl.com/wp-content/uploads/papers/ecah2018/ECAH2018_40599.pdf.

Annan, Nancy. 2014. "Violent Conflicts and Civil Strife in West Africa: Causes, Challenges and Prospects." *Stability: International Journal of Security and Development* 3, 1, 1–16.

Arewa, Olufunmilayo B. 2017. "Nollywood Pirates and Nigerian Cinema." In Kate Darling and Aaron Perzanowsky, eds., *Creativity Without Law: How Communities and Markets Challenge the Assumptions of Intellectual Property Law*. New York: New York University Press, pp. 228–248.

2016. "Constructing Africa: Chinese Investment, Infrastructure Deficits, and Development." *Cornell International Law Journal* 49, 101–139.

2006. "TRIPs and Traditional Knowledge: Local Communities, Local Knowledge and Global Intellectual Property Frameworks." *Marquette Intellectual Property Law Review* 10, 2, 156–180.

Arewa, Olufunmilayo B. and Ayodeji O. Fakolade. 2021. "Law and the Regulation of New Technologies in Africa." (Chapter 15) In The Routledge *Handbook of African Law*, Muna Ndulo and Cosmas Emeziem, eds. New York: Routledge.

Arowolo, Dare. 2011. "Fiscal Federalism in Nigeria: Theory and Dimensions." *Afro Asian Journal of Social Sciences* 2, 2.2.

Arsan, Andrew. 2014. *Interlopers of Empire: The Lebanese Diaspora in Colonial French Africa*. Oxford: Oxford University Press.

Asante, Eric Appau, Alice Korkor Ebeheakey, Kwame Opoku-Bonsu, and John Cornah, Jr. 2019. "The Unwritten Historical Perspectives of Akan Spokespersons Staffs." *African Journal of History and Culture* 11, 1, 1–10.

Asomugha, Ephraim E. Maduelosi. 1994. *Company Law in Nigeria under the Companies and Allied Matters Act*. Lagos: E.M. Asomugha.

Austin, Gareth. 2005. *Labour, Land and Capital in Ghana*. Rochester: University of Rochester Press.

1993. "Indigenous Credit Institutions in West Africa, c. 1750–c.1960." In Gareth Austin and Kaoru Sugihara, eds. *Local Suppliers of Credit in the Third World, 1750–1960*. New York: Palgrave Macmillan, pp. 93–159.

Ayandele, E.A. 1967. "Background to the 'Duel' between Crowther and Goldie on the Lower Niger, 1857–1885." *Journal of the Historical Society of Nigeria* 4, 1, 45–63.

Babalola, Joel B., Geoffrey Lunwangwa, and August A. Adeyinka. 1999. *McGill Journal of Education* 34, 1, 79–98.

Baer, Tobias. 2019. *Understand, Manage, and Prevent Algorithmic Bias: A Guide for Business Users and Data Scientists*. New York: Apress.

Banner, Stuart. 2005. "Why *Terra Nullius?* Anthropology and Property Law in Early Australia." *Law and History Review* 23, 1, 95–131.

Bannerman, Sara. 2013. *The Struggle for Canadian Copyright: Imperialism to Internationalism, 1842–971*. Vancouver: UBC Press.

Barbieri, Chiara, Mário Vicente, Sandra Oliveira, Koen Bostoen, Jorge Rocha, Mark Stoneking, and Brigitte Pakendorf. 2014. "Migration and Interaction in a Contact Zone: mtDNA Variation Among Bantu-Speakers in Southern Africa. *PLoS ONE* 9, 6 e99117.

Barlet, Olivier. 2012. "The Ambivalence of French Funding." *Black Camera* 3, 2, 205–216.

Barnes, Andrew. 2018. "Samuel Ajayi Crowther: African and Yoruba Missionary Bishop." Oxford Research Handbook, African History, https://oxfordre.com/africanhistory/view/10.1093/acrefore/9780190277734.001.0001/acrefore-9780190277734-e-278.

Barnes, Sandra T. 1986. *Patrons and Power: Creating a Political Community in Metropolitan Labor*. London and New York: Routledge. Google Books edition, published 2019.

Barraclough, B. 1954. "The Anglo-Saxon Writ." *History* 39, 137, 193–215.

Bauer, P.T. 1963. *West African Trade: A Study of Competition, Oligopoly and Monopoly in a Changing Economy*. New York: Routledge.

Beegle, Kathleen, Luc Christiaensen, Andrew Dabalen, and Isis Gaddis. 2016. *Poverty in a Rising Africa*. Washington, DC: World Bank.

Begashaw, Belay. 2020. "Strategies to Deliver on the Sustainable Development Goals." Achieving the Sustainable Development Goals: The State of Play and Policy Options. Foresight Africa, www.brookings.edu/wp-content/uploads/2020/01/ForesightAfrica2020_Chapter1_20200110.pdf.

Benkler, Yochai. 2006. *The Wealth of Networks: How Social Production Transforms Markets and Freedom*. New Haven and London: Yale University Press.

Bennett, T.W. 2019. "Comparative Law and African Customary Law." In Mathias Reimann, and Reinhard Zimmermann, eds., *The Oxford Handbook of Comparative Law*. Oxford: Oxford University Press, pp. 652–680.

Benton, Lauren and Benjamin Straumann. 2010. "Acquiring Empire by Law: From Roman Doctrine to Early Modern European Practice." *Law and History Review* 28, 1, 1–38.

Bernal, Victoria. 2014. *Nation as Network: Diaspora, Cyberspace, and Citizenship*. Chicago: University of Chicago Press.

Bernault, Florence. 2019. *Colonial Transactions: Imaginaries, Bodies, and Histories in Gabon*. Durham and London: Duke University Press.

Berry, Sara. 1993. *No Condition is Permanent: The Social Dynamics of Agrarian Change in Sub-Saharan Africa*. Madison: University of Wisconsin Press.

Bessen, James and Michael J. Meurer. 2008. *Patent Failure: How Judges, Bureaucrats, and Lawyers Put Innovators at Risk*. Princeton: Princeton University Press.

Beth, Loren P. 1977. "The Judicial Committee as Constitutional Court for the British Empire 1833–1971." *Georgia Journal of International and Comparative Law* 7, 1, 47–84.

Beveridge, Andrew. 1974. "Economic Independence, Indigenization, and the African Businessman: Some Effects of Zambia's Economic Reforms." *African Studies Review* 17, 3, 477–490.

Birla, Ritu. 2011. "Law as Economy: Convention, Corporation, Currency." *University of California Irvine Law Review* 1, 3, 1015–1037.

Birnhack, Michael D. 2012. *Colonial Copyright: Intellectual Property in Mandate Palestine*. Oxford: Oxford University Press.

Bischoff, Lizelle. 2009. "Sub-Saharan African Cinema in the Context of FESPACO: Close-Ups on Francophone West Africa and Anglophone South Africa." *Forum for Modern Language Studies* 45, 4, 441–454.

Bivar, A.D.H. 1961. "The Wathiqat Ahl Al-Sudan: A Manifesto of the Fulani Jihad." *The Journal of African History* 2, 2, 235–243.

Bogdanor, Vernon. 2007. Tarunabh Khaitan and Stefan Vogenauer. "Should Britain Have a Written Constitution?" *The Political Quarterly* 78, 499–517.

Bostoen, Koen. 2007. "Pots, Words and the Bantu Problem: On Lexical Reconstruction and Early African History." *Journal of African History* 48, 173–199.

Bregu, Elvis, Armela Animali, and Bitila Shosha. 2019. "The Diffusion of M-Pesa in Developing Countries: Convergence Program Lead Vodafone Albania Sh.a, Tirane, Albania." *European Journal of Economics and Business Studies* 5, 2, 43–47.

Brempong, Arhin. 2000. "The Role of Nana Yaa Asantewaa in the 1900 Asante War of Resistance." *Ghana Studies* 3, 1, 97–110.

Bruton, Henry J. 1998. "A Reconsideration of Import Substitution." *Journal of Economic Literature* 36, 2, 903–936.

Buchan, Bruce. 2005. "The Empire of Political Thought: Civilization, Savagery and Perceptions of Indigenous Government." *History of the Human Sciences* 18, 2, 1–22.

2001. "Subjecting the Natives: Aborigines, Property and Possession Under Early Colonial Rule." *Social Analysis: The International Journal of Anthropology* 45, 2, 143–162.

Button, Kenneth, Alberto Brugnoli, Gianmaria Martini, and Davide Scotti. 2015. "Connecting African Urban Areas: Airline Networks and Intra-Sub-Saharan Trade." *Journal of Transport Geography* 42, 84–89.

Buolamwini, Joy and Timnit Gebru. 2018. "Gender Shades: Intersectional Accuracy Disparities in Commercial Gender Classification." Proceedings of the 1st Conference on Fairness, Accountability and Transparency, *Proceedings of Machine Learning Research* (PMLR) 81, 77–91, http://proceedings.mlr.press/v81/buolamwini18a.html.

Breunig, Peter. 2017. *Exploring the Nok Culture*. Joint Research Project of Goethe University Frankfurt/ Main, Germany and National Commission for Museums and Monuments, Nigeria, January 2017, http://araf.studiumdigitale.uni-frankfurt.de/attachments/110_Nok%20Broschüre%20Exploring%20the%20Nok%20Culture%20online.pdf.

1996. "The 8000-year Old Dugout Canoe from Dufana (NE Nigeria)." In Gilbert Pwiti and Robert Soper. Harare, eds., *Aspects of African Archaeology: Papers from the 10th Congress of the Pan-African Association for Prehistory and Related Studies*. Harare: University of Zimbabwe Publications, pp. 461–468.

Burrell, Jenna. 2012. *Invisible Users: Youth in the Internet Cafés of Urban Ghana*. Cambridge: MIT Press.

Caenegem, R.C. van. 1988. *The Birth of the English Common Law*, 2nd edition. Cambridge: Cambridge University Press.
Campos-Serrano, Alicia. 2013. "Extraction Offshore, Politics Inshore, the Role of the State in Equatorial Guinea." *Africa* 83, 2, 314–339.
Cannandine, David. 2001. *Ornamentalism: How the British Saw Their Empire*. London: Penguin Books.
Carletto, Gero. 2010. Improving the Availability, Quality and Policy-Relevance of Agricultural Data: The Living Standards Measurement Study – Integrated Surveys on Agriculture. Development Research Group. Washington, DC: The World Bank, www.fao.org/fileadmin/templates/ess/pages/rural/wye_city_group/2010/May/WYE_2010.2.1_Carletto.pdf.
Carpenter, Jennifer F. and Robert F. Whitelaw. 2017. "The Development of China's Stock Market and Stakes for the Global Economy." *Annual Review of Financial Economics* 9, 233–255.
Castillo, Lisa Earl. 2016. "Mapping the Nineteenth-Century Brazilian Returnee Movement: Demographics, Life Stories and the Question of Slavery." *Atlantic Studies* 13, 1, 25–52.
Cell, John W. 1989. "Lord Hailey and the Making of the African Survey." *African Affairs* 88, 353, 481–505.
Chanock, Martin. 1998. *Law, Custom, And Social Order: The Colonial Experience in Malawi and Zambia*. Cambridge: Cambridge University Press.
1978. "Neo-Traditionalism and the Customary Law in Malawi." *African Legal Studies* 16, 80–90.
Chiroma, Isa H. 1993. "Conflict Between Islamic Law and Common Law on the Testamentary Powers [Waṣiyyah]: The Attitude of Nigerian Courts." *Islamic Studies*. 32, 3, 339–349.
Christensen, Clayton. 1997. *The Innovator's Dilemma: When New Technologies Cause Great Firms to Fail*. Boston: Harvard Business Review Press.
Christopher, A.J. 1988. "'Divide and Rule': The Impress of British Separation Policies." *Royal Geographic Society* 20, 3, 233–240.
Chukwuma, Kodili Henry. 2020. "Constructing the Herder–Farmer Conflict as (in)Security in Nigeria." *African Security* 13, 1, 54–76.
Chuma-Okoro, Helen. 2018. "Nigerian Copyright Reform and Implications for Access to Teaching and Learning Materials (TLMs) in the Digital Age." *The African Journal of Information and Communication* (AJIC) 22, 1–28.
Churchill, Winston. 1902. *The River War: An Account of the Reconquest of the Sudan*. London: Longmans.
Cloonan, Martin. 2006. "Popular Music Censorship in Africa." In Michael Drewett and Martin Cloonan, eds., *Popular Music and Censorship in Africa*. Aldershot: Ashgate, pp. 3–21.
Cohen, Julie E. 2017. "Law for the Platform Economy." *University of California Davis Law Review* 51, 133–204.
Colonial Office. 1927. Report by His Britannic Majesty's Government to the Council of the League of Nations on the Administration of the British Sphere of Togoland for the Year 1926. Google Books edition.
Colson, Elizabeth. 1971. "The Impact of the Colonial Period on the Definition of Land Rights." In Peter Duignan, L.H. Gann and Victor Turner, eds., *Colonialism in Africa 1870–1960. Volume 3 Profiles of Change: African Society and Colonial Rule*. Cambridge: Cambridge University Press, pp. 193–215.
Comaroff, John L. 1997. "Images of Empire, Contests of Conscience: Models of Colonial Domination in South Africa." In Frederick Cooper and Ann Laura Stoler, eds., *Tensions*

of *Empire: Colonial Cultures in a Bourgeois World*. Oakland: University of California Press, pp. 163–197.

Conrad, Sebastian. 2012. *German Colonialism: A Short History*. Cambridge: Cambridge University Press.

Coolidge, Jacqueline and Susan Rose-Ackerman. 1997. *High-Level Rent-Seeking and Corruption in African Regimes*. World Bank Policy Research Working Paper 1780. June 1997. Washington, DC: World Bank. http://documents1.worldbank.org/curated/en/855031468767966104/pdf/multi-page.pdf.

Cooper, Allan D. 2006. "Reparations for the Herero Genocide: Defining the Limits of International Litigation." *African Affairs* 106, 42,2, 113–126.

Cooper, Frederick. 2002. *Africa Since 1940: The Past of the Present*. New York: Cambridge University Press.

Cottrell, Jill. 1972. "Law Reports in Nigeria." *African Law Studies* 7, 63–72.

Cox, Kate, William Marcellino, Jacopo Bellasio, Antonia Ward, Katerina Galai, Sofia Meranto, and Giacomo Persi Paoli. 2018. Social Media in Africa: A Double-Edged Sword for Security and Development, November 2018. UNDP, www.africa.undp.org/content/dam/rba/docs/Reports/UNDP-RAND-Social-Media-Africa-Research-Report_final_3%20Oct.pdf.

Cranenburgh, Oda van. 2008. "'Big Men' Rule: Presidential Power, Regime Type and Democracy in 30 African Countries." *Democratization*, 15, 5, 952–973.

Craven, Matthew. 2015. "Between Law and History: The Berlin Conference of 1884–1885 and the Logic of Free Trade," *London Review of International Law* 3, 1, 31–59.

Crowder, Michael. 1964. "Indirect Rule—French and British Style." *Journal of the International African Institute*, 34, 3, 197–205.

Dalrymple, William. 2019. *The Anarchy: The Relentless Rise of the East India Company*. New York: Bloomsbury Publishing.

Darkoh, Michael B.K. and Mohamed Ould-May. 1992. "Cash Crops Versus Food Crops in Africa: A Conflict Between Dependency and Autonomy." *Transafrican Journal of History* 21, 36–50.

Davis, Kevin E., Benedict Kingsbury, and Sally Engle Merry. 2012. "Introduction: Global Governance by Indicators." In Kevin E. Davis, Angelina Fisher and Benedict Kingsbury, eds., *Governance by Indicators: Global Power Through Quantification and Rankings*. Oxford: Oxford University Press, pp. 3–28.

Demarest, Leila, Arnim Langer, and Ukoha Ukiwo. 2020. "Nigeria's Federal Character Commission (FCC): A Critical Appraisal." *Oxford Development Studies* 48, 4, 315–328 .

Desrosiers, Marie-Eve and Haley J. Swedlund. 2018. "Rwanda's Post Genocide Foreign Aid Relations: Revising Notions of Exceptionalism." *African Affairs* 118, 472, 435–462.

Diamond, Jared. 1997. *Guns, Germs and Steel: The Fates of Human Societies*. New York: W. W. Norton.

Dike, Kenneth Onukwa. 1956. *Trade and Politics in the Niger Delta, 1830–885: An Introduction to the Economic and Political History of Nigeria*. Oxford: Clarendon Press.

Dixon-Fyle, Mac. 1989. "The Saro in the Political Life of Early Port Harcourt, 1913–49." *Journal of African History* 30, 125–138.

Donohue, Laura K. 2015. "High Technology, Consumer Privacy, and U.S. National Security." *American University Business Law Review* 4, 1, 11–48.

Doshi, Rush, Judith G. Kelley, and Beth A. Simmons. 2019. "The Power of Ranking: The Ease of Doing Business Indicator and Global Regulatory Behavior." *International Organization* 73, 611–643.

Drahos, Peter and Ruth Mayne, eds. 2002. "Introduction." In Peter Drahos and Ruth Mayne, eds., *Global Intellectual Property Rights: Knowledge, Access and Development*. Houndmills, England: Palgrave Macmillan, pp. 1–12.

Du Bois, W.E. Burghardt. 1915. "The African Roots of War." *The Atlantic Monthly Magazine*, May, pp. 115, 5, 707–714.

Dzahene-Quarshie, Josephine. 2011. "Language Policy, Language Choice and Language Use in the Tanzanian Parliament." *Legon Journal of Humanities* 22, 27–69.

Easterly, William. 2003. "IMF and World Bank Structural Adjustment Programs and Poverty." In Michael P. Dooley, Jeffrey A. Frankel, Michael Thomson, Alexander Kentikelenis, and Thomas Stubbs, eds., *Managing Currency Crises in Emerging Markets*. Chicago: University of Chicago Press, pp. 361–391.

Eaton, Richard M. 2011. "From Bidar to Timbuktu: Views from the Edge of the 15th Century Muslim World." *Medieval History Journal* 14, 1, 1–20.

Edgerton, Robert B. 2010. *The Fall of the Asante Empire: The Hundred-Year War for Africa's Gold Coast*. New York: Free Press.

Eglash, Ron. 1999. *African Fractals: Modern Computing and Indigenous Design*. New Brunswick: Rutgers University Press.

Ekechi, F.K. 1978. "The Missionary Career of the Venerable T. J. Dennis in West Africa, 1893–1917." *Journal of Religion in Africa* 9, 1–26.

Ekekwe, Ndubuisi. 2017. "How Digital Technology Is Changing Farming in Africa." *Harvard Business Review*, May 18, accessed March 14, 2021, https://hbr.org/2017/05/how-digital-technology-is-changing-farming-in-africa.

Egobueze, Anthony and Callistus U. Ojirika. 2018. "Corruption and Fiscal Federalism in Nigeria: Analysis of the Federal Budgetary Process, 1999–2016." *African Journal of Political Science and International Relations* 12, 10, 191–207.

Ekeh, Peter Palmer. 2005. *Warri City and British Colonial Rule in Western Niger Delta*. Urhobo Historical Society.

Elaigwu, J. Isawa. 1988. "Nigerian Federalism Under Civilian and Military Regimes." *Publius* 18, 173–188.

Elias, Taslim Olawale. 1963. *The Nigerian Legal System*. London: Routledge.

1954. *Groundwork of Nigerian Law*. London: Routledge.

Englebert, Pierre. 2000. "Solving the Mystery of the AFRICA Dummy." *World Development* 28, 1821–1835.

Enweremadu, David U. 2013. "Nigeria's Quest to Recover Looted Assets: The Abacha Affair." *Africa Spectrum* 48, 2, 51–70.

Erhagbe, Eddy O. 2012. "The Dynamics of Inter Group Relations in Pre-Colonial Nigeria: Nupe Activities in Etsakoland C. 1860–1897." *Canadian Social Science* 8, 2, 209–218.

Erikson, Emily. 2014. *Between Monopoly and Free Trade: The English East India Company, 1600–1757*. Princeton: Princeton University Press.

Espeland, Wendy Nelson and Michael Sauder. 2016. *Engines of Anxiety: Academic Rankings, Reputation, and Accountability*. New York: Russell Sage Foundation.

Everett, Caleb. 2013. *Linguistic Relativity: Evidence Across Languages and Cognitive Domains*. Berlin and Boston: De Gruyter Mouton.

Ezeh, Alex and Jessie Lu. 2019. Transforming the Institutional Landscape in Sub-Saharan Africa: Considerations for Leveraging Africa's Research Capacity to Achieve Socioeconomic Development, CGD Policy Paper 147, July 2019. Washington, DC: Center for Global Development, www.cgdev.org/sites/default/files/transforming-institutional-landscape-sub-saharan-africa-considerations-leveraging-africa.pdf.

Ezejiofor, Gaius. 1973. "The Law of Patents in Nigeria: A Review." *The Journal of Legal Pluralism and Unofficial Law* 5, 9, 39–60.
Ezenwe, Uka. 1993. "The African Debt Crisis and the Challenge of Development." *Intereconomics* 28, 1, 35–43.
Ezepue, Ezinne M. 2020. "The New Nollywood: Professionalization or Gentrification of Cultural Industry." *Sage Open* (July–September), 1–10.
Ezera, Kalu. 1964. *Constitutional Developments in Nigeria*. 2nd ed. Cambridge: Cambridge University Press.
Fajana, Ade. 1972. "Colonial Control and Education: The Development of Higher Education in Nigeria 1900–1950." *Journal of the Historical Society of Nigeria* 6, 3, 323–340.
Falola, Toyin. 2009. *Colonialism and Violence in Nigeria*. Bloomington: Indiana University Press.
Fanon, Frantz. 1967. *Black Skin, White Masks*. New York: Grove Press.
Fassbender, Bardo and Ann Peters. 2012. "Introduction: Towards a Global History of International Law." In Bruno Fassbender and Ann Peters, eds., *The Oxford Handbook of the History of International Law*. Oxford: Oxford University Press, pp. 1–24.
Ferguson, James and Akhil Gupta. 1978. "Spatializing States: Toward an Ethnography of Neoliberal Governmentality." *American Ethnologist* 29, 4, 981–1002.
Ferguson, Niall. 2003. *Empire: How Britain Made the Modern World*. New York: Penguin.
Ferguson, Phyllis and Ivor Wilks. 1970. "Chieftaincy in Northern Ghana. In Michael Crowder and Obaro Ikimẹ, eds., *West African Chiefs: Their Changing Status Under Colonial Rule and Independence*. Ile-Ife: University of Ife Press, pp. 326–369.
Fieldhouse, D.K. 1994. *Merchant Capital and Economic Decolonization: The United Africa Company 1929–1987*. Oxford: Clarendon.
Food and Agriculture Organization of the United Nations. 2019. *Food Security and Nutrition in the World: Safeguarding Against Economic Slowdowns and Downturns*, www.fao.org/3/ca5162en/ca5162en.pdf.
Fombad, Charles Manga. 2005. "The Separation of Powers and Constitutionalism in Africa: The Case of Botswana." *Boston College Third World Law Journal* 25, 2, 301–342.
1999. "Cameroonian Bi-Juralism: Current Challenges and Future Prospects." 22 *Fundamina* 5, 22–43.
Foucault, Michel. 1991. "Governmentality" trans. Rosi Braidotti and revised by Colin Gordon. In Graham Burchell, Colin Gordon and Peter Miller, eds., *The Foucault Effect: Studies in Governmentality*. Chicago, IL: University of Chicago Press, pp. 87–104.
Fox, Eleanor M. and Mor Bakhoum. 2019. *Making Markets Work for Africa: Markets, Development, and Competition Law in Sub-Saharan Africa*. Oxford: Oxford University Press.
French, Howard W. 2014. *China's Second Continent: How a Million Migrants Are Building a New Empire in Africa*. New York: Random House.
Freund, Bill. 2007. *The African City: A History*. Cambridge: Cambridge University Press.
Friedman, Uri. 2014. "How Nigeria Became Africa's Largest Economy Overnight." *The Atlantic*, April 7, www.theatlantic.com/international/archive/2014/04/how-nigeria-became-africas-largest-economy-overnight/360288/.
Fuchs, Christian and Eva Horvath. 2008. "Africa and the Digital Divide." *Telematics and Informatics* 25, 2, 99–116.
Gann, Lewis H. and Peter Duignan. 1978. *The Rulers of British Africa 1870–1914*. Stanford, CA: Stanford University Press.
Garba, Abubakar. 1996. "The Architecture and Chemistry of a Dug-Out: The Dufana Canoe in Ethno-Archeological Perspective." *Berichte des Sonderforschungsbereichs* 268, 8, 193–200.

Garbacza, Christopher and Herbert G. Thompson, Jr. 2007. "Demand for Telecommunication Services in Developing Countries." *Telecommunications Policy* 31, 5, 276–289.

Gastineau, Bénédicte and Valérie Golaz. 2016. "Being Young in Rural Africa: Introduction." *Afrique contemporaine* 259, 3, 9–22.

Gathii, James Thuo. 2020. "The Companies Act, 2015: Assessing Its Borrowed Origins." In *Kenya's Company Law Under the 2015 Companies Act*. Sheria Publishing House (draft manuscript).

1998. "Representations of Africa in Good Governance Discourse: Policing and Containing Dissidence to Neo-Liberalism." *Third World Legal Studies* 15, 1, 65–108.

Geertz, Clifford. 1972. *The Interpretation of Cultures*. New York: Basic Books.

Gertzel, Cherry. 1962. "Relations Between African and European Traders in the Niger Delta 1880–1896." *The Journal of African History* 3, 2, 361–366.

Gewald, Jan-Bart. 1994. "The Great General of the Kaiser." *Botswana Notes and Records* 26, 67–76.

Ghai, Yash. 1991. "The Role of Law in the Transition of Societies: The African Experience." *Journal of African Law* 35, 1/2, 8–20.

Giddens, Anthony. 1984. *The Constitution of Society*. Berkeley: University of California Press.

Glass, Lisa-Maria and Jens Newig. 2019. "Governance for Achieving the Sustainable Development Goals: How Important Are Participation, Policy Coherence, Reflexivity, Adaptation and Democratic Institutions?" *Earth System Governance* 2, 1–14.

Glickman, Harvey. 2005. "The Nigerian "419" Advance Fee Scams: Prank or Peril?" *Canadian Journal of African Studies* 39, 3, 460–489.

Golub, Stephen and Faraz Hayat. 2015. "Employment, Unemployment, and Underemployment in Africa." In Célestin Monga and Justin Yifu Lin, eds., *Context and Concepts*. Oxford: Oxford University Press, pp. 136–153.

Gomber, Peter. 2017. Jascha-Alexander Koch and Michael Siering. "Digital Finance and FinTech: Current Research and Future Research Directions." *Journal of Business Economics* 87, 537–580.

Goodhart, Arthur L. 1930. "Case Law in England and America." *Cornell Law Review* 15, 2, 173–193.

Goon, Patricia and Allison Craven. 2003. "Whose Debt? Globalisation and Whitefacing in Asia." *Intersections: Gender, History and Culture in the Asian Context*, 9, http://intersections.anu.edu.au/issue9/gooncraven.html.

Gorwa, Robert. 2019. "What Is Platform Governance?" *Information, Communication & Society* 22, 6, 854–871.

Hailey, William Malcolm. 1947. "Native Administration in Africa." *International Affairs* 23, 3, 336–342.

1938. *An African Survey: A Study of Problems Arising in Africa South of the Sahara*. London: Oxford University Press.

Harrington, John A. and Abreena Manji. 2003. "The Emergence of African Law as an Academic Discipline in Britain." *African Affairs* 102, 405, 109–134.

Harsch, Ernest. 1993. "Structural Adjustment and Africa's Democracy Movements." *Africa Today* 40, 4, 7–29.

Headrick, Daniel R. 1981. *The Tools of Empire: Technology and European Imperialism in the Nineteenth Century*. Oxford: Oxford University Press.

Heldring, Leander and James Robinson. 2017. "Colonialism and Economic Development in Africa." In Carol Lancaster and Nicolas van de Walle, eds., *The Oxford Handbook on the Politics of Development*. Oxford: Oxford University Press, pp. 295–327.

Herskovits, Melville and Frances S. Herskovits. 1998. *Dahomean Narrative: A Cross Cultural Analysis*, 2nd ed. Evanston, IL: Northwestern University Press.

Herzog, Tamar. 2018. *A Short History of European Law: The Last Two and a Half Millennia*. Cambridge: Harvard University Press.

Hicks, Dan. 2020. *The Brutish Museums: The Benin Bronzes, Colonial Violence and Cultural Restitution*. London: Pluto Press.

Higazi, Adam. 2011. *The Jos Crisis: A Recurrent Nigerian Tragedy*. Discussion Paper No. 2, accessed October 23, 2020, Friedrich-Ebert Stiftung, http://library.fes.de/pdf-files/bueros/nigeria/07812.pdf.

Himbara, David. 2016. *Kagame's Economic Mirage*. North Charleston, SC: CreateSpace Independent Publishing Platform.

Hochschild, Adam. 1998. *King Leopold's Ghost: A Story of Greed, Terror, and Heroism in Colonial Africa*. Boston and New York: Houghton Mifflin.

Hood, Kirsty. 2007. *The Conflict of Laws Within the UK*. Oxford: Oxford University Press.

Hopkins, Antony G. 1976a. "Imperial Business in Africa, Part I: Sources." *Journal of African History* 17, 1, 29–48.

1976b. "Imperial Business in Africa, Part II: Interpretations." *Journal of African History* 17, 2, 267–290.

1968. "Economic Imperialism in West Africa: Lagos, 1880–92." *The Economic History Review* 21, 3, 580–606.

Howlett, Michael. 2019. *Designing Public Policies: Principles and Instruments*. New York: Routledge.

Hung, Ho-fung. 2015. *The China Boom: Why China Will Not Rule the World*. New York: Columbia University Press

Hunt, Tristam. 2014. *Cities of Empire: The British Colonies and the Creation of the Urban World*. New York: Holt.

Hunter, David. 2019. "Handel Manuscripts and the Profits of Slavery: The 'Granville' Collection at the British Library and the First Performing Score of Messiah Reconsidered." *Notes* 76, 1, 27–37.

Hunter-Gault, Charlayne. 2007. *New News Out of Africa*. Oxford: Oxford University Press.

Ibahwoh, Bonny. 2007. *Imperialism and Human Rights: Colonial Discourses of Rights and Liberties in African History*. Albany: State University of New York Press.

Ibrahim, Muhammed Baba. 1988. Arabic Manuscripts in the Early Nupe Kingdom. Master's Thesis (Library Science), Ahmadu Bello University.

Igbafe, Philip A. 1970. "The Fall of Benin: A Reassessment." *Journal of African History* 11, 3, 385–400.

Igboanusi, Herbert. 2008. "Empowering Nigerian Pidgin: A Challenge for Status Planning?" *World Englishes* 27, 1, 61–82.

Igboanusi, Herbert and Peter Lothar. 2005. *Languages in Competition: The Struggle for Supremacy Among Nigeria's Major Languages, English and Pidgin*. Frankfurt am Main: Peter Lang.

Igboanusi, Herbert and Martin Pütz. 2008. "The Future of French in Nigeria's Language Policies." *Journal of Multilingual & Multicultural Development* 29, 3, 235–259.

Ijere, M.O. 1974. "Colonial Policy in Nigerian Agriculture and Its Implementation." *Agricultural History* 48, 2, 298–304.

Ikime, Obaro. 1965. "Chief Dogho: The Lugardian System in Warri 1917–1932. *Journal of the Historical Society of Nigeria* 3, 2, 313–333.

Imhonopi, David and Ugochukwu Moses Urim. 2011. "The Development of Labor Movements and State Interference: The Nigerian Experience." *Journal of Sustainable Development in Africa* 13, 2, 235–253

International Crisis Group. 2014. *Curbing Violence in Nigeria (II): The Boko Haram Insurgency*, Africa Report No. 216, accessed May 25, 2015, www.crisisgroup.org/~/media/Files/africa/west-africa/nigeria/216-curbing-violence-in-nigeria-ii-the-boko-haram-insurgency.pdf.

Ipara, Isaac and Bob Mbori. 2009. "The Role of Kiswahili in Enhancing the Potential of Science and Technology." *The Journal of Pan African Studies* 2, 8, 139–150.

Ismi, Asad. 2004. *Impoverishing a Continent: The World Bank and the IMF in Africa*. Ottawa: Canadian Centre for Policy Alternatives.

Iwobi, Andrew Ubaka. 2019. The Regulation of Electronic Commerce in Nigeria: An Object Lesson in Legislative Ineptitude. Draft Paper.

2017. "Stumbling Uncertainly into the Digital Age: Nigeria's Futile Attempts to Devise a Credible Data Protection Regime." *Transnational Law and Contemporary Problems* 26, 1, 14–61.

Iwayemi, Akin. 2008. "Nigeria's Dual Energy Problems: Policy Issues and Challenges." *International Association for Energy Economics* 53, 17–21, www.iaee.org/en/publications/newsletterdl.aspx?id=53

Iyer, Venkhat. 2018. "Separation of Powers: The UK Experience." *Journal of International and Comparative Law* 5, 2, 507–527.

Jallow, Baba G. 2014. *Leadership in Postcolonial Africa: Disruption of Traditional Frameworks and Patterns*. New York: Palgrave.

Jedwab, Rémi, Edward Kerby, and Alexander Moradi. 2017. "How Colonial Railroads Defined Africa's Economic Geography." In Stelios Michalopoulos and Elias Papaioannou, eds., *The Long Economic and Political Shadow of History. Volume II. Africa and Asia*. London: CEPR Press, pp. 88–97.

Jerven, Morten. 2013. *Poor Numbers: How We Are Misled by African Development Statistics and What to Do About It*. Ithaca: Cornell University Press.

Johnson-Odim, Cheryl and Nina Emma Mba. 1997. *For Women and the Nation: Funmilayo Ransome-Kuti of Nigeria*. Urbana, IL and Chicago: University of Illinois Press.

Joireman, Sandra Fullerton. 2001. "Inherited Legal Systems and Effective Rule of Law: Africa and the Colonial Legacy." *The Journal of Modern African Studies* 39, 4, 571–596.

Joseph, Richard A. 1987. *Democracy and Prebendal Politics in Nigeria*. Cambridge: Cambridge University Press.

Jules Roger, Sombaye Eyango. 2018. Inside the Virtual Ambazonia: Separatism, Hate Speech, Disinformation and Cameroonian Diaspora in the Anglophone Crisis. Master of Arts Thesis (International Studies), University of San Francisco.

Jung, Woo S. and Gyu Lee. 1986. "The Effectiveness of Export Promotion Policies: The Case of Korea." *Weltwirtschaftliches Archiv* 122, 2, 340–357.

Kabir, Md. Humayun. 2011. "Swaziland Corporate Governance with Regard to the New Companies Act of 2009." *Procedia – Social and Behavioral Sciences* 25, 36–45.

Kahn, Paul. 1999. *The Cultural Study of Law*. Chicago: University of Chicago Press.

Kaufmann, Miranda. 2018. *Black Tudors*. London: Oneworld.

Kayaoglu, Turan. 2010. *Legal Imperialism: Sovereignty and Extraterritoriality in Japan, the Ottoman Empire, and China*. Cambridge: Cambridge University Press.

Keith, Arthur Berriedale. 1924. *The Constitution, Administration and Laws of the Empire*. London: W. Collins.

Kenney, Martin and John Zysman. 2016. "The Rise of the Platform Economy." *Issues in Science and Technology* 32, 3, https://issues.org/the-rise-of-the-platform-economy/.
Kiango, John G. 2005. "Tanzania's Historical Contribution to the Recognition and Promotion of Swahili." *Asia & Africa* 5, 157–166.
Kirk-Greene, A.H.M. 1980. "The Thin White Line: The Size of the British Colonial Service in Africa." *African Affairs* 79, 314, 25–44.
Kiye, Mikano E. 2015. "The Repugnancy and Incompatibility Tests and Customary Law in Anglophone Cameroon." *African Studies Quarterly* 15, 2, 85–101.
Klaaren, Jonathan, Simon Roberts, and Imraan Valodia, eds. 2017. *Competition Law and Economic Regulation: Addressing Market Power in Southern Africa*. Johannesburg: Wits University Press.
Kofi, Tetteh A. 1972. "The Elites and Underdevelopment in Africa: The Case of Ghana." *Berkeley Journal of Sociology* 17, 97–115.
Kopytoff, Jean Herskovits. 1965. *A Preface to Modern Nigeria: The "Sierra Leonians" in Yoruba, 1830–1890*. Madison: University of Wisconsin Press.
Korieh, Chima J. 2001. "The Invisible Farmer? Women, Gender, and Colonial Agricultural Policy in the Igbo Region of Nigeria, c. 1913–1954." *African Economic History* 29, 117–162.
Kramer, Larry. 1990. "Rethinking Choice of Law." *Columbia Law Review* 90, 2, 277–345.
Kusimba, Chapurukha. 2018. "Ancient Trade Between China and East Africa." In Akshay Sarathi, ed., *Early Maritime Cultures in East Africa and the Western Indian Ocean*. Oxford: Archaeopress Publishing, pp. 83–102.
Kusimba, Sibel. 2021. *Reimagining Money*. Stanford: Stanford University Press.
Kuwali, Dan. 2014. "Decoding Afrocentrism: Decolonizing Legal Theory." In Oche Onazi, ed., *African Legal Theory and Contemporary Problems: Critical Essays*. New York: Springer, pp. 71–92.
Kwarteng, Kwasi. 2011. *Ghosts of Empire: Britain's Legacies in the Modern World*. London: Bloomsbury.
Kyerematen, A. 1969. "The Royal Stools of Ashanti." *Journal of the International African Institute* 32, 1, 1–10.
LaFrance, Adrienne. 2016. "Facebook and the New Colonialism." *The Atlantic*, February 11, 2016, accessed October 23, 2020, www.theatlantic.com/technology/archive/2016/02/facebook-and-the-new-colonialism/462393/.
Lall, Somik Vinay, J. Vernon Henderson, and Anthony J. Venables. 2017. *Africa's Cities: Opening Doors to the World*. Washington, DC: International Bank for Reconstruction and Development/World Bank.
Langdon, Steven. 1986. "Industrial Dependence and Export Manufacturing in Kenya." In John Ravenhill, ed., *Africa in Economic Crisis*. London: Palgrave Macmillan, pp. 181–212.
Larkin, Brian. 2008. *Signal and Noise: Media, Infrastructure, and Urban Culture in Nigeria*. Durham: Duke University Press.
Lawan, Mamman. 2014. "Islamic Law and Legal Hybridity in Nigeria." *Journal of African Law* 58, 2, 303–327.
Lawrance, Benjamin N., Emily Lynn Osborn, and Richard L. Roberts. 2006. "Introduction: African Intermediaries and the 'Bargain' of Collaboration." In Benjamin N. Lawrance, Emily Lynn Osborn and Richard L. Roberts, eds., *Intermediaries, Interpreters, and Clerks: African Employees in the Making of Colonial Africa*. Madison: University of Wisconsin Press, pp. 3–34.
Lawrence, Margaret. 1993. The Families and House of Oxenhoath, West Packham. *Archeologia Cantiana* 11, 1, 237–262.

Le Billion, Philippe. 2006. "Fatal Transactions: Conflict Diamonds and the (Anti)Terrorist Consumer." *Antipode* 38, 4, 778–810.

Lee, Ching Kwan. 2017. *The Specter of Global China: Politics, Labor, and Foreign Investment in China*. Chicago: University of Chicago Press.

Lee, Christopher J. 2011. "Jus Soli and Jus Sanguinis in the Colonies: The Interwar Politics of Race, Culture, and Multiracial Legal Status in British Africa." *Law and History Review* 29, 2, 497–522.

2005. "The 'Native' Undefined: Colonial Categories, Anglo-African Status and the Politics of Kinship in British Central Africa, 1929-38." *Journal of African History* 46, 455–478.

Leibold, James. 2020. "Surveillance in China's Xinjiang Region: Ethnic Sorting, Coercion, and Inducement." *Journal of Contemporary China* 29, 121, 46–60.

Leke, Acha, Mutsa Chironga, and Georges Desvaux. 2019. "The Innovations Closing Africa's Electric Power Gap." *Harvard Business Review*, January 16, 2019, https://hbr.org/2019/01/the-innovations-closing-africas-electric-power-gap.

LeLaw Barristers & Solicitors. 2021. "Protections: A Commentary on Trade Secrets in Nigeria." Lexology, February 21, www.lexology.com/library/detail.aspx?g=38343fb5-4282-4446-b217-e895c176eeed.

Lennox, Corinne and Matthew Waites. 2013. *Human Rights, Sexual Orientation and Gender Identity in The Commonwealth*. London: University of London Press.

Lequiller, François and Derek Blades. 2014. *Understanding National Accounts*, 2nd ed. Paris: OECD Publishing, www.oecd.org/sdd/UNA-2014.pdf.

Lessig, Lawrence. 2006. *Code: Version 2.0*. New York: Basic Books.

1995. "The Regulation of Social Meaning." *University Chicago Law Review* 62, 943–1045.

LeVan, A. Carl. 2014. *Dictators and Democracy in African Development: The Political Economy of Good Governance in Nigeria*. Cambridge: Cambridge University Press.

Levtzion, Nehemia. 1980. *Ancient Ghana and Mali*. New York: Africana.

LiPuma, Edward and Benjamin Lee. 2004. *Financial Derivatives and the Globalization of Risk*. Durham: Duke University Press.

Lobato, Roman. 2010. "Creative Industries and Informal Economies: The Case of Nigerian Video." *International Journal of Cultural Studies* 13, 4, 337–354.

Locke, John. 1689. *Two Treatises of Government*. Book II, Chapter XVIII, Section 202. Liberty Fund Online Library of Liberty, https://oll.libertyfund.org/pages/john-locke-two-treatises-1689.

Loewenson, Rene. 1993. "Structural Adjustment and Health Policy in Africa." *International Journal of Health Services* 23, 4, 717–730.

Lugard, Frederick. 1922. *The Dual Mandate in British Tropical Africa*. Edinburgh and London: William Blackwood and Sons.

Lydon, Ghislaine. 2012. *On Trans-Saharan Trails: Islamic Law, Trade Networks, and Cross-Cultural Exchange in Nineteenth-Century Western Africa*. Cambridge: Cambridge University Press.

Lynn, Martin. 2006. "British Business and the African Trade: Richard & William King Ltd. of Bristol and West Africa, 1833–1918." *Business History* 34, 4, 20–37.

1995. "Law and Imperial Expansion: The Niger Delta Courts of Equity, c.1850–85." *The Journal of Imperial and Commonwealth History* 23, 1, 54–76.

1992. "Trade and Politics in 19th-Century Liverpool: The Tobin and Horsfall Families and Liverpool's Africa Trade." *Transactions of the Historic Society of Lancashire & Cheshire* 146, 2, 99–120.

1981. "Change and Continuity in the British Palm Oil Trade with West Africa, 1830–55." *The Journal of African History* 22, 3, 331–348.

Lyons-Padilla, Sarah, Hazel Rose Markus, Ashby Monk, Sid Radhakrishna, Radhika Shah, Norris A. "Daryn" Dodson IV, and Jennifer L. Eberhardt. 2019. "Race Influences Professional Investors' Financial Judgments." *Proceedings of the National Academy of Sciences* 116, 35 (August), 17225–17230.

Maiangwa, Benjamin, Muhammad Dan Suleiman, and Chigbo Arthur Anyaduba. 2018. "The Nation as Corporation: British Colonialism and the Pitfalls of Postcolonial Nationhood in Nigeria." *Peace and Conflict Studies* 25, 1, article 3, https://nsuworks.nova.edu/pcs/vol25/iss1/3.

Maine, Henry Sumner. 1861. *Ancient Law*. London: J.M. Dent.

Makinde, Abdul-Fatah 'Kola and Philip Ostien. 2012. "Legal Pluralism in Colonial Lagos: The 1894 Petition of the Lagos Muslims to the British Colonial Masters." *Die Welt des Islams* 52, 1, 51–68.

Malu, Linus Nnabuike. 2019. "Violent Conflicts in Africa: Types, Trends, Challenges and the International Criminal Court." In *The International Criminal Court and Peace Processes*. Cham, Switzerland: Springer Naturalizations Switzerland, pp. 75–91.

Mamdani, Mahmood. 1996. *Citizen and Subject: Contemporary Africa and the Legacy of Late Colonialism*. Princeton: Princeton University Press.

Man, Sin Wai and Chu Yiu Wai. 1999. "Whose Rule of Law? Rethinking (Post) Colonial Legal Culture in Hong Kong." *Social and Legal Studies* 8, 147–169.

Mann, Charles C. 1990. "Choosing an Indigenous Official Language for Nigeria." In *"Language and Nation," British Studies in Applied Linguistics* 91–103.

Marechera, Dambudzo. 1978. *The House of Hunger*. Long Grove, IL: Waveland Press (reissued in 2013).

Maret, Pierre de. 2018. "Archaeologies of the Bantu Expansion." In *The Oxford Handbook of African Archaeology*, eds., Peter Mitchell and Paul J. Land. Oxford: Oxford University Press.

Marston, Sallie A., Keith Woodward, and John Paul Jones, III. 2007. "Flattening Ontologies of Globalization: The Nollywood Case." *Globalizations* 4, 45–63.

Martin, Phyllis. 1995. *Leisure and Society in Colonial Brazzaville*. Cambridge: Cambridge University Press.

Mastercard Foundation and International Finance Corporation. 2018. Digital Access: The Future of Financial Inclusion in Africa, www.ifc.org/wps/wcm/connect/96a4f610-62b1-4830-8516-f11642cfeafd/201805_Digital-Access_The-Future-of-Financial-Inclusion-in-Africa_v1.pdf?MOD=AJPERES&CVID=mdz-QFo.

Matera, Marc, Misty L. Bastian, and Susan Kingsley Kent. 2011. *The Women's War of 1929: Gender and Violence in Colonial Nigeria*. New York and London: Palgrave Macmillan

Mathew, W.M. 1968. "The Imperialism of Free Trade: Peru 1820–70." *The Economic History Review* 21, 3, 562–579.

Mattes, Robert. and Alejandro Moreno. 2018. "Social and Political Trust in Developing Countries: Sub-Saharan Africa and Latin America." In Eric M. Uslaner, ed.,*The Oxford Handbook of Social and Political Trust*. Oxford: Oxford University Press, pp. 357–382.

Mattingly David J. 2013. *Imperialism, Power, and Identity: Experiencing the Roman Empire*. Princeton: Princeton University Press.

Mavhunga, Clapperton Chakanetsa. 2014. *Transient Workspaces: Technologies of Everyday Innovation in Zimbabwe*. Cambridge: MIT Press.

Mazrui, Ali A. and Alamin M. Mazrui. 1998. *Language and Governance in the African Experience*. Chicago: University of Chicago Press.

Mbaku, John and Chris Paul. 1989. "Political Instability in Africa: A Rent-Seeking Approach." *Public Choice* 63, 63–72.

Mbakwe, Paul Uche. 2015. "The Impact of Colonial Rule on the Agricultural Economy of Mbaise, Imo State, 1500–1960." *African Journal of History and Culture* 7, 6, 133–140.

Mbembe, Achille. 2001. *On the Postcolony*. Berkeley: University of California Press.

McConnell, Allan and Simon Tormey. 2020."Explanations for the Brexit Policy Fiasco: Near-Impossible Challenge, Leadership Failure or Westminster Pathology?" *Journal of European Public Policy: Special Issue: The Brexit Policy Fiasco* 27, 5, 685–702.

Mcintosh, Susan Keech. 2012. "West African Savanna Kingdoms: Introduction." In Neil Asher Silberman, ed., *The Oxford Companion to Archeology*, 2nd ed. Oxford: Oxford University Press, volume 3, pp. 369–372

McQueen, Rob. 1999. "Of Wigs and Gowns: A Short Story of Legal and Judicial Dress in Australia." *Law in Context: A Socio-Legal Journal* 16, 1, 31–58.

McQueen, Rob and W. Wesley Pue. 1999. "Misplaced Traditions: British Lawyers, Colonial People." *Law in Context: A Socio-Legal Journal* 16, 1, 1–16.

Meredith, Martin. 2005. *The Fate of Africa: A History of Fifty Years of Independence*. New York: PublicAffairs.

Merry, Sally Engle. 1988. "Legal Pluralism." *Law and Society Review* 22, 5, 869–896.

Meyer, Birgit 1999. "Popular Ghanaian Cinema and 'African Heritage'." *Africa Today* 46, 93–114.

Meyerson, Denise. 2004. "The Rule of Law and the Separation of Powers." *Macquarie Law Journal* 4, 1–6.

Mgbeoji, Ikechi. 2014. "The Comprador Complex: Africa's IPRs Elite, Neo-Colonialism and the Enduring Control of African IPRs Agenda by External Interests." Osgoode Legal Studies Research Paper Series Paper 43, http://digitalcommons.osgoode.yorku.ca/olsrps/43.

Michael, C. Ogwezzy. 2016. "Communication of an Interpreter and Fair Trial Under Nigerian Criminal Justice System." *International Journal of Legal Discourse* 1, 1, 213–233.

Michaels, Ralf. 2017. "Jurisdiction, Foundations." In Jürgen Basedow, Gisela Rühl, Franco Ferrari, and Pedro De Miguel Asensio, eds., *The Max Planck Encyclopedia of European Private Law*. Cheltenhem: Edward Elgar, pp. 1042–1051.

2012. "Legal Culture." Forthcoming In Basedow, Hopt and Zimmerman, eds., *Oxford Handbook of European Private Law* . Oxford: Oxford University Press. https://scholarship.law.duke.edu/faculty_scholarship/2390/.

Mngomezulu, Bhekithemba R. 2020. *Foreign Policy Posture in Post-Apartheid South Africa*. Cambridge: Cambridge Scholars Publishing.

Mochizuki, Katsuya. n.d. Resources, Conflict and Human Insecurity in African Context: An Insight from Experiences of Nigeria, Institute of Developing Economies, [https://perma.cc/5KV3-3BWT].

Modi, Renu and Ian Taylor. 2017. "The Indian Diaspora in Africa: The Commodification of Hindu Rashtra." *Globalizations* 14, 6, 911–929.

Mommsen, W.J. and J.A. de Moor, eds. 1992. *European Expansion and Law: The Encounter of European and Indigenous Law in the 19th and 20th Century Africa and Asia*. Oxford: Berg Publishers.

Monson, Jamie. 2009. *Africa's Freedom Railway: How a Chinese Development Project Changed Lives and Livelihoods in Tanzania*. Bloomington: Indiana University Press.

Moore, Henrietta L. and Megan Vaughan. 1994. *Cutting Down Trees: Gender, Nutrition, and Agricultural Change in the Northern Province of Zambia 1890–1990*. Portsmouth, NH: Heinemann.

Moore, Sally Falk. 1986. *Social Facts and Fabrications: "Customary" Law on Kilimanjaro, 1880–1980*. Cambridge: Cambridge University Press.

Mordi, Mark. 2011. "Towards Trademark Law Reform in Nigeria: A Practitioner's Note." *NIALS Journal of Intellectual Property [NJIP]* 193–216.

Morgan, Lewis Henry. 1877. *Ancient Society*. New York: Holt.

Morier-Genoud, Eric. 2020. "The Jihadi Insurgency in Mozambique: Origins, Nature and Beginning." *Journal of Eastern African Studies* 14, 3, 396–412.

Morrock, Richard. 1973. "Heritage of Strife: The Effect of Colonialist 'Divide and Rule' Strategy upon the Colonized People." *Science & Society* 37, 2, 129–151.

Mosa, Imad A. and Nisreen Noosa. 2019. "Conditionality and Structural Adjustment Programmes." In *Eliminating the IMF*. New York: Palgrave Macmillan, pp. 55–87.

Mudimbe, V.Y. 1988. *The Invention of Africa: Gnosis, Philosophy, and the Order of Knowledge*. Bloomington, IN and Indianapolis: Indiana University Press.

Mukerjee, Subhayan. 2016. "Net Neutrality, Facebook, and India's Battle to #SaveTheInternet." *Communication and the Public* 1, 3, 356–361.

Mulligan, Michael. 2009. "Nigeria, the British Presence in West Africa and International Law in the 19th Century." *Journal of the History of International Law* 11, 2, 274–301.

Munir, Arshad and Godwin Onuh Odeh. 2014. "The Establishment of the Nigerian Sokoto Caliphate: An Inquest into the Background History of the 1804 Jihad in Hausa Land, 210 Years After." *Al-Qalam* 19, 2, 61–71 (December).

Munslow, Barry. 1983. "Why Has the Westminster Model Failed in Africa?" *Parliamentary Affairs* 36, 1, 218–228.

Murphy, James T. and Pádraig Carmody. 2015. *Africa's Information Revolution: Technical Regimes and Production Networks in South Africa and Tanzania*. West Sussex: John Wiley & Sons Ltd.

Muthuri, Robert, Francis Monyango, and Wanjiku Karanja. 2018. Biometric Technology, Elections, and Privacy: Investigating Privacy Implications of Biometric Voter Registration in Kenya's 2017 Election Process, Strathmore University Centre for Intellectual Property and Information Technology Law, May 2018, https://cipit.strathmore.edu/wp-content/uploads/2020/05/PDF-4.pdf.

Murthy, Dhiraj. 2013. *Twitter: Social Communication in the Twitter Age*. Cambridge, MA: Polity Press.

Mwalimu, Charles. 2009. *The Nigerian Legal System, Volume 2: Private Law*. New York: Peter Lang.

Mwaura, Stephen. 2011. "Enhancing Financial Inclusion Through Technological Innovations." The Fletcher School, Tufts University, Leadership Program for Financial Inclusion, Policy Memoranda, pp. 37–40.

Ndemo, Bitange and Tim Weiss, eds. 2017. *Digital Kenya: An Entrepreneurial Revolution in the Making*. London: Palgrave Macmillan.

Ndulo, Muna. 2011. "African Customary Law, Customs, and Women's Rights." *Indiana Journal of Global Legal Studies* 18, 1, 87–120.

2003. "The Democratization Process and Structural Adjustment in Africa." *Indiana Journal of Global Legal Studies* 10, 1, 315–367.

https://sites.tufts.edu/flpfi/files/2017/08/FLPFI_PolicyMemoranda_2011.pdf.

Nest, Michael. 2011. *Coltan*. Cambridge: Polity Press.

Neuwirth, Robert. 2012. *The Stealth of Nations: The Global Rise of the Informal Economy*. New York: Anchor.

Ngũgĩ wa Thiong'o. 1986. *Decolonising the Mind: The Politics of Language in African Literature*. London: James Currey.

Niekerk, Gardiol van. 2015. "Multilinguialism in South African Courts: The Legislative Regulation of Language in the Cape During the Nineteenth Century." *Fundamina* 21, 2, 372–391.

Nixon, Rob. 2011. "Pipe Dreams: Ken Saro-Wiwa, Environmental Justice, and Micro-Minority Rights." In *Slow Violence and the Environmentalism of the Poor*. Cambridge, MA: Harvard University Press, pp. 103–127.

Njoh, Ambe J. 2008. "Colonial Philosophies, Urban Space, and Racial Segregation in British and French Colonial Africa." *Journal of Black Studies* 38, 4, 579–599.

Noah, Monday Efiong. 1989. "Inland Ports and European Trading Firms." *African Affairs* 88, 350, 25–27.

1987. "After the Warrant Chiefs: Native Authority Rule in Ibiobioland 1931–1951. *Phylon* 48, 1, 77–90.

Noble, Safiya Umoja. 2018. *Algorithms of Oppression: How Search Engines Reinforce Racism*. New York: New York University Press.

Nolte, Insa, Rebecca Jones, Khadijeh Taiyari, and Giovanni Occhiali. 2016. "Research Note: Exploring Survey Data for Historical and Anthropological Research: Muslim–Christian Relations in South-West Nigeria." *African Affairs* 115, 460, 541–561.

Northrup, David. 1976. " The Compatibility of the Slave and Palm Oil Trades in the Bight of Biafra." *The Journal of African History* 17, 3, 353–364.

Notais, Toussaint. 2020. "Access Granted: Facebook's Free Basics in Africa. *Media, Culture & Society* 42, 3, 329–348.

Notshulwana, Mxolisi. 2011. "State Fragility in Africa: Methods Chasing Problems or Problems Chasing Methods in Political Discourse." *International Journal of African Renaissance Studies – Multi-, Inter- and Transdisciplinarity* 6, 2, 81–99.

Nour, Samia Satti Mohamed. 2017. Africa Bridging the Digital Divides. Nordiska Afrikainstitutet, Policy Note No. 4, www.diva-portal.org/smash/get/diva2:1146536/FULLTEXT01.pdf.

Nunn, Nathan. 2008. "The Long-Term Effects of Africa's Slave Trades." *Quarterly Journal of Economics* 123, 139–176.

Nunn, Nathan and Leonard Wantchekon. 2011. "The Slave Trade and the Origins of Mistrust in Africa." *American Economic Review* 101 (December), 3221–3252.

Nwabueze, Remigius N. 2001. "The Evolution of Conflict of Laws in Nigeria." *ILSA Journal of International and Comparative Law* 8, 31–60.

Nwagbara, Eucharia Nwabugo. 2007. "The Igbo of Southeast Nigeria: The Same Yesterday, Today and Tomorrow?" (In Memory of Professor V. C. Uchendu), *Dialectical Anthropology* 31, 99–110.

Nwocha, Matthew Enya. 2016. "Customary Law, Social Development and Administration of Justice in Nigeria. *Beijing Law Review* 7, 430–442.

Nwokeabia, Hilary. 2001. *Why Industrial Revolution Missed Africa: A Traditional Knowledge Perspective* U.N. Economic Commission for Africa, ECA/ESPD/WPS/01/02, https://repository.uneca.org/bitstream/handle/10855/457/Bib.%206930_I.pdf?sequence=1&isAllowed=y.

Nyabola, Nanjala. 2018. *Digital Democracy, Analogue Politics: How the Internet Era Is Transforming Politics in Kenya*. London: Zed.

Oba, A.A. 2002. "Islamic Law as Customary Law: The Changing Perspective in Nigeria." *The International and Comparative Law Quarterly* 51, 4, 817–850.

Obarrio, Juan. 2014. *The Spirit of the Laws in Mozambique*. Chicago: The University of Chicago Press.

Ochieng'Opalo, Ken. 2020. *Legislative Development in Africa: Politics and Postcolonial Legacies*. Cambridge: Cambridge University Press.

Ochonu, Moses E. 2014. *Colonialism by Proxy: Hausa Imperial Agents and Middle Belt Consciousness in Nigeria*. Bloomington: Indiana University Press.

O'Connor, Anthony. 1983. *The African City*. London: Hutchinson.

Of the Holy Bible for the Use of the Negro Slaves in the British West-India Islands. 1807. London: Law and Gilbert.

Ogbuigwe, Anthony. 2018. "Refining in Nigeria: History, Challenges and Prospects." *Applied Petrochemical Research* 8, 181–192.

Oguamanam, Chidi. 2020. "Nollywood Phenomenon: 'The Nollywood Phenomenon: Innovation, Openness, and Technological Opportunism in the Modeling of Successful African Entrepreneurship'." *The Journal of World Intellectual Property* 23, 3-4, 518–545.

Ojo, Olatunji. 2016. "Forced Marriage, Gender, and Consent in Igboland, 1900–1936." In Annie Bunting, Benjamin N. Lawrence, and Richard L. Roberts, eds., *Marriage by Force: Contestation over Consent and Coercion in Africa*. Athens, OH: University Press, pp. 65–88.

2007. "'Èmú' (Àmúyá): The Yoruba Institution of Panyarring or Seizure for Debt." *African Economic History* 35, 31–58.

Okediji, Ruth L. 2006. *The International Copyright System: Limitations, Exceptions and Public Interest Considerations*. International Centre for Trade and Sustainable Development Issue Paper No. 15. Geneva: ICTSD.

Okekeocha, Chinelo and Andrew I.E. Ewoh. 2014. "Questioning the Constitutionality of Sharia Law in Some Nigerian States." *African Social Science Review* 6, 1, 15–28.

Okenyodo, 'Kemi. 2018. *Judicial Oversight in Nigeria*. Bonn: Friedrich Ebert Stiftung.

Okome, Onookome, ed. 1999. *Before I am Hanged: Ken Saro-Wiwa, Literature, Politics, and Dissent*. Trenton, NJ: Africa World Press.

Okoye, Chike. 2020. "Of Pidgin, Nigerian Pidgin Poetry, and Minority Discourses." In Tanure Ojaide and Joyce Ashuntantang, eds., *Routledge Handbook of Minority Discourses in African Literature*. London: Routledge, pp. 121–134.

Olsen, Gorm Rye. 1998. "Europe and the Promotion of Democracy in Post Cold War Africa: How Serious Is Europe and for What Reason? *African Affairs* 97, 343–367.

Oluya, Donatus Sunday. 2012. Bini Customary Law of Inheritance: Shift in "Igiogbe" as a Case Study. Master of Arts Thesis (History), Dalarna University Falun, Sweden.

Omenka, Nicholas. 1986. "The Role of the Catholic Mission in the Development of Vernacular Literature in Eastern Nigeria." *Journal of Religion in Africa* 16, 2, 121–137.

Omwansa, Tonny K. and Nicholas P. Sullivan. 2012. *Money, Real Quick: The Story of M-Pesa*. London: Guardian Books.

Opeibi, Tunde Olusola. 2012a. "Investigating the Language Situation in Africa." In Lawrence M. Solan and Peter M. Tiersma, eds., *The Oxford Handbook of Language and Law*. Oxford: Oxford University Press, pp. 272–285.

2012b. "Language Countertrading in Courtroom Exchanges in Nigeria: A Discursive Study." *International Journal of Applied Linguistics and English Literature*, 1, 5, 49–63.

Opoku, Kwame. 1974. "Traditional Law under French Colonial Rule." *Verfassung und Recht in Übersee / Law and Politics in Africa, Asia and Latin America* 7, 2, 139–153.

Orisakwe, Irish Ebere, Chiara Frazzoli, Cajetan Elochukwu Ilo, and Benjamin Oritsemuelebi. 2019. "Public Health Burden of E-Waste in Africa." *Journal of Health & Pollution* 9, 22, 19061.0, www.ncbi.nlm.nih.gov/pmc/articles/PMC6555250/.

Orr, Charles A. 1966. "Trade Unionism in Colonial Africa." *The Journal of Modern African Studies* 4, 1, 65–81.

Ortner, Sherry B. 2006. *Anthropology and Social Theory: Culture, Power, and the Acting Subject*. Durham, NC: Duke University Press.

Otiso, Kefa M. and Bisola Falola. 2017. "Introduction." In Toyin Falola and Bisola Falola, eds., *The African Metropolis: Struggles over Urban Space, Citizenship, and Rights to the City*. New York: Routledge, pp. 1–18.

Oyedemi, Toks Dele. 2019. "Global Digital Capitalism: Mark Zuckerberg in Lagos and the Political Economy of Facebook in Africa." *International Journal of Communication* 13, 2045–2061.

Oyedepo, Olusegun. 2012. "Patent and Economic Development in Nigeria." *Nigeria Law Journal* 16, 144–155.

Palan, R. and G. Mangraviti. 2016. "Troubling Tax Havens: Tax Footprint Reduction and Jurisdictional Arbitrage." In I. Hay and J. Beaverstock, eds., *International Handbook of Wealth and Super-Rich*. Cheltenhem: Edward Elgar, pp. 422–442.

Pam, Adamu Audu and John Ishaku Mantu. 2019. An Appraisal of the Legal Framework on Confidential Information and Trade Secrets in Nigeria. Working Paper, May 20, 2019, https://ssrn.com/abstract=3422302.

Partridge, C. 1911. "Native Law and Custom in Egbaland." *Journal of the Royal African Society* 10, 4, 422–433.

Pascoe, Bruce. 2018. *Dark Emu: Aboriginal Australia and the Birth of Agriculture*. London: Scribe UK.

Pasquale, Frank. 2018. "Two narratives of platform capitalism." *Yale Law & Policy Review* 35, 1, 309–319.

Paton, Bill. 1995. "Tanzania: A Successful Labour-Retention Policy." In *Labour Export Policy in the Development of Southern Africa* London: Palgrave Macmillan, pp. 181–207.

Pearson, Scott R. 1971. "The Economic Imperialism of the Royal Niger Company." *Food Research Institute Studies in Agricultural Economics, Trade, and Development* 10, 69–88.

Pedler, Frederick. 1974. *The Lion and the Unicorn in Africa: The United Africa Company 1787–1931*. London: Heinemann.

Pennycock, Alistair and Sinfree Makoni. 2005. "The Modern Mission: The Language Effects of Christianity." *Journal of Language, Identity & Education* 4, 2, 137–155.

Perham, Margery. 1950. "Editor's Introduction." In *The Nigerian Legislative Council*. Joan Wheare. London: Faber.

Petzell, Malin. 2012. "The Linguistic Situation in Tanzania." *Moderna språk* 106, 1, 135–144.

Pierskalla, Jan H. and Florian M. Hollenbach. 2013. "Technology and Collective Action: The Effect of Cell Phone Technology on Political Violence in Africa." *American Political Science Review* 107, 2, 207–224.

Piketty, Thomas. 2017. *Capital in the Twenty-First Century*. Cambridge: Belknap.

Pistor, Katharina. 2019. *The Code of Capital: How Law Creates Wealth and Inequality*. Princeton and Oxford: Princeton University Press.

Plankensteiner, Barbara. 2016. "The Benin Treasures: Difficult Legacy and Contested Heritage." In Brigitta Hauser-Schäublin and Lyndel V. Prott, eds., *Cultural Property and Contested Ownership: The Trafficking of Artefacts and the Quest for Restitution*. Oxford and New York: Routledge, pp. 133–155.

Pollard, Edward and Okeny Charles Kinyera. 2017. "The Swahili Coast and the Indian Ocean Trade Patterns in the 7th–10th Centuries CE." *Journal of Southern African Studies*, 43, 5, 927–947.
Postema, Gerald J. 2007. "Custom in International Law: A Normative Practice Account." In Amanda Perreau-Saussine and James Bernard Murphy, eds., *The Nature of Customary Law*. Cambridge: Cambridge University Press, pp. 279–306.
Prunier, Gérard. 2009. *Africa's World War: Congo, the Rwandan Genocide, and the Making of a Continental Catastrophe*. Oxford: Oxford University Press.
Rahmatian. Andreas. 1996. "Termination of Marriage in Nigerian Family Laws: The Need for Reform and the Relevance of the Tanzanian Experience." *International Journal of Law, Policy and the Family* 10, 281–361.
Ralston, Richard D. 1969. "The Return of Brazilian Freedmen to West Africa in the 18th and 19th Centuries. *Canadian Journal of African Studies* 3, 3, 577–593.
Rand, Dafna Hochman. 2013. *Roots of the Arab Spring*. Philadelphia: University of Pennsylvania Press.
Ranger, Terence. 1992. "The Invention of Tradition in Colonial Africa." In Eric Hobsbawm and Terence Ranger, eds., *The Invention of Tradition*. Cambridge: Cambridge University Press, pp. 211–262.
Rautenbach, Christa. 2010. "Deep Legal Pluralism in South Africa: Judicial Accommodation of Non-State Law." *The Journal of Legal Pluralism and Unofficial Law* 42, 60, 143–177.
Rawls, John. 1999. *A Theory of Justice*. Belknap: Harvard University Press.
Read, James S. 1979. "Studies in the Making of Colonial Laws: An Introduction." *Journal of African Law* 23, 1, 1–9.
Reinstein, Robert J. 2009. "The Limits of Executive Power." *American University Law Review* 59, 2, 259–337.
Reisberg, Arad. 2010. "Corporate Law in the UK after Recent Reforms: The Good, the Bad and the Ugly." *Current Legal Problems* 63, 1, 315–374.
Richard, Brilliant and Sumenenua Suzi Nwizug. 2017. "A Critical Discourse Analysis of Courtroom Proceedings in Nigeria." *International Journal of Arts and Humanities* 6, 4, 93–102.
Richards, Paul. 1996. *Fighting for the Rain Forest: War, Youth and Resources in Sierra Leone*. London: International African Institute.
Richens, Peter. 2009. "The Economic Legacies of the 'Thin White Line': Indirect Rule and the Comparative Development of Sub-Saharan Africa." *African Economic History* 37, 33–102.
Roberts, Richard and Kristin Mann. 1991. "Law in Colonial Africa." In Kristin Mann and Richard Roberts, eds., *Law in Colonial Africa*. Portsmouth, NH: Heineman, pp. 3–58.
Rodney, Walter. 1972. *How Europe Underdeveloped Africa*. Baltimore: Black Classic Press.
Rodrik, Dani. 1996. "Understanding Economic Policy Reform." *Journal of Economic Literature* 34, 1 (March), 9–41.
Rosenthal, Caitlin. 2018. *Accounting for Slavery: Masters and Management*. Cambridge: Harvard University Press.
Ross, Robert. 2014. "Cape of Good Hope and the World Economy, 1652–1835." In Richard Elphick and Hermann Giliomee, eds., *The Shaping of South African Society, 1652–1840*, 2nd ed. Hanover and London: Wesleyan University Press, pp. 243–282.
Rotimi, Kemi and Adetunji Ojo Ogunyemi. 2016. "Justice, Due Process and the Rule of Law in Nigeria: The Story Constable Thomas Shorunke, 1940–1946." *West Bohemian Historical Review* 6, 2, 309–322.

Roy, Ananya. 2018. "In/Exclusion: The Question of Inclusion." In Bill Maurer, Smoki Musaraj, and Ivan V. Small, eds., *Money at the Margins: Global Perspectives on Technology, Financial Inclusion, and Design*. New York: Berghahn Books, pp. 19–21.

Rugege, Sam. 2007. "Judicial Independence in Rwanda." *Global Business & Development Law Journal* 19, 411–425.

Rusalem, Rollin F. 2016. "The Colonial Foundations of State Fragility and Failure," *Polity* 48, 4 (October), 445–495.

Sacks, Vera. 2000. "Can Law Protect Language? Law, Language and Human Rights in the South African Constitution." *International Journal of Discrimination and the Law* 4, 343–368.

Said, Edward. 1993. *Culture and Imperialism*. New York: Vintage.

1979. *Orientalism*. New York: Pantheon.

Sautman, Barry. 1994. "Anti-Black Racism in Post-Mao China*." *The China Quarterly* 138, 413–437.

Sanya, Brenda Nyandiko. 2013. "Disrupting Patriarchy: An Examination of the Role of E-technologies in Rural Kenya." *Feminist Africa* 18, 12–24.

Saroxe "*Saro*"-Wiwa, Noo. 2012. *Looking for Transwonderland: Travels in Nigeria*. New York: Soft Skull Press.

Sarr, Dominique and Richard Roberts. 1991. "The Jurisdiction of Muslim Tribunals in Colonial Senegal, 1857–1932." In Kristin Mann and Richard Roberts, eds., *Law in Colonial Africa*. Portsmouth, NH: Heinemann, pp. 131–145.

Sarr, Felwine and Bénédicte Savoy. 2018. The Restitution of African Cultural Heritage. Toward a New Relational Ethics, November 2018, http://restitutionreport2018.com/sarr_savoy_en.pdf.

Sauer, Matthew E. 1992. "Nigeria and India: The Use of Film for Development-Whispers in a Crowd. *Africa Media Review* 6, 25–33

Saxenian, Anna Lee. 1996. *Regional Advantage: Culture and Competition in Silicon Valley and Route 128*. Cambridge, MA: Harvard University Press.

SB Morgen. 2020. Nigeria's Kidnap Problem: The Economics of the Kidnap Industry in Nigeria, May, www.sbmintel.com/wp-content/uploads/2020/05/202005_Nigeria-Kidnap.pdf.

Schaller, Dominik J. 2010. "Genocide and Mass Violence in the 'Heart of Darkness': Africa in the Colonial Period." In Donald Bloxham and A. Dirk Moses, eds., *The Oxford Handbook of Genocide Studies*. Oxford: Oxford University Press, pp. 345–364.

Schierup, Carl-Ulrich. 2016. "Under the Rainbow: Migration, Precarity and People Power in Post-Apartheid South Africa." *Critical Sociology* 42, 7–8, 1051–1068.

Schumpeter, Joseph A. 1951. *Imperialism and Social Classes*. Cleveland: The World Publishing Company.

1942. *Capitalism, Socialism and Democracy*. London: [George Unwin].

Schwarz, Daniel. 2017. "The Internationalization of Competition Law in Africa." Competition Policy International, www.competitionpolicyinternational.com/wp-content/uploads/2017/08/Africa-Column-August-Full.pdf.

Scott, David. 1999. *Refashioning Futures: Criticism After Postcoloniality*. New Haven: Yale University Press.

Scott, Francis Reginald. 1944. "The End of Dominion Status." *American Journal of International Law* 38, 1, 34–49.

Scott, James C. 1999. *Seeing Like a State: How Certain Schemes to Improve the Human Condition Have Failed*. New Haven: Yale University Press.

Seidman, Robert B. 1981. "Law, Development, and Legislative Drafting in English Speaking Africa." *The Journal of Modern African Studies* 19, 1, 133–161.
Seleti, Yona Ngalaba. 1992. "Entrepreneurship in Colonial Zambia." In Samuel N. Chipungu, ed., *Guardians in Their Time: Experiences of Zambians Under Colonial Rule 1890–1964*. London: Macmillan, pp. 147–179.
Sen, Amartya. 2009. *The Idea of Justice*. Cambridge: Belknap.
2000. *Development as Freedom*. New York: Anchor.
Seraile, William. 1972. "Black American Missionaries in Africa: 1821–1921." *Social Studies* 63, 5, 198–202.
Sharkey, Heather J. 2003. *Living with Colonialism: Nationalism and Culture in the Anglo-Egyptian Sudan*. Berkeley: University of California Press.
Shasore, Olasupo. 2016. *Possessed: A History of Law and Justice in the Crown Colony of Lagos, 1861–1906*. Lagos: Quramo Publishing Ltd.
Shelley, Toby. 2004. *Endgame in the Western Sahara: What Future for Africa's Last Colony?* London and New York: Zed Books.
Shepperson, George. 1985. "The Centennial of the West African Conference of Berlin, 1884–1885. *Phylon* 46, 1, 37–48.
Shepperson, George and St. Clare Drake. 1986. "The Fifth Pan-African Conference, 1945 and the All African People's Congress, 1958." *Contributions in Black Studies* 8, 5, 35–66.
Sherwood, Marika. 2007. *After Abolition: Britain and the Slave Trade Since 1807*. New York: I. B. Tauris.
Shih, Chi-Yu. 2013. "Harmonious Racism: China's Civilizational Soft Power in Africa." In *Sinicizing International Relations: Self, Civilization, and Intellectual Politics in Subaltern East Asia*. New York: Palgrave Macmillan, pp. 33–39.
Shivji, Issa G. 1982. "Semi-Proletarian Labour and the Use of Penal Sanctions in the Labor Law of Colonial Tanganyika (1920–38)." In Colin Sumner, ed., *Crime, Justice and Underdevelopment*. Aldershot: Heinemann, pp. 40–60.
Shyllon, Folarin. 2018. "BENIN DIALOGUE GROUP: Benin Royal Museum–Three Steps Forward, Six Steps Back." *Art Antiquity & Law* 23, 4, 341–346.
2003. "Negotiations for the Return of Nok Sculptures from France to Nigeria – An Unrighteous Conclusion." *Art Antiquity & Law* 8, 2 (June), 133–148.
Siems, Mathias. 2018. *Comparative Law*, 2nd ed. Cambridge: Cambridge University Press.
Simmel, Georg. 1950. *The Sociology of Georg Simmel*, Kurt H. Wolff trans., Glencoe, IL: The Free Press.
Siollun, Max. 2015. "How Goodluck Jonathan Lost the Nigerian Election." *The Guardian*, April 1, accessed May 25, 2015, www.theguardian.com/world/2015/apr/01/nigeria-election-goodluck-jonathan-lost.
2013. *Soldiers of Fortune: A History of Nigeria (1983–1993)*. Abuja: Cassava Republic Press.
Smillie, Ian. 2010. *Blood on the Stone: Greed, Corruption and War in the Global Diamond Trade*. Ottawa: Anthem Press.
Smith, Adam. 1904. "Of Colonies." In *An Inquiry into the Nature and Causes of the Wealth of Nations, Volume 2*. Book IV. 3rd edition. London: Methuen & Co., pp. 58–140.
Smith, Edwin W. 1926. *The Golden Stool: Some Aspects of the Conflict of Cultures in Modern Africa*. London: Holborn.
Smith, Robert Sydney. 1989. *Warfare and Diplomacy in Pre-Colonial West Africa*. 2nd ed. Madison: University of Wisconsin Press.
1988. *Kingdoms of the Yoruba*, 3rd ed. Madison: University of Wisconsin Press.
1979. *The Lagos Consulate, 1851–1861*. Berkeley: University of California Press.

Smith, Roger. 2005. "Constitutional Reform, the Lord Chancellor, and Human Rights: The Battle of Form and Substance." *Journal of Law and Society* 32, 1, 187–201.

Smyth, Rosalyn. 1979. "The Development of British Colonial Film Policy, 1927–1939, with Special Reference to East and Central Africa." *Journal of African History* 20, 437–450.

Snyder, Francis G. 1981. "Colonialism and Legal Form: The Creation of 'Customary Law' in Senegal." *Journal of Legal Pluralism* 19, 49–90.

Soest, Christian von and Fabian Bohnenberger. 2016. External Intervention to Strengthen Democracy in Africa. GIGA Focus Africa. October 2016, www.giga-hamburg.de/en/system/files/publications/gf_afrika_1604_en.pdf.

Spear, Thomas. 2003. "Neo-Traditionalism and the Limits of Invention in British Colonial Africa." *Journal of African History* 44, 1, 3–27.

Stauder, Jack. 1974. "The 'Relevance' of Anthropology to Colonialism and Imperialism." *Race* 16, 1, 29–51.

Stern, Philip J. 2013. "'Bundles of Hyphens': Corporations as Legal Communities in the Early British Modern Empire." In L. Benton and R.J. Ross, eds., *Legal Pluralism and Empires, 1500–1850*. New York: New York University Press, pp. 21–48.

Stevens, Joanna. 1997. "Colonial Relics I: The Requirement of a Permit to Hold a Peaceful Assembly." *Journal of African Law* 41, 1, 118–133.

Stocking, George W., Jr. 1968. "The Dark-Skinned Savage: The Image of Primitive Man in Evolutionary Anthropology." In *Race, Culture and Evolution: Essays in the History of Anthropology*. Chicago: University of Chicago Press, pp. 110–132.

Suberu, Rotimi. 2018. "Legislative Development and Decadence in the Fourth Republic National Assembly." In Carl Levan and Patrick Ukata, eds., *The Oxford Handbook of Nigerian Politics*. Oxford: Oxford University Press, pp. 221–237.

1991. "The Struggle for New States in Nigeria, 1976–1990. *African Affairs* 90, 499–522.

Sumner, Colin. 1982. "Crime, Justice and Underdevelopment: Beyond Modernisation Theory." In Colin Sumner, ed., *Crime, Justice and Underdevelopment*. Aldershot: Heinemann, pp. 1–39.

Suri, Tavneet and William Jack. 2016. "The Long-Run Poverty and Gender Impacts of Mobile Money." *Science* 354, 6317 (December 8), 1288–1292.

Sutton, Inez. 1989. "Colonial Agricultural Policy: The Non-Development of the Northern Territories of the Gold Coast." *The International Journal of African Historical Studies* 22, 4, 637–669.

Taoua, Phyllis. 2018. *African Freedom: How Africa Responded to Independence*. Cambridge: Cambridge University Press.

Tamuno, Tekena N. 1969. "The Role of the Legislative Council in the Administration of Lagos, 1886–1913." *Journal of the Historical Society of Nigeria* 4, 4, 555–570.

Taneja, Hermant. 2019. "The Era of Move Fast and Break Things Is Over," *Harvard Business Review*, January 22, https://hbr.org/2019/01/the-era-of-move-fast-and-break-things-is-over.

Taplin, Jonathan. 2017. *Move Fast and Break Things: How Facebook, Google, and Amazon Cornered Culture and Undermined Democracy*. New York: Little Brown.

Tar, Usman A. 2009. "Organized Labor and Democratic Struggles in Nigeria." *Information, Society and Justice* 2, 2, 165–181.

Taylor, Christopher C. 2002. "The Cultural Face of Terror in the Rwandan Genocide of 1994." In Alexander Laban Hinton, ed., *Annihilating Difference: The Anthropology of Genocide*. Berkeley: University of California Press, pp. 137–178.

Teferra, Anbessa. 2008. "Amharic: Political and Social Effects on English Loan Words." In Judith Rosenhouse and Rotem Kowner, eds., *Motives for Adopting English Vocabulary in Other Languages*. Bristol: Channel View Publications, pp. 165–186.

Tetteh, E. Kofi. 1971. "Law Reporting in Anglophone Africa." *The International and Comparative Law Quarterly* 20, 1, 87–98.

Thomas, Martin and Andrew S. Thompson. 2018. "Rethinking Decolonization: A New Research Agenda for the Twenty-First Century." In Martin Thomas and Andrew S. Thompson, eds., *The Oxford Handbook of the Ends of Empire*. Oxford: Oxford University Press, pp. 1–22.

Thomson, Michael, Alexander Kentikelenis, and Thomas Stubbs. 2017. "Structural Adjustment Programmes Adversely Affect Vulnerable Populations: A Systematic-Narrative Review of Their Effect on Child and Maternal Health. *Public Health Reviews* 38, 13.

Thornton, John. 1984. "The Development of an African Catholic Church in the Kingdom of the Kongo, 1491–1750." *Journal of African History* 25, 2, 147–167.

Tijani, Hakeem Ibikunle. 2012. *Union Education in Nigeria: Labor, Empire and Decolonization Since 1945*. New York: Palgrave Macmillan.

Tilley, Helen. 2011. *Africa as a Living Laboratory: Empire, Development, and the Problem of Scientific Knowledge, 1870–1950*. Chicago and London: University of Chicago Press.

Tom, Edet J. and Amadu J. Attai. 2014. "The Legislature and National Development: The Nigerian Experience." *Global Journal of Arts Humanities and Social Sciences* 2, 9, 64–78.

Trivedi, Raj Kumar. 1971. "The Role of Imperial British East Africa Company in the Acquisition of East African Colony in the Second Half of the Nineteenth Century." *Proceedings of the Indian History Congress* 33, 616–623.

Tuori, Kaius. 2010. "Legal Pluralism and Modernization: American Law Professors in Ethiopia and the Downfall of the Restatements of African Customary Law." *Journal of Legal Pluralism*, 62, 43–70.

Twitter, Initial Public Offering Prospectus. 2013. Filed with the United States Securities and Exchange Commission on November 7, 2013, accessed October 23, 2020, www.sec.gov/Archives/edgar/data/1418091/000119312513431301/d564001d424b4.htm.

Tylor, Edward B. 1871. *Primitive Culture*. London: John Murray.

Ugor, Paul. 2007. "Censorship and the Content of Nigerian Home Video Films." *Postcolonial Text* 3, 1–22.

Ukpabi, S.C. 1970. "The British Colonial Office Approach to the Ashanti War of 1900." *African Studies Review* 13, 3, 363–380.

Umahi, Okechukwu Timothy. 2011. "Access to Medicines: The Colonial Impacts on Patent Law of Nigeria." Working Paper, accessed May 25, 2015, http://ssrn.com/abstract=1975928.

UNCTAD. 2013. Economic Development in Africa: Intra-African Trade: Unlocking Private Sector Dynamism, accessed October 23, 2020, https://unctad.org/en/PublicationsLibrary/aldcafrica2013_en.pdf.

2008. Creative Economy Report 2008: The Challenge of Assessing the Creative Economy Towards Informed Policy-Making, accessed October 23, 2020, https://unctad.org/system/files/official-document/ditc20082cer_en.pdf.

United Nations Department of Economic and Social Affairs. 2019. Population Division, World Population Prospects 2019—Highlights, accessed October 23, 2020, https://population.un.org/wpp/Publications/Files/WPP2019_Highlights.pdf.

UNICEF. 1989. The State of the World's Children 1989, www.unicef.org/about/history/files/sowc_1989.pdf.

Vail, Leroy. 1976. "Mozambique's Chartered Companies: The Rule of the Feeble." *Journal of African History* 17, 3, 389–416.

Vansina, Jan. 2010. *Being Colonized: The Kuba Experience in Rural Congo, 1880–1960*. Madison and London: University of Wisconsin Press.

Vaughan, Olufemi. 2018. "Sharia Politics, the 1999 Constitution, and the Rise of the Fourth Republic. In Carl LeVan and Patrick Ukata, eds., *The Oxford Handbook of Nigerian Politics*. Oxford: Oxford University Press, pp. 239–256.

Vile, M.J.C. 1998. *Constitutionalism and the Separation of Powers*. Indianapolis: Liberty Fund.

Voeltz, Richard A. 1988. German Colonialism and the South West Africa Company, 1884–1914. *Africa Series Number* 50. Athens: Ohio University Center for International Studies.

Watson, Alan. 1996. "Aspects of the Reception of Law." *American Journal of Comparative Law* 44, 335–351.

1993. *Legal Transplants: An Approach to Comparative Law*. Athens: University of Georgia Press.

Watson, Ruth. 2003. *'Civil Disorder Is the Disease of Ibadan': Chieftaincy and Civic Culture in a Yoruba City*. London: James Currey.

Watts, Michael J. and Thomas J. Bassett. 1986. "Politics, the State and Agrarian Development: A Comparative Study of Nigeria and the Ivory Coast." *Political Geography Quarterly* 5, 2, 103–125.

Wei, Yuwa. 2008. "Maximising the External Governance Function of the Securities Market: A Chinese Experience." *International Company and Commercial Law Review* 3, 19, 111–116.

Weisbord, Robert G. 2003. "The King, the Cardinal and the Pope: Leopold II's Genocide in the Congo and the Vatican." *Journal of Genocide Research* 5, 1, 35–45.

Weller, Katrin, Axel Bruns, Jean Burgess, and Merja Mahrt. 2013. *Twitter and Society*. New York: Peter Lang Publishers.

West, Francis James. 1999. "The Colonial History of the Norman Conquest?" *History* 84, 274, 219–236.

Wiebe, Robert H. 1967. *The Search for Order 1877–1920*. New York: Hill and Wang.

Wilentz, Amy. 2013. *Farewell, Fred Voodoo: A Letter from Haiti*. New York: Simon & Schuster.

Williams, Geo W. 1890. An Open Letter to His Serene Majesty Leopold II, King of the Belgians and Sovereign of the Independent State of Congo.

Williams, Robert N., Duncan Wright, Alison Crowther, and Tim Denham. 2020. "Multidisciplinary Evidence for Early Banana (*Musa* cvs.) Cultivation on Mabuyag Island, Torres Strait." *Nature Ecology and Evolution*, August 10, www.nature.com/articles/s41559-020-1278-3.

Wolton, Suke. 2000. *Lord Hailey, The Colonial Office and the Politics of Race and Empire in the Second World War*. London: Palgrave Macmillan.

World Bank. 2018. *Learning to Realize Education's Promise. World Bank 2018 Human Development Report*. Washington, DC: The World Bank.

1989. *Sub-Saharan Africa: From Crisis to Sustainable Growth*. Washington, DC: The World Bank.

World Economic Forum. 2017. *The Africa Competitiveness Report 2017*. Geneva: World Economic Forum.

Wucherpfennig, Julian, Philipp Hunziker, and Lars-Erik Cederman. 2016. "Who Inherits the State? Colonial Rule and Postcolonial Conflict." *American Journal of Political Science* 60, 4, 882–898.

Zhao, Wayne Xin, Jing Jiang, Jianshu Weng, Jing He, Ee Peng LIM, Hongfei Yan, and Xiaoming Li. 2011. "Comparing Twitter and Traditional Media Using Topic Models."

European Conference on Information Retrieval (ECIR) Working Paper, accessed October 23, 2020, www.mysmu.edu/faculty/jingjiang/papers/ECIR%2711.pdf.

Zuboff, Shoshana. 2019. *The Age of Surveillance Capitalism: The Fight for a Human Future at the New Frontier of Power*. New York: PublicAffairs.

Zulu, Bheki, Maanda Phosiwa, and Mehluli Ncube. 2018. CIPC to Introduce Substantive Search and Examination, February 1, accessed October 23, 2020, www.derebus.org.za/cipc-introduce-substantive-search-examination/.

Index